PREHISTORIC MAN ON THE GREAT PLAINS

PREHISTORIC

ON

GREAT

MAN

THE

PLAINS

WALDO R. WEDEL

UNIVERSITY OF OKLAHOMA PRESS : NORMAN

The publication of this work has been aided by a grant from The Ford Foundation

Library of Congress Catalog Card Number: 61-9002

Copyright 1961 by the University of Oklahoma Press,
Publishing Division of the University.
First edition, August, 1961.
Second printing, by offset, February, 1964.
Manufactured in the U.S.A.

TO MILDRED

PREFACE

MANY BOOKS HAVE BEEN WRITTEN about the Indians of the North American Plains. In large part, these have been concerned with the Indians of the last century or two—chiefly, perhaps, with the war-bonneted horse-riding raiders and buffalo hunters of the short-grass country, secondarily with the more peaceably inclined farming tribes whose picturesque villages and cornfields once stood on the banks of the Missouri, Platte, and other waterways of the region. The fiction-writer, the historian, the geographer, and the anthropologist have tirelessly mined the great and still unexhausted store of information left us about these natives by explorers, traders, artists, and scientists, beginning in the mid-sixteenth century. And, because the Plains were in a sense the last great frontier in America and their native residents remained independent long after most tribes had come under the white man's thumb, anthropologists for many years have found the region a particularly rewarding one in which to conduct investigations into the social organization, religion, and ways of life of its original inhabitants.

As to what or who preceded the historically observed tribes or how long they had been in the region, there was little or nothing on which sound judgments could be based, other than inferences from Indian traditions or from comparative studies and distributions. By contrast with the great burial and temple mounds of the eastern United States, the cliff dwellings and ruined pueblos of the Southwest or the shell heaps of the Atlantic and Pacific coasts, the Plains had few conspicuous antiquities; and until perhaps thirty years ago, they remained the least-known area of any size in the United States, archaeologically speaking. Since that time, increasing field researches in all sections and especially the widespread work-relief programs of the 1930's and the current salvage operations connected with the federal water-control program, have made it abundantly clear that the history of human occupation in the Plains extends thousands of years back into the past.

This book has been written with two primary objectives in mind. It undertakes, first, a review of the human prehistory of the North American Plains, as this has been revealed by some three decades of systematic and sustained archaeological research. Obviously, any attempt to condense into a few hundred pages the story of some 10,000 years or more of human activities in more than 800,000 square miles of valley and plain has necessarily involved the slighting of some important facts and the omission of a great wealth of detail. For the serious reader or the student interested in further and more detailed information, or the one who prefers to make his own interpretation of the data, I have given references liberally and have also supplied a comprehensive, but not all-inclusive, bibliography. It should not be necessary to emphasize the fact that field and laboratory work are going forward everywhere in the Plains region, and that this work may at any time sharply modify or overturn present views and interpretations.

A second objective is that of presenting the story in a manner which will not deter or repel the nonspecialist, but without sacrifice of clarity and accuracy. For this I have sought to avoid the overuse of technical terms and specialized expressions. As in any other field, however, so here the reader may find an occasional term that is not immediately familiar to him—a term for which there is no ready circumlocution and which he may therefore as well learn. Whether I have in any appreciable manner been successful in meeting the complaint of the non-archaeologist that Plains archaeologists "write only for other archaeologists" and not for the general reader, I must leave to the reader's judgment.

Not all parts of the Plains region, as defined in this book, are equally well known with regard to their prehistory, because field work or publication, or both, have lagged behind that on other sections. It is manifestly impossible, too, for any one individual to know all parts of the region equally well, nor is it to be expected that the views and interpretations of other workers will necessarily parallel or coincide exactly with all those advanced herein. My own firsthand knowledge, based on several seasons of field work for the Nebraska State Historical Society, the University of Nebraska, and the Smithsonian Institution, beginning in 1930, is greatest for the Central Plains of Nebraska, Kansas, and western Missouri. Close participation in the River Basin Surveys salvage work of the Smithsonian, first as field director of the Missouri Basin Project from 1946 through 1949 and then as a field party chief on the Middle Missouri during the seasons of 1951, 1955, 1956, and 1957, provided a broadened perspective on Northern Plains problems and the opportunities to discuss these matters at formal and informal meetings with specialists in various sections. For other parts of the Plains where my knowledge is not first-hand, I have, of course, leaned the more heavily on the work of a host of professional colleagues and co-workers, most of whose names will be found in the bibliography.

It is a pleasure to acknowledge the help of many individuals who have responded generously to my appeals for information where little or none existed on the printed page or who have pro-vided guidance and discussed problems in areas where my own knowledge was inadequate or who have helped in other ways. They must not be held accountable for any misuse I may have made of this assistance. They include especially the following: Carl H. Chapman, Paul L. Cooper, Roger T. Grange, Jr., James H. and Dolores A. Gunnerson, Jack T. Hughes, Harold A. Huscher, Jesse D. Jennings, Thomas F. and Alice B. Kehoe, Mar-vin F. Kivett, Alex D. Krieger, William Mulloy, Carlyle S. Smith, G. Hubert Smith, Harry E. Weakly, Fred Wendorf, W. Ray-mond Wood, and Alan Woolworth. Where problems led me northward beyond the forty-ninth parallel, Richard S. MacNeish,

Richard G. Forbis, and William J. Mayer-Oakes gave invaluable assistance; and Mr. MacNeish very generously made available unpublished manuscripts and field reports filed in the National Museum of Canada.

It has been my good fortune to have been able to talk over various problems of Plains ethnohistory, prehistory, and physical anthropology with John C. Ewers, George S. Metcalf, Marshall T. Newman, and T. Dale Stewart, Smithsonian associates for many years; and these discussions have helped greatly to clarify, strengthen, or modify views of my own. I must acknowledge also the always pleasant and uniformly profitable associations with several men who strongly influenced my thinking during my early years of work in the Plains, notably A. T. Hill, W. D. Strong, G. F. Will, and C. R. Keyes. And, as always, my obligation is especially heavy to my wife, Mildred Mott Wedel, for her endless patience, constructive criticism, and constant encouragement, and for her untiring help in the mechanical process of readying the manuscript for the publisher.

Photographs from which some of the illustrations were prepared, and supporting data, have been supplied by the following individuals and organizations: M. F. Kivett, Nebraska State Historical Society; Russell Reid, W. Raymond Wood, and Norman Paulson, North Dakota Historical Society; Robert L. Stephenson, River Basin Surveys, Lincoln; Frank H. H. Roberts, Jr., Bureau of American Ethnology; Kenneth E. Kidd, Royal Ontario Museum; Jack T. Hughes, Panhandle-Plains Museum; and Emil W. Haury, Arizona State Museum. Others have come from the photographic collections of the Division of Archeology, U. S. National Museum, and from my personal files. For permission to reproduce line drawings previously published elsewhere, I am indebted to the editors of the *American Anthropologist* and *El Palacio*.

This book could have been organized and written in any of several different ways, as I am acutely aware now that the manuscript is about to leave my hands. What I have tried to do is to write the kind of book I think I would have welcomed thirty-five years ago, when arrow points and pottery fragments picked up on the prairies of central Kansas awakened the first stirrings of curiosity about Plains prehistory. Another, writing the book, would undoubtedly have done it differently. This, with the indispensable help of many professionals and nonprofessionals, is my version.

WALDO R. WEDEL

Washington, D. C.
May 25, 1961

CONTENTS

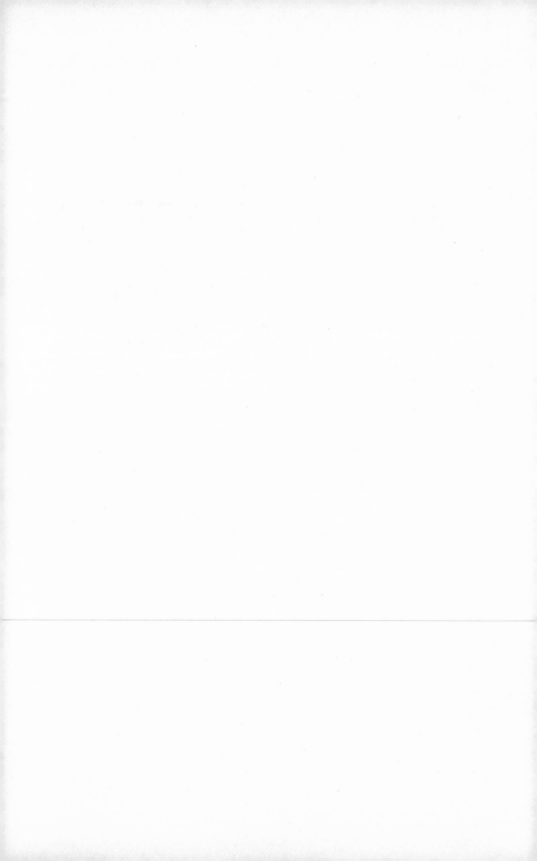

PLATES

FIGURES

PREHISTORIC MAN ON THE GREAT PLAINS

CHAPTER ONE

TOOLS OF THE ARCHAEOLOGIST

ARCHAEOLOGY HAS BEEN DEFINED RECENTLY as "the systematic study of antiquities as a means of reconstructing the past." With this there can be no quarrel, only an emphatic reaffirmation of the second part of the definition. To a good many well-intentioned people, archaeology still implies little more than a preoccupation with antiquities—that is, the collecting of arrowheads, pottery fragments, and bones, and the assembling or restoration of such materials in the laboratory. It is this, to be sure, but it is also much more. In simplest terms, archaeology is the study of how men lived in the past. It is not geology or fossil-hunting, though geological and paleontological considerations inevitably enter into certain aspects of archaeological research.

In the Great Plains, as generally throughout North America, the archaeologist deals principally with the remains of preliterate peoples, who perforce left no written records of any sort. The chief testimony of their former presence lies in their village and camp sites, refuse deposits and burial grounds, and in the artifacts and skeletons that are found in these locations. Thus, if the archaeologist seems to be extraordinarily absorbed with sorting and counting pottery fragments or in measuring and describing bits of bone and stone, it is because those odds and ends are usually the only surviving clues to the identity, way of life, and social activities of the people who made them and to the relations of those people with the environment in which they lived.

It is a basic tenet of the archaeologist that wherever man has carried on his domestic and community activities for any length of time, some traces of his former presence will usually be left. Under favorable conditions, his garbage heaps, discarded or lost implements and utensils, his house ruins—often even the remains of the people themselves—will be preserved indefinitely. If these deposits were laid down over a sufficiently long period of time, the products of human workmanship undergo changes from the bottom to the top. Sometimes, after these villages and camp sites had been abandoned for a time and were partially covered over by action of wind, water, or other natural agencies, another people with different house, artifact, and burial types, and perhaps even a different physical appearance, reoccupied the same location. Their refuse left a second layer, separated from the earlier by a stratum of wind-blown or water-laid soil. Such successive reoccupations of a given spot by different peoples may be repeated more than once throughout a period of decades, centuries, or millennia. As with geological strata, so here we may assume, in the absence of evidence to the contrary, that the topmost layer was put down last and that the successively deeper layers are of progressively greater age. Through careful examination of such stratified sites, we may learn the order in which different, and often unrelated, peoples followed one another in a given locality. This, of course, is only an extension of the well-known principle in geology sometimes called the law of superposition.

Sites of archaeological interest can be found in a great variety of situations. Isolated finds of arrowpoints or other objects, perhaps lost by Indian travelers or as a result of hunting and raiding forays, may be found almost anywhere. In the Eastern Plains, most village and burial sites are located on terraces along the watercourses, large and small, or on the nearby bluffs overlooking the bottoms. Older sites frequently occur at depths of several to many feet underground, where stream action, road building, or other agencies have cut into the terrace formations. Workshop sites littered with the results of flint-chipping activities are often found on exposed hilltops, as are pits for eagle catching. Farther west, sites buried in streamside terraces are also fairly common;

4

and temporary camps with hearths can be found far from any visible source of surface water or other obvious attraction to residence. Caves, rock shelters, and pictograph sites are much more common throughout the Western Plains than in the Eastern, as are various kinds of rock alignments and bison traps. The nature and distribution of these various kinds of antiquities will be further discussed elsewhere in this book. What has just been said is intended mainly to show that archaeological materials may be found almost anywhere if one searches closely enough.

Having located or selected a promising site, the archaeologist goes through a series of more or less standard procedures. He maps it, photographs it, and stakes out the area to be dug, according to some system of co-ordinates. He then excavates, carefully recording his findings and observations in terms of his system of horizontal and vertical controls. The exact location of each specimen and its relation to changing soil and cultural formations must be noted. In theory, at least, he digs and removes his materials in such fashion that the entire site—be it mound, village ruin, camp, or cemetery—could be exactly rebuilt, with every feature and every artifact replaced precisely where it was originally found. If this method seems needlessly painstaking and time-consuming, it must be remembered that the archaeologist learns by destroying. Once a site is dug, it is gone forever; it cannot be re-examined or the job done over, like a questionable experiment or one gone wrong in a laboratory test tube. Therefore, the investigator seeks to surround himself and his operations with as many safeguards as possible in order to prevent loss or misinterpretation of evidence.

Back in his laboratory, the archaeologist reworks his field data. The artifacts must be classified, analyzed, and described, and then correlated with the data on house units, cache or storage pits, burials, and other cultural and natural features. Plant and animal remains must be identified to determine what they show about man's utilization of the contemporary natural environment, the comparative importance of hunting and gathering as compared to horticulture, etc. Perhaps the collections include pottery fragments from distant areas, whereby trade relations can be worked out and chronological correlations established; or there may be glass and metal objects which will similarly offer clues to contacts with other peoples, this time with white traders or travelers. All of this requires endless time and patience, and frequent consultation with persons intimately familiar with the archaeology of other areas or with certain specialized technological matters on which the archaeologist himself lacks information. Normally, the end product of all this effort is a published report in which the findings and interpretations of the archaeologist are made generally available to his colleagues and to that section of the interested public able to make its way with comprehension through the report, murky and toilsome though the path may be at times.

Whatever the immediate interests of the archaeologist, a principal goal of archaeology is the extension of history back in time. It is concerned with a series of events, the clues to which are the artifacts and their associations. Those events took place at varying times; and the archaeologist is faced with the problem of establishing a framework of time into which the inferred events can be fitted. Chronology, as someone has said, becomes the nerve electrifying the dead body of history. In the area with which we are here concerned, as already noted, there are no written records, no calendric systems, and few or no direct aids toward the establishment of chronological perspective. Most of the methods currently in use give us indirect or relative, rather than absolute, chronology. They tell us which event came before or after another, rather than the precise time at which it occurred.

Many of the Indian tribes living in the Great Plains were for years in contact with white men. Their villages and camps were visited again and again by traders, missionaries, army personnel, scientists, and other travelers. From the journals, reports, and letters left by these visitors, we can often determine the location of the Indian communities they saw, estimate the time when these communities were occupied, and identify them with specific archaeological sites. Then, by excavating at village sites known through these historical documents to have been inhabited by, say, the Pawnees or the Mandans or the Cheyennes, it is possible

6

to determine the characteristics that distinguish the remains of one tribe from those of another.

The differences noted by the archaeologist in types of houses or pottery or burial methods and in other particulars can often be specifically verified from historical records. By combining the information derived from historical sources, from archaeological investigation, and from observations on tribes still in possession of parts of their native culture, we can often project our interpretations back in time to progressively earlier sites. Unfortunately, the number and reliability of historical records drops off rapidly before the year 1800. Moreover, the distinctiveness of the remains of many of these peoples lessens as we approach the older time levels, so that it is no longer safe to apply modern tribal names to the earlier groups. Nevertheless, prudent use of this direct historical approach, as it has sometimes been termed, offers an excellent device for tying in the archaeological record at its upper end with written history and ethnography. Moreover, it represents a logical approach from the known (historical) to the unknown (prehistoric) peoples of the region.

Historic sites—those dating from approximately 1550 on, when the Indians were in contact with white men—may be dated with varying accuracy by the relative amounts of Caucasian trade materials they contain or by the presence of datable European or American objects whose period of manufacture is known. Thus, a village site on the Missouri River occupied after 1800 will normally contain much more European and American iron and glass than will another that was abandoned before 1700. Again, where two sites yield gun parts or glass bottles or silver ornaments, the types of guns, bottles, or ornaments may enable us to say that one site was receiving trade items of a later period than the other. There are pitfalls in these operations, but they can be avoided or allowance made for them.

This historical approach has been used with much success in the Great Plains, but not yet on all tribes or with equal persistence everywhere. By its use, it has been possible to date and identify the remains of several tribes in various parts of the region, and as

7

far back as the Coronado period of the mid-sixteenth century in central Kansas.

Nowhere in the Great Plains did white men meet the Indians before 1541, and in most localities, the date of the initial contact is a century or more later. Thus, the period for which historic documents or other aids can be used is generally under four hundred years. This is a small fraction of the ten thousand years or more of man's estimated presence in the region. It is not surprising, then, that for every site which can be dated or identified by historic means, there are scores or hundreds that were undoubtedly abandoned before 1541. And when we come to deal with these, the problem of chronology is much more difficult.

The most satisfactory method of establishing relative chronology where prehistoric sites are concerned is stratigraphy. This we have already touched upon briefly. Stratigraphy is based on the familiar geological principle that, unless strata or beds have lost their original position through disturbance, the order in which they lie on one another is their order of age—the lowest is the oldest, the one at the top is the youngest. If the same order can be established at several or many locations, there is good reason to believe that it represents the correct sequence of events for the region.

The principle is sound, but its application in the field is not always easy. Rarely in the Great Plains are the different layers of occupation sharply separated. More often, they lie directly one on top of another and can be separated only by careful observation. Too, where successive peoples have occupied the same spot, the later ones often sank their fireplaces, habitations, storage pits, graves, and other dug features into or through the older levels. The objects placed in these later diggings may thus come to rest deeper beneath the surface than are other items which were actually deposited long before. Man's predilection for scratching in the soil for one purpose or another, including modern agriculture and construction, can in this way mix the evidence until all the ingenuity of the archaeologist is required to bring order into the picture.

8

When stratigraphic methods are inapplicable, other devices may be used. Seriation is one of these. It uses variations in pottery and other artifacts as a guideline. Over a long period of time, the kinds of pottery made in any given region will show changes in their style of decoration, surface finish, vessel shapes, fabric, tempering, and other details. One kind appears, reaches a maximum of popularity, then dwindles and gives way to another kind. No single site will show the entire range of pottery types used in the region; but the pottery fragments it yields will show varying amounts of the several kinds being made while the site was inhabited. There may be a few sherds, let us say, of type A, many of type B, fewer of type C. The same kinds may be present in about the same proportions at other sites nearby, from which it is inferred that all were inhabited at about the same time. Sites in another group may yield a few sherds of type B, more of type C, and fewer of type D. These, it may be suggested, were partly contemporaneous with the first group; but the presence of a new kind of pottery, type D, indicates that the occupation may have begun earlier, or lasted later, than the sites in which this kind does not occur. If, now, in yet another group of sites, type D becomes the dominant pottery and we find in these sites consistent indication of white-trade goods dating from 1550–1600, we conclude that these villages were occupied later than those without such items and lacking, or having only a small amount of, type D pottery. It thus becomes possible to arrange the sites in a series based on changing pottery types A to D and ending at a time level that can be dated by other means. The method here crudely illustrated may be used also for projectile points, or for any other artifacts that occur fairly plentifully at all sites and show measurable changes in shape, size, and other particulars.

Still other methods are of varying usefulness and dependability in establishing relative chronology. As is well known, some sites are much better preserved than others; and, by the uninitiated, these are frequently presumed to be later in time. But the preservation of house ruins, artifacts, and sites generally depends upon a great variety of factors—for example, their location with respect

9

to drainage and weathering, the length of their occupation or use, whether they were burned on abandonment or simply left to deteriorate, and the extent of subsequent molestation by plow or other destructive agencies. The state of preservation alone is seldom a reliable clue to the age of antiquities. Again, it is often supposed that crudely made artifacts or primitive-looking constructions are necessarily older than those of more advanced or finished type. This may frequently be the case, but it must not be forgotten that most native arts among the Plains Indians deteriorated rapidly after the white conquest, and also that there were inept and slipshod craftsmen even among the prehistoric peoples who otherwise turned out highly competent and well-made work. A few attempts have been made to identify and classify sites on the basis of native legends; but until these identifications have been confirmed through excavation and analysis, they cannot be unreservedly accepted as valid. Where the earlier prehistoric peoples are concerned, the association of their artifacts and other remains with the bones of animals now extinct, or their occurrence in stream terraces or otherwise in formations that can be dated relatively by geologists, are important clues. The earliest known hunting peoples in the Great Plains, we can now be sure, made use of several kinds of large animals, such as the American elephant, that died out in early postglacial times.

The "dating" methods considered to this point, so far as they relate to prehistoric materials, do not tell us whether a given site or group of remains is five hundred years old or two thousand. They make it possible only to divide archaeological time into a series of consecutive periods, into a chronological framework within which archaeological events may be arranged in their proper order of time. There are other chronological devices that permit more exact dating, and these must be considered briefly. Two are of principal interest to us—dendrochronology, or tree-ring analysis, and radiocarbon dating. Neither has yet been widely applied in the Great Plains.

Dendrochronology makes use of the well-known fact that certain trees add a well-marked growth ring each year and of the second fact that where precipitation is a strong limiting factor in tree growth, as it is in much of the Great Plains, the width of the successive rings may vary greatly. A dry year or period produces narrow rings; a wet period, wide rings. These variations form discernible patterns, which are usually exhibited by all trees growing under the same conditions. It is common knowledge that the age of a tree can be ascertained more or less accurately by simply counting its growth rings, though occasional double or missing rings may interpose complications. Since, however, few living trees are old enough to carry the ring record back more than a century or two, they must be supplemented by older wood. This may come from stumps of trees cut many years ago by early settlers, from timbers used in the building of forts, trading posts, and other historic buildings, or from long-dead buried stumps found in canyons and valley fills. By matching a distinctive series of wide and narrow rings near the center of a wood sample whose outermost ring or cutting date is exactly known with a similar series near the outer part of a timber from an early historic building, the sequence of annual rings can be extended far back beyond the lifetime of any single tree. By counting back from the known starting point, the exact year in which each ring in such a succession grew can be determined and an absolute date assigned to it. By the similar overlapping of additional older specimens, eventually including wood from Indian house ruins or campfires, the latter can be given a date in terms of the Christian calendar. When a house or other aboriginal feature has been thus dated, it is still necessary to establish that the artifacts found in or with that feature belong to it; in other words, that the association is a direct one, not accidental. If the artifacts do belong to the feature, then they, too, may be considered dated.

In the American Southwest, where wood was extensively used by the Indians for house construction throughout many centuries of time and where climatic conditions are unusually favorable for preservation of such timbers, dendrochronology has been used with conspicuous success. Hundreds of village sites have been dated, going as far back as the early years of the Christian Era.

The tree-ring sequences, transcribed as lines of varying length on graphs, are backed up by large numbers of wood samples, and the validity of the master charts so produced has been firmly established. Also, the time span during which various pottery types were in use has been quite accurately delimited. When sherds from one of these dated types, say in the upper Río Grande Valley, are found at sites in the Great Plains, they furnish helpful clues to the probable time when the latter were occupied. This method is called cross dating.

In the Great Plains, dendrochronology has been seriously attempted only in the North Platte locality in western Nebraska and in the area around Bismarck, North Dakota.[1] The scarcity of suitable timber in much of the region will doubtless severely limit its usefulness on a wide scale, but its applicability certainly deserves further testing. It should perhaps be emphasized that dendrochronology, besides the promise it offers for dating Indian sites, is also an important gauge of past climatic conditions because the variations in width of rings reflects the varying precipitation from time to time in the past. These variations, of course, can be dated as precisely as can any of the Indian sites falling within the range of the dated ring sequence.

Radiocarbon dating is a comparatively new method.[2] Its results have opened new vistas in prehistory and promise to open more; but the inconsistent and unacceptable dates that turn up from time to time suggest technical difficulties, contamination, or other adverse factors which still place limits on the reliability of the method. It determines the age of organisms that lived during the past twenty to forty thousand years by measuring the amount of

[1] H. E. Weakly, "Tree Rings as a Record of Precipitation in Western Nebraska," *Tree-Ring Bulletin*, Vol. VI, No. 3 (1940), 18–19. Weakly, "A Tree-Ring Record of Precipitation in Western Nebraska," *Journal of Forestry*, Vol. XLI, No. 11 (1943), 816–19; G. F. Will, "Tree-Ring Studies in North Dakota," *Bulletin 338*, Agricultural Experiment Station, North Dakota Agricultural College (1946).

[2] D. Collier, "New Radiocarbon Method for Dating the Past," Chicago Natural History Museum *Bulletin*, Vol. XXII, No. 1 (1951), 6–7; F. Johnson, "Radiocarbon Dating," *Memoirs* of the Society for American Archaeology, No. 8 (1951); W. F. Libby, *Radiocarbon Dating* (2nd ed., 1955).

carbon 14 they contain. All living things absorb from the atmosphere minute amounts of this form of carbon, and it has been experimentally determined that the proportion of carbon 14 in all living matter is a constant. At death, the organism ceases to take on any more C_{14}, and that which it already contains begins immediately to disintegrate at a uniform rate. Half of the C_{14} disintegrates in 5,568 years, half of the remainder in another like period, and so on. Thus, by reducing a sample of organic material —wood, charcoal, burned bone, or other substance—to carbon, measuring its radioactivity, and then computing the proportion of C_{14} present to that in living things, it is possible to calculate the time which has elapsed since the material under study ceased to live. Despite some lingering doubts in regard to the dependability of this method, its possibilities for determining the time of events in the remote past are great. It lacks the preciseness of dendrochronology, to be sure, but it can be used on materials far too old to be dated by tree rings.

In the pages immediately preceding, there were outlined briefly the objectives of archaeology and some of the methods employed by archaeologists in achieving their goal. In the next chapter, we will review the principal characteristics of the natural environment as it exists in the Great Plains today and as it has existed in the recent historic past. Since, however, our survey of human prehistory involves men's activities through some ten thousand years of time, some consideration must be given the matter of environmental conditions, particularly the climate, in the past. This entails more than simple recognition of the fact that the earliest plainsmen had to cope with a cooler and more moist climate attending the proximity of the last ice sheet on the northern margin of our area and the common supposition that postglacial climate has consisted of little more than a progressive warming and drying. The picture is, in fact, a good deal more complex than this.[3] The ever widening and intensifying scrutiny into the nature of

[3] H. Shapley, *Climatic Change: Evidence, Causes, and Effects;* C. E. P. Brooks, "Geological and Historical Aspects of Climatic Change," *Compendium of Meteorology,* ed. by T. F. Malone (1951), 1004-18.

climate since the last glaciation has been a fruitful one; but it has also indicated clearly that the problems are exceedingly complicated, involving a wide variety of considerations of geology, geography, atmospheric physics, and, ultimately, solar activity. It is entirely probable that man's adjustment to the Great Plains environment, in the remote prehistoric past as in the more recent historic past, has been in considerable part a problem of adapting his subsistence economies and ways of life to a variable and often extremely trying climate.

The recent past provides dramatic evidence of climatic instability in the Great Plains. Still fresh in the memory of men are the widespread droughts of the 1930's and the early 1950's with their spectacular dust storms, their crop failures, and their aftermath of human misery. Weather records, which unfortunately go back less than one hundred years in most of the region, remind us of several severe droughts in the nineteenth century, notably those of the 1860's and 1870's in the central section.

This record has been considerably extended by analysis of tree rings in two localities—North Platte, Nebraska, and Bismarck, North Dakota. The North Platte sequence[4] is derived largely from buried juniper stumps and logs found in the canyons along the North Platte River Valley. The tree growth registered in these rings reveals numerous dry and wet periods, some short and others longer. Droughts of ten years or longer are indicated in the following periods: 1439–68 (thirty years); 1539–64 (twenty-six years); 1587–1605 (nineteen years); 1688–1707 (twenty years); 1761–73 (thirteen years); 1822–32 (eleven years); and 1880–95 (sixteen years.) Some of these "would have been very severe on the present population of aboriginal farmers. Several of the drouths were of sufficient severity to very largely depopulate the plains even now ...."[5]

For the northern Plains, the Bismarck series offers a climatic

[4] Weakly, "A Tree-Ring Record of Precipitation in Western Nebraska," *loc. cit.*, 816–19.

[5] Weakly, cited in W. R. Wedel's "Environment and Native Subsistence Economies in the Central Great Plains," Smithsonian *Miscellaneous Collections*, Vol. CI, No. 3 (1941), 25.

record of approximately equal length.[6] Here again marked climatic fluctuations are indicated, including dry periods in 1406–15 (nine years), 1438–52 (fourteen years), 1471–85 (fourteen years), 1488–1501 (thirteen years), 1505–18 (thirteen years), 1562–76 (fourteen years), 1596–1611 (fifteen years), 1633–49 (sixteen years), 1836–51 (fifteen years), etc. Wet periods are indicated in 1415–33 (eighteen years), 1452–71 (nineteen years), 1611–23 (twelve years), 1663–1702 (thirty-nine years), etc. Comparison of the two published records from these tree-ring observations shows that the sequences lack the close correlation that would be expected if they reflected climatic fluctuations involving synchronous events in the Northern and Central Plains. If both sequences prove valid as further tree-ring studies progress, they will afford additional proof of the historically observed fact that climatic variations do not necessarily coincide over the entire Plains region, that a severe drought in one section may occur while normal or above-normal precipitation is enjoyed in other sections.

A longer period is covered in a chart compiled by Brooks to show climatic variations during the Christian Era.[7] This is based on world-wide correlation of various lines of evidence, including among other considerations the fluctuations of lake levels and rivers, the growth of peat bogs and the succession of vegetation types they show, the growth rates of trees as shown by annual rings, and the advances and retreats of glaciers. From these, six dry periods and as many wet ones have been recognized for the western United States. From a pre-Christian wet period that began before 660 B.C. and reached its maximum between 480 and 250 B.C., climate at the beginning of the Christian Era is judged to have been about what it is at present. Dry periods are indicated in the fourth and fifth centuries; around A.D. 700 to 800; in the tenth, the twelfth, the thirteenth, and the fifteenth centuries; and around 1900. Increased rainfall occurred around A.D. 600; in the latter part of the ninth century; in the eleventh century ("very

6 Will, "Tree-Ring Studies in North Dakota," *loc. cit.*
7 Brooks, *loc. cit.*, 1009.

15

rainy"); and about 1300, 1600, and 1800. How these inferred fluctuations, or which of them, affected the Great Plains specifically, or any part of the region, is not indicated; but as we shall see later, certain of these variations appear to coincide with events in human prehistory that may have had some basis in environmental changes.

In the arid lands of the western United States, beyond the Rockies, dead and dying lakes with their telltale abandoned shore lines and beaches, have long served as gauges of past climatic changes. Unfortunately, equally informative indicators of this sort do not exist in most of the Great Plains, except perhaps in the Pleistocene basins at their northern and southern extremities. In eastern North Dakota, however, Devils Lake and its chain of lesser lakes provides noteworthy information. At the risk of oversimplification, the situation here may be outlined as follows: Since white settlement of the region, there has been a steady and marked reduction in the size of the lakes, which appear to have attained their highest levels about 1830. Abandoned shore lines and lake sediments, as well as tree lines bordering the lakes, indicate that the shrinkage has been underway for a long time, possibly with occasional brief halts or temporary recoveries. In the beds of several of the lakes, notably Stump Lake, North and South Washington lakes, and Lake Coe, there are stumps of oak trees which grew when the lakes were dry, or substantially so, some time before the 1830 level, and which were drowned when the waters rose again. Some of these trees, unquestionably rooted in the lake bed, showed one hundred or more annual growth rings—eloquent testimony to the length of time during which the lake floors were dry. Growth-ring studies on one of the stumps indicate a strong probability that this tree ceased to grow in 1541.[8] This compares favorably with another rooted stump for which an age of 500, plus or minus 200 years, has been determined by radiocarbon dating.[9] Since the Devils Lake system occupies a basin of internal

[8] Will, "Tree-Ring Studies in North Dakota," *loc. cit.*, 16.
[9] S. Aronow, "On the Postglacial History of the Devils Lake Region, North Dakota," *Journal of Geology*, Vol. LXV, No. 4 (1957), 422.

drainage, the changing lake levels are believed to reflect fluctuations in rainfall involving at least the following developments: (1) a high water level in late glacial time; (2) a dry warm period, lasting at least one hundred years and ending perhaps in the fifteenth or sixteenth century; (3) a cool period with heavy precipitation and rising lake levels, culminating probably about 1830; (4) a drier, warmer period with falling lake levels, culminating in a partial rejuvenation since 1947. At the moment, the climatic fluctuations here established cannot be correlated with tree-ring or other records for the Missouri River or other more westerly sections of the Eastern Plains, and there is no other evidence of the protracted drought represented by the timber that once grew on the dry lake beds of the Devils Lake district.

Important indications of past climatic conditions are found also in the buried or "fossil" soils and in deep deposits of wind-blown materials which often overlie them. Both features are often associated with archaeological sites in the Great Plains. Buried soils are manifested as dark horizontal bands exposed where stream action, road construction, or other disturbances have laid bare a cross section of the subsurface deposits. They occur commonly in Kansas and Nebraska and in adjacent states in and around the Great Plains. Some are clearly of recent origin, since in and on their surfaces can be found village and camp sites, potsherds, stone artifacts, and other materials left by man from six or seven centuries to two or three millennia ago.[10] Others are far older, probably dating from one or another of the interglacial periods and offering further testimony to the prehuman antiquity of the plains and prairie grasslands. It can be inferred that these buried soil horizons represent periods when the land surface was relatively stable, allowing man to dwell upon it and vegetation to flourish long enough and luxuriantly enough to build up a humus layer.

Blanketing these old soil surfaces are lighter-colored materials that were evidently laid down by wind action. They were de-

[10] J. L. Champe, "Ash Hollow Cave," University of Nebraska *Studies*, new ser., No. 1 (1946), 58–82.

posited so rapidly, or under such adverse climatic circumstances, that little or no humus was able to develop. Thus, they suggest a sparse cover of vegetation, presumably climatically induced, in the area from which the materials were carried in, if not in the locality where they were finally deposited. Such deposits may be only a foot or two deep and, because they overlie datable archaeological materials, can be shown to be no more than a few centuries old. Others, as at Signal Butte in western Nebraska, probably precede the Christian Era by some hundreds of years.[11] Still others, as at Lime Creek in southwestern Nebraska, are much thicker and suggest events operating on a much grander scale and at a more remote time period.[12] We shall have occasion to refer to these matters again and in more detail.

Most of the inferred climatic fluctuations for which we now have some evidence in the Great Plains cannot, on present knowledge, be safely interpreted as widespread events. It is entirely possible that some of these episodes did affect considerable areas, but this has not yet been established. Much painstaking work will be needed to fit the scattered bits of data into a larger and lasting framework. The lack of agreement between the Nebraska and North Dakota tree-ring sequences is a case in point. On an earlier time level, there is reason to be skeptical also about some of the river-terrace correlations and their inferred climatic implications in portions of the Central Plains.

Before we leave the subject of past or paleoclimates, attention should be focused briefly on one major event in geological history that undoubtedly did manifest itself in the Great Plains, and that within the time of man's demonstrable presence here. This is the warm, dry interval of some two thousand years or more that marked the maximum of warmth in the northern hemisphere since the retreat of the last ice sheet. Several independent lines of evidence confirm this maximum, from approximately 4,000 or

[11] W. D. Strong, "An Introduction to Nebraska Archeology," Smithsonian *Miscellaneous Collections*, Vol. XCIII, No. 10 (1935), 224–28.
[12] C. B. Schultz, *et al*, "Preliminary Geomorphological Studies of the Lime Creek Area," *Bulletin*, University of Nebraska State Museum, Vol. III, No. 4 (1948), Pt. 1, p. 38.

4,500 B.C. to 2,000 B.C.,[13] since which time the climate is believed to have become cooler and more moist to the present. Various names have been applied to this period—the Climatic Optimum, the Altithermal, the Thermal Maximum, the Hypsithermal, etc. —and it has been termed by Flint the "outstanding fact of so-called postglacial climatic history." Under any name, the warm, dry conditions by which it was distinguished brought about extensive adjustments in native vegetational and faunal distributions in most of the central and western United States, and it undoubtedly had an important bearing on prehistoric events in the Great Plains.

Our discussion has by no means exhausted the subject of past climates of the Plains, nor has it touched on several other important avenues of approach to the problem. Enough has been said, however, to indicate the complexity of the problem, and also to demonstrate the truism that variability has been the rule rather than the exception. The droughts which devastated large areas of the Southern and Central Great Plains in the 1930's and again in the 1950's are seen to be only the most recent and vivid expressions of a regional, climatic pattern of very long standing. From this it follows that prehistoric man, like his modern successor, has found it necessary to adjust his ways of life to this overriding fact—or be defeated in his attempt to settle the Great Plains region.

[13] R. F. Flint, *Glacial Geology and the Pleistocene Epoch*, 487; *see also* G. I. Quimby, "Cultural and Natural Areas Before Kroeber," *American Antiquity*, Vol. XIX, No. 4 (1954), 318–19; E. Antevs, "Geologic-Climatic Dating in the West," *American Antiquity*, Vol. XX, No. 4 (1955), 328–29; E. S. Deevey and R. F. Flint, "Postglacial Hypsithermal Interval," *Science*, Vol. CXXV, No. 3240 (1957), Table 1.

CHAPTER TWO

LAND OF SUN AND WIND AND GRASS

THE GEOGRAPHICAL LIMITS OF THE Great Plains have been defined
in various ways by different writers and observers. To most, the
Rocky Mountains have served as a convenient boundary on the
west, since at their base the characteristic natural vegetation and
terrain of the Plains change perceptibly. On the east, however,
there are no easily recognized "natural" borders, but rather zones
of transition from one physiographic or vegetational or climatic
province to another. The hundredth meridian has often been used
as a boundary line, since it coincides, but again very roughly, with
the line of twenty-inch annual average rainfall, west of which
agriculture is precarious and difficult except by specialized methods and with specialized crops.

The physiographer, using land forms and the manner in which
they were created as his guide, sets the eastern margin of the Great
Plains along an imaginary line that starts on the Canadian border
at longitude 103 degrees west, thence curves east to 99 degrees in
the Dakotas, to 97 degrees in Nebraska and northern Kansas, and
finally southwest to 101 degrees in west central Texas.[1] The student of native vegetation finds a more satisfactory limit somewhat
farther to the east, approximately paralleling the ninety-seventh
meridian in the north and the ninety-eighth meridian in the south.
The changes in vegetation beyond this line reflect, in part, corresponding soil changes, since the "humid" soils found generally
east of the above vegetational line lack the zone of carbonate

[1] N. M. Fenneman, *Physiography of Western United States*, Plate 1.

accumulation found to the west.[2] This is approximately the eastern boundary followed by the President's Great Plains Committee in its 1936 study of drought conditions and the economic future of the region.[3]

In popular usage, of course, exact definitions are seldom attempted, and the term Great Plains connotes the generally flat, semiarid grasslands lying west of the Mississippi-Missouri Valley. Vague and impressionistic as this view is, it is a concession to the very real difficulty of defining precisely the Great Plains region. Moreover, it reflects tacitly a viewpoint properly emphasized long ago by Webb,[4] who held that, in discussing the region from the standpoint of its utilization by man, the concept of a Great Plains environment may be more satisfactory than that of a Great Plains region. The outstanding characteristics of this environment he considers to be a comparatively level (flat) surface of great extent, treelessness, and a subhumid or semiarid climate in which rainfall is insufficient for the sort of agriculture practised in humid lands. Each of these characteristics is found over a great part of the United States. The region in which all three coincide and dominate the land constitutes the Great Plains.

The environmental forces that give the heart of the area its distinctiveness thus represent a combination of factors, each transcending any set of lines we may draw on a map to delimit the Great Plains. Man's use of the Plains does not, and did not formerly, change immediately when he crossed the hundredth meridian or the boundary between the short grass and the tall grass. Rather, he gradually shifted his emphases and values, and modified his techniques from those found adequate in the adjacent regions to others better adapted to the Plains environment.

It is perhaps worth noting that the Plains culture area of the ethnologist likewise disregards the physiographic and vegetational

[2] H. L. Shantz, "The Natural Vegetation of the Great Plains Region," *Annals of the Association of American Geographers*, Vol. XIII, No. 2 (1923), 81–82, 98–100, Fig. 1.
[3] "The Future of the Great Plains," Report of the Great Plains Committee, Washington, 1936.
[4] W. P. Webb, *The Great Plains*, 1–9.

boundaries indicated above for the Great Plains. As usually defined,[5] its eastern limits extend nearly to the junction of the Mississippi-Missouri rivers; its western, well beyond the Rockies into the Basin and Plateau regions. Such tribes as the Iowa and Osage, marginal Woodland hunters and horticulturists, assuredly differed sharply in many details from the Utes, Bannocks, and other tribes west of the Rockies; yet they also shared a significant number of basic Plains traits with each other and with such tribes as the Blackfeet, Crows, and Comanches of the short-grass plains. The way of life based on this combination of traits—including heavy emphasis on bison hunting, well developed skin-working, dog and horse transport, the tipi, sign language, etc.—was a distinctive one, and is so recognized in the concept of a Plains culture area.

The Great Plains may be defined in yet another way. They comprise a major portion of the vast, roughly triangular tract in the heart of temperate North America which has been designated the central North American grassland.[6] The irregular base of this grassland triangle rests on the west against the foot of the Rocky Mountain highland, with its apex meeting in the east the deciduous forests of the Mississippi Valley. Originally, this great grassland stretched more than 1,500 miles from the Río Grande northward to the coniferous forest of Canada and, including the prairie peninsula of Iowa, Illinois, and Indiana, had an east-to-west dimension of nearly 1,000 miles.

Within these general limits, our discussion of Plains prehistory will be concerned with a somewhat more restricted area. Its extent is indicated in Figure 1. The western limit coincides in general with the base of the Rockies. On the north, it includes somewhat more than the Palliser triangle, "having for its base the 49th parallel from longitude 100° to 114° W, with its apex reaching the 52nd parallel of latitude." The eastern limit shown runs a little east of south from approximately the ninety-eighth meridian at

[5] Clark Wissler, *The American Indian*, 218–21, Fig. 59; R. H. Lowie, "Indians of the Plains," *Anthropological Handbook No. 1*, American Museum of Natural History (1954), 2–9, Fig. 2.
[6] J. R. Borchert, "The Climate of the Central North American Grassland," *Annals* of the Association of American Geographers, Vol. XL, No. 1 (1950), 1–39.

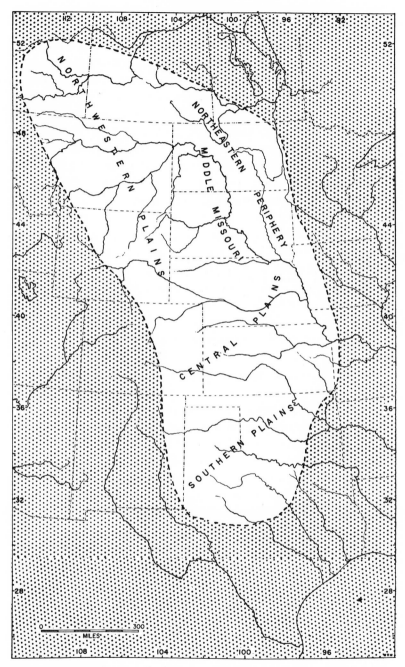

FIG. 1. *Map of the North American Plains area* (heavy broken line) *and its subareas.*

the Canadian boundary, south through western Minnesota and Iowa to west central Missouri. Here it turns southwest past the Ozark Mountains, crosses Oklahoma to leave aside the Ouachita Mountains, and enters Texas at the western Cross Timbers. On the south, the line curves around the Staked Plains and then turns northward east of, and parallel to, the Pecos River. In terms of modern political units, it includes all of Kansas, Nebraska, and South Dakota, and parts of Texas, Oklahoma, New Mexico, Colorado, Missouri, Wyoming, Iowa, Montana, North Dakota, and the three Prairie Provinces of Canada—Manitoba, Saskatchewan, and Alberta.

No implication is intended here that the extensive region thus delineated is environmentally or archaeologically homogeneous, or that it constitutes a distinctive prehistoric "culture" area. As we shall see, the native cultures and ways of life have varied greatly from section to section, as well as from time to time within each section. Nonetheless, there are certain broad uniformities of environment in the region encompassed. Where these are most pronounced, there were direct responses to them in man's way of doing things. Native culture, in other words, changed through zones of transition; and, so, any line is more or less arbitrary. Other observers, with differing bias or information than mine, would doubtless shift the line here and there and would have no difficulty justifying their revisions.

Having delimited our area of interest, we must next examine its physical basis. In the popular view, the term Great Plains has long carried an implication of monotonous uniformity of landscape, of an endless expanse of flat, featureless country covered with grass. It has often been described in deficiency terms. Thus, in the broadest outline, it may be characterized as a land of low relief, few trees, and little rainfall—of sun and wind and grass. But this characterization is not complete, nor is it altogether accurate; and it masks a good many details of the natural environment which, through the centuries, have had bearing, directly or indirectly, on man's use of the land. Because the prewhite peoples with whose activities we shall be mainly concerned lacked the

24

technological advantages of the later European and American invaders, their ways of life represented a closer response to the opportunities and limitations of the land on which they lived. Thus the shape of the land surface, the distribution and quantity of water resources, its plants and animals must be considered.

The Great Plains have their physical basis in long-standing processes of geology and climate. There is no need to detail the geological history of the region, since it is, after all, the surface in which we are primarily interested here. This surface is largely a result of repeated, widespread uplifts of the Rocky Mountain region occurring in Tertiary time, ten million years or more ago, and continuing into Pleistocene time.[7] Ultimately, this upwarping of a zone hundreds of miles across, produced elevations of ten to eleven thousand feet along the Continental Divide. As the land rose, the streams descending from the heights became increasingly active in widening, deepening, and lengthening their valleys. Enormous quantities of eroded materials were carried from the highlands, to be deposited as gravels, sands, clays, and silts where the overloaded and slowing streams reached more gentle grades east of the mountains. Here their channels gradually became choked with sediments; and the streams, constantly seeking the lowest places to drop their loads, shifted from side to side as they made their way across the growing alluvial fans. Eventually, the accumulating deposits merged and lengthened into an immense apron of waste, many hundreds of feet thick and sloping gently eastward from the base of the mountains.[8] In the north, this apron of sediments covered the southern parts of the Prairie Provinces of central Canada, much of Montana and eastern Wyoming, and most of North and South Dakota to a distance of fifty to seventy-five miles beyond the present Missouri River, where its approximate limit is marked by the Coteau du Missouri. In the Central Plains, most of Nebraska and more than half of Kansas was mantled, in the areas now classed as the High Plains and the Plains

[7] C. O. Dunbar, *Historical Geology*, 406–17.

[8] W. D. Johnson, "The High Plains and Their Utilization," U. S. Geologic Survey *Twenty-first Annual Report*, Pt. 4 (1900), 607–741.

25

Border. Farther south, the outwash belt may have included central and western Oklahoma, but the Great Plains province today narrows appreciably and is best shown in the Staked Plain of Texas and its southernmost extension, the Edwards Plateau.

Over most of the region, the surface of this great outwash plain has been modified in some measure by subsequent erosion. Probably its original character, if not necessarily its original surface, is best exemplified by the High Plains section, extending from the southern boundary of South Dakota nearly to the Río Grande.[9] Here, broad and phenomenally flat uplands, "as flat as any land surface in nature," are characteristic of the interstream areas. The Tertiary mantle in its upper portion consists largely of porous materials which readily absorb the limited precipitation; and where these upper materials have been cut through by streams that reach the underlying impervious formations, permanent springs and seeps frequently occur. Only a few streams—the Canadian, the Arkansas, and the two forks of the Platte—cross the High Plains belt, running over sandy beds in bluff-lined, flat-floored valleys. Other streams rise within the region or along its eastern edge, which from Texas to Kansas presents a highly irregular, deeply indented margin. Among the few surface features are shallow depressions of varying size and depth, ranging from "buffalo wallows" a few feet in diameter to larger depressions of several hundred acres. Some of the latter may hold rain water for weeks or months during a rainy season; and like the springs, they were important focuses of interest to the native populations on their hunting forays into the buffalo country.

Sandy areas occur in several localities—along the Cimarron and Arkansas rivers in western Kansas, between the Republican headwaters and the South Platte in southwestern Nebraska and northeastern Colorado, and locally elsewhere. By far the largest area lies north of the Platte in central Nebraska, where some 20,000 square miles are covered with active and inactive dunes.

Northward, the High Plains develop an increasingly rolling and uneven surface. They end at the Pine Ridge, a prominent and

[9] N. M. Fenneman, *Physiography of Eastern United States*, 559–630.

picturesque north-facing escarpment that is best developed south of the Black Hills between the Niobrara and White rivers and becomes less conspicuous toward the east and west.

Beyond, are the northern Great Plains or, in physiographic terms, the Missouri Plateau.[10] Owing to widespread and prolonged erosion, this area differs markedly in appearance from the High Plains. Their seemingly endless smooth, flat surfaces here give way to a series of terraced plains, the valleys are often wide and indefinitely set off from interstream areas, and there is a good deal of rough country. Isolated mountain masses of diverse origins are widely scattered over the Missouri Plateau, including such features as the Black Hills, the Big Snowy, Little Rocky, and Bear Paw mountains, and the Sweetgrass and Cypress hills. Considerable areas of badlands occur along the Missouri, Yellowstone, Little Missouri, and White rivers, and locally to a lesser extent. Elsewhere, there are rugged, often picturesque ridges, hills, cliffs, and breaks, as well as flat-topped buttes whose gravel-capped summits, often many hundreds of feet above the surrounding plains, are a dramatic reminder of the extent to which the ancient outwash plain has been stripped away to create the present surface.

Bordering the physiographic Great Plains on the east is a landscape of still different origin and character, the Central Lowland, which also merits some attention here.[11] In the Dakotas, the dividing line is the Coteau du Missouri, a belt of hills fifty to seventy-five miles east of the Missouri River, roughly paralleling that stream, and continuing into southern Saskatchewan from the northwestern corner of North Dakota. East and north of the Coteau belt, the bedrock has been deeply buried by glacial debris and the land surface owes its form primarily to the activity of the continental ice sheets from the north. The last major ice advance here may have taken place no longer ago than ten or twelve thousand years; and the mantle of debris it left has not yet been greatly altered by subsequent erosion. Thus, the surface is essen-

[10] W. C. Alden, "Physiographic Development of the Northern Great Plains," *Bulletin*, Geological Society of America, Vol. XXXV (1924), 385–423.
[11] Fenneman, *Physiography of Eastern United States*, 559–630.

tially a gently rolling to hilly plain. There are few rivers and they are mostly widely spaced, with few and unimportant tributaries. In pre-agricultural days, this poorly drained plain was dotted with innumerable lakes, along with marshy areas and boulder fields. Along the Red and Souris rivers, level expanses of lake sediments mark the former locations of extensive bodies of water impounded behind the retreating ice sheet. Ridges of earth and rock dropped along the edge of the ice sheet are a prominent feature of the landscape. The great Altamont moraine, marking the outermost limits of the Mankato advance, last of the ice sheets in the region, forms a conspicuous system paralleling the Missouri River, between it and the Coteau du Missouri.

Southward, the Central Lowland glaciated area extends to the Kansas River in a zone ending roughly one hundred miles or less west of the Missouri River. Here earlier glaciation is mainly involved, and there has been ample time since for extensive modification of the old landscape. Moreover, a thick blanket of wind-deposited loess, extending from Iowa far into Nebraska and sometimes attaining a thickness of one hundred feet or more, has obscured the Great Plains–Central Lowland relationships. Along the Missouri is the deeply eroded, hilly zone known as the Drift Hills. Farther west, erosion is less advanced; but, while the horizon line is often level and plainslike in character, there are many well-developed stream valleys, and the relief is considerable. East of the Nebraska Sand Hills are the rolling Loess Hills. South of the Platte, the loess mantle extends as a flat plain far to the west, lapping onto the High Plains and thinning southward into northern Kansas. The soils developed on the loess have great fertility, as do the alluvial terraces lining most of the streams in this section. This, as we shall see later, may have contributed heavily to utilization of the region in aboriginal times.

From the Kansas River to central Texas, the Central Lowland was never subjected to glaciation, and the landscape is more varied in character. Basically, it has been developed on a surface of alternating hard- and soft-rock strata that slope downward toward the west. The hard formations have given rise to a series of east-facing escarpments, of which the Flint Hills of Kansas are an excellent example, whereas the less resistant beds between have resulted in plains. This scarped landscape continues south through eastern Oklahoma, giving way westward to the Redbeds Plains—a gently rolling lowland of slight relief in the central part of the state, and finally to the more subdued escarpments and plains of the Gypsum Hills. Belts of sand dunes border many of the streams of western Oklahoma. Still farther south, in Texas, plains remain the dominant feature, but the escarpments are more pronounced and major stream valleys are often more deeply entrenched.

The stream valleys of the Great Plains have strongly influenced man's activities, those of ancient man no less than modern. In a land of limited precipitation and scanty surface water, where native peoples lacked the know-how and technological equipment for tapping the deep-lying ground waters, the rivers, creeks, and springs were of great importance. Besides supplying the elemental need for water, the valleys also provided food for fuel and building purposes, shelter from the rigorous winters, and a fairly sure supply of meat and fur animals. To the prehistoric horticultural peoples, of course, the stream valleys were doubly important since, except in localities climatically or otherwise unsuitable, they furnished cultivable bottom lands for garden plots. Moreover, in a region where man has moved since time immemorial by land rather than by water, the valleys were easy and convenient routes of travel and trade.

The principal streams pursue easterly courses, following the general slope of the land surface. In the far north, drainage is by way of the Saskatchewan and Assiniboine river systems into Lake Winnipeg and, ultimately, to Hudson Bay. From the Canadian border to northern Kansas and Colorado, the waters drain into the Missouri, master stream for the greater part of our area. From central Kansas to northern Texas, the Arkansas, Canadian, and Red rivers carry the waters into the Mississippi; and in the extreme south, the Trinity, Brazos, and Colorado empty directly into the Gulf of Mexico.

The major through-flowing streams that rise in the mountains, as the Saskatchewan, Missouri, Platte, Arkansas, and Canadian, have entrenched themselves in flat-floored valleys several hundred feet below the general surface level and varying in width from one to several miles. Narrow canyons or gorges characterize some of their upper tributaries. An important feature of the streams, large and small, is the presence of well-marked terraces. These often occur at various levels, and provided man with safe flood-free living sites. The valley floors are frequently well wooded, but in the drier sections in the west, the timber is reduced to occasional groves or disappears entirely. The numerous lesser streams originating in the Plains often carry little or no water in their upper reaches, but along many of them there are excellent springs, and in their lower courses water can usually be found except in times of drought.

The climatic characteristics of the Plains region have affected its human utilization no less than has the form of the land surface —perhaps, indeed, more so. Considering the region as a whole, its outstanding climatic features are the low precipitation, especially limited in winter; the irregular and uncertain distribution of moisture received over long and short periods; the pronounced daily and seasonal temperature ranges; the low relative humidity, high rate of evaporation, and frequent droughts; the abundant sunshine; and the persistent winds of relatively high velocity. In general, these characteristics become increasingly marked from east to west, and are especially typical of the High Plains.[12]

In the area of interest to us here, the average annual precipitation diminishes from a high of forty inches in southeastern Kansas to about fourteen inches in eastern Colorado and New Mexico and about ten inches in southern Alberta and Saskatchewan. Westward, the annual amount diminishes fairly regularly as far as the twenty-inch line, very roughly at the hundredth meridian. Beyond this, irregularities in the land surface increasingly bring

[12] J. B. Kincer, "The Climate of the Great Plains as a Factor in Their Utilization," *Annals* of the Association of American Geographers, Vol. XIII, No. 2 (1923); C. G. Bates, "Climatic Characteristics of the Plains Region," in *Possibilities of Shelterbelt Planting in the Plains Region,* U. S. Forest Service (1935), 82–110; Borchert, *loc. cit.*

about local variability. Thus, on the High Plains of the Texas Panhandle, there is an increase of five or six inches which bends the twenty-inch line considerably toward the west. The Black Hills in South Dakota induce an increase of six to eight inches over the moisture received by the surrounding plains. Similar, though lesser, increases have been noted on the slightly elevated, upland divide between the Platte and Republican rivers in southwestern Nebraska, in the Bear Paw Mountains, on the Cypress Hills, and elsewhere. These variations, it may be surmised, are of significance not only to the modern economy of the localities concerned, but, by their effects on the natural vegetation and on the animal life it supported, would doubtless have affected in some measure the pre-agricultural native populations as well.

To native man, as perhaps in even greater degree to his modern successor, the distribution of moisture received was as important as its amount. Where corn-growing economies were or are concerned, the normal seasonal distribution is generally favorable, since sixty-five to seventy-five per cent of the precipitation occurs in the growing season of spring and early summer. This is an important point, since the scanty winter precipitation throughout the region leaves very little stored moisture in the soil upon which growing crops may draw. Basically, this fact is reflected in the native vegetation: grasses are shallow-rooted and quickly utilize the scant rainfall, while trees, dependent on stored water, find survival difficult.

Averages do not tell the whole story, of course. There are wide variations in the rainfall from year to year, and likewise in the length in which these variations persist. Without attempting a definition of what constitutes a drought or semiaridity, we may point up the foregoing by a quotation from Thornthwaite:

The year 1905 was one of the rainiest in the history of the Great Plains, and semiarid climate disappeared from the region altogether except in a small island in southeastern Colorado. Moist subhumid climate, normal to Iowa and western Illinois, occupied most of Montana and extended in two great lobes westward across Nebraska and Oklahoma. Humid climate, characteristic of Ohio,

31

pushed into the Plains in two places. The years 1910 and 1934 were two of the driest on record. In 1910 desert climate covered most of the southern Plains; there were a few islands of desert climate in the northern Plains, and semiarid climate was displaced by arid as far as Wisconsin. In 1934 nearly half of the area of the Great Plains experienced desert climate.[13]

These fluctuations are a recurrent feature of the Plains climate; and when subnormal precipitation persists over several years, they result in the droughts familiar to us from the 1930's and the 1950's. Everywhere, the moisture fluctuations add greatly to the agricultural uncertainties of the region. This is true especially west of the ninety-seventh or ninety-eighth meridian. Here the normal yearly average is very close to the minimum required for successful corn-growing, hence any marked decrease in precipitation may have disastrous consequences. Not only are the fluctuations of variable duration, extent, and intensity, but they come in no regular succession nor can they be predicted with accuracy. They do not always affect the entire region simultaneously or in equal measure; and there are certain localities that seem particularly prone to repeated and persistent moisture deficiencies. Thus, southwestern Kansas, if not perennially drought-ridden, is certainly a notoriously dry spot. So also is central South Dakota eastward from the Black Hills along the broad valley of the Cheyenne to and beyond the Missouri River. The steppe region of southern Saskatchewan and Alberta is still another example.

Summer precipitation in the Plains comes mainly as thunderstorms, often of great violence and short duration, much less frequently as hail. Downpours of three to six inches, or more, have been recorded, the amount falling in a single storm sometimes exceeding the normal precipitation for the month in which it occurs. These rains may come in such force that the ground surface is puddled, and most of the water runs off before it can be absorbed by the thirsty soil. Further, the storms are mostly local in nature, having short, erratic paths that leave a small area drenched

[13] C. W. Thornthwaite, "Climate and Settlement in the Great Plains," *Yearbook of Agriculture 1941: Climate and Man,* 183.

while nearby surrounding sections receive little or no moisture. Widespread "million-dollar" rains also occur, especially in the spring; and dry periods not uncommonly end with heavy precipitation and destructive floods.

The great expanses of unbroken topography and the absence of surface impediments give the winds a free sweep. In consequence, the average wind velocities in the Plains are exceeded in only a few places in the United States. The prevailing directions are from the northwest in winter, and from the south in summer. Violent and destructive winds, but usually of short duration, are associated with the thunderstorms that develop locally in the late afternoons or evenings and move eastward across the countryside. The strong southerly winds that usually accompany droughty conditions and prolonged high temperatures in summer, have a pronounced drying effect, and their high velocity induces rapid evaporation. Especially destructive for the corngrower are the "hot winds" which sometimes accompany shade temperatures of 100 to 110 degrees F. They have been appropriately likened to the blast from a hot furnace, and often cause heavy damage to crops and much discomfort to animal life. When they strike during critical stages in crop development, as when corn is tasselling, immense havoc may be wrought within a few hours. If they continue through several days, man and beast alike suffer intensely, widespread crop failure ensues, and even the native vegetation withers.

A few other characteristics of the Plains climate that have affected man's occupation of the region may be briefly noted. Relative humidity is lowest near the mountains, highest toward the northeast and southeast, so that at any given latitude it tends to decrease from east to west. Evaporation, on the other hand, being strongly affected by temperature and wind movement, is much greater in the south. The northward decrease in rate of evaporation is such that fifteen inches of precipitation on the Canadian line is approximately equivalent to twenty-two inches in Texas.

Temperatures show a wide annual range, with the upper thermometer readings generally decreasing somewhat and the lower readings increasing from south to north. Annual means drop fairly regularly from 65 degrees F. in Texas to 35 degrees F. in southern Alberta and Saskatchewan. Extreme summer temperature readings of 110 degrees F. or more have been recorded from Texas to Alberta in the Western Plains, though they are of course more common in the south. Minimum readings range from −16 degrees F. in the south to −55 degrees F. in southern Canada. There are also frequent sharp changes that sometimes exceed 45 degrees F. within a twenty-four-hour period. These may occur anywhere in the region; but, except for those induced on the northwestern margin by the chinook winds, they seem especially marked in the central portion and the Dakotas.

Of more direct concern than these annual temperature means to the aboriginal inhabitants of the Great Plains, particularly to those peoples who undertook the cultivation of corn, beans, and squash, was the length of the growing season. The domestic plants were all essentially warm-weather forms, sensitive to frost. In the Southern and Central Plains, about as far north as the Platte River, the period between the last spring frost and the first fall frost was normally in the neighborhood of 140 to 200 days. Farther north, unseasonable and unpredictable frosts occur with increasing frequency, and the growing season is likely to be drastically shortened in some years. Figure 2 indicates the limits of the areas within which the frost-free season is likely to be 120 and 100 days in four years out of five. In historic times, prior to reservation days, there is apparently no record of native corn agriculture beyond the 100-day line shown for the Northern Great Plains.

The natural vegetation of the Great Plains consists principally of grasses.[14] Except along the watercourses, trees grow sparsely and there are no sizable areas of forest. The grasses are of various kinds and associations, reflecting in their changes from east to west the diminishing precipitation and progressively greater aridity. On the west, extending in a broad belt from the South Saskat-

[14] Shantz, *loc. cit.*; J. M. Aikman, "Native Vegetation of the Region," in *Possibilities of Shelterbelt Planting in the Plains Region*, U. S. Forest Service (1935), 155–74.

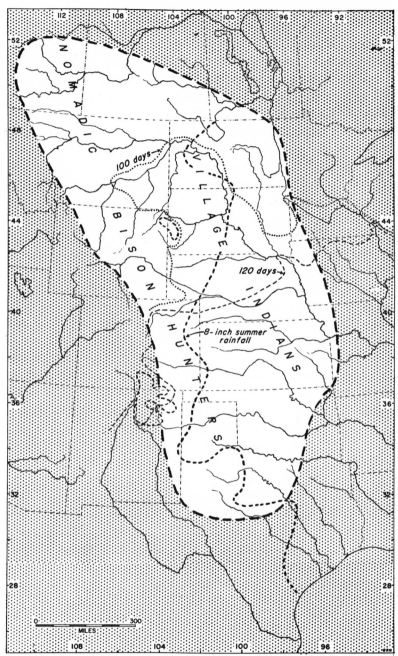

Fig. 2. *Map indicating some climatic factors that influence corn-growing in the Plains area, showing the line of eight-inch summer rainfall* (June to August), *and the limits of 100 and 120 frost-free growing days in four years out of five.* (Generalized from *Atlas of American Agriculture.*)

chewan Valley into Montana and western North Dakota, thence southward to Texas, are the short-grass plains, or steppe. This area includes large tracts of sand hills dominated by tall grasses; and on poor soils with low rainfall in Montana and in central and western Wyoming, there are extensive stands of sagebrush.

In the short-grass plains, the subsoil is permanently dry and moisture is at a premium. The characteristic grasses are grama and buffalo grass. These are low-growing, shallow-rooted, sod-forming types, capable of quick growth on the spring moisture after which they may pass into a dormant stage when the rains cease. Moreover, they have the property of curing, without cutting, into a palatable and highly nutritious winter forage, thus providing in the old days an immense natural pasture for bison and antelope.

On the east was the tall-grass region, or true prairie. Here the subsoil is permanently moist under the heavier precipitation, and tall-growing, luxuriant, deep-rooted grasses like bluestem, wheat grass, and other bunch grasses are dominant. Between this prairie zone and the steppe was a transitional belt where the short grasses characteristic of the west are conspicuous in dry years and on dry, high locations, whereas taller grasses are dominant in wet periods and on low, moist habitats. This belt lies between the ninety-eighth and hundredth meridians from South Dakota to Oklahoma, but bends toward the west at both ends. In Texas, the short-grasses and mixed-grass formations give way to mesquite and desert-grass savanna. On the north, a strip of tall grass, grading northward into the aspen-grove park land, separates the short-grass plains from the northern forest lands of Canada.

Although grasses dominated the Plains landscape everywhere, herbaceous flowering plants are an important and conspicuous part of the natural vegetation. Many of these were of varying economic significance to native man—as foods, as medicinal items, as dyestuffs, as fibers, or for other reasons.[15] There was, for ex-

15 M. R. Gilmore, "Uses of Plants by the Indians of the Missouri River Region," Bureau of American Ethnology *Thirty-third Annual Report* (1919), 43–154; P. A. Vestal and R. E. Schultes, *The Economic Botany of the Kiowa Indians;* G. G. Carlson and V. H. Jones, "Some Notes on Uses of Plants by the

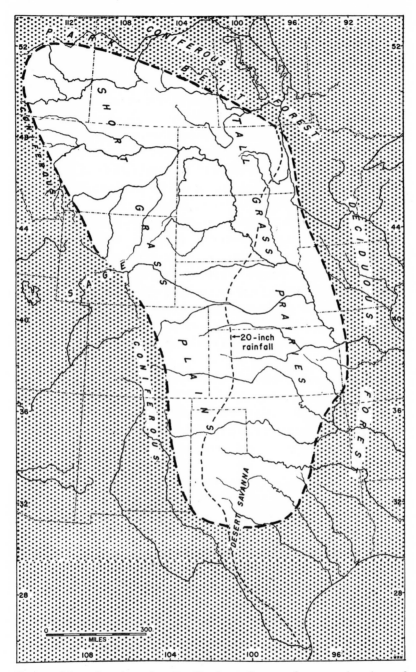

Fig. 3. *Map showing the distribution of natural vegetation in and around the Great Plains.* (Generalized from *Atlas of American Agriculture.*)

ample, the Indian turnip or tipsin (*Psoralea esculenta*), the *pomme blanche* of the *voyageurs,* whose starchy roots were eaten fresh or dried for winter use by tribes throughout the length and breadth of the Plains. In the eastern Plains, the tubers of the groundnut (*Apios tuberosa*), which grew like beads on a string and so were termed *les racines des chapelets* by the French, were gathered to be boiled or roasted, as were those of the water-loving *Sagittaria,* or arrowhead. The underground caches of the prairie vole were robbed for their stores of nutritious ground beans (*Falcata comosa*). Many of the western tribes, in times of famine, fell back on the huge, but not very palatable, roots of the bush morning-glory (*Ipomoea leptophylla*). Plantain, milkweed, purple coneflower, sunflower, and numerous other species furnished remedies for a wide variety of ailments and discomforts among the Indians. Fibers for cordage and sewing materials were obtained from the dogbane, or Indian hemp, from certain species of milkweed, and from the nettle. This list of "weeds" upon which the Plains Indians drew for one purpose or another could be greatly extended.

To the traveler from the forested lands of the east, one of the most striking characteristics of the Plains region is the sparseness of tree growth. With exception of mesquite chaparral in the south, a belt of oak savanna in east central Oklahoma and its southward extension in the Texas Cross Timbers, and a few limited stands of pine and juniper in the north, there is virtually no natural upland timber in the Plains region. On mountainous, hilly, or rugged lands, such as the Black Hills of South Dakota, the Rawhide Buttes in Wyoming, the Piney Buttes and larger, isolated masses of elevated land in Montana, and the Cypress Hills, coniferous and/or deciduous trees flourish. These, however, are not typical Plains habitats and the tree growth reflects slightly increased rainfall, more favorable soil conditions, or topographic factors that tip the scales in favor of trees as against grasses.

Throughout the region generally, trees are closely correlated

Comanche Indians," *Papers* of the Michigan Academy of Science, Arts, and Letters, Vol. XXV (1940), 517-42.

with availability of water. In the prairie belt, where fires have probably helped the grasses hold their ground against trees, the latter occur as long, branching ribbons of forest extending far to the west along the watercourses. Along the Missouri and other major streams, and southward along the eastern part of our area, these belts are from two to ten miles wide, covering the valley bottoms, fringing the bluffs, and sometimes extending onto the adjacent uplands. Towards the west, these ribbons narrow, the thinning stands of timber are entirely restricted to the valleys, and such species as oak, hickory, walnut, and sycamore disappear. Beyond the ninety-ninth meridian, aside from the ubiquitous cottonwood and willow, about the only species present are the elm, ash, hackberry, and the box elder, and these trees are greatly reduced in size and luxuriance of growth. In response to the increasingly adverse climate, trees tend to grow in greatest abundance on slopes facing north and east, where they have maximum protection against the strong drying winds and intense sunlight of midsummer, and where moisture from winter snows and summer rains is retained longest by the soil. Throughout the Plains, such locations frequently support limited stands of shrubs of various kinds. Away from these favored spots, the dry, cold winters, high winds, and irregular precipitation discourage seedlings, and the better-adapted grasses assert their dominance.

Among the shrubs and smaller trees of the region, we must take note of a number of species that were of direct economic importance to the native peoples. Edible fruits and berries were available in one form or another over a great part of the Plains and in bordering regions. In the north, the wild currant, gooseberry, saskatoon or serviceberry, and the pembina or high-bush cranberry were much sought after. Farther south were the buffalo berry, chokecherry, and wild plum. In the southeast, the nuts of the hickory, the black walnut, pecan, and hazelnut were gathered; and the papaw was certainly used, its characteristic flattened seeds having been found archaeologically at several sites. We may suppose that the persimmon was also utilized, though archaeological evidence is lacking. Among the historic tribes, the sap of the box

39

elder was boiled to produce a sugar. The wood of the Osage orange, native to the southern plains of Texas and Oklahoma, was widely traded for the manufacture of bows. From the inner bark of the slippery or red elm came fibers for making ropes and cords. Other species could be added, but those listed are illustrative.

No summary of the plant life of the Great Plains, such as that given above, can convey to the casual visitor or to the outsider an adequate impression of the land. Only those who have lived there, or who have seen it repeatedly in its varying moods, will believe that it is not everywhere and always a drab and monotonous spectacle. In a favorable year, the short grasses of the steppe resemble a smooth, velvety, soft, green carpet or a well-kept pasture. The prairie grasses, where they still remain in large stands, are like a luxuriant meadow or a field of waving grain. The varying greens of the different grasses usually fade by late summer to browns and russets. But throughout the spring, and again in fall, the grassland is a constantly changing panorama of flowering forms. The delicate-hued prairie rose, the evening primroses, the Canada and Mariposa lilies, the coreopsis and sunflower, the blue vervain, and in fall, the composites in a variety of colors and shapes, all delight the eye. Many special habitat areas have their own flowering plants: the creamy-white, bell-shaped flowers of the yucca on dry hillsides everywhere, the red and yellow blooms of the prickly pear on the uplands, the purple beeweed of the roadside and other disturbed areas, the spurge, and the showy white prickly poppy. Even the gloomy and forbidding gumbo wastes of the Dakotas are brightened by the delicate gumbo lily, and even more for the fortunate observer, by the fragrant and strikingly lovely evening star.

The principal native game resources of the Great Plains are so well known that extended discussion here is unnecessary. They included no forms unique or wholly restricted to the region. However, some of them, like the bison, flourished here in an abundance unsurpassed anywhere else on the continent. They made of the Great Plains, before the coming of the white man, one of the world's greatest hunting grounds for big game.

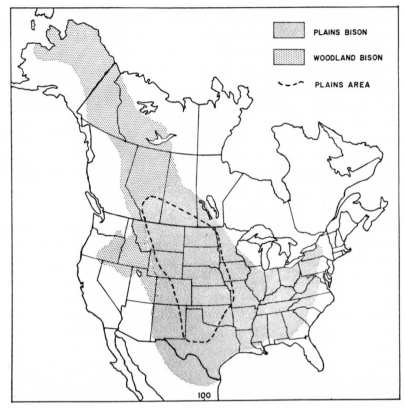

FIG. 4. *Map of the distribution in recent time of the Plains and Woodland bison in relation to the Plains area.* (Modified from Skinner and Kaisen.)

Native to the steppe and the mixed-grass areas were the bison, pronghorn antelope, and mule deer. They shared the uplands and open valleys with the gray wolf, coyote, kit fox, and jack rabbit—all fleet of foot, keen of eye, and thrifty in their water requirements—and with such typical burrowing animals as the prairie dog and badger. The plains grizzly, now believed to be extinct, ranged from western Kansas to the Prairie Provinces of Canada; and the bighorn sheep, now driven to the fastnesses of the Rockies, was once found as far east as the Little Missouri badlands. With excep-

41

tion of the last two species, the bones of all these forms have been identified in the refuse deposits at numerous archaeological sites.

Of first importance to man, of course, was the bison. Before 1800, this animal ranged from the Atlantic seaboard to the Rockies, and from northern Mexico deep into Canada. It was most numerous, however, in the Great Plains where the millions of acres of natural pastureland supported a well-nigh inexhaustible supply of beef. Upon this supply the Indian drew for a substantial part of his subsistence through thousands of years, with clothing, shelter, and a variety of household utensils of bone, horn, skin, hair, and sinew as important by-products. To any human group within reach of the herds, the size and abundance of the bison must have been an irresistible attraction. Its migratory habits meant that there would be periods of scarcity as well as of feasting, but development of methods of drying and storing the meat in times of plenty went far toward offsetting this disadvantage. Pursuit of the bison, first by stalking or by driving herds over cliffs or into compounds or by fire drives, and later by surrounds or running on horseback, was carried on by the Indian in varying degree from a dim and undated past until the final near-extermination of the animal in the 1870's. In its influence on native man, the bison outranked all other animals of the Plains combined.

Almost equally widespread, but probably present in lesser numbers, was the pronghorn, swiftest of all North American quadrupeds and, often to his undoing, one of the most inquisitive. Normally an inhabitant of the open plains, gifted with keen vision, and possessing great powers of endurance, the antelope was less easily taken by hunters than was the bison. Moreover, its weight seldom exceeded 120 pounds, as against 700 to 1,200 pounds for the female and 1,500 to 2,000 pounds for the male bison, and so its taking netted much less sustenance per animal. Its bones and horns occur in small quantities in the refuse deposits of Indian camp and village sites.

Supplementing these Plains forms, and at times rivaling them in importance to native man, were the woodland game animals that followed the narrow, winding ribbons of timber up the stream valleys far westward into the grasslands. This happy juxtaposition of widely varying habitats—open, grassy uplands and wooded valley bottoms—added such major food animals as the white-tailed deer and the elk. Here, too, were black bear, cougar, wildcat, beaver, otter, mink, raccoon, and numerous smaller fur-bearers that could be drawn on for food in times of scarcity among the larger mammals.

There was also a surprisingly varied and abundant bird life. In addition to its own more or less distinctive subspecies or varieties, the Plains region was a meeting ground for many species whose principal ranges extended far to the east or west. Some of these were taken for food, others for their feathers or for bones to be fashioned into ornaments and tools. Still others figured in the legends and myths of the historic tribes, and doubtless also in those of earlier times. Wild geese, ducks, and other aquatic birds nested in immense numbers on the lakes and marshes from Nebraska to Canada. Their seasonal migrations down the Missouri flyway brought them within easy reach of Indians residing along the rivers and creeks of the central and southern Plains. The prairie chicken and grouse flourished everywhere in the grasslands; the sage hen, from Wyoming northward. The wild turkey occurred in large numbers along the eastern margin of our area from Texas to northern Iowa and the Coteau des Prairies, ranging west with the oak forests far across Oklahoma and Kansas, into Nebraska, and up the Missouri River to the Big Bend in South Dakota. Hawks and owls were abundant, as were the bald and golden eagles and the great horned owl, all sought for their feathers.

Among the bird bones found sparingly in archaeological sites, as refuse or as worked items, are those of the great blue heron, whooping and sand-hill cranes, white pelican, crow, and raven. Absent are remains of the numerous passerine and other small birds of the region, which presumably did not figure in the native subsistence economies. And, interestingly enough, the Carolina paroquet, which formerly ranged into Kansas and Colorado, and the passenger pigeon, reported historically from as far west as western

43

North Dakota, have not been identified in the bones from archaeological sites west of the Missouri.

Of varying importance to the successive aboriginal economies in the Great Plains were fish, turtles, and shellfish. Among the historic Plains hunting tribes, there were widespread restrictions on the eating of fish; but along the Missouri, the Arikaras and their neighbors used hooks and weirs to take the large river catfish and occasional gar pike. Farther west and south, on the lesser streams, some of the prehistoric peoples angled for catfish and buffalo fish. The bones of snapping, soft-shelled, painted, and box turtles are occasionally found in Indian trash heaps, but are nowhere abundant. Mussels from the clearer, unsilted streams and creeks may or may not have been eaten, but their shells were certainly much used for the manufacture of beads, ornaments, spoons, hoes, paint receptacles, and other items. Among some peoples, they were burned or crushed for addition to the clay used in pottery-making.

In closing our review of the natural setting, it should be observed that various theories have been advanced regarding the origin of the grasslands of which the Great Plains are a part, indeed the heartland. They have been attributed to fires,[16] climate, the immense herds of bison, and to other causes. It seems most probable, however, that they have their basis, as does the climate in part, in the geological events that initiated the Great Plains land surface. According to this view, the grassland originated in Tertiary times, long before the advent of man and his fire drives, and was a result of the uplift of the western cordillera. Paleontological evidence indicates that extensive hardwood forests once extended across the present northern plains, with such warm-temperate life forms as palms and alligators common as far north as the Dakotas.[17] With uplift of the mountains to the west, the

[16] C. O. Sauer, "A Geographic Sketch of Early Man in America," *Geographical Review*, Vol. XXXIV, No. 4 (1944), 540–54; O. C. Stewart, "Why the Great Plains Are Treeless," *Colorado Quarterly*, Vol. II, No. 1 (1953), 40–50; W. R. Wedel, "The Central North American Grassland: Man-made or Natural?" *Studies in Human Ecology* (1957), *Social Science Monographs, III*, 39–69.

[17] Dunbar, *op. cit.*, 431.

climate became more diversified and extreme, the moisture-bearing winds from the Pacific were cut off, and rainfall east of the Rockies was limited to moisture derived from the Gulf of Mexico. So, there developed east of the Rockies "a region of low summer rainfall and still drier winters." In such a climate, tree growth was impossible, and the forests gradually disappeared. They were replaced by a vegetation of herbaceous plants, chiefly grasses. This vegetation persists today on the great prairies and plains.[18]

That the Great Plains grassland is of great antiquity is indicated by the frequent occurrence of buried, or fossil, soils in the Pleistocene and early Recent formations of Kansas, Nebraska, Iowa, and adjacent states, these showing the characteristics of grassland, not forest, soils.[19] Moreover, fossil seeds in Tertiary times have been cited as evidence of the widespread existence of grasses at that time. With the spread and development of the grasses in late Tertiary times was associated the evolution and wide dispersal of the large plains-dwelling grazing animals—for example, the horse, bison, camel, and others—whose dentition was specialized for feeding on the coarse prairie grasses.[20]

Thus, in broadest outline, was the stage set for man's appearance in the North American grasslands.

[18] H. A. Gleason, "The Vegetational History of the Middle West," *Annals of the Association of American Geographers*, Vol. XII (1922), 39–85.

[19] W. R. Wedel, "The Central North American Grassland: Man-made or Natural?" *loc. cit.*, 47–49.

[20] Dunbar, *op. cit.*, 492.

CHAPTER THREE

✋ THE EARLY BIG-GAME HUNTERS

NEITHER THE TIME of man's first coming to the New World, nor the routes over which he traveled, nor the nature of the cultural equipment he brought along, are known. To all of these problems, the answers are still hidden in the mists of remote antiquity, and archaeology has thrown no direct light on them. At present, therefore, we can speak only in generalities—in terms, that is, of what probably or possibly happened.

There is, of course, no evidence whatsoever that man originated in America. Biologically speaking, all of his near relatives in the animal kingdom belong to the Old World. Informed students generally accept the view that the peopling of the New World was principally from Asia by way of a former connection in the present Bering Strait locality. Geologists have pointed out that an upwarping of the earth's crust here, or, conversely, a lowering of the ocean level, by 180 feet would lay bare a broad strip of relatively flat land connecting Siberia and Alaska and extending as a fringe along the adjacent coasts of both continents. This sort of lowering of the sea level is known to have occurred during each glacial age, when immense quantities of water were drawn from the ocean to nourish the widespread continental ice sheets.[1]

It may be supposed that with the Arctic waters blocked off by

[1] W. A. Johnston, "Quaternary Geology of North America in Relation to the Migration of Man," in D. Jenness' *The American Aborigines, Their Origin and Antiquity*, Fifth Pacific Science Congress (1933), 11–45; D. M. Hopkins, "Cenozoic History of the Bering Land Bridge," *Science*, Vol. CXXIX (1959), 1519–28; D. S. Byers, "The Bering Bridge—Some Speculations," *Ethnos*, Nos. 1–2 (1957), 20–26.

46

PLATE I. *Upper:* The Lindenmeier site in northern Colorado. Figure stands on level of Folsom occupation ten thousand years ago. (Courtesy F. H. H. Roberts, Jr.). *Lower:* Excavating a deeply buried early-big-game-hunter site (lower right) on Lime Creek in southwestern Nebraska. (River Basin Surveys, Smithsonian Institution).

PLATE II. *Upper:* Signal Butte in western Nebraska. The soil cap contains the stratified remains of successive human occupations running from about 2000 B.C. to A.D. 1700. (Photograph by C. L. Dow). *Left:* Buried fireplaces of the Woodland people at Sterns Creek in eastern Nebraska.

PLATE III. *Upper:* Aerial view of two square Upper Republican house floors (top and center) on Medicine Creek in southwestern Nebraska, dated about A.D. 1400. (River Basin Surveys, Smithsonian Institution). *Lower:* Aerial view of three square Upper Republican house floors (left center, top center, and lower right) on Medicine Creek in southwestern Nebraska, dated about A.D. 1400. (River Basin Surveys, Smithsonian Institution).

PLATE IV. *Upper:* Floor of circular Pawnee earth lodge near Leshara, Nebraska. (Nebraska State Historical Society). *Lower:* Rectangular house floor of the Upper Republican people, about A.D. 1200–1400, on Medicine Creek in southwestern Nebraska. (Nebraska State Historical Society).

PLATE V. Some Central Plains pottery wares. *Upper left:* Historic
Pawnee, about A.D. 1800; *Upper right:* Lower Loup, about sixteenth
century; *Middle left:* Great Oasis; *Middle right:* Oneota; *Lower left:*
Upper Republican, about A.D. 1400; *Lower right:* Valley focus Woodland. (Nebraska State Historical Society, except *lower left*, Smithsonian Institution).

PLATE VI. Some Central Plains pottery wares. *Upper left:* Great Bend aspect, Kansas, about sixteenth century; *Upper right:* Dismal River, about A.D. 1700; *Lower left:* Kansas City Hopewell, about A.D. 200–400; *Lower right:* Woodland vessel, Platte County, Nebraska. (*Upper right and lower right*, Nebraska State Historical Society).

PLATE VII. Stone and pottery pipes from the Central Plains. (Nebraska State Historical Society and Smithsonian Institution).

PLATE VIII. *Upper:* Petroglyphs near Blackbird Hill, Thurston County, Nebraska. (Nebraska State Historical Society). *Lower:* Petroglyphs at Spriggs Rocks, Rice County, Kansas. (Smithsonian Institution).

such a land bridge, the warmer waters of the Pacific would have tempered somewhat the climate of the southern portions of the isthmus. From what is known of the contours of the ocean floor in and about Bering Strait, it has been further suggested that the land bridge would probably have appeared as a gently rolling plain, perhaps sprinkled with lakes and ponds, intersected by small streams, and clothed with lush prairie grasses that would have provided abundant pasturage for mammoths, bison, horses, and other large grazing animals of the time. Whatever the exact nature of this land bridge and the manner of its formation, it is evident that across such a connection moved a great host of large mammals in Pleistocene time and earlier—horses and camels from America westward into Asia; elephants, bison, bears, deer, and other forms from Asia into America. Through these intercontinental exchanges, the valleys and plains of North America came to be occupied by the most diversified big-game fauna in their history —as varied and impressive an assemblage of game animals as those of modern East Africa, and including many animals of greater size than their modern representatives.[2]

It is possible that the first men to set foot on New World soil were hunters following the migrating game animals in a direction that would take them away from the competition of others of their own kind. Or, they may have made the crossing of the frozen strait long after, drawn by some attraction or driven by some force we do not yet comprehend. In any case, whatever their motivation or the time of their coming, we know that some of these early hunters arrived while the plains of America were still inhabited by such great Pleistocene mammals as the elephant, horse, camel, and ground sloth, all of which were extinct when the first Europeans finally made their way into the North American interior in the sixteenth century.

Once these early human arrivals reached the American mainland, there were several possible routes by which they could have dispersed themselves over the New World.[3] The great central

2 Dunbar, *op. cit.*, 484–93; Sauer, *loc. cit.*, 539–40.
3 Flint, *Glacial Geology*, 534–35; Sauer, *loc. cit.*, 535–36, 554–57.

47

plateau of Alaska and the lowlands along the Arctic coast, both accessible from the land bridge, were too low and dry to support glaciers, though the high mountains bordering them were extensively iced. Thus, men and the game animals upon which they subsisted could have moved up the Yukon Valley and crossed over to the Mackenzie River, thence passing southward by way of an intermittently ice-free corridor along the east base of the Rocky Mountains. In times of partial deglaciation during the last (Wisconsin) major ice age, other low-level routes were probably open through the interior of British Columbia, along the valleys between the Coast Ranges and the Rockies. This intermontane passage would have given access to the Plateau and Great Basin regions of the United States. That east of the Rockies, which one student of the problem has called "the central axis from which the dispersal of early man took place,"[4] led directly to the High Plains and an easy road south. The stream valleys coursing eastward from the Rockies diverted some of this traffic into the eastern sections of the United States. In all likelihood, the regions into which the early pedestrian traffic east and west of the Rockies first debouched—the Plateau–Great Basin on the west, the High Plains on the east, were subject to much heavier rainfall than they receive today, and thus offered greater inducements to the early hunting and gathering peoples.

The early migrations to America should be visualized not as a headlong rush or a purposeful move by large numbers of people headed for a known destination. Rather, there was a slow, long-continued, and probably intermittent movement by many small bands of hunter folk. If we may trust the evidence of the radio-carbon clock, early hunting and food-gathering peoples had established themselves in the southern United States, four thousand miles or more from Bering Strait, as early as twelve to fifteen thousand years ago, and perhaps as much as twenty-five thousand years ago; and they had reached the southern tip of South America, more than ten thousand miles from the port of entry, by eight thousand years ago. No one supposes that these dates mark the

[4] Sauer, *loc. cit.,* 555.

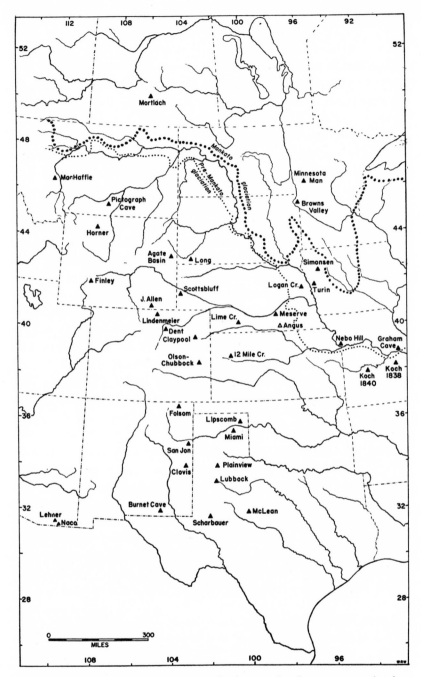

FIG. 5. *Map of the early-big-game-hunter and other preceramic sites in and around the Great Plains.*

time of arrival of the first comers, nor does anyone know how much earlier man may have been present. A recent geologic estimate suggests that man in America may date as far back as forty to sixty thousand years.[5] There are archaeologists and geographers who regard this estimate as conservative.

Of the cultural baggage with which man entered the New World, we can be reasonably sure a priori on several points. In the first place, pedestrian travel through the high latitudes of Asia and America, even during an interglacial period, would have necessitated familiarity with fire, the manufacture of clothing, and the construction of shelters. If subsistence was fundamentally by hunting of large game, the use of spears for thrusting or hurling, of other weapons, and of appropriate butchering tools must also be inferred. In regard to the precise character of these tools and weapons, we still know nothing. Neither do we know whether these peoples possessed the dog, either for hunting, for transport of baggage, or for food; but it may be significant that no dog remains have been reported among the bones identified from the earliest American sites we now know.

The view that the movement of early peoples from the Old World to the New was a long-drawn-out process may help explain some of the marked physical variations seen among the American Indians. Long classed as a branch of the Mongoloid race, the American aborigines exhibit many departures from that Old World stock. This is true of peoples represented by skeletal remains known from their archaeological associations to be of some antiquity, and also of certain more recent groups occupying marginal or "refuge" areas in North and South America. In considerable measure, these differences may have arisen after man's arrival in the New World, thus reflecting adaptations to varying environmental circumstances.[6] Some anthropologists, on the other hand, have suggested that the Mongoloid peoples of Asia may be

[5] Flint, *Glacial Geology*, 534.

[6] M. T. Newman, "The Application of Ecological Rules to the Racial Anthropology of the Aboriginal New World," *American Anthropologist*, Vol. LV (1953), 324.

a comparatively recent evolutionary development, and that they were preceded by different racial stocks with Caucasoid or other non-Mongoloid characteristics.[7] Thus, early peoples drifting into Alaska at various times over a period of many millennia and perhaps originating in various sections of Asia, may well have been drawn from more than one racial stock. The descendants of such immigrants, when they turn up in archaeological situations, would show much less similarity to the "classic" Mongoloid stock than do the recent Indians who are presumably descendants of later arrivals from the Old World. The presence of such deviant groups, and the growing suspicion that they perhaps betoken an earlier non-Mongoloid New World population, should prompt a more thoughtful answer by the professional to the widely asked and time-worn question—who preceded the Indian in America?

In an estimable attempt to distinguish broadly the earlier native peoples of America from those who left the much more abundant remains of later times, archaeologists and other students have from time to time had recourse to various designations—the Old Hunters, the Ancient Hunting Peoples, and, probably the most widely used of all, the familiar Paleo-Indian. To the extent to which the term Indian itself has built-in racial connotations, that is, implies a Mongoloid relationship, the designation Paleo-Indian is admittedly of doubtful accuracy or applicability. On the other hand, if by "Indian" we understand simply one of the aboriginal or native peoples of the New World, with no further implication of race, then the qualifier "paleo-" (meaning old) seems both permissible and useful. It is in this latter sense that the term Paleo-Indian appears here and there throughout this book. For the immediate purposes of the present chapter, however, Sauer's casual designation of the Paleo-Indians as the "early big-game hunters"[8] seems more adequately expressive of what little we know about these very early Americans. This rubric conveniently accommodates both the hunters of the elephant and the later hunters of

[7] J. B. Birdsell, "The Problem of the Early Peopling of the Americas as Viewed from Asia," in *The Physical Anthropology of the American Indian*, (1949), 63.
[8] Sauer, *loc. cit.*, 556.

51

large bison, but it carries no implication that the subsistence economy of the men involved was based solely on the pursuit of these
large quadrupeds. Like the much later equestrian bison-hunters
of the western Plains, these early men must have supplemented
their livelihood with vegetable and other products when circumstances required.

ELEPHANT HUNTERS OF THE SOUTHERN PLAINS

Archaeological evidence that men and elephants existed together in the New World has been found at a number of localities
in the United States. Indeed, the first New World sites where the
claim was raised for a direct or primary association of human artifacts and the remains of animals now extinct involved one of the
American Proboscidea, the mastodon. The earliest was Koch's discovery in 1838, in the bottomlands of the Bourbeuse River, in Gasconade County, Missouri, of a half-burned mastodon skeleton and
eight chipped stone artifacts; the second, also by Koch but in 1840,
was his find of another mastodon with five chipped artifacts, this
time in the Pomme de Terre Valley in Benton County, Missouri[9]
(Figure 5). Some of the artifacts from the Gasconade County find
have proven, on further study by competent present-day scholars,
to be of forms elsewhere associated with more recent prehistoric
horizons of the Midwest, and their primary association with the
mastodon is consequently questioned. The implements from the
later find have not been located; they are nowhere described in
detail, and their appearance is unknown; and so the significance
of the reported association cannot be evaluated in light of the
much more precise information now available on early man and
his manufactures, and on the animals with which he may have
been associated.

No such uncertainties surround a series of more recent discoveries, most of them made in the past twenty-five years in the

[9] H. Gross, "Mastodons, Mammoths, and Man in America," *Bulletin*, Texas
Archeological and Paleontological Society, Vol. XXII (1951), 115–16, 103–10,
124–25; H. M. Wormington, *Ancient Man in North America* (4th ed., 1957),
101–102.

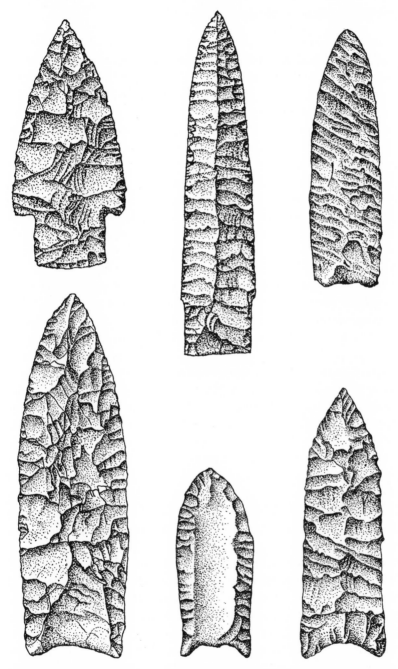

FIG. 6. *Some weapon points of the early big-game hunters, from seven to twelve thousand years ago. Top row* (left *to* right) *Scottsbluff, Eden Angostura; bottom row* (left *to* right), *Clovis Fluted, Folsom Fluted, Plainview.*

Southern Plains and in the adjacent Southwest. In these, the initial finds were accidental, to be sure; but the follow-up work was by competent scientists excavating under careful controls and recording their observations meticulously. As a result, the associations have been solidly established.

In comparison with the village sites and burial mounds of the later American aborigines, the locations attributed to early man have not produced artifacts in large numbers or in great variety. This is not surprising, for people who live by the chase and move about on foot seldom encumber themselves with nonessentials. The marks of their passage must be read chiefly in a few obscure game kills and camp sites, where occasional stone and bone tools were dropped, lost, or otherwise escaped the eyes of their owners when they moved on.

In the case of the early elephant-hunters, recognition of their erstwhile presence is made easier for the archaeologist by the consistent finding of a distinctively fashioned kind of spear point. To this spear point has been assigned the name *Clovis Fluted*, to distinguish it from a variety of other forms sometimes found in slightly younger associations. Clovis Fluted points vary somewhat in details, but all are leaf-shaped in outline, fairly heavy in cross section, with parallel or slightly convex edges and a concave base. On one or both sides they have a broad, shallow channel, or flute, that runs from the base about half way to the tip. The edges above the base are usually blunted by grinding. In length, these points range from one and one-half to about five inches, and their width is about one-third to a little less than one-half the length. The flaking is not remarkable for either fineness or precision. It is these points that are usually found in association with elephant remains.

Other artifacts are much less common and also less distinctive. They include large flakes, sometimes triangular in outline, and having retouched edges, which were presumably cutting or scraping tools like those not uncommonly found in many later sites. There are a few circular or oblong, slightly flattened hammerstones, and a few specimens of worked bone. The latter in-

54

clude cylindrical shaftlike pieces, nine to ten inches long and slightly more than one-half inch in diameter, which were beveled at one or both ends. It has been suggested that these were perhaps foreshafts from spears or possibly spear points.

For this very limited series or assemblage of artifacts, and for such other characteristics as may be inferred regarding the way of life of the people who made and used them, the term *Llano complex* has been suggested.[10] The materials at hand are insufficient to justify use of the term *culture*, which usually implies a much more detailed knowledge of the tool assemblage and way of life of the peoples concerned. Perhaps a clearer idea of the difficulties that confront the archaeologist on this very early time-level can be derived from brief descriptions of some of the principal sites from which the evidence has come to date.

The first of these finds was made near Dent, Colorado, some thirty-five miles north and slightly east of Denver.[11] Here, flood-waters in 1932 exposed a deposit of large animal bones in a terrace of the South Platte River. Systematic excavation subsequently revealed parts of at least twelve mammoths, most of them females and immature animals, and some in partial articulation. Among the bones were found two Clovis Fluted spear points, as well as numerous large stones which were otherwise scarce in the vicinity. A mass kill is suggested, though there were no butchering tools.

In the following year, on the High Plains near Miami, Texas, deep plowing brought to light a number of bone fragments.[12] Investigation disclosed parts of no less than five dismembered mammoth skeletons, representing both immature and mature animals. All were in the upper layers of what is believed to have been a filled-in pond. From among the scattered bones, tusks, and teeth were taken three projectile points and a scraper. It is suggested that disease, hunger, or drought may have brought the animals to a dwindling waterhole, where some perhaps died from

10 E. H. Sellards, *Early Man in America*, 17–46.

11 Wormington, *Ancient Man in North America*, 43–44.

12 Sellards, *Early Man in America*, 18–29; Sellards, "Artifacts Associated with Fossil Elephant," *Bulletin*, Geological Society of America, Vol. XLIX (1938), 999–1010.

natural causes and others were finished off by man. As at Dent, there is no evidence here of campfires or of other features suggesting that men had camped on the spot; nor is there a satisfactory explanation as to why no remains of animals other than the mammoth would occur in or around the ancient waterhole, if drought brought them there.

Other finds of prime importance for the problems of the early elephant-hunters come from the well-known Clovis-Portales district on the Staked Plains of eastern New Mexico.[13] Here is a series of shallow dry basins, locally known as Blackwater Draw, and believed to represent ancient lakes or marshes dating from a period of heavier precipitation than the present. With climatic desiccation, these lakes dwindled and finally disappeared, and their beds were filled with sand. Subsequently, wind and water have eroded these deposits in varying degrees. The surface sands have been rearranged into dunes, exposing a more resistant gray or bluish-gray stratum which contains animal bones and artifacts. The bones of extinct bison are very plentiful; and mammoth bones, both scattered and as nearly complete skeletons, are also common. Along with both these forms, there are Clovis Fluted points, a few scraping or cutting tools, and occasional bone implements. Hearths have also been found. The remains of horses and camels are present, but these have not been reported in definite association with artifacts or other evidence of man. Snail shells from the bluish-gray sands and charcoal from the hearths are regarded as indicating a cooler and more moist climate than the present. On the available evidence, man is believed to have been camping and hunting the mammoth along Blackwater Draw during a period of heavy rainfall and reduced temperatures corresponding to the end of the Pleistocene. The camp fires, the assemblages of stone tools, and the associated animal bones date

[13] Sellards, *Early Man in America*, 29–31; E. B. Howard, "Evidence of Early Man in North America," *Museum Journal*, Vol. XXIV, Nos. 2–3 (1935), 79–100; J. L. Cotter, "The Occurrence of Flints and Extinct Animals in Pluvial Deposits Near Clovis, New Mexico," *Proceedings*, Academy of Natural Sciences of Philadelphia, Vol. LXXXIX (1937), 2–16; Wormington, *Ancient Man in North America*, 47–51.

from that period, from which, however, we have as yet no radio-carbon dates.

Two other recent discoveries, though they lie outside the area of main interest here, deserve comment for the added light they shed on the activities of the early elephant-hunters. These are the Naco and Lehner mammoth sites in southern Arizona, only a few miles from the International Boundary.[14] Both were initially exposed by arroyo erosion. The Naco find included the skull, fore parts, and other bones of a single animal, possibly not quite full grown. With these remains were associated eight points, identified as Clovis Fluted. None was embedded in bone; but all lay between the skull base and the fore part of the rib cage, and one was directly at the base of the skull, where the spinal cord was most vulnerable. The concentration of points in the vital area of the beast is regarded as evidence that they were from spears used in making the kill. No tools suitable for skinning or butchering the animal came to light. The sands in and on which the bones lay are identified as deposits by a perennial stream. Overlying silts and clays are interpreted as reflecting drying of the climate and impoverishment of the plant cover. Charcoal samples from among the bones have given a radiocarbon date of 9,250, plus or minus 300 years before present, whereas geological considerations lead to an estimated antiquity of ten to eleven thousand years ago.

The Lehner site, located only a few miles northwest of the Naco site, is a bone bed which has yielded parts of at least nine mammoths, in addition to the extinct bison, tapir, and probably the horse. Among the bones were found thirteen points and eight chipped cutting or scraping tools, presumably used in skinning or dressing the kills. It is inferred that ponded waters drew the animals, some of which were killed and butchered by man from time to time. Two hearths are evidence that the hunters camped for a time at the scene. Charcoal from these has been variously

---

[14] E. W. Haury, *et al,* "Artifacts with Mammoth Remains, Naco, Arizona," *American Antiquity,* Vol. XIX, No. 1 (1953), 1–14; Haury, *et al,* "The Lehner Mammoth Site, Southeastern Arizona," *American Antiquity,* Vol. XXV, No. 1 (1959), 2–39.

dated at between seven and twelve thousand years ago, with the latter figure regarded as probably most nearly correct.

In and around the Great Plains, there have been other finds involving either elephant remains or large fluted points, or both. Since these add little to what can be inferred from the records reviewed above, they merit no more than passing notice here. Thirty miles southwest of Abilene, Texas, at the McLean site, a fluted point was found embedded in the soil near the lower jaw of an elephant; but there is no evidence that the point was in any way connected with the death of the animal. A fluted point from Burnet Cave, in the Guadalupe Mountains of southern New Mexico, appears to be within the range of the Clovis type; but among the apparently associated animal bones, which included extinct bison and a musk ox-like animal, there were no elephant bones. The Angus, Nebraska, find remains inadmissible as evidence of association because the circumstances of discovery of the point have never been cleared up. East of the Plains, fluted points have not been found in association with extinct animals or in situations which would permit geological estimates of age.

Of the several kinds of elephants that inhabited North America during Pleistocene times, the one that has been most frequently identified in association with artifacts of early man is the Columbian mammoth (*Mammuthus [Parelephas] columbi*). All of the associations we have just reviewed for the Great Plains and the adjacent Southwest, so far as satisfactory identification of species has been made, appear to be with this form.[15] Like the Imperial mammoth, another common resident of the Southern Plains and Great Basin, it was a giant among the mammals of its time and would have been such today. Both these species exceeded in size the modern elephants, standing as much as thirteen or fourteen feet high at the shoulder and possessing great curving tusks of nearly the same length. The food requirements of beasts of this bulk must have been far too great to have been met by the short steppe grasses that now dominate much of their former habitat, and a much more luxuriant vegetative cover than exists at present

[15] Sellards, *Early Man in America*, 109–10.

must therefore be inferred. The heavier rainfall deduced by geologists from the soil formations in which the elephant remains occur, as at Clovis, may have been reflected in a lush prairie grassland where there is now steppe or desert.

It is important to note that at all of the sites we have briefly reviewed, the remains of several animals were found. This does not necessarily mean that all were slain at the same time, or that man availed himself of an abundance of meat made suddenly available by some turn of fate. At most of these localities there were both scattered skeletons and others in partial articulation, suggesting that the beasts perished at intervals rather than en masse. Moreover, a surprisingly large proportion of the skeletons have been identified as those of young and immature animals. From this we may infer that the early hunters, like the Plains Indian bison-hunters of one hundred years ago, selected their quarry with care and took the animals that were easier to kill and better for eating.

The methods employed by the early American elephant-hunters, armed with stone-tipped spears, in bringing down their giant prey can only be conjectured.[16] A young animal or one already incapacitated by accident or illness, once isolated successfully from the herd, could doubtless have been dispatched by a group of experienced spearmen without undue risk to themselves. Or, animals trapped at a creek-bottom water hole, on the marshy edge of an upland pond, in broken terrain, or at a slippery stream crossing, could have been successfully attacked. Repeated kills of individual animals at especially favored hunting spots over periods of a few months or years could account for the situation found by the archaeologist at any one of the stations we have considered. There is no indication of pits or traps, that poison was used, or of communal drives such as were certainly practiced by the later bison-hunters in the Plains. Neither is there any shred of evidence in any of the known associations of man and the elephant that the latter were the victims of a fire drive.

[16] For an excellent discussion of this point, see Haury, *et al*, "The Lehner Mammoth Site, Southeastern Arizona," *loc. cit.*, 27–29.

59

BISON HUNTERS OF THE WESTERN PLAINS

With the disappearance of the elephant from the Southern Plains, the early hunting peoples of the region turned to the smaller but vastly more abundant grazing animals that remained. Their chief source of meat became the bison. This was probably represented by several species. The one most frequently hunted, to judge from the archaeological record, is that which has been variously described as *Bison taylori, Bison antiquus,* and *Bison occidentalis.*[17] It was somewhat larger in body size than the modern bison, *Bison bison,* from which its remains are most readily distinguished by greater skull size and larger, straighter horn cores. Where the skull and horn cores are missing, final identification of the species is seldom satisfactory.

The remains of these early bison-hunters are more plentiful and more widespread in the Great Plains than are those of the earlier elephant hunters. The camp sites and mass kills from which the most substantial data come are rare, although surface finds of typical points occur widely. They have been found from the Prairie Provinces southward to Texas and New Mexico, and from the Rockies eastward into the western Dakotas, Nebraska, and Kansas. Related or similar artifacts occur also in the eastern United States, but not in association with extinct animals.

As in the case of the elephant hunters, so the bison hunters provided themselves with weapon heads of more or less distinctive types. Taking these as a rough guide, it is possible to set apart several different complexes which judged by the associated animal remains and their geological context and radiocarbon dates, can be further arranged in a tentative chronological framework.

On the present evidence, the Folsom complex is the oldest of the bison-hunting groups. It takes its name from the locality in northern New Mexico where its highly distinctive spear points

---

[17] It has been suggested that Bison *occidentalis* was "a later animal on the plains of North America than *antiquus*, but was the successful surviving species that gave rise to the recent plains bison," See M. F. Skinner and O. C. Kaisen, "The Fossil Bison of Alaska and Preliminary Revision of the Genus," *Bulletin*, American Museum of Natural History, Vol. LXXXIX (1947), 171.

were first found in undisputed association with the remains of an extinct form of bison. The points, known as *Folsom Fluted*, are generally smaller and lighter than the Clovis Fluted previously described, and often show more painstaking workmanship on the part of the ancient flintsmith. They are more or less leaf-shaped in outline, broadest toward the tip which is either rounding or tapering, and have a concave base. The base frequently has two sharp rearward projections and sometimes a small nipple-like protuberance in the center. Highly characteristic is a broad groove on one or both faces, which runs from the base for two-thirds or more of the distance toward the tip, and results in two lateral ridges paralleling the edges of the blade. In cross section, this gives a biconcave appearance to the points. The edges have a fine secondary retouching, after which the base and the edges for about one-third of the length of the blade were blunted. In length, Folsom Fluted points range from less than one inch to about three inches.

The type locality for the Folsom Fluted points, as we have noted, is in New Mexico—specifically, in Union County.[18] Here, on a tributary of the Cimarron, eight miles west of Folsom, nineteen finely-flaked fluted points were recovered among the bones of twenty-three large, wide-horned bison. The bones and artifacts were in a dark-gray clay stratum believed to represent an old water hole or bog, which had presumably attracted the animals to the spot. Most of the skeletons lacked the tail bones, from which it is inferred that the people who made the kill had removed the hides with the tails attached. Except for a scraper and part of a flake knife, however, there were no tools which might have been used in flaying the bison. It is now generally accepted that the fluted points were not knives but spearheads from the weapons used in dispatching the quarry.

The inventory of tools and other artifacts possessed by these hunters has been extended considerably by several later discoveries, notably those at the Clovis-Portales locality, at the Lipscomb bison quarry, and at the Lindenmeier site. At Clovis, for example,

[18] Wormington, *Ancient Man in North America*, 23–29.

Folsom Fluted points, other points similar in size and outline but without fluting, and various forms of end and side scrapers have been found stratigraphically above the formations we have previously noted as containing elephant bones and Clovis Fluted points.[19] The scrapers are a varied lot and show no marked differences from some of those commonly found in later sites of the Plains Indians.

At the Lipscomb bison quarry, sixteen miles north of Canadian, Texas, eighteen projectile points, several side scrapers, an end scraper, two flake knives, and a number of chips were found in association with a mass of fossil bison skeletons. Charcoal and ashes were noted among the bones, as well as indications of hearths; and some of the bones had been split and cut. Many of the skeletons are reported to have been in articulation, including fourteen with skulls in an area measuring but twelve by twenty feet. Of these, it was said that the "skeletons were headed chiefly in an easterly or southerly direction and overlapped one another considerably." It has been suggested that the animals may have been a herd which, caught perhaps in a snow storm, wandered into a depression, stopped, and perished by the hand of man.[20]

The most substantial additions to our knowledge of the way of life of the Folsom hunters comes from the Lindenmeier site, some twenty-two miles north of Fort Collins, Colorado.[21] It is in an old valley, from which the bordering ridge on the south has been removed by erosion so that the former valley floor remains as a sort of terrace. Some thousands of years ago, there were doubtless meadows and marshes here which attracted bison and other animals from the Plains not far to the east. On the old surface, buried beneath two to seventeen feet of alluvial deposits, are traces of old

[19] Sellards, *Early Man in America*, 54–58.

[20] C. B. Schultz, "Some Artifact Sites of Early Man in the Great Plains and Adjacent Areas," *American Antiquity*, Vol. VIII, No. 3 (1943), 244–48.

[21] F. H. H. Roberts, Jr., "A Folsom Complex: Preliminary Report on Investigations at the Lindenmeier Site in Northern Colorado," Smithsonian *Miscellaneous Collections*, Vol. XCIV, No. 4 (1935); Roberts, "Additional Information on the Folsom Complex: Report on the Second Season's Investigations at the Lindenmeier Site in Northern Colorado," Smithsonian *Miscellaneous Collections*, Vol. XCV, No. 10 (1936).

camps, with the debris of stone-working activities, refuse animal bone, and various stone and bone artifacts.

Conspicuous among the artifacts are the fluted points and a few fluted knives, both of which are distinctive types for the complex here represented. There are also end scrapers and side scrapers, many of them differing little from the scraping tools of later times in the Plains. Flint flakes with the ends or sides chipped to scraping edges are present. Other chipped implements include concave-edged scrapers or "spoke shaves," various cutting and chopping tools, large blades, drills, and flakes with one or more small graver points probably intended for scratching fine lines on bone, wood, or other surfaces. The channel flakes produced in fluting the spear points were sometimes retouched and utilized as flake knives. Hammerstones, grooved sandstone blocks for smoothing down shafts, rubbing stones, small sandstone tablets for grinding or mixing paints, and red and yellow ocher for pigments were also found. Objects of bone included awls and punches, small needle-like objects with an eye, incised tubular beads (?), small gambling pieces with incised markings, and a disk with a finely ticked edge.

From the same soils that yielded the foregoing artifacts were taken the bones of the extinct bison, *Bison taylori*, the American camel, and such smaller forms as the deer, pronghorn, wolf, fox, and rabbit, which have survived without significant change to the present time. There were also elephant bones, but none of these was in direct association with the artifacts and other evidences of human activity.

The archaeological zone at Lindenmeier is in a dark soil resulting from heavy vegetation, and thus is presumed to reflect a period of heavier precipitation than the present. Grazing animals drawn to the spot by the lush grass and water would surely have attracted the men who preyed upon those animals. An assured water supply, the presence of gravels that offered materials suitable for manufacture of tools and implements, and a sheltered camping location would have induced men to linger as long as there was game available and to return to it as often as the animals visited it.

63

As surface finds, Folsom Fluted points have been found over a considerable portion of the Great Plains. Two additional occurrences require notice. One is near Lubbock, Texas, where a lake fill yielded Folsom points, a scraper, and burned bison bone from a well-defined stratum approximately fifteen feet underground. Radiocarbon tests on some of the burned bone indicate an age of 9,883, plus or minus 350 years, and the associated Folsom points are presumed to be of comparable age. At the MacHaffie site, near Helena, Montana, Folsom points occurred in the lowermost of three occupational levels. With them were several scrapers, flaked knives, and retouched flakes. Associated bison bones have not been identified, though they are thought to be from animals larger than the modern forms.[22]

In contrast to the sites from which have come the typical fluted Clovis and Folsom points, is another group of early hunter-sites characterized instead by leaf-shaped points of various kinds, but all without fluted faces. Some of these may be as old as Folsom sites, others are certainly later. They constitute a complicated and difficult area, since it involves many more finds whose age, distribution, and associations almost defy simplification. A good many of the finds have not yet been reported in detail, and the information at hand is far from satisfactory. To the nonspecialist, there appears to be a great deal of confusion regarding the identification and classification of the point types, of associated animal remains, and in other critical details. No general over-all synthesis has yet been produced; and the familiar device of inventing rubrics into which a variety of differing materials may be forced and thus seemingly made more manageable has not helped clear the confusion. Too, there is the sobering thought that archaeologists here are still very much in the fact-gathering stage, that almost every new discovery may produce data that will contradict established dogma and thus call for new interpretations.

Apparently somewhat later in time than the materials ascribed to the Folsom complex were the unfluted points now designated

[22] R. G. Forbis and J. D. Sperry, "An Early Man Site in Montana," *American Antiquity*, Vol. XVIII, No. 2 (1952), 127–32.

as *Plainview*. These take their name from a locality near Plainview, Texas (Figure 5), where eighteen specimens were found among the bones of one hundred or more bison provisionally identified as *Bison taylori*.[23] The bones had evidently accumulated within a fairly short time in a shallow water hole or pond along an old watercourse. From the number of skeletons present, it is thought the animals might have been stampeded into attempting to cross the stream, became disabled in the attempt, and were dispatched by man. In addition to the points, there were also end and side scrapers and a small flake knife, presumably representing implements employed in dressing out the kill. The points may be described as more or less lanceolate in outline, with parallel or slightly convex edges and concave bases. They show some similarity to Clovis points, but lack fluting. There is usually some thinning of the base, however, and the edges near the base are ground smooth.

Plainview points, or points classed as Plainview, are reported to have a wide distribution in and around the Plains; but such published records as are available provide little detailed information concerning the associated tools or the way of life of their makers. An exception may be the Red Smoke site in Frontier County, Nebraska, where other stone artifacts and probably hearths are reported in association with Plainview points, and stratigraphically beneath other archaeological materials dated by radiocarbon at 8,862, plus or minus 230 years ago. This figure compares favorably with the older of two radiocarbon dates from the Plainview site—one of 7,100 plus or minus 160 years ago, the other of 9,172, plus or minus 500 years ago.

Another important group of early materials are those formerly designated as "Yuma," from their initial recognition in Yuma County, Colorado. In this locality, and then more widely throughout the Plains, these points were found in wind-scoured areas, or blowouts, during the drought of the 1930's. Sometimes they were

---

[23] Sellards, *et al.* "Fossil Bison and Associated Artifacts from Plainview, Texas, with Description of Artifacts by Alex D. Krieger," *Bulletin*, Geological Society of America, Vol. LVIII (1947), 927–54.

found in the same blowouts with Folsom Fluted points, and in the same general localities were noted the remains of fossil bison or elephants. Since most of the early records were of surface finds, it was impossible to judge their true chronological position. In due course, some of these points began to turn up in geological context, in fossil quarries with bison bones, and otherwise under circumstances that suggested a very respectable antiquity. Many of these early finds of subsurface specimens involved only one or two pieces, and there were conflicting reports on the identity of the associated animal species. So, the position of the "Yuma" materials in time and space remained cloudy. As late as 1949, one of our foremost anthropologists observed that "the Yuma points, though some of them probably possess a respectable antiquity, are a group of poor cousins of the Folsom culture, by whose fame they were carried into a degree of prominence."[24]

In the past decade, the nature of the "Yuma" complex has become measurably clearer; but the term has, perhaps unfortunately, fallen into professional disrepute. It is obvious now that "Yuma" is distinct from the Folsom complex; and there is good evidence, stratigraphic and otherwise, that it is later in general or survived longer. That it existed earlier than Folsom has not yet been established.

Two principal point types which are involved with the "Yuma" materials are the *Eden* and the *Scottsbluff* forms. The Eden point is long and narrow, with slightly convex edges and pronounced ridges down the center of each face which result in a markedly diamond-shaped cross section. The base is usually straight; above it, is the stem which is set off from the blade by a very slight shoulder. The length ranges up to about five inches, with the blade from one-fourth to one-seventh as wide as it is long. The flaking is often very well done, and the edges show fine secondary retouching. The finest examples of the Eden type show a superlative measure of skill and craftsmanship on the part of their makers. The Scottsbluff point is proportionately broader and shorter, biconvex in cross section, with more prominent shoulders to set off

[24] A. L. Kroeber, *Anthropology*, 684.

the stem, and with coarser flaking and retouching. As thus defined, here and elsewhere, the two types are fairly easily distinguishable; actually, in a large series, there is likely to be an almost complete gradation from the "typical" Scottsbluff to the "typical" Eden. It seems quite likely that both types could have been produced by the better flintsmiths of the groups concerned.

Eden points have a restricted distribution, occurring essentially in the High Plains and northward, with isolated examples reported still farther north. Scottsbluff points are much more widely distributed, perhaps partly because of the readiness of some observers to place a liberal construction on what constitutes a Scottsbluff point.

Three sites are of principal interest in connection with these materials—the Finley and Horner sites in Wyoming and the Clovis-Portales locality in New Mexico.

The Finley site is in the Bridger Basin in southwestern Wyoming, about five miles east and south of Eden and twenty-five or thirty miles southwest of historic South Pass. The Bridger Basin is the most westerly of a series of interconnected desert and semi-desert plains and valleys lying astride the Continental Divide and collectively known as the Wyoming Basin. In this sector, the Rocky Mountain spine bordering the Great Plains is interrupted by a local sag, and the mountains have been largely covered with sediments. The resulting basin is actually a plateau whose floor connects eastward with the Great Plains through an opening between the Bighorn and Laramie Mountains and southward with the Colorado Plateau and Great Basin by another gap east of the Uinta Mountains. In both directions, the land surface has a comparatively gentle slope, and there are no serious topographic hindrances to passage across the divide. Through this Wyoming gap, modern railroads, highways, and airlines make an easy transit, following the routes traversed a century ago by the emigrant traffic on the Oregon and Overland trails. Through it, the sagebrush and greasewood of the Great Basin–Colorado Plateau deserts spills into the grasslands of the Great Plains in central Wyoming; and through it, as we shall see, men carrying a desert way of life some thousands of years ago spread into the western margin of the Great Plains. Through it, too, we may suppose, the early big-game hunters passed from the High Plains corridor into the transcordilleran land of lakes that we now know as the Great Basin.

The Finley site is on an old valley of Pacific Creek, a tributary of the Little Sandy River. The archaeological zone is a buried soil in the upper part of the second of three sandy layers.[25] Twenty-four points, including sixteen found *in situ* and representing both Eden and Scottsbluff types, were associated here with the bones of an unidentified species of bison. Most of the skeletal remains were limb bones, particularly those of the front and lower legs, split foot bones, and a few teeth and jaw fragments. Some of the bones were scorched and fire-blackened. Several broad triangular-bladed stemmed points may have been knives, and there were also a few chips and flakes. There were no hearths or other traces of camping activity, and it is presumed that the occurrence represents a kill or butchering ground. The shells of fresh-water snails in the archaeological horizon include species partial to ponds and swampy places. The evidence suggests a former pond or water hole, probably bordered by grass on which the bison fed, and in all likelihood reflecting a period of moister climate than characterizes the immediate neighborhood at present. Ecological conditions may have resembled those in the Great Plains today. As a result of subsequent desiccation, the surface water has disappeared and the water table has dropped; increased wind action has buried the artifact- and bone-bearing layer beneath dune sands and a desert vegetation of sagebrush has established itself. From the geological evidence, a date of seven to nine thousand years ago has been suggested for emplacement of the artifacts at this site.

The Horner site is about 4 miles northeast of Cody, Wyoming,

25 E. B. Howard, "Discovery of Yuma Points, *In Situ*, Near Eden, Wyoming," *American Antiquity*, Vol. VIII, No. 3 (January, 1943), 224–34; L. Satterthwaite, "Stone Artifacts At and Near the Finley Site, Near Eden, Wyoming," *Museum Monographs*, University Museum, University of Pennsylvania, 1957; J. H. Moss, "Early Man in the Eden Valley," *Museum Monographs*, The University Museum, University of Pennsylvania, 1951.

near the junction of Sage Creek and the Shoshone River, and approximately 175 miles north of the Finley site. It is in the north-western part of the Bighorn Basin, a semiarid sagebrush plain resembling the basins to the south more closely than the Great Plains of eastern Wyoming. The site is a former butchering ground covering several thousand square feet, and including scattered hearths and other indications that men camped for a time, or at times, on the spot. The remains of nearly 200 bison littered the area just beneath the ground surface, and with them were a few bones of antelope, deer, wolves, and other smaller forms. There were no complete skeletons and few examples of articulated limbs or other parts. Many of the bones were broken, and the skulls in nearly all cases lacked the upper part.

From the ages of the animals at the time of death, it has been inferred that they were killed within a period of a few weeks in the fall or early winter, or that there was a succession of kills made annually at that time over a period of years. Whether the scattered and fragmentary nature of the bones is entirely the result of man's work or, alternatively, reflects in part the activity of wolves, bears, or other animals drawn to the scene by offal is uncertain.

In direct association with the bones were more than two hundred stone tools of various kinds. These included complete and fragmentary projectile points, representing both Eden and Scottsbluff and intergrading types. There were also plano-convex end scrapers, side scrapers, several kinds of knives, fine-pointed gravers similar to those at the Lindenmeier Folsom site, spoke-shaves, choppers, and rubbing stones. A distinctive form of cutting implement, sometimes termed the Cody knife, has a triangular blade with a transverse or oblique cutting edge, a single tang or shoulder, and a stem for hafting. Numerous small, paper-thin flakes and larger chips attest to stoneworking on the spot. A favorite stone was a maroon chert, similar to that which occurs in nodular form in the Bighorn Mountains some seventy-five miles to the east of the site. A few bones bore scratches or light incisions, but no definite implements of bone have been recognized here.

Preliminary geological estimates of the age of this butchering ground and temporary camp site placed it between 5,000 and 9,000 years ago. Subsequently, charred bison bones gave a carbon 14 date of 6,876, plus or minus 250 years ago, and charcoal from a heavily burned area believed to represent a fireplace gave two figures averaging out to 6,920, plus or minus 500 years ago.[26]

Strongly reminiscent of the artifact assemblage just noted for the Horner site is another discovered at the Claypool site in Washington County, Colorado. Here the remains of human activity were found in a sandy layer which, as a result of extensive wind erosion during the 1930's, revealed various kinds of artifacts and the bones of extinct animals. Among the materials found in place during controlled excavations were points of Eden and Scottsbluff types, with variants of these; oblique-edged Cody knives; end scrapers; grooved sandstone blocks presumed to be shaft smoothers; and finely pointed gravers. Mammoth bones weathering from an underlying formation, and surface finds of Clovis and Folsom Fluted points, suggest the possibility of an earlier occupation. There are no radiocarbon dates, but geological considerations have led to an estimated antiquity of between seven and nine thousand years for the artifact-bearing horizon.[27]

At the Clovis-Portales locality, as we have already seen, two horizons with fluted points have been recognized—the lowermost and oldest with Clovis points and elephant remains; the next above with Folsom points and extinct bison. Still higher in the stratigraphic sequence are artifacts of yet another kind. They include straight-based leaf-shaped points, a few of which show some superficial similarity to the Eden type, and none of which was fluted. The illustrated points do not impress one as part of the complex represented at the Horner and Claypool sites, though they are certainly closer to that than to the Folsom or Clovis assemblages, and seem likely to belong to the same general time level. A few scrapers and worked flakes were also found at this level, which contained a "great quantity of skeletons of bison."

[26] G. L. Jepsen, "Ancient Buffalo Hunters," *Princeton Alumni Weekly*, Vol. LIII, No. 25 (1953), 10–12; Libby, *op. cit.*, 125.
[27] Wormington, *Ancient Man in North America*, 128–32.

To this group of items the name *Portales complex* has been given.[28] Bones from the archaeological zone have yielded two radiocarbon dates—one of 6,300, plus or minus 150 years ago, the other at 6,230, plus or minus 150 years ago. These determinations suggest an antiquity of roughly the order indicated by radiocarbon tests for the Horner site, and the general equivalence in time between the Wyoming and New Mexico finds seems plausible.

Two locations in the general vicinity of the Black Hills also appear to belong to the post-Folsom hunting occupations of the Great Plains. One of these is the Long site, a buried living level excavated by the Smithsonian River Basin Surveys in the Angostura reservoir. Its discovery came about as a result of erosion by a small gully tributary to Horsehead Creek, some miles from Angostura Dam. Excavation disclosed the presence of small circular hearths made on the old living surface and unaccompanied by stones. The characteristic projectile point is lanceolate in form, with the sides narrowing to a straight or slightly concave base. Fine ribbon flaking, often oblique, is manifested; and the basal edges are ground smooth. Many of these points, first termed "Long" points and later renamed *Angostura points*, were made of quartzite presumably obtained from one or another of the aboriginal quarries found in the southern Black Hills a few miles to the west and northwest. The finding of quantities of thin, small flakes is evidence that at least some of the chipping was done on the spot. Other artifacts include knives of plate chalcedony, medium to large bifacially chipped blades, end and side scrapers, drills, flake scrapers, subrectangular manos, and small fragments of rock with remnants of grinding surfaces suggesting broken metates. Noteworthy is the presence of one point suggesting a crude Plainview point. The inventory of stone tools suggests heavy reliance on hunting by the former inhabitants of the site; but distressingly little bone refuse was found in the excavations. Charcoal from two different sections of the site yielded radiocarbon dates of 7,073, plus or minus 300 years and 7,715 plus or minus 740 years ago. A third sample was dated at 9,380, plus or

[28] Sellards, *Early Man in America*, 72–74.

minus 500 years ago. Publication of the full report on this site may alter in some measure the interpretations so far based only on preliminary statements and summary reports.[29]

The second site is a bison kill in the Agate Basin, some forty miles west of the Long site on a tributary of the Cheyenne River in Niobrara County, Wyoming. Animal bones and artifacts were in a stratum now twenty feet above the floor of an eroding gully but originally possibly on the edge of a marsh or meadow. The number of animals represented is unknown, but all bones were reported to be those of modern bison. More than seventy points and fragments are known from the kill, including thirty-two specimens recovered *in situ*. Despite considerable range in size, the form is remarkably consistent. They are long and slender, with narrowed straight or rounded base and fine marginal retouching. A few may be described as having the shape of a willow leaf. There is some resemblance to points from the Long site, but the *Agate Basin* series exhibits superior workmanship and many of the points are larger. A few end and side scrapers were also found. No geological or radiocarbon dating of the site has been attempted. From such illustrations of the artifacts as are available, it seems unlikely that the Agate Basin points are the weapons of the same people who dwelt at the Long site, though some sort of relationship undoubtedly exists.[30]

Notable additions to our knowledge of the ancient bison-hunters have come from extensive excavations at a group of sites in southwestern Nebraska that may be collectively termed the Lime Creek sites. These include the Lime Creek and Red Smoke sites, situated a few hundred yards apart on Lime Creek, and the Allen site, on the right bank of Medicine Creek below the mouth of Lime Creek.[31] All three are in the lower portion of a terrace

[29] J. T. Hughes, "Investigations in Western South Dakota and Northeastern Wyoming," *American Antiquity*, Vol. XIV, No. 4, Pt. 1 (April, 1949), 270–71; Wormington, *Ancient Man in North America*, 138–41.

[30] Roberts, "A New Site," in "Notes and News," *American Antiquity*, Vol. VIII, No. 3 (1943), 300.

[31] C. B. Schultz and W. D. Frankforter, "Preliminary Report on the Lime Creek Sites: New Evidence of Early Man in Southwestern Nebraska," *Bulletin*, University of Nebraska State Museum, Vol. III, No. 4, Pt. 2 (1948), 43–62; E. M.

fill designated as *Republican River Terrace 2 A* and provisionally dated as of Mankato age, that is, late Pleistocene.

At the Lime Creek site, the archaeological materials occurred principally on top of a dark carbonaceous layer that may represent an old beaver meadow. Overlying this layer were some forty-seven feet of silts and loess, streaked at intervals with dark layers and with soil zones near the top. Archaeological materials were most plentiful in the basal first foot of the fill, with chips and charcoal scattered here and there for another six or eight feet up. Large, roughly-chipped jasper blades, four to seven inches long, were common, as were large numbers of flakes and spalls. This suggests workshop activities, the jasper perhaps having been quarried from local veins and roughed into blanks for later completion. Other items included end scrapers, hammerstones, fragments of a grooved sandstone shaft-smoother, and some worked bone and antler. With these artifacts were associated the bones of seventeen mammalian forms, including much beaver material, as well as those of reptiles, birds, and amphibians. A Scottsbluff point also came from this horizon.

Eight feet above was another occupational layer in which were two hearths, fragments of bone, various cutting and chopping tools, and two points described as resembling specimens from the Plainview bison kill.

Charcoal from one to two feet below the lower zone, but said to be in the "same sedimentary unit," has been dated by radiocarbon at 9,524, plus or minus 450 years.

The Red Smoke site, roughly one-half mile up the creek from the preceding site, was found to consist of eight successive strata containing evidences of human activity. Most of the artifacts, including practically all the diagnostic points, came from a middle layer. The points, with some exceptions, are said to conform in

Davis and C. B. Schultz, "The Archeological and Paleontological Salvage Program at the Medicine Creek Reservoir, Frontier County, Nebraska," *Science*, Vol. CXV, No. 2,985 (March 14, 1952), 288–90; P. Holder and J. Wike, "The Frontier Culture Complex, A Preliminary Report on a Prehistoric Hunters' Camp in Southwestern Nebraska," *American Antiquity*, Vol. XIV, No. 4, Pt. 1 (April, 1949), 260–66.

all important essentials to the Plainview type. The exceptions include specimens in which the edges of the blade taper abruptly from the stem to the tip. To this form the term *Meserve* point has been assigned; two such points were found near Grand Island, Nebraska, in association with *Bison occidentalis*. Bison bones were associated with all levels; hearths, with several. Charcoal from a hearth in the uppermost level yielded radiocarbon dates averaging 8,862, plus or minus 230 years.

The Allen site yielded cultural materials and camp remains from a level about three feet thick beneath some twenty feet of terrace fill. Two strata of concentrated refuse and stained soil were separated by a lighter colored intermediate zone in which much less material occurred. Most of the artifacts and about half of the fireplaces uncovered were in the lower level, termed *Occupational Level I*. Here were numerous animal bones, including those of bison, antelopes, deer, coyotes, rabbits, mice, rats, and prairie dogs, as well as occasional reptiles, birds, and amphibians. Many of the larger bones had been cut or broken up. The associated artifacts included leaf-shaped projectile points with a concave base, reminiscent of the Angostura type; trapezoidal scrapers, some with gougelike bits; lanceolate and ovoid blades; drills; abrading or grinding stones; a flattened stone spheroid with an encircling groove; eyeleted bone needles; crude bone awls, a bi-pointed bone object; and various cut and otherwise worked bone fragments. Burned nests of the mud-dauber wasp were found throughout the occupational layers; most had been broken open, presumably in pursuit of the larvae. Since the mud dauber nests from May to September, a summer camp or summertime residence might be inferred. The hearths, of which twenty were noted, were simple affairs built on the ground surface; some, to judge from the degree of reddening of the underlying soil, must have been maintained for a considerable period of time. A relatively permanent hunting camp, perhaps recurrently occupied during the late spring to early fall months, is suggested.

There are three radiocarbon dates for the Allen site. Two are from the lower occupational zone—8,274, plus or minus 500 years ago, and 10,493, plus or minus 1,500 years ago. The third, from a mixture of charcoal from both horizons, is much more recent—5,256, plus or minus 350 years ago. No reason for these marked inconsistencies has yet been advanced.

There are other early bison-hunter locations to which attention might be drawn, but for present purposes they would add little to what can be inferred from the examples already reviewed. All suggest a way of life probably not greatly different from that of the earlier elephant hunters, except that the small, scattered human groups were relying principally upon the bison herds rather than on the elephant for their sustenance. Well-defined and long-used hearths at the Allen site and perhaps those at the Horner site indicate camps of some permanence, or else repeated short-term residence, probably at spots near some unusually favorable hunting ground. Mass kills can be inferred at the Lipscomb, Plainview, and Horner sites, perhaps also at other locations; and man, if not wholly responsible for the slaughter, was certainly on hand to leave his weapon points and other tools among the slain animals.

Again, as with the earlier elephant hunters, we do not know the methods used by the bison hunters. That lack of horses and guns imposed no serious handicaps to these Stone Age foot hunters is clearly indicated in the sixteenth-century Spanish accounts of the Southern Plains Indians. The *Relacion del Suceso*, an anonymous narrative by a member of the Coronado expedition, tells us that the Spaniards "found that the best weapon for killing [bison] was a spear for hurling at them."[32] In 1599, Mendoca observed the Plains Indians of eastern New Mexico using weapons "of flint and very large bows" and also "some arrows with long thick points, although few, for the flint is better than spears to kill cattle." With these weapons, the Spaniards saw the Indians "kill them at the first shot with the greatest skill, while ambushed in brush blinds made at the watering places."[33] It is likely that hunting from an ambush or from blinds near water holes was a common method as

[32] G. P. Hammond and A. Rey, "Narratives of the Coronado Expedition, 1540–1542," *Coronado Historical Series*, Vol. II (1940), 289.

[33] H. E. Bolton, "Spanish Exploration in the Southwest, 1542–1706," *Original Narratives of Early American History* (1916), 230.

75

well in the much earlier period with which we are here concerned. There may also have been stalking of the bison by single hunters disguised in the skins of wolves and other predators to whose presence in their vicinity the herds were accustomed.

The mass kills imply something different—either that man was an opportunist who took advantage of herds trapped in storms or through other natural phenomena, or else that he engineered stampedes for his own ends. In the latter event, the fire drive would undoubtedly have been the most successful device, though we have no direct evidence from archaeology that it was used. The grasslands of the Plains, as is well known from historic records for the tall-grass prairies, were well suited to the use of fire in hunting. Dry seasons, high, steady winds, and extensive areas of flat unbroken terrain permitted grass fires to sweep for miles across country. Herds of large grazing animals in the path of such fires, if unable to escape, would have left dead and maimed beasts, with survivors perhaps finding refuge at upland ponds and lakes or in the breaks along a watercourse or drain way. The headlong flight of the herds might have carried them into ravines or water holes, where injured and blinded animals could have been easily dispatched. Such kills, like the surrounds and falls of the later Plains Indians, may well have exceeded the requirements of the hunters for meat and hides, so that many of the carcasses would have been left unbutchered, their skeletons to endure in more or less complete articulation. That such a method could have been effectively employed, even by small groups of hunters, is highly probable; and its use has been strongly argued by Sauer,[34] who cites the Lipscomb bison quarry as an illustration. What sort of archaeological evidence one should expect from a fire-drive kill, in contrast to a mass kill resulting from storms or other natural events, I am unable to suggest.

As the review of selected early hunter sites has noted, some of the artifact associations are with extinct forms—for example, the elephant, horse, and *Bison taylori*—whereas in others, they are with species of bison still living. The early big-game hunters, thus,

[34] Sauer, *loc. cit.*, 540–45.

76

from their still undated beginnings up to a time about seven thousand years ago, were on the scene during the period when the last of the great Pleistocene mammals were dying out. The causes of this extinction are not known, and we shall not undertake here a venture into what is not primarily an archaeological problem. It may be relevant, however, to take note of two explanations that seek to fix the responsibility in large part on man.

One of these views suggests that disappearance of the Folsom bison "could as well have occurred a hundred as a thousand or ten thousands years before Columbus," once human groups "centered their subsistence on it."[35] Perhaps it could; but with the addition of more primary field data and the development of a better chronology than was available twenty-five years ago, we know that the Folsom bison did not survive until anything like one thousand years ago in the Plains, although the intriguing suggestion has been made that the Wood Buffalo (*Bison bison athabascae*) found in the Upper Mackenzie River drainage in the last century may have represented "at least in a mixed form, the last of that Ice Age bison which early man had hunted in the western plains."[36]

Another thesis suggests that the fire drives of the early hunters materially hastened the extinction of the larger mammals.[37] This has been ably disputed by Eiseley,[38] and we may accept his verdict that the Folsom bison did not vanish "because he gazed too long and stupidly at man-made fires." This is not to say that man may not have contributed in some small measure to the slaughter, just as his fire drives at the prairie margin doubtless affected locally the distribution of forest and grassland; but it is not now evident that man was the prime destroyer of the large game animals of the

[35] Kroeber, "Cultural and Natural Areas of Native North America," University of California *Publications in American Archeology and Ethnology*, Vol. XXXVIII (1939), 88.

[36] L. C. Eiseley, "Did the Folsom Bison Survive in Canada?" *Scientific Monthly*, Vol. LXVI, No. 5 (1943), 468–72.

[37] Sauer, *loc. cit.*, 540–45.

[38] Eiseley, "Archeological Observations on the Problem of Post-glacial Extinction," *American Antiquity*, Vol. VIII, No. 3 (1943), 209–17; Eiseley, "The Fire-Drive and the Extinction of the Terminal Pleistocene Fauna," *American Anthropologist*, Vol. XLVIII, No. 1 (1946), 54–59; Eiseley, "The Fire and the Fauna," *American Anthropologist*, Vol. XLIX, No. 4, Pt. 1 (1947), 678–80.

terminal Pleistocene any more than he was the creator of the North American grasslands.

In closing this chapter, it must be observed that at none of the sites here considered have human remains been found, and in no case do we know the physical appearance of any of the people involved. There have been finds for which considerable antiquity was once claimed or suggested or seemed possible, as for example, in the case of four crevice burials found near Torrington, Wyoming, or of *Homo novusmundus* of northern New Mexico;[39] but for none of these finds has real antiquity been demonstrated. The lone exception to date is the fragmentary skull from a sand blowout at the Scharbauer site near Midland, Texas. Long and narrow in form, with an estimated cranial index of 68.8, this skull is not unlike other early longheaded skulls previously found in southern Texas and elsewhere in the New World. In the absence of associated artifacts, it is impossible to assign the Midland skull to any of the early hunters or to any other people of whom we now have record. Its age is uncertain; but it is believed to date from pre-Folsom times, perhaps in the eleven-to-twelve-thousand-year range, or older.[40]

[39] W. W. Howells, "Crania from Wyoming Resembling 'Minnesota Man'," *American Antiquity*, Vol. III, No. 4 (1938), 318–26; J. D. Figgins, "New World Man," *Proceedings*, Colorado Museum of Natural History, Vol. XIV, No. 1 (1935).
[40] F. Wendorf, *et al*, *The Midland Discovery;* F. Wendorf and A. D. Krieger, "New Light on the Midland Discovery," *American Antiquity*, Vol. XXV, No. 1 (1959), 66–78.

CHAPTER FOUR

THE CENTRAL PLAINS

STRETCHING FROM THE Rockies to the Missouri, and from the Niobrara to the Upper Arkansas River Basin, are the Central Plains. For our purposes, they include the states of Kansas and Nebraska, eastern Colorado, and the southeastern corner of Wyoming. Approximately bisected by the hundredth meridian, they are probably the best-known section of the Plains, archaeologically speaking.

Their western portion is in the High Plains, that thirsty, windswept, sun-drenched region of short-grass flatlands, dotted with ephemeral ponds and lakes, and relieved at infrequent intervals by wide, shallow streams and sandy creeks with occasional stands of cottonwood and willow along their banks. This is the heart of what the early American explorers termed the "Great American Desert," unaware that for thousands of years its nutritious grasses had provided natural pasturage for countless multitudes of bison. In the nineteenth century, it was the hunting range from north to south of the Dakotas, Cheyennes, Arapahoes, Comanches, Kiowas, and Apaches. The way of life of these groups was tersely described on Stephen Long's map of 1819 by the notation:

"The Great Desert is frequented by roving bands of Indians who have no fixed places of residence but roam from place to place in quest of game."

North of the Platte River, the High Plains merge eastward into the Sand Hills of Nebraska. Like the High Plains, this is an area of

79

little timber or surface water, and of limited arable land; but the thousands of cattle grown annually on its grassy dunes would perhaps have surprised the early-day observer whose opinion is perpetuated on the Perrin du Lac map of 1802, in the following words:

> "A great desert of moving sand where there is neither timber nor soil nor rock nor water nor animals except some small varicolored tortoises."

We may suppose that this has always been primarily a hunting ground, with native human occupancy centered along the valleys of such perennial streams as the Loup, Calamus, and Dismal rivers, and about the shores of the innumerable small lakes of the western and northern portions. In such localities, the light, open-textured soils could probably have supported a small-scale corn agriculture in aboriginal times under such climatic conditions as prevail today.

East of the hundredth meridian, the landscape shows marked changes. The eastern third of Nebraska is mantled by loess deposits which have been increasingly dissected by creeks and rivers as one travels toward the Missouri. South of the Platte, the loess plains extend west to the High Plains; on the south they merge into the deeply eroded Plains Border of central Kansas and, farther east, into the gently rolling prairies known as the Osage Plains. Nearly everywhere there are heavier precipitation, much more surface water, and more abundant and varied plant and animal life than in the High Plains. To native peoples who were inclined toward crop-growing, the fertile, well-watered alluvial bottoms and terrace-lined valleys offered many inducements to settlement—shelter, wood for fuel and building purposes, flood-free benches for village sites, potable water, game, and easily worked soils. And here, from the earliest days of white contact, were concentrated the semisedentary corn-growing Village tribes —the Poncas and Omahas in northeastern Nebraska and the Pawnees of east central Nebraska; the Otos on the Lower Platte and adjacent Missouri; the Kansas and Osages of northeastern and

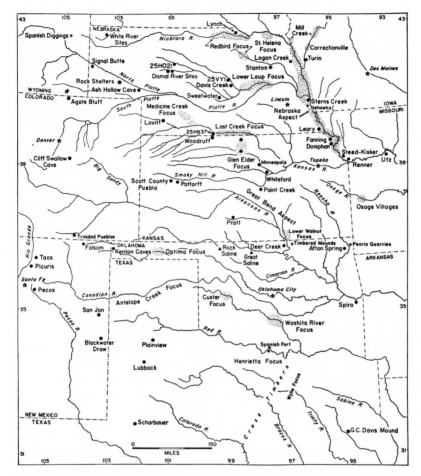

FIG. 7. *Map of the Central and Southern Plains, showing location of certain archaeological sites and complexes.*

eastern Kansas, and the Wichitas in central Kansas. The archaeological record furnishes abundant proof that these tribes were only the last in a series of peoples who, through still uncounted centuries, inhabited the land.

Most of what we know about the prehistory of the Central Plains comes from work done since 1925; but notable contribu-

81

tions to knowledge were made long before.[1] Indeed, shortly after 1800, when American exploration of the newly acquired Louisiana Territory was getting under way, Lewis and Clark, Long, and other early travelers noted the remains of ancient villages and mounds on their way up the Missouri. The opening of a burial mound by the Reverend Isaac McCoy near Fort Leavenworth, in 1830, may have been the first archaeological excavation of which a record survives in the Kansas-Nebraska region.

In post-Civil War days, as geographical and geological explorations pushed into the West along with the advancing frontier, the traces of former human occupancy attracted more and more attention. There were, of course, no trained archaeologists at the time, and the burden of recording and reporting fell on the geologists and naturalists, and on enthusiastic amateurs who often lacked any sort of scientific training. Out of this background, there came in the 1870's reports by Todd on supposed aboriginal chert quarries in eastern Nebraska, by Hayden on village sites along the Platte, Loup, and Blue rivers, by Aughey on an artifact with elephant bones near Omaha, by Mudge on sherd-littered sites in northern and central Kansas, and by Curtiss on mound explorations near Marion, Kansas. During the 1880's, Udden worked a large village site near Lindsborg, Kansas, and suggested, on the basis of a piece of chain mail found there, that the site might have been visited by Coronado. In the 1890's paleontologists Williston and Martin investigated a pueblo ruin in Scott County, Kansas, and also reported the discovery of a projectile point in association with fossil bison at Twelve-Mile Creek in Logan County; and J. V. Brower devoted several years of time and considerable money to "proving" that the province of Quivira was located in eastern Kansas.

Not until after the turn of the century did professional anthropologists take note of the antiquities of the Central Plains. The

---

[1] W. D. Strong, "An Introduction to Nebraska Archeology," *loc. cit.,* 40–55; Wedel, "An Introduction to Kansas Archeology," *Bulletin 174,* Bureau of American Ethnology, (1959), 82–98; Wedel, "Culture Sequence in the Central Great Plains," Smithsonian *Miscellaneous Collections,* Vol. C (1940), 291–352.

stimulus was the finding of human skeletal remains in 1902 near Lansing, Kansas, and in 1906 on Long's Hill near Omaha, Nebraska, under circumstances suggesting considerable geological antiquity. Both finds were critically investigated by geologists and anthropologists; neither is now accepted as evidence of ancient man. Probably as a result of the wide interest aroused at this time, however, important investigations were begun soon after in some of the mounds and village sites with which this stretch of the Missouri abounds. Gilder, of Omaha, Sterns, of Harvard's Peabody Museum, and Fowke, of the Bureau of Ethnology were the principal figures involved; but none carried his researches more than a few miles beyond the main stem. Farther west, it remained for a few dedicated and inquiring private individuals, such as Blackman and Hill in Nebraska, Schultz and Jones in Kansas—all lacking formal training and thus unhampered by the professional dogma of their time—to give the lie to the widespread misconception that there could have been no fixed Indian settlements and therefore no archaeology more than one hundred miles west of the Missouri. It is no reflection upon the character or accomplishment of professional archaeologists of the past three decades to observe that if we today see a little farther and somewhat more clearly than those who preceded us, it is in large measure because we stand with one foot on their shoulders.

Archaeological remains in the Central Plains are both abundant and varied, though not often conspicuous in character. In the east, where environmental conditions favored heavier populations and both food-collecting and food-producing economies yielded a good living, there are many village sites. Before the days of intensive agriculture, these were sometimes marked by trash heaps and house rings. Mounds, usually small and unimpressive, formerly occurred in some numbers. Because they usually stood on the edges of the bluffs or on hilltops, they were easily seen; and most were dug early, unsystematically, and without adequate record. Beyond the ninety-eighth meridian in Kansas and the ninety-ninth in northern Nebraska, there are few or no mounds; and village sites, essentially restricted to the few perennial streams,

83

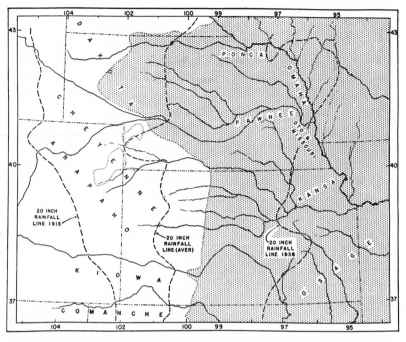

FIG. 8. *Map of the Central Plains. Broken lines indicate twenty-inch annual precipitation in average, wet (1915), and dry (1936), years. Stippling, tall-grass prairies (bluestem, bunch grass, etc.); unstippled, short-grass plains (grama, buffalo grass). Tribal locations as in approximately 1825.*

American Anthropologist

are found in diminishing numbers. On the High Plains, traces of former human activity may be found on the dry shores of one-time ponds that were probably seasonal in nature. Even in the sandy tracts among the dunes can be found broken bone, artifacts, and occasional fireplaces. A characteristic feature of most streams is the terraces that line their banks; and where these have been cut by lateral erosion, older materials may be exposed in dark, humus-stained strata that represent ancient living surfaces long since covered by wind- or water-laid deposits. Some of these buried sites are of great antiquity, long antedating the pottery-bearing sites near or on the surface, and harking back to the days of the ancient big-game hunters or of the hunters and gatherers who followed them.

The oldest known traces of human activity in the Central Plains occur mainly in the western section and are attributable to the early big-game hunters. They include numerous projectile points of Folsom, Plainview, Scottsbluff, Eden, and other early types, which have been reported as surface finds from widely scattered localities in eastern Colorado and Nebraska, and in lesser number and variety from Kansas. Moreover, as we have already noted elsewhere, there are several important sites at which these and other artifacts have been found in place, usually in association with remains of extinct species of animals. Mostly, these associations are with fossil bison; but the finding of large Clovis Fluted points with mammoth skeletons near Dent, Colorado, suggests that the earliest people here were hunters of the elephant, probably ten thousand years ago, or more.

On a somewhat later time level were the people whose camp sites and game kills have been found in Colorado at Lindenmeier, Olson-Chubbuck,[2] and several sites in Yuma and Washington counties; at Lime Creek and the Scottsbluff bison quarry in western Nebraska; at the Long site in southwestern South Dakota; and perhaps at Twelve Mile Creek in western Kansas. Here, so far as the animal bones have been identified, those of the bison predominate, and at most localities they apparently represent extinct species. While the problems of dating have not been worked out everywhere to complete satisfaction, it seems likely that these sites represent the hunter folk who, in small, scattered groups, were roaming the Western Plains from about ten to seven thousand years ago.

Much later came the butte dwellers whose remains occur in some abundance on Signal Butte, in the North Platte Valley of western Nebraska. Here they constitute the lowest and oldest of

[2] J. Chubbuck, "The Discovery and Exploration of the Olsen-Chubbuck Site (CH-3)," *Southwestern Lore*, Vol. XXV, No. 1 (1959), 4–10; see also *American Antiquity*, Vol. XXIV (1959), 337–38.

three culture-bearing strata.[3] Charcoal, animal bones, burned stones, artifacts, and other occupational debris occur in a dark layer one foot or more thick. Hearths, some of them lined with stones, are present and also small pits possibly used for storage; but there is no sign of habitations. Hunting was evidently of great importance, as shown by the quantities of broken, split, and burned animal bone, including bison of modern species only. Projectile points of lanceolate, stemmed, and other forms are abundant, as are scrapers, drills, and other chipped stone tools, and crude but efficient bone awls. A way of life primarily concerned with bison hunting is indicated; but doubtless there was also some gathering of vegetal products for reduction to food by grinding. Radiocarbon dates have placed these remains at between 3,000 and 3,500 years ago—long after the time of the early big-game hunters.

Of the later peoples who must have hunted and gathered in the western Central Plains before the introduction of pottery-making, we know as yet very little. They are possibly represented by the second, or middle, level at Signal Butte, which is separated from the lowermost by some eighteen inches of wind-blown soil. Their traces may include also some of the cemeteries with tightly flexed burials and boat stones, but without pottery, that have been found at various localities in the North Platte drainage of western Nebraska. Farther south, the flexed burials near Scott County State Park in western Kansas, accompanied by simple bone and chipped-stone artifacts, may be yet another example. Until further work has been done at camp sites that can be linked with these burials, it will be impossible to speak with confidence of the chronological position of the remains now known or to assess their significance in Plains prehistory.

Neither can we yet say very much about the archaeology of the Eastern Plains during the long period before the beginning of the Christian Era and the appearance of pottery makers. Hunting peoples were undoubtedly present. There have been occasional finds of large stemmed or notched projectile points and other artifacts that resemble forms attributed farther east and south to the Ar-

[3] Strong, "An Introduction to Nebraska Archeology," *loc. cit.*, 224–39.

chaic and Early Woodland cultures, and these may be evidence of the hunters of the pre-Christian Era; but until very recently there have been no sites or artifact assemblages that could certainly be so classified. Possibly some of the large, coarsely chipped implements—choppers, knives, blades, scrapers, and points—that formerly occurred in such extraordinary numbers in the Kansas Valley where it traverses the Flint Hills upland, and from which Winchell once argued for a Paleolithic culture here, date back to an early pre-pottery era.

Bearing directly on this point is the recent work by Kivett on a pre-pottery habitation site on Logan Creek in Burt County, eastern Nebraska.[4] Here four occupation levels are indicated, all thought to represent a single culture or way of life. Among the features reported are stone-filled and plain hearths, medium to large points with wide shallow notches, side-notched or stemmed plano-convex scrapers, milling stones, bone awls and tubular beads, and a curved bone fishhook. Animal bones, especially those of bison still unidentified as to species, are common, as are freshwater mussel shells. Charcoal from the second level down has been radiocarbon dated at 4674 B.C.; by how much the two underlying levels antedate this we do not know. The points from Logan Creek show strong similarities to others reported from the Simonsen bison kill near Quimby, Iowa, in direct association with remains of the extinct *Bison occidentalis* and there dated, also by radiocarbon, at 6471 B.C.[5] This suggests that at a time when the early big-game hunters and their successors in the western Plains were making various forms of lanceolate and unnotched weapon points, contemporary big-game hunters in the east were fashioning dissimilar forms characterized by notches on the sides near the base. The relationships of the Logan Creek peoples were apparently with the ancient hunters of the Eastern Woodlands rather than with the early big-game hunters of the Western Plains.

[4] M. F. Kivett, in "Notes and News," *American Antiquity*, Vol. XXIII (1958), 337; and report presented at the Seventeenth Plains Conference, Nov. 27, 1959, Lincoln, Nebraska.

[5] G. A. Agogino and W. D. Frankforter, "A Paleo-Indian Bison-Kill in Northwestern Iowa," *American Antiquity*, Vol. XXV, No. 3 (1960), 414–15.

We cannot yet say exactly when pottery-making and corn-growing reached the prehistoric inhabitants of the Central Plains, nor do we know whether the two practices arrived simultaneously or at different times. The oldest dated archaeological remains with which corn has been found in unquestioned association are the Hopewellian sites along the Missouri near Kansas City, which were probably inhabited during the second or third centuries of the Christian Era. Closely related remains have been found in the lower Kansas River drainage as far west as Junction City, Kansas, but insufficient work has as yet been carried out in these westerly manifestations.

In the Kansas City Hopewell village sites, a fairly heavy mantle of village refuse and abundant trash-filled pits originally used for storage suggest an occupation of some permanence and duration rather than transient camps.[6] Not much is known about the size and arrangement of the community, but the villages seem to have been small. No posthole patterns or other structural remains have been recognized from which the type of dwelling could be inferred, but probably an eastern type of pole and mat structure was used. Burial mounds of earth, containing rectangular dry masonry chambers with short-walled entrances, occur in some numbers on the bluffs near the villages and are believed to be directly connected with them.

The trash found in the pits and in the refuse mantle includes much broken pottery, worked stone, bone, and other materials, as well as considerable animal bone representing chiefly deer, bear, and other woodland forms. Bison and the dog are sparingly represented. The subsistence economy evidently involved hunting, gathering, and some crop-growing. Maize and beans are directly indicated; but the bone hoe so characteristic of most later Plains agricultural peoples is absent. The kind of milling implement used is unknown.

Implements of hunting and warfare are represented by large

[6] Wedel, "Archeological Investigations in Platte and Clay Counties, Missouri," U. S. National Museum *Bulletin 183* (1943), 15–62, 106–37, 193–208.

stemmed or corner-notched stone points and socketed conical bone or antler points, presumably used on darts or throwing spears, grooved and ungrooved axes of polished stone, and numerous chipped knives. For skin-working, there were stemmed and unstemmed scrapers of various kinds and sizes; lumps of pumice gathered along the river bank; bone beaming or dehairing tools made from the leg bone or hipbone of the deer, eyed sewing needles, turkey bone awls, and punches. Large flat bone needles may have been used in sewing rush mats. Polished stone gorgets, imitation perforated bear teeth of bone, and pierced toe bones of the deer may have been used for adornment of the dress or person. Small funnel-shaped objects of stone and clay remain unidentified as to use. Platform pipes of stone are indicated.

Pottery is plentiful on these sites. It includes large jars with pointed bases, small globular pots, occasional shallow bowls and lobed jars, miniature vessels, and some modeling of animal and bird forms. Much of the pottery is plain surfaced; a small proportion bears allover cord-roughening. Rims frequently have a crisscross pattern of incised lines below which a row of shallow punctates encircle the vessel. Zigzag patterns, made by a notched or unnotched wheel or roulette, frequently cover much of the vessel exterior.

The Hopewell materials of the Missouri Valley and their westward extension up the Kansas River are clearly a watered-down version of the culture which, farther east, was responsible for many of the great, well-stocked burial mounds of the Ohio Valley. There are closer relationships to materials well known in Illinois. Practically no evidence of the Hopewell people has been found on the Missouri beyond the northern boundary of Kansas, but related materials are known in eastern Kansas and in northeastern Oklahoma. It is of particular interest as representing the first evidence, on the margin of the Plains, of a people whose subsistence rested in part on the cultivation of domestic crops.

At about the time the Hopewellian communities were flourishing along the Missouri, other peoples with a simpler way of life inhabited the Plains farther west and northwest. These were the bearers of what has long been called the Plains Woodland culture.[7] Archaeologists have recognized several variants which are distinguished from one another by differences, often minute, in the nature of the artifacts and other remains. The principal variants now known include: the Sterns Creek focus along the Missouri River in eastern Nebraska and western Iowa; the Loseke Creek focus in northeastern Nebraska, Iowa, and southern South Dakota; the Valley focus, widespread in Nebraska and Kansas; and the Keith focus in central and western Nebraska, western Kansas, and eastern Colorado. All of these have pottery; but other than squash remains in Sterns Creek and a few grains of corn in a Loseke Creek site, there is no acceptable evidence of crop-growing. The sites are usually small and inconspicuous, and may be deeply buried in stream terraces. They are most abundant in the Eastern Plains, but have a wide distribution westward along the smaller rivers and creeks of Kansas and Nebraska, and beyond.

House remains, if not absent, are scanty and inconclusive. In some Nebraska sites have been found shallow basins up to fifteen or eighteen feet in diameter, which may contain fireplaces and possibly represent dwellings made of light poles covered with perishable material of which no traces have survived. At other sites, such as Walker Gilmore (Sterns Creek) in Cass County, scattered post molds and masses of reeds and bark suggest small, thatched structures, presumably of an Eastern Woodlands type. Small pits nearby probably served for storage.

Pottery and other artifacts are not plentiful by comparison with Hopewell and later sites. The pottery is characteristically heavy and coarse, with large, wide-mouthed jars that have a more or less pointed bottom and were roughened on the outside with a cord-wrapped tool. Simple decorative effects were sometimes obtained

[7] Kivett, "Woodland Sites in Nebraska," Nebraska State Historical Society *Publications in Anthropology,* No. 1 (1952); A. T. Hill and M. F. Kivett, "Woodland-Like Manifestations in Nebraska," *Nebraska History Magazine,* Vol. XXI, No. 3 (July-September, 1940), 147–243; Champe, "Ash Hollow Cave," *loc. cit.,* 66–82; Strong, "An Introduction to Nebraska Archeology," *loc. cit.,* 184–97, 267; Wedel, "An Introduction to Kansas Archeology," *loc. cit.,* 542–57.

through a row of low bosses, made by punching the soft clay with a round-ended stylus, and encircling the vessels below the rim. In later times, more elaborate triangular or rectilinear designs were produced on vessel rims or upper bodies by impressing tightly-twisted single cords into the clay.

Artifacts of stone and bone were principally those required in hunting and gathering, and in processing the results of such activities. Stemmed projectile points, scrapers, knives, and choppers were flaked out of stone. Grinding slabs suggest the crushing of vegetal foods. Grooved sandstone blocks used as abraders and pebble hammerstones served in the making of tools and weapons. From a site in Valley County, Nebraska, came part of a bison leg bone pierced at the end for insertion of a handle, perhaps the earliest instance of the bone-digging stick tips that became much more plentiful in later times among the Plains Village Indians to the north and south. Here, too, were found broken fleshing tools of deer or antelope bone, finely toothed at the tip much like those of elk and bison bone so widely used in later times. Awls and needles were used in skin-working and, perhaps, in basket making, of which there is no evidence, however. For personal adornment, there were tubular bone beads, either plain or incised, as well as various kinds of simple shell pendants and disk beads. There is not much evidence of smoking, though crude, curved clay pipes may have been in use. Such typical later Plains artifacts as the bison shoulder-blade hoe, the diamond-shaped bevel-edged chipped knife, the bone fishhook, and well-shaped sandstone arrow-shaft smoothers used in pairs, are absent.

Disposal of the dead was accomplished in various ways. Single or double burials in the flesh, usually flexed, were sometimes made in small pits in or near the camp-site area. More characteristic, especially in the Upper Republican River drainage, were ossuary pits of varying size into which the dismembered remains of several or many individuals were placed, along with shell ornaments and great numbers of disk beads.[8] In eastern Kansas and Nebraska,

[8] Kivett, "The Woodruff Ossuary, A Prehistoric Burial Site in Phillips County, Kansas," Bureau of American Ethnology *Bulletin 154 River Basin Surveys Papers No. 3* (1953), 103–41.

small, round-topped mounds situated singly or in small groups on the valley margin bluffs are believed to belong to one or another of the several Woodland peoples. These mounds, of earth or of earth and stones, commonly have a shallow basin, or one or more small pits, under the base; and these contain poorly preserved human remains, often very fragmentary and fire-blackened, and with few or no mortuary offerings.

Along the Lower Kansas and Republican River valleys, some of the mounds are larger, and the human remains in them may include flexed and extended burials. Tubular bone beads, both plain and incised, shell disk beads, and small chipped arrow points may occur in some numbers. There are also stone platform pipes, drilled imitation bear teeth, and other items that suggest relationships with the Hopewellian peoples farther east. It has been suggested that these sites perhaps reflect the influence of Hopewell burial and other practices on a people with a less advanced culture who may have been in the region for some time previously.[9]

It is impossible to say how early the Woodland occupancy of the Central Plains began, or when it ended. For the remains we have here briefly reviewed, there are several radiocarbon dates. The earliest, from a site in Valley County, Nebraska, is 1872 B.C. Others range from 122 B.C. to A.D. 828. For the related, but more advanced, Hopewell materials near Kansas City, dates range from A.D. 8 to A.D. 687, with one other impossibly late date of A.D. 1270. All of these materials, of course, have their roots in older cultures widely distributed east of the Missouri, in the lower Missouri drainage, and in the Upper Mississippi and Ohio valleys. On present evidence, they must be regarded as peripheral manifestations of peoples more abundantly represented in the Eastern Woodlands rather than as the traces of an ancestral group or groups passing through the Plains on their way to the eastern United States.

Some time after perhaps A.D. 1000, but certainly several cen-

[9] F. Schultz and A. C. Spaulding, "A Hopewellian Burial Site in the Lower Republican Valley, Kansas," *American Antiquity*, Vol. XIII, No. 4 (1948), 306–13.

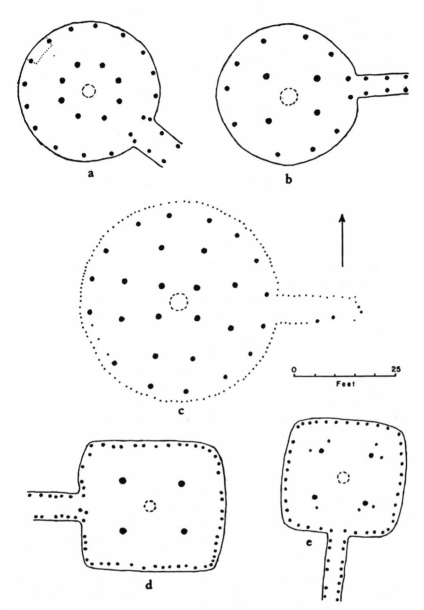

Fig. 9. *Some Central Plains house floor plans, showing characteristic shapes and posthole patterns, but with subfloor cache pits omitted.* a. *Historic Pawnee, about* 1800; b. *and* c. *Lower Loup focus, about* 1500–1700; d. *Upper Republican, about* 1100–1400; e. *Nebraska aspect, probably about* 1300–1450. *Arrow points north.*

turies before the first white men arrived, the Plains Woodland and Hopewellian peoples were replaced or succeeded by others who left remains of a different character. In these there is direct and convincing evidence of cultivation, as well as of hunting and fishing; pottery is comparatively plentiful; and the artifact inventory otherwise is usually much more extensive and varied than among the earlier Woodland groups.

Here, too, the archaeologists take note of several regional variants, each with certain features that distinguish it from the remains in other localities.[10] Perhaps the best known is the Upper Republican culture, or aspect, of western Kansas and Nebraska. First recognized in the Republican River Valley of southern Nebraska, it is found also to the south and is widely distributed in the Loup River drainage to the north. Along the Missouri in northeastern Kansas and on the eastern edge of Nebraska is the Nebraska culture, or aspect, known across the river in western Iowa as the Glenwood culture. In eastern and north central Kansas, and perhaps extending northward, are numerous sites for which the name Smoky Hill culture, or aspect, has recently been proposed. All of these regional variants can be included in a larger classificatory grouping, the Central Plains phase.

Highly characteristic of all these people are remains of substantial earth-covered dwellings. These were usually square or rectangular in floor plan, with rounded corners and long, covered entrance passages facing away from the prevailing winter winds. In the center of the floor was a simple, unlined fireplace; midway between the fireplace and each of the corners was a stout post, or else two or more closely-set lighter posts. Other closely-set smaller posts along the edge of the floor carried the outer edge of the roof and the top of the wall. In the east, these structures commonly stood in and over deep pits, with the floor from two to five feet below ground; in the west, the pits were usually shallower or entirely lacking.

---

[10] Strong, "An Introduction to Nebraska Archeology," *loc. cit.*, 69–114, 124–75, 245–67; Wedel, "An Introduction to Kansas Archeology," *loc. cit.*, 557–71, and references cited therein.

Villages show little or no evidence of planning. In the Nebraska culture they consisted of house units strung irregularly along the tops of ridges and bluffs; others may have been scattered on lower terraces, where their arrangement is now obscured by slope wash or other factors. Upper Republican villages, like many of those in the Lower Kansas River drainage, were generally on creek terraces, where the topography permitted more latitude in the disposition of the lodges. Typically, they consisted of single houses, randomly scattered at intervals of a few yards to several hundred feet, or of clusters of two to four lodges, similarly separated from other small clusters or single units. Storage pits are usually present beneath the floor, and small refuse dumps often occur not far outside the door. There is no evidence of defensive works.

For these small rural hamlets, whose population probably seldom exceeded fifty to one hundred persons, the adjacent creek bottoms and ravines would have provided ample garden space. Here, on easily worked alluvial soils, the plots of corn, beans, squash, and sunflowers were tilled with hoes made from the shoulder blade of the bison. Crop surpluses were stored in the caches. Milling stones, on which corn and other vegetal foods were crushed, occur frequently in Kansas sites, less so in Nebraska. Wooden mortars and pestles may have been used also, but of these there is no evidence. Deer and small game were available to foot hunters in the brushy valleys; antelope and bison could be taken at water holes, stalked along the broken valley margins, or killed in numbers by communal drives over cliffs and steep banks. Curved bone fishhooks were widely used at least as far west as Signal Butte. Along the Missouri, where larger fish were available, the Nebraska culture people also used a harpoon with a toggle head of bone or antler. Wild fruits, seeds, berries, and roots were undoubtedly collected in season. The dog was the only domestic animal.

Weapons included the bow and arrow, the latter tipped with small triangular side-notched points quite unlike those most characteristic of the earlier Woodland hunters. For skin-working there were small snubnose end scrapers, side scrapers, various kinds of chipped knives (including four-edged beveled forms), bone awls,

95

bodkins, eyed needles, and occasionally bone beamers or dehairing tools similar to those of the earlier Hopewellian people. There is no evidence concerning the dress, woven textiles, or basketry of these peoples, except for impressions of coiled baskets on a few Nebraska culture pottery fragments. Red and yellow minerals for pigment, along with thinly scraped bracelets, gorgets, pendants, and beads of bone, and a few shell ornaments served for personal adornment. Pipes were usually equal-armed and of stone among the Upper Republican people; in the Nebraska culture, there are curved clay pipes, sometimes with human faces or other features molded on the bowl, as well as stone pipes of various kinds.

Pottery was plentiful among all these groups. Upper Republican potters usually made large, round-bottomed jars whose exteriors were almost invariably cord-roughened, and whose characteristic thickened, wedge-shaped rims were often incised on their outer surface. Nebraska culture vessels were commonly globular, with simple out-curved rims; the exteriors were either left smooth or were treated with a cord-wrapped paddle. Small handles or lugs were often affixed to the rims of Nebraska culture pots, but are generally absent on Upper Republican pieces. Where the Nebraska culture potters came into contact with alien peoples, as in southeastern Nebraska and northeastern Kansas, some of their pottery carried incised decoration on the vessel bodies, and small animal effigies are sometimes perched on the rims.

The dead were disposed of in various ways. Among the Upper Republican peoples, the corpse seems to have been exposed for a time and the dismembered bones subsequently placed in large communal pits situated on the bluffs overlooking the village sites. Broken pottery identifiable with the wares found in the village sites is sometimes present, as are small numbers of shell disk beads, pendants, and occasional chipped-stone artifacts. Such ossuaries have been examined along the Republican Valley, and others are known in the Loup River drainage to the north. They somewhat resemble the ossuaries of the earlier Keith focus Woodland groups of the same region; but unlike the latter, the Upper Republican ossuaries never contain the great numbers of shell disk beads and the triangular shell pendants characteristic of the earlier burials. From one burial site have been recovered small wooden disks covered with sheet copper, presumably obtained from contemporary peoples to the east. The burial practices of the Nebraska culture peoples are not very well known; but it appears likely that they too exposed the corpses and afterwards placed the bones in haphazard fashion in or under low mounds, or in small natural elevations.

Farther south, in Kansas, there is also not much evidence. Near Salina, in association with a rambling settlement of earth lodges, more than 140 burials, closely massed and accompanied by shell ornaments, chipped flint knives and other artifacts, and with cord-roughened pottery vessels, undoubtedly belong to the general time and cultural level we are considering. This cemetery also yielded a large fragment of a pottery bowl identifiable with wares made on the Lower Arkansas Valley. Trade or other contacts by way of the Neosho, Verdigris, or Arkansas rivers are suggested here.

The accumulating evidence makes it clear that the prehistoric earth-lodge dwellers of the Central Plains were in contact with alien peoples with whom they doubtless traded and intermarried, and from whom they certainly borrowed ideas. In southeastern Nebraska and northeastern Kansas, for example, are found animal-effigy pottery handles, modeled clay figurines, pottery "trowels," and certain kinds of incising on pottery that strongly suggest practices occurring more commonly among peoples farther east in the central Mississippi Valley. We know that along the east side of the Missouri above Kansas City there were settlements of these Middle Mississippi people, whose ultimate relationships were with the builders of Cahokia and other well-known mounds near St. Louis. Although not much excavation has yet been done here, it appears that the Middle Mississippi peoples lived in villages that included some earth lodges similar to those of the Nebraska culture; that they cultivated maize, beans, squash, and sunflowers with shell hoes; that they buried their dead in large mounds and also in hilltop cemeteries, with pottery and other offerings; and

97

that they made shell-tempered pottery in a variety of shapes, including large jars, water bottles, bean-pot forms, and bowls, commonly with animal-effigy handles.[11]

Many of the items found on this time level are also shared with prehistoric peoples to the north and south. There are relationships with rectangular house communities yet to be noted in southeastern South Dakota and on the Missouri farther west; and with cultures to the south in Oklahoma and the Texas Panhandle. Some of the materials to the north seem to be earlier, if we may trust radiocarbon findings; but the exact relationships are still to be worked out.

Whether, or to what extent, some of the prehistoric communities beyond the northeastern margin of our immediate area were instrumental in the shaping of Central Plains cultures is not yet clear. We may take notice, however, of an interesting and important complex that flourished in nearby northwestern Iowa during a long period which, to judge from radiocarbon findings, may have begun before the Upper Republican and Nebraska cultures assumed the form by which we know them. This is the Mill Creek culture, represented by some fifteen village sites on the Big and Little Sioux rivers and some of their lesser tributaries.[12] The Broken Kettle, Kimball, and Phipps sites are probably the best known. The villages are characteristically small, consisting of an oval or rectangular refuse heap covering less than two acres of ground and varying in depth up to twelve feet. The people are thought to have lived on the accumulating trash heap, but the shape and construction of the houses have not yet been determined; and there seem to have been from ten to twenty houses on each site. Artificial ditches, presumably backed up by a palisade on an earthen embankment along the inner edge, protected the communities. No cemeteries have been found. The refuse

11 Wedel, "Archeological Investigations in Platte and Clay Counties, Missouri,"," *loc. cit.*, 62–98, 208–14.

12 C. R. Keyes, "Prehistoric Indians of Iowa," *The Palimpsest*, Vol. XXXII, No. 8 (1951), 340–43; R. J. Ruppé, "Archeological Investigations of the Mill Creek Culture of Northwestern Iowa," American Philosophical Society *Year Book 1955* (1956), 335–38.

comprising the mounds, or "tells," includes great quantities of animal bone, especially bison; and there is evidence that corn, beans, and other crops were cultivated. Bone artifacts, including the shoulder-blade hoe, are very plentiful, and there are also considerable quantities of chipped and ground stone, antler, and shell artifacts. Flourishing communities are indicated, with an ample and assured food supply and consequently with relatively well-developed arts and industries. Perhaps the comparative affluence manifested eventually necessitated the defensive works which feature some of the sites.

Pottery from the lower levels of some of these sites is said to resemble closely that from Middle Mississippi sites on the lower Missouri, whereas in the upper levels its similarities are with Middle Missouri Valley pottery wares. As Keyes long ago suggested, the Mill Creek sites appear to be the "remains of a culture that was in process of change from a former home in the South to a new habitation area on the edge of the northern Plains." There are broad similarities to some of the Central Plains people whose remains we have been considering, but even more striking ones with prehistoric village communities on the Middle Missouri in the Dakotas, about which more will be said in a later chapter. The time span of the Mill Creek culture is estimated as "about A.D. 800 until a short time before the historic period." While it is not possible to identify the sites with any historic tribe, it has been conjectured that they may represent the locality from which the ancestral Mandans started their movement into the Plains and up the Missouri to their historic habitat in the Dakotas. It has also been suggested that the Omahas may have been among the descendants of the Mill Creek people.

Much is still to be learned about the prehistoric earth-lodge dwellers of the Central Plains. We do not know, for example, when or where they first appeared in the region, how rapidly they spread westward up the stream valleys, or what their relationships may have been to such historic Village tribes as the Pawnees and their Siouan-speaking neighbors along the Missouri. Their remains are well enough known, however, to permit reasonable inferences about their way of life; and a few radiocarbon dates, ranging from A.D. 1138 to 1458, give some indication of the probable time span involved. It seems clear, too, that this small-town pattern of settlement, based partly on crop-growing and partly on hunting, fishing, and gathering, in one form or another extended itself westward about as far as soils and climate permitted creek-bottom gardening, streams or springs could be depended upon for water, and suitable timber for building purposes could be found. The widely scattered little Upper Republican sites represent, so far as we now know, the first people who established fixed villages and undertook cultivation of the soil west of the hundredth meridian.

We do not even know yet what eventually became of these people. At none of the Upper Republican and Nebraska culture sites investigated to date is there any trace of contacts with white men. From this we infer that the innumerable little square-house settlements strung along the Missouri River bluffs and scattered over the creek terraces for more than four hundred miles to the west were given up by A.D. 1500—a good half-century or more before the first Europeans came on the scene.

The reason for this abandonment of the Western Plains by semihorticultural peoples is not altogether clear. It has been suggested that the arrival of nomadic hunting tribes, perhaps the Plains Apaches in the fifteenth or early sixteenth century, may have been responsible.[13] Such newcomers, if numerous, warlike, or hard pressed for food, would undoubtedly have found the corn caches of the peaceful little farming communities a tempting prize and their relative defencelessness an invitation to pillage. If forced to give up or barter away their limited reserves of stored food, the village dwellers might then have retreated toward the east, gathering into larger towns for mutual protection against the new menace from the west and eventually becoming the Pawnees and other tribes of history.

Another view, taking note of the fact that much of the former Upper Republican territory lies in a region of low, uncertain rain-

[13] G. E. Hyde, *Indians of the High Plains*, 23–24.

fall and that many of the western sites are thickly covered with deposits of wind-blown soil, sees a possible explanation in drought and its adverse effects on the farming communities. It is not likely that the little prehistoric garden plots would have escaped the high temperatures and hot searing winds that usually accompany droughts in this region, any more than did the bottomland corn-fields of the historic Pawnees and other Eastern Plains tribes during the severe droughts of the 1860's and 1870's. I suspect that prolonged, intense, and widespread drought might also have affected the movements of the large herd animals, such as the bison, thus further weakening the subsistence basis on which the welfare of the human communities depended. There are sites in northeastern Nebraska which show a mixing of Upper Republican and Nebraska culture materials, along with other features usually regarded as belonging to a later period. This may mean that when the Western Plains for some reason became undesirable for the prehistoric farmers, they moved east and northeast in search of better watered and more reliable corn-growing lands.[14]

The character of the native human occupations of the western part of the Central Plains in late prehistoric times, say between A.D. 500 and 1400, still awaits investigation and clarification. It should be an interesting study in human ecology in a region that has been somewhat uncritically regarded for years as a most uninviting one for non-horse using peoples. I know of no published evidence, for example, that the creeks draining the High Plains and Colorado Piedmont of eastern Colorado have been carefully examined in recent years or the springs and seeps at their heads thoroughly searched for signs of prehistoric man. Yet, as Renaud's surveys in the early 1930's first clearly showed, there are many sites in the region which apparently represent both pottery-making and nonpottery peoples.[15]

[14] Wedel, "Environment and Native Subsistence Economies in the Central Great Plains," Smithsonian *Miscellaneous Collections*, Vol. CI, No. 3 (1941), 1–29; Wedel, "Some Aspects of Human Ecology in the Central Plains," *American Anthropologist*, Vol. LV, No. 4 (1953), 499–514.

[15] E. B. Renaud, "Archeological Survey of Eastern Colorado," *First Report* (1931), *Second Report* (1932), *Third Report* (1933), Department of Anthropology, University of Denver.

More recently, pottery, projectile points, and other remains apparently related to the Upper Republican aspect have been found in the rock shelters in the Nebraska Panhandle, in the upper level at Signal Butte, in southeastern Wyoming, in the rock shelters at Agate Bluff in northern Colorado, in the South Platte and Republican river drainages of northeastern Colorado, and to the south in the Arkansas River basin. At Agate Bluff, excavations have shown that Upper Republican materials apparently followed in time an earlier Woodland occupation, and the finding of a kernel of dent corn four and one-half feet underground with Upper Republican materials is of particular interest. At Cliff Swallow Cave in the South Platte drainage southeast of Denver, Woodland-like pottery was associated with projectile points much more strongly resembling Upper Republican forms.[16]

Until more of this westerly material has been collected, analyzed, and published in detail, it is impossible to judge to what extent these sites represent seasonal hunting stations used over a period of several or many years by people normally residing farther east or, alternatively, were semipermanent settlements where some small scale crop-raising may have been attempted. It is conceivable, too, that some of these locations mark the passage of people formerly relying in part on corn-growing farther east but here attempting the transition from a food-producing to a primarily bison-hunting Plains subsistence economy.

Written history in the Central Plains begins, of course, with the march of Coronado in 1541 from the Río Grande to the fabled land of Quivira. The summer before, at the easternmost pueblo of Cicuye (Pecos), the Spaniards met two Plains Indians who were captives of the Pueblos—one a Pawnee whom they called the Turk, the other a native of Quivira named Isopete. The men-

16 E. H. Bell and R. E. Cape, "The Rock Shelters of Western Nebraska," in *Chapters in Nebraska Archaeology*, No. 5 (1936), 357–99; Champe, "Ash Hollow Cave," *loc. cit.*, 47–50; Strong, "An Introduction to Nebraska Archeology," *loc. cit.*, 229; C. Irwin and H. Irwin, "The Archeology of the Agate Bluff Area, Colorado," *The Plains Anthropologist*, No. 8 (1957), 15–33; H. C. Morton, "Excavation of a Rock Shelter in Elbert County, Colorado," *Southwestern Lore*, Vol. XX, No. 3 (1954), 30–41; A. M. Withers, "University of Denver Archeological Fieldwork, 1952–1953," *Southwestern Lore*, Vol. XIX, No. 4 (1954), 1–3.

dacious Turk, both at Cicuye and in winter quarters at Tiguex, regaled the Spaniards with fanciful tales of the riches of Quivira far to the northeast, and of Harahey beyond. The next spring, Coronado led his hopeful army eastward by way of Pecos, across the Llano Estacado to the vicinity of Palo Duro Canyon. Thence, with a reduced retinue of thirty men, he continued northward across the Arkansas River and down its great bend to the settlements of Quivira in central Kansas. Here he spent several weeks exploring the region before returning to Tiguex by another route.

In the chronicles of this remarkable journey[17] we have our first glimpse of the Indians of the Great Plains, before their way of life had begun to change by reason of the horses, guns, alcohol, and other innovations introduced by Europeans. Moreover, what we can extract from these records has direct bearing on the archaeologists' interpretations of the late prehistoric and early historic (protohistoric) remains in the region, and is therefore of first importance.

Two or three weeks out of Pecos, the Spaniards met wandering bands of people who had no fixed settlements, did no planting, and were without pottery. They sustained themselves by following the herds of bison, eating the meat raw or drying it in strips, using the skins for tent covers, clothing, and robes, and residing in large well-constructed skin tents, supported on poles tied together at the top and spread at the bottom. Large dogs transported their baggage and supplies, and dragged the tent poles from place to place. The natives painted their bodies and faces, used bows and arrows, and were "very skillful in the use of signs." In winter, some traveled to the pueblos, others to Quivira to trade hides, robes, and meat for corn. The Spaniards recognized two kinds of these wanderers, the Querechos and the Teyas, noting also that they were far more numerous than the Pueblos. Relations between the Plains hunters and the people of the terraced houses were not always amicable, however, for the Teyas were said to have destroyed several towns near Pecos sixteen years earlier and even to have besieged the latter unsuccessfully.

[17] Hammond and Rey, *loc. cit.*

To the northeast, where the land was more broken and productive, the Spaniards found settlements of another kind. Here, along some small streams, Coronado reported not more than twenty-five towns of round straw houses, "clustered together." Of woven blankets, cotton, and fowls (turkeys) there were none; but unlike the Querechos and Teyas, the "people of Quivira have the advantage over the others in their houses and in the growing of maize." There were also beans and calabashes; and bison were available close at hand in unlimited numbers. The only metal seen was a copper gorget or breastplate. There is no mention of pottery or of milling stones, both of which were mentioned by Oñate when he visited Quivira sixty years later and described its settlements and flourishing corn fields in greater detail.[18]

Of the Querechos and Teyas, who were probably among the people later known as Plains Apaches, the Spanish were to learn much more in the next two hundred years. It is clear, however, that, in 1541, they were already experienced plainsmen; and in the Coronado narratives there is clear proof of their primary dependence on the bison herds and their use of dog traction, the conical skin tipi, leather clothing, jerked meat, pemmican, the bow and arrow, body painting, and sign language. It would be another century before these people had horses and guns, and would advance from the austerity of pedestrian hunters to a share in the richer and more colorful life of the equestrian bison-hunters. Nevertheless, they show that a hunting economy based upon the bison was possible in the Plains in prehorse days. Unfortunately, as long as they remained migratory hunters, there would not be much for the archaeologist to uncover on their short-lived and frequently changed camp sites; and his spade would turn up little concrete evidence as to how long these hunters had been in the Plains before Coronado first reported them.

The Spanish documents relating to the Western Plains for a century or more after Coronado all seem to confirm what archaeology has shown—that there were no fixed villages of farming Indians west of the great bend of the Arkansas or in other words,

[18] H. E. Bolton, *Spanish Exploration in the Southwest, 1542–1706,* 250–65.

the ninety-ninth meridian. Whether all of this region, once the western part of the Upper Republican range, had been taken over by Plains Apache hunters, we do not know, for few white men saw the region north of the Arkansas before the eighteenth century. At any rate, the permanent communities whose way of life rested in part on corn-growing all seem to have lain farther to the east, in what Coronado designated as Quivira and Harahey.

The earliest archaeological materials in the Central Plains showing contact with white men are in central Kansas, between the Smoky Hill River and the great bend of the Arkansas. They consist of numerous sites, some of them large and prolific, scattered along Cow Creek, the Little Arkansas and Walnut Rivers, and on other tributaries of the major streams. Best known, probably, is the Paint Creek site in McPherson County, investigated between 1881 and 1889 by Professor J. A. Udden, of Bethany College, and described by him in an excellent monograph published in 1900.[19] Much sporadic digging and surface-collecting took place in later years at this and other sites; and in 1940, the U. S. National Museum made limited excavations at the Tobias, Thompson, and Malone sites in Rice County, and at a series of closely related sites on both banks of the lower Walnut near Arkansas City.[20]

All of the sites mentioned are large, covering from twenty-five to one hundred acres, or more. Like others that have not yet been studied, they are usually marked by low mounds and areas of concentrated refuse; and it is likely that trash mounds occurred commonly before modern farming operations broke the sod and leveled the ground surface. There is no evidence of house sites, either on the surface or in the excavation done to date; and it seems likely that the dwellings were of perishable nature, grass houses presumably, with floors so near the ground surface that all traces have been obliterated by repeated plowing. On a few sites there are large, ditched circles, ninety to one hundred feet in diameter, with mounded centers. At one of these, excavation has disclosed

[19] J. A. Udden, "An Old Indian Village," Augustana Library *Publication*, No. 2 (1900).
[20] Wedel, "An Introduction to Kansas Archeology," *loc. cit.*, 211–377, 571–89.

curving, dug basins containing post molds, fireplaces, successive floor levels, large lumps of pole- and grass-impressed baked clay, quantities of artifacts, and scattered human bones. Locally termed "council circles" and never numbering more than one per village site, these may have been specialized ceremonial structures of more permanent character than the ordinary dwellings.

There are great numbers of cache pits, some as much as eight or ten feet in depth and diameter, and characteristically with sharply constricted openings. From these have come charred corn and beans, along with bones of bison, antelope, and other animals, and artifacts. Milling stones and bone hoes are common. Small, triangular, unnotched arrow points, end and side scrapers, ovate, diamond-shaped, and two-edged side-notched knives, frequently with beveled edges, bone fleshers, drills, perforators, and awls occur in large numbers, suggesting heavy reliance on hunting and a well developed skin-working industry. Wedge-shaped pieces of cancellous bone served as paint brushes to decorate leather articles. Twisted vegetal fiber cordage and coiled basketry are directly indicated.

Other common artifacts include grooved mauls; small sandstone disks with or without central perforation; well-made sandstone arrow-shaft smoothers, shaped like nail buffers and used in pairs; shaft straighteners or wrenches fashioned of bison rib; ribs with transverse grooves or notches that have been variously identified as tallies, musical rasps, and pottery-finishing tools; flakers of antler tip; bone tubes, and beads; and long, slender, curved strips of bone or horn, perforated at one end and notched at the other. Shell was not extensively used, though there are a few spoons or scrapers and simple ornaments.

Trade or other relationships with people in several directions are indicated by obsidian thought to be from New Mexico or Colorado, by pleasingly banded varicolored flint from native quarries on the Kansas-Oklahoma line east of the Arkansas River, and by Minnesota catlinite, used for simple ornaments and for pipes. The latter include a high-bowled L-shaped type and other forms.

Pottery is quite plentiful on all sites, but represents mostly a simple utilitarian ware. The usual form is a jar somewhat higher than wide, with a constricted neck and a simple, flaring or out-curved rim without ornamentation. In Rice and McPherson counties, the pottery is mostly sand-tempered; the Cowley County ware is almost exclusively shell-tempered. Handles, usually two on a vessel, and flat disk bases occur throughout, but are more characteristic of the southern shell-tempered pottery. Vessel surfaces are generally left plain; but in the north there is some use of the grooved paddle to produce a ridged or corrugated effect, and fillets of clay encircling the upper part of the pot may have oblique incisions suggesting a twisted rope. Certainly of foreign manufacture are sherds from central Nebraska, the lower Arkansas, and the Río Grande, all giving further evidence of contacts with alien peoples and helping to fix the local culture in time.

The central Kansas materials we have just reviewed have been classed by archaeologists as the Great Bend aspect. Their position in time seems well established, in part through the discovery of glaze-paint pottery identified with wares made on the Upper Río Grande during the sixteenth and seventeenth centuries, and in part by finds of chain mail and other white-trade items in very limited quantities. The Great Bend communities, in short, were apparently flourishing during the very period when Coronado, Bonilla and Humaña, and Oñate were exploring the Upper Río Grande Valley and pressing on for gold, glory, and converts in the Plains to the northeast. I believe, along with Bolton, that the Great Bend aspect materials in Rice and McPherson counties can be identified with the province of Quivira to which Coronado journeyed; and further, that such of the larger sites as Malone, Tobias, and Paint Creek were very likely among the grass-house villages whose dusky inhabitants greeted the bearded and travel-worn strangers from the south on that memorable day in early July of 1541.[21]

[21] Bolton, *Coronado, Knight of Pueblos and Plains*, 282–304; Wedel, "Archeological Remains in Central Kansas and Their Possible Bearing on the Location of Quivira," Smithsonian *Miscellaneous Collections*, Vol. CI, No. 7 (1942).

When Coronado reached the end of Quivira and asked his hosts what lay beyond, they informed him that there was only Arahey, or Harahey, and that it was the same sort of place as Quivira. The general, says Jaramillo, sent for the chief of these settlements, who appeared at the head of a company of two hundred men armed with bows and wearing "some sort of things on their heads." The chief, a large man, was called Tatarrax; he and his band have been generally regarded as Pawnees, linguistic kindred of the Wichitas and evidently already living somewhere north of the latter at that time.

Although the Pawnee villages from which Coronado's visitors came cannot be definitely identified, it seems likely that they may have been somewhere in east central Nebraska, rather than in northern Kansas as some would have it. At any rate, on the banks of the Loup and Platte rivers, mostly within thirty miles of their confluence, there is a group of a dozen or more large and important village sites that were certainly inhabited into and during an early period of contact with white men. These sites are particularly numerous on the north bank of the Loup, extending almost without interruption from Looking Glass Creek westward to a point beyond Genoa. Nearly all are in or very near the major stream valleys in contrast to the predilection of the prehistoric groups for the lesser creeks. From the known distribution of these materials, they have been designated the Lower Loup focus.[22]

These sites range in area from less than fifteen to more than one hundred acres, and most are on elevated terraces or on the bluffs bordering the stream valleys. In the early days of white settlement, house rings and refuse mounds without number abounded in this stretch; and broken pottery, animal bones, and other vestiges of human industry littered the ground surface. Extensive excavations have been made at some of the locations, mainly by the Nebraska State Historical Society and the University of Ne-

[22] M. L. Dunlevy, "A Comparison of the Cultural Manifestations of the Bur- kett (Nance County) and the Gray-Wolfe (Colfax County) Sites," in *Chapters in Nebraska Archeology*, No. 2 (1936), 147–247; Wedel, "The Direct-Historical Approach in Pawnee Archeology," Smithsonian *Miscellaneous Collections*, Vol. XCVII, No. 7 (1938), and references cited therein.

braska; but, unfortunately, these are still largely unpublished.

In contrast to the settlements of the Great Bend aspect, much evidence is at hand regarding the Lower Loup communities. They consisted of numerous medium to large earth lodges from twenty-five to fifty feet in diameter, always circular in plan, and with the floor one or two feet below the ground surface. The fireplace was a simple basin in the center, and four large posts about midway between the fireplace and the wall provided the main roof support. A second series of smaller posts, eight to sixteen in number, commonly stood three feet or so inside the wall, and on the stringers connecting their tops rested the outer ends of the rafters. Closely set smaller poles, sometimes planted in the floor at the base of the pit wall and at other times set on the ground surface at the pit edge, formed the frame of the sloping wall closing in the house. The entrance was a long, covered passage opening away from the prevailing winds, often but not invariably toward the east. Cache pits were dug into the floor; and many of the structures had a small altar platform against the rear wall opposite the door. There is, of course, considerable variation in details of construction. From their size and judging by analogy with historic accounts of such lodges, it is likely that each unit housed from ten to twenty persons.

At some sites faint traces of defensive works such as earth walls and ditches are still visible, or have been revealed by excavation. In many cases, however, the houses were scattered over such a large area that fortification was impractical or else was considered unnecessary because of the strength of the available defending force. In and near some of these sites have been found burials, usually those of individuals interred in the flesh in single graves and sometimes accompanied by a few offerings.

In most respects, the way of life followed by the Lower Loup peoples paralleled closely that inferred from the Great Bend remains. Horticulture was important, with maize, beans, and squash directly evidenced, and the bone hoe of very common occurrence.

The abundance and size of cache pits suggests a highly productive crop-growing economy and considerable crop surpluses to be cared for. Milling stones for grinding corn are less plentiful than in the Great Bend sites, suggesting that wooden mortars and pestles may have been known. There is no indication of fishing, but hunting with the bow and flint- or bone-tipped arrow was extensively practised. There is no evidence of horses, either in the bone refuse or in the artifact complex; but dogs were plentiful, and some of these, as among the Great Bend people, were large, powerful brutes that may well have served as draft animals during hunting trips or when household equipment or other baggage had to be transported.

The stone and bone tools were mostly those in use also by the Great Bend peoples, but the Lower Loup craftsmen were perhaps not as accomplished flintsmiths. Leather-working gear included knives, scrapers, drills, reamers, L-shaped elkhorn scrapers with stone blade, toothed fleshers, needles, and bone paint brushes. Coarse, twined bags were made of vegetal materials and may have been used for storage of corn. Catlinite and other suitable stone was used for ornaments and for several kinds of pipes.

Pottery is very abundant on all sites. Like the Great Bend pottery, it is grit-tempered, but much of it is far superior to and much more varied in form than the Kansas wares. Many of the vessels have handles, a particularly distinctive feature being the use of many small handles which give a cloistered or arcaded effect to the rim. Vessel surfaces are usually treated with a grooved paddle to give a corrugated effect. Incised decoration is frequently found on the upper body, most commonly as a series of triangular areas filled with diagonal lines, the lines in contiguous triangles slanting in opposite directions. Some of this resembles, as we shall see presently, pottery produced in large quantities on the Missouri River in South Dakota during the fifteenth, sixteenth, and seventeenth centuries; and the basic design motif of hatched triangles has, of course, a wide distribution in the Missouri and the Mississippi-Ohio valleys in late prehistoric and early historic times.

That the Lower Loup people were at least partly contemporaneous with the Great Bend people in central Kansas is indicated not only by the general similarity of the artifacts used by both, but also by cross finds of pottery. Thus, sherds exhibiting the distinctive cloistered rim on some Lower Loup pottery have been found in refuse mounds and cache pits at the Paint Creek site near Lindsborg, Kansas; and conversely, fragments of a large shell-tempered flat-bottomed jar probably made on the Arkansas or Walnut rivers were recovered from a Lower Loup lodge at the Gray site near Schuyler, Nebraska.[23] As far as I am aware, no puebloan pottery has yet been found in any of the Lower Loup sites. I suspect, however, that some of these communities may extend back in time about as far as the Great Bend sites, at any rate to the sixteenth century if not earlier. It can probably also be safely predicted that seriation of the large collections of artifacts and careful analysis of all other data on hand from the Lower Loup sites will ultimately show a clear and unbroken line of development leading to the historic Pawnee culture that occupied substantially the same locus and for which there are many historical accounts by white travelers after the year 1800.

In the High Plains of western Kansas and eastern Colorado, and extending northward into the Sand Hills of Nebraska, are numerous camp and village sites assigned to the Dismal River culture. This was first recognized as a distinct unit through work at the forks of the Dismal River in Nebraska. Its principal features are best known from excavations at the Lovitt site, in Chase County, White Cat Village in Harlan County, and Site 25 HO21 in Hooker County, all in Nebraska, and at the Scott County State Park in Kansas.[24] Otherwise it is represented almost entirely from small surface collections.

Dismal River sites have been found on stream terraces, around the shores of Sand Hill lakes and ponds, in blowouts, and in rock shelters. They vary considerably in size, from an acre or two to

[23] Wedel, "An Introduction to Kansas Archeology," *loc. cit.*, 576, 586.
[24] A. T. Hill and G. Metcalf, "A Site of the Dismal River Aspect in Chase County, Nebraska," *Nebraska History Magazine*, Vol. XXII, No. 2 (April-June, 1941), 158–226; Champe, "White Cat Village," *American Antiquity*, Vol. XIV, No. 4, Pt. 1 (April, 1949), 285–92; J. H. Gunnerson, "An Introduction to Plains Apache Archeology—The Dismal River Aspect," Bureau of American Ethnology *Bulletin 173*, *Anthropological Papers, No. 58* (1960), 131–260; Wedel, "An Introduction to Kansas Archeology," *loc. cit.*, 422–68, 589–99.

as many as sixty or seventy acres. Aside from scattered artifacts, potsherds, bone refuse, and other occupational detritus, the surface indications are usually unobtrusive. There are no refuse mounds, fortifications, hut rings, or other structural remains, nor have any burials been found.

Not much is known about the houses in which the Dismal River people lived, but the earth lodge was apparently not used. Excavations have disclosed circular and pentagonal patterns of postholes that are presumed to be house ruins. These must have been small affairs, probably of poles with grass, thatch or skin covering. It has been suggested that the pentagonal post-mold groupings may represent a structure somewhat like the Navaho hogan of a century ago. Shallow irregular basins of unknown function also occur. Distinctive of the Dismal River people are baking pits from two to three feet deep, three to five feet across the floor, with a constricted mouth and heavily burned walls and floors. No such features have been recorded from any other Plains culture, but identical structures have been found in post-Spanish levels at the pueblo ruin of Pecos, New Mexico.

The Dismal River people were principally hunters, with only a secondary interest in corn-growing. Among their stone and bone tools there was a preponderance of items probably or certainly associated with hunting, butchering, and skin-working. These include knives of several kinds, scrapers, chopping tools, drills, and an abundance of small, triangular stone arrow points, as well as bone awls, needles, toothed fleshing tools made of bison leg bones, rib arrow-shaft wrenches, bone paint "brushes," and hemispheric hide rubbing tools made from the rounded joint ends of large buffalo bones. Conversely, devices from which horticulture and the processing of crops can be inferred—bone hoes, metates, and manos—are limited in kind and number. The virtual absence of cache pits, in marked contrast to their abundance and size at the sites of the semihorticultural Indians in the Eastern Plains, suggests that crop surpluses were much smaller. We must assume the extensive use of berries, roots, and other wild vegetal foods; but there is no evidence whatever of fishing. At some sites the bones of small animals are relatively plentiful, suggesting that at times, perhaps when bison and other primary foods were in short supply, the people foraged for whatever they could find to sustain life.

The Dismal River people also made pottery in some quantity. Characteristically, it is a thin, hard, dark ware, fashioned into jars with constricted necks, and usually without handles or decoration. Much of it contains an abundance of mica particles, and strongly resembles the utility pottery made at Taos, Picuris, and other frontier pueblos on the Upper Río Grande.

Many of the artifacts of the Dismal River people were identical with those used by the Great Bend and Lower Loup peoples farther east. Others show evidence of contacts with puebloan peoples on the Río Grande, as in the occasional finds of turquoise, obsidian, bone flageolets, glaze-painted potsherds, finely incised bone tubes, arrow-shaft polishers of fine-grained stone, and incised tubular pottery pipes, sometimes with flared or otherwise elaborated bits.

The Dismal River sites about which we know most through excavation have all been dated, either through tree rings or by cross finds of datable Southwestern potsherds, at approximately A.D. 1700, plus or minus twenty-five to fifty years. The sites occur in the region where, to judge from historical documents, the Spanish working into the Plains from the Río Grande settlements came into repeated contact with the Plains Apaches around 1700. The French, pushing westward from the Mississippi-Missouri Valley, like Bourgmond in 1724, met the same groups and designated them the Padoucas. It is now generally accepted that the Plains Apaches and the Padoucas of the seventeenth and early eighteenth centuries were one and the same people, and that the Dismal River materials represent the archaeological remains of these people. Nothing in Dismal River archaeology contradicts what the documents have to say about the Plains Apaches or the Padoucas.

Archaeology as yet tells us little, directly, about the nature of Plains Apache culture in earlier times; but we can perhaps surmise that it was not unlike that of the Dismal River people stripped of their agriculture, pottery, and the special tools and practices associated therewith. As we have seen, the Spanish documents leave us in no doubt that the Apaches, as wandering hunters rather than part-time corngrowers, were already south of the Arkansas when Coronado and Oñate marched from the Upper Río Grande into the buffalo plains. The free-roving life described for the Querechos and Teyas, lacking domestic crops, pottery, or fixed settlements, is not one that would leave much to reward the archaeologist; but the hunting and skin-working they did, could have been carried on as well with the bone and stone tools of the Dismal River people as with any others. That this was actually the case is suggested by the finding in the rubbish heaps at Pecos, gateway between the Pueblos and the Plains, of many bone and stone artifacts unmistakably of Plains origin; and these occur in levels dating from the sixteenth century and after. They reflect increasingly close contacts between the Pueblos and the plainsmen from the east, doubtless including the Apaches as well as more distant peoples. Some of these items, indeed, may well have been left by the Apaches when, at the approach of spring, they broke camp at their wintering grounds beneath the walls of Pecos and betook themselves again to the buffalo plains.[25]

The Dismal River sites probably represent the high-water mark in the Apache occupation of the Central Plains. In the century and a half since their first notice by the Spaniards, the way of life of the Apaches had undergone notable and far-reaching changes. Many of them, especially in the Southern Plains, had taken over the horse, provided themselves and their mounts with leather armor, and, equipped with iron-tipped lances, were for a time the scourge of the Spanish, the Pueblos, and the settled horticultural tribes on the southeastern margin of the Plains.[26] Sometime during the latter part of the seventeenth century, other groups in northeastern New Mexico and southeastern Colorado adopted

[25] D. A. Gunnerson, "The Southern Athabascans: Their Arrival in the Southwest," *El Palacio*, Vol. LXIII, Nos. 11–12 (1956), 346–65.

[26] F. R. Secoy, "Changing Military Patterns on the Great Plains," *Monographs of the American Ethnological Society*, No. 21 (1953).

maize agriculture, ditch irrigation, and pueblo-like house types. Beginning around the time of the Pueblo Revolt of 1680, several groups of Pueblo Indians fled to the Apache country, evidently as far as western Kansas, speeding up, if they did not initiate, the adoption of crop-growing among the Plains people hundreds of miles northeast of the Upper Río Grande settlements.

I have already suggested, perhaps prematurely, that the Dismal River culture developed principally in prehorse days, the horse having been acquired not long before the displacement of the Apaches by the invading Comanches on horseback.[27] There is no direct evidence, in the form of bones, gear, or trappings, that the horse was known at any of the sites so far excavated. Neither Ulibarri in 1706, nor Valverde in 1719, mention horses among the Apaches they visited north of the Arkansas, though the latter commented on "the dogs, on which were loaded the poles for tents and other utensils used." On the other hand, one of Ulibarri's officers declared later that the captain of the *ranchería* of El Cuartelejo "wore on the neck of his horse a little silver bell with lettering which read: *Jesus Maria.*" Moreover, when Bourgmond met the Padoucas in north central Kansas in 1724, he noted that they were provided with horses and were, in fact, the source of supply for the Kansas and other village tribes to the north and northeast. It seems likely, therefore, that there were some horses among the Dismal River people, despite the negative evidence from archaeology, and that these animals were available for hunting, warfare, and trading. At the same time, the indicated heavy reliance on dogs as beasts of burden suggests that the Apaches had not yet made the full change-over from a prehorse to an equestrian hunting economy.

Since none of the Dismal River sites has been dated after *circa* 1725, we conclude that the occupation they represent ended at about that time. This coincides nicely with what the Spanish doc-

[27] Wedel, "An Introduction to Kansas Archeology," *loc. cit.*, 635. According to Forbes, however, "the arrival of the horse in western Kansas can be dated at least as early as *circa* 1640," which would invalidate this point. (J. D. Forbes, "The Appearance of the Mounted Indian in Northern Mexico and the Southwest, to 1680," *Southwestern Journal of Anthropology*, Vol. XV, No. 2 [1959], 200.)

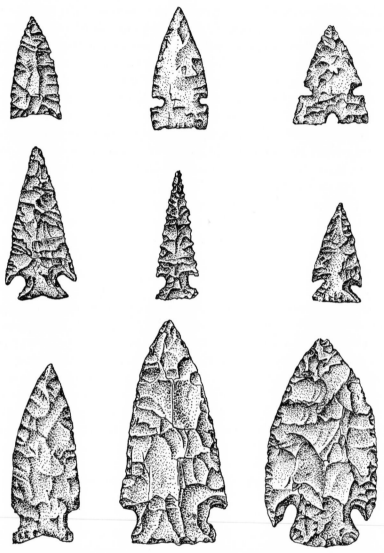

FIG. 10. *Some Central Plains weapon points.* Top row, left, *Dismal River, about* A.D. 1700; top center and right, *Upper Republican about* 1200–1400; middle row, left and center, *Schultz focus Woodland, estimated about* A.D. 400; middle and bottom row, right, *Keith focus Woodland, about* A.D. 600; bottom row center, *Hopewellian, about* A.D. 200–400; bottom row, left, *Logan Creek Archaic, about* 4500 B.C.

uments tell us about the Comanches, who soon after 1700 descended out of the Colorado Rockies to acquire horses and become full-fledged Plains hunters and warriors. Raiding Indian and white communities alike, the elusive Comanches struck with particularly telling effect on the scattered and unprotected Apache settlements. By the second quarter of the eighteenth century, they had broken the Apache hold on the Central Plains and were themselves in full control. Most of the Apaches withdrew far to the south; others seem to have retired northward, beyond the Platte, to the upper reaches of the Niobrara, and perhaps yet farther.

Along the eastern margin of the Plains yet another major archaeological culture makes its appearance during this period. This, the Oneota aspect, may be characterized as a Prairie rather than a Plains entity. Oneota materials occur principally in Iowa, southern Minnesota, Wisconsin, Illinois, and Missouri. West of the Missouri River, in eastern Nebraska and northeastern Kansas, not more than half a dozen sites have been recorded, and none of these is more than fifty or sixty miles west of the main stem. Most extensively worked and best known are the Leary site, at the mouth of the Nemaha River in extreme southeastern Nebraska, and the Fanning site, fifteen miles to the south in Doniphan County, Kansas.[28] Some data are also available from the Ashland site in Saunders County, Nebraska, where both Oneota and non-Oneota materials occur. Not yet reported in full is the Stanton site on the Elkhorn River, where the problem of disentangling the Oneota remains from earlier Upper Republican and later Omaha materials is a thorny one.

With respect to the western Oneota sites, the area of occupation varies considerably; at Leary it covers upwards of one hundred acres, whereas at Fanning it is less than fifteen. Refuse heaps are, or formerly were, to be found in some numbers; cylindrical and bell-shaped cache pits are very plentiful. Evidence of fortifications or other earthworks is lacking, though the Oneota

[28] A. T. Hill and Wedel, "Excavations at the Leary Indian Village and Burial Site, Richardson County, Nebraska," *Nebraska History Magazine*, Vol. XVII, No. 1 (1936), 2–73; Wedel, "An Introduction to Kansas Archeology," *loc. cit.*, 131–72.

people sometimes placed their dead in nearby mounds constructed by earlier peoples. No cemetery areas have been found; but at Leary, the bodies seem usually to have been laid out at full length in individual graves dug in unoccupied spots in the general village area and with few or no grave offerings.

From the considerable quantities of refuse on the sites, we infer a prolonged and intensive residence—villages of some permanence, that is, rather than short-lived hunting camps. Earth-lodge remains are present; but they appear to have been uncommon, and it is likely that the usual form of habitation was a less substantial structure of poles and mats, that is, a wigwam of eastern type.

Like the Lower Loup and Great Bend peoples, the Oneotas subsisted partly by growing corn, beans, and other crops, which were tilled with the bone hoe; and partly by hunting and gathering. The bones of deer, bear, and other marginal woodland animals usually outnumber those of bison, however; and unlike their western contemporaries, the Oneota people also fished, presumably with straight gorge fishhooks of bone or chipped stone.

The artifact inventory likewise generally parallels that of the westerly groups; and many of the stone and bone tools of the Oneotas are indistinguishable from those of the Lower Loup and Great Bend peoples. Such characteristic Plains implements as the toothed bone flesher, the adz-shaped elkhorn hide scraper, and the bone paint "brush" are, however, lacking in Oneota; and most of the sites seem to have much less bonework in general than did the groups to the west. Conical antler-tip arrow points with socketed base and large, flat mat-sewing needles are present, reflecting the eastward relationships of the Oneota. There is no evidence of woven textiles or basketry, but twisted cordage, preserved by charring, has been found at Leary. Also from Leary is a small, conical copper object which may be of native origin, the source of the metal perhaps being to the east or northeast where native copper was obtainable in the glacial drift deposits of Iowa or, further away, in the Lake Superior region.

An important domestic activity of the Oneota people was the

manufacture of pottery, and their products are usually readily distinguishable from other pottery wares of the Central Plains. Characteristically, the clay contains much pounded or burned shell. Vessels vary in size up to several gallons capacity; and they were generally full-bodied with a round base, a constricted neck, an outcurved rim with a plain or notched lip, and had two or four handles set in the angle between the rim and the body. In some vessels from Leary, the length exceeds the width, and the shape is elliptical, as is also true at Oneota sites in northern Iowa and Minnesota. Vertical, horizontal, or diagonal incised or trailed lines often decorate the rounding shoulder and upper body, with the lines in adjacent blocks running in different directions. Downward-pointing chevrons, blocks of round punch marks, and short dashed lines of incising also occur, as do, rarely, concentric circles or curved lines. The pottery from the Leary site is far better made and much more varied than that from the later Fanning site.

That the Oneota materials were in part contemporary with Lower Loup materials is indicated not only by the general similarity in many of the artifacts, but also by the finding of several cloistered rimsherds at Fanning which almost certainly were made in the Loup-Platte locality or by a potter with knowledge of the clays, tempering, and styles typical of that locality. It should be noted, also, that at some of the older Lower Loup sites there are a few oblong or elliptical pottery vessels, whose shape is almost certainly copied from Oneota forms. Strangely enough, few or no sherds certainly traceable to Leary or Fanning have yet been recognized in the Lower Loup or Great Bend sites.

The Oneota materials, both east and west of the Missouri River, include both sites that yield limited quantities of white-contact goods and others that do not. Thus, while we do not yet know how far back into prehistoric times the culture extends, we must conclude that some of the sites were inhabited when Europeans came on the scene. In the east, much of the material is, in fact, concentrated in localities where early historic documents or Indian traditions, or both, tell us that specific tribes resided—for example, the Iowas and Otos in northern Iowa and Minnesota, the Winnebagos in Wisconsin, and the Missouris in central Missouri.[29] Midwestern archaeologists thus generally accept the view that the Oneota materials represent the remains of Siouan-speaking peoples.

West of the Missouri, the situation is less clear. The Leary site shows many similarities to northern Iowa and Minnesota sites; but there is no trace of white contact, the site has not been dated by tree rings or radiocarbon, and it is impossible to say with any degree of assurance whether the Otos, the Iowas, the Kansas, or some other tribe dwelt here. The Fanning site has yielded small metal items and glass beads in some quantity; it was very likely inhabited between 1650 and 1700, roughly speaking; and it is in or near the locality where the Kansas were presumably living at about that time. The Oneota materials at Stanton and Ashland remain unidentified in regard to tribe.

That the Oneota culture is relatively late is certain; that it developed after 1600, as some have argued, is still unproved. The presence of square earth-lodge remains at Leary suggests that its inhabitants may have had some contacts with Upper Republican or related prehistoric groups. Moreover, occasional pottery vessels from Nebraska culture sites recall Oneota pottery. It is possible, of course, that both the Upper Republican and the Nebraska culture lasted later in this locality than is usually supposed. I think it equally likely that the Oneota culture preceded, and perhaps by some little time, the suggested 1600 date line.

The four major cultures we have been considering by no means represent all of the archaeological remains we know of in the Central Plains during the sixteenth to eighteenth centuries. In the Republican River drainage of northern Kansas and southern Ne-

---

[29] M. Mott, "The Relation of Historic Indian Tribes to Archeological Manifestations in Iowa," *Iowa Journal of History and Politics*, Vol. XXXVI, No. 3 (1938), 227–314; W. C. McKern, "Preliminary Report on the Upper Mississippi Phase in Wisconsin," *Bulletin*, Milwaukee Public Museum, Vol. XVI, No. 3 (1945), 109–285; C. H. Chapman, "Culture Sequence in the Lower Missouri Valley," in J. B. Griffin's *Archeology of Eastern United States* (1952), 147–49; Wedel, "An Introduction to Kansas Archeology," *loc. cit.*, 610–12.

braska, for example, there are several small sites whose content has not yet been published in full and whose cultural and chronological positions thus remain unclear. In some respects, they are reminiscent of the Oneota culture, though for the most part they differ widely from all described sites of Oneota. Much of their artifact inventory parallels that of the protohistoric Lower Loup and Great Bend peoples, but this may mean only that the people responsible for the remains were sharing a way of life common to all groups in the area at that time. It has been suggested that some of these remains, as represented at Glen Elder and on White Rock Creek in northern Kansas,[30] may have been an early group related to the Kansa Indians; but there is nothing to support this view, nor has any other attribution been made that carries much conviction.

Farther north on the headwaters of the Elkhorn and on the Lower Niobrara have been found other small villages in which are the remains of circular earth lodges. The pottery shares certain characteristics with that of the Lower Loup, others with sites on the Missouri in South Dakota, and still others with Oneota pottery. The other artifacts apparently parallel again those of the Lower Loup people. Once regarded as possibly of Ponca origin, these sites are now thought to be those of a people related to the Pawnees, presumably of the period A.D. 1600–1700[31]

South of the great bend of the Arkansas, on the upper Ninnescah River, is at least one site of great potential interest. Some of the bone and stone artifacts resemble those of the Great Bend people; others point southward toward late prehistoric cultures of the Oklahoma area. The pottery is a curiously mixed lot, including little that can be considered typical of the Great Bend sites. Moreover, there are also potsherds of Southwestern origin, including Biscuit ware "with a time span from about 1425–50 to 1525–50," and Río Grande glaze-paint sherds dated from 1450 to

[30] M. K. Rusco, "The White Rock Aspect," unpublished M. A. thesis, University of Nebraska (1955); Wedel, "An Introduction to Kansas Archeology," *loc. cit.*, 612–14.

[31] W. R. Wood, "The Redbird Focus," unpublished M. A. thesis, University of Nebraska (1956).

1475.[32] Systematic investigations are urgently needed here to determine more fully the nature of the remains and their relationships to other materials in the Southern and Central Plains.

On the fully historic level, after *circa* 1800, where it is possible to identify archaeological sites with Indian villages visited and described by white men, the Pawnees are much the best known tribe in the Central Plains.[33] Investigations have been made on a smaller scale at sites believed to have been inhabited by some of their contemporaries, such as the Omahas, Poncas, Otos, and Kansas, but the results here have either been inconclusive or else remain undescribed in print.

As revealed by archaeology, the material culture of the Pawnees after 1800 shows many parallels to the remains from the protohistoric Lower Loup towns, but can be described as generally much inferior in quality. The way of life, we may infer, was essentially the same. Villages were, apparently, fewer in number but of even larger size than formerly. Some of them were reported by contemporary observers to contain from 150 to 200 circular earth lodges and from 2,000 to 3,000 inhabitants. Usually they were located on the second bottom on the immediate banks of the Loup and Platte rivers, with a few towns located for a time on the Blue and the Republican to the south. Protection against the hostile Dakotas and other enemies was furnished by the steep river banks and by earth walls and ditches. The livelihood was about equally divided between hunting and agriculture. Using bone or iron hoes, the women tilled their small plots of maize, beans, squash, and sunflowers, scattered widely over the bottoms and sometimes as much as five or ten miles from the villages. The underground cache pit was still in use, but seldom reached the great size of the earlier pits.

There is direct archaeological as well as eyewitness evidence of the upright wooden mortar and pestle; flat milling stones are rare or absent, but smaller anvil stones for crushing dried meat, berries,

[32] Wedel, "An Introduction to Kansas Archeology," *loc. cit.*, 503-12, 630.
[33] Wedel, "An Introduction to Pawnee Archeology," Bureau of American Ethnology *Bulletin 112* (1936).

and the like are common. The jawbone of the deer was used for scraping corn off the cob. Bison were sought in regular organized summer and winter hunts in which entire villages participated for months at a time. During these trips, which were usually directed toward the west or northwest, or southward to the Arkansas Valley, the Pawnees lived in tipis and followed the same sort of life practiced by such full-fledged, bison-hunting nomads as the Dakotas and Comanches. Large herds of horses were to be seen around every village and camp, and dogs were common.

Weapons included some firearms, as well as the bow and iron-tipped arrow, lance, war club, tomahawk, and knife. Work in stone and bone was on a much more restricted scale and often of poorer quality than in earlier days. Nevertheless, at most sites can still be found small, chipped end and side scrapers, drills and reamers, knives, and large chopping or hide scraping tools. The large L-shaped elkhorn scraper, toothed flesher of bison leg bone, and paint "brush" of cancellous bone were still present. Clothing, except for textiles obtained by trade, was of skins, and there is evidence of bison haircloth and cordage. Bone plume holders and roach spreaders, widespread among the nineteenth-century tribes, have been found archaeologically. Fragments of twined rush or corn-husk matting sometimes turn up in burned houses or otherwise where conditions for their preservation were unusually favorable. Spoons were made of bison horn, less commonly of mussel shell; and wooden trays have come to light. Tobacco pipes, always made of stone, were fairly common and took various forms. The large, well-made catlinite pipe bowl, sometimes with an animal effigy carved on the stem end, has been found in graves dating perhaps as early as 1800 or soon thereafter. Imported glass beads and metal trinkets of various kinds were replacing the native articles of bone, shell, and stone for personal adornment. Long, shell hair pipes, originating in New Jersey and in great demand in the Indian trade, also began to appear soon after 1800.

The dead were buried, usually in a flexed position, in single dug graves located on the hilltops overlooking the villages. Grave furniture includes quartz crystals, occasional pottery vessels, stone balls, whetstone-like objects, and catlinite pipes; and, in perhaps greater abundance, glass beads, lead rings, metal knives, and other odds and ends that originated with white men. Tastefully incised bone quirt handles, bone and wood objects studded with brass-headed tacks, and other items are present. Of interest, too, are the rare peace medals and such unusual pieces as a wildcat skull with a brass military button set into each eye socket. The last named item, taken from a grave at the Hill site where Pike visited the Pawnees in 1806, was doubtless a personal or family fetish.

These nineteenth-century sites generally yield far fewer potsherds than do the older ones, reflecting the deterioration of the native potter's art in the face of a growing flood of metal pots and kettles brought in by the white traders. The pottery, moreover, is generally much cruder, though it still retains the basic vessel shapes, the thickened wedge-like rim with incised decoration, and the ridged body surfaces with or without incised decoration. Small pottery figurines, having a sort of fishtail base and decorated with incised lines and dots, have been found at a few late sites, but their use is unknown. There are also occasional crude representations in clay of horses, saddles, and other items.

As we have elsewhere noted, there remains little doubt in the minds of many students that the Pawnees visited after 1800 by Pike, Long, Frémont, and others, and among whom Dunbar and Allis labored for years as missionaries, were directly descended from the Lower Loup peoples who had resided in the same locality from two or three centuries earlier. The way of life was basically the same, and this is also true of the pottery, the house types, and the material culture generally. Interestingly enough, in some details the older Lower Loup materials conform more closely to Pawnee traditions than do the remains of the nineteenth-century sites. For example, the Pawnees traditionally built their houses with the doorway opening to the east, and used four center posts as the main supports. These two features characterize the great majority of Lower Loup houses, with but rare exceptions, whereas historic Pawnee houses face other directions as often as they do east and usually have six, eight, or more center posts. Thus, in the nineteenth century, the Pawnees were doing lip service to ritual requirements that had been carefully observed a century or two earlier, but which were no longer scrupulously adhered to after 1800. Equally intriguing is the fact that there are hints in the Pawnee legends of a time when the Pawnees lived in many villages, some said to have been on the Elkhorn where there is no historic evidence of the tribe's residence. One wonders whether this refers perhaps to that remote period when the little Upper Republican communities were scattered along many of the little creeks outside as well as in the Loup River drainage. It should be noted, however, that the Pawnees can be traced back with reasonable assurance only as far as the Lower Loup people. Their relationship to the earlier Upper Republican peoples has not been convincingly worked out as yet.

In contrast to the little we still know regarding the archaeology of the Siouan Village tribes in eastern Nebraska and northeastern Kansas, much information is on record about the Missouri and Osage tribes.[34] Both were, in a sense, marginal to our area of primary interest; but in later times, their customs and pursuits were strongly oriented toward the Plains Indian way of life and they had, of course, many contacts with the people of the bison area. Both tribes, moreover, had their roots partly in older cultures that also have their counterparts in the Eastern Plains.

The villages of the Missouri, since their first recorded notice in history in 1673, were along or near the Missouri River, below the mouth of the Kansas. Most of these locations have been verified by archaeology. The best known is the Utz site in Saline County, which appears to have been inhabited from prehistoric times into the first half of the eighteenth century. Cache pits are abundant and productive; and at least three cemetery areas are known. There is no trace of earth lodges, but good evidence that the subsistence economy included agriculture, hunting, fishing, and gathering. The pottery, which is plentiful and almost entirely shell-tempered, is mostly of the Oneota type, closely resembling in many particulars the wares from Leary and from northern

[34] Chapman, loc. cit., 145–49.

Iowa. There are also indications of influence from the potters of the Mississippi Valley in the vicinity of Cahokia or related Middle Mississippi centers. Bone, stone, and shell artifacts are consistent with the pottery picture; and, as in the Oneota sites farther west, show the result of cultural borrowing from peoples of the Eastern Plains. European trade goods are much less common than in the later and smaller sites farther upstream, where the native manufactures were clearly declining in importance. We do not know how long the Missouris had been living in this locality when they first came into contact with whites, or how populous and powerful a group they may have been at that time. Not long before 1800, however, harried by the Sauks and Foxes and decimated by smallpox, the Missouris were broken up and their remnants scattered among the Osages, Otos, and Kansas.

The Osage villages were situated principally on the banks of the Upper Osage River and on the Missouri River in north central Missouri. Their communities, large and unfortified, consisted of long ridged or domed houses of poles covered with rush matting or bark, with each sheltering several families. There is no evidence of the earth lodge. Agriculture and hunting were both important, with seasonal hunts on a tribal basis made into the bison country to the west. The known sites date mostly from the latter eighteenth and nineteenth centuries, by which time considerable quantities of Spanish and French trade goods were reaching the tribe and supplanting the native products. Pottery from some of the sites somewhat suggests Oneota ware in its use of shelltempering and incised decoration; but the relationships are probably still closer to late prehistoric materials found in the general region and southward. Among the bone and stone artifacts are the agricultural, hunting, and skin-working implements so characteristic of the historic Pawnees and other semihorticultural, bison-hunting tribes of the Eastern Plains. Although no pre-1700 village sites of the Osages have been found and their culture in prewhite days remains more or less conjectural, it appears likely that it was strongly rooted in locally-distributed prehistoric archeological assemblages in the area where Missouri, Arkansas,

Oklahoma, and Kansas adjoin, with a later overlay or infusion of Oneota culture perhaps derived from the close contacts of the Osages with the Missouri and Oto Indians. Probably like the Kansas, then, the Osages were originally a prairie or marginal Woodland people who, in course of time acquired a strong Plains bias, adopted many of the typical artifacts and practices of their westerly neighbors, and finally assumed an active role in the equestrian bison-hunting life of the semihorticultural peoples to whom they were geographically marginal.

Minor antiquities in the Central Plains that deserve brief mention before we move on include petroglyphs and aboriginal quarries. Petroglyphs—outline figures that were pecked, rubbed, or ground on stone ledges—are not common. Most known examples are in eastern Nebraska and in north central Kansas, where there are extensive outcrops of soft, readily worked brown to red-brown Dakota sandstone.[35] On these surfaces, using thin-edged or pointed tools, the native artists could quickly and easily inscribe their simple designs. Outside the sandstone area, rocky ledges are uncommon, usually very soft and calcareous in nature, and offered scant inducement to the Indians.

The petroglyphs include life forms, both human and animal; unreal or fanciful creatures; and various simple geometrical and straight-line patterns. Among the human figures there are two-horned characters, others that seem to be costumed as if for dances or ceremonies, and occasional horsemen. Geometrical figures include triangles, squares, hourglass and ladder-like designs, zigzags, circles or drilled pits with radiating lines, vertically bisected circles, deer and bird tracks, and many others.

Some of the carvings occur singly or in twos and threes, and may be in isolated spots far from water or village sites. On the other hand, there are some notable groups, such as Inscription Rock or Indian Hill near Ellsworth, Kansas; a cave near Blackbird Hill, on which the notorious Omaha chief was buried, near

[35] A. T. Hill and Paul Cooper, "The Archeological Campaign of 1937," *Nebraska History Magazine*, Vol. XVIII, No. 4 (1938), 347, plates 24–25; Wedel, "An Introduction to Kansas Archeology," *loc. cit.*, 482–94.

Macy, Nebraska; and another cave near Toronto, Kansas. None of these groups, unfortunately, has been adequately described or illustrated.

We can only guess at the age and purpose of the carvings, and at the identity of the artist. Where horses, guns, flags, flat-brimmed hats, and similar items appear, it is evident we are dealing with relatively late postwhite-contact creations. It is tempting to correlate others, when found near a culturally identifiable village or camp site, with the inhabitants of that site; but usually there is little or no proof of such association. It has been suggested that some of the carvings near Blackbird Hill are of Omaha Indian origin.

The motives behind the carvings undoubtedly varied as much as their age and cultural or tribal identity. Some of the grotesque creatures may have had legendary or ceremonial significance. Bonneted horsemen and groups of dancing (?) figures possibly memorialize some otherwise unrecorded event, important to the artist or to his group. Some of the figures in secluded spots might have been made by lonely vision-seekers, or by members of a raiding or hunting party who sought thus to enhance their chances of success.

Aboriginal chert quarries include two principal groups—one in eastern Nebraska, the other in southern Kansas. The first is in the Weeping Water district in Cass County, where the origin of hundreds of partially filled trenches and pits has long been in dispute. Most were well sodded over at the time of earliest white settlement, and in many there are growing trees one foot or more in diameter, all of which suggests some antiquity. Some of the limestone strata here contain nodules of bluish-gray chert, finely speckled with white; and artifacts and refuse of this easily recognized stone occur in abundance in the prehistoric sites of eastern Nebraska. There is little question that this "Nehawka" flint was obtained somewhere in the locality and in considerable quantities, and the old pits along the valley margin seem a likely source.[36]

The Kansas quarries are in the Flint Hills upland near Maple

[36] Strong, "An Introduction to Nebraska Archeology," *loc. cit.*, 43–44, 203–205.

City, a few miles north of the Oklahoma line.[37] Here, as at the Timbered Mounds in Kay County, Oklahoma, and also to the north, are groups of pits, some well sodded over and having the appearance of considerable age, others still fresh-looking and littered with broken limestone, chert nodules, and other refuse. Characteristic of these nodules, assigned by geologists to the Permian Florence flint, are *Fusulina* fossils, which have a wheat-grain shape, and a strong pink, buff, or gray banding. As artifacts and refuse, this material occurs plentifully in the Great Bend (Quivira) sites and in lesser quantities in many other districts in Kansas. Most of the known finds date from the fifteenth century or later; how much earlier the quarries may have been worked is not yet clear. A few smaller and apparently older quarries have been found farther north in the Flint Hills; and the blue-gray stone used by many of the natives of northern and northeastern Kansas very likely came from this zone, though the ancient diggings have not yet been located or recognized.

Farther west other kinds of stone were more commonly used, but not much is known about their sources. In the Republican drainage a yellow to brown jasper was extensively worked into knives, celts, and other artifacts. This was available in thin seams along the lesser creek beds. Extensive quarries have been reported in Nebraska near Beaver City, and in Kansas east of Norton, and again west of Bird City. Near Norton there are also exposures of soft, whitish to pink limestone identical with that often used by Upper Republican people for pipe-making, and early settlers asserted there were formerly indications of quarrying operations in this locality.

[37] Wedel, An Introduction to Kansas Archeology," *loc. cit.*, 476–82.

CHAPTER FIVE

THE SOUTHERN PLAINS

SOUTH OF THE THIRTY-SEVENTH PARALLEL, in Oklahoma, Texas, and eastern New Mexico, are the Southern Plains. As the term is here used, they include most of Oklahoma, with the exception of the rugged easterly portions that belong physiographically with the Ozark Plateau and Ouachita Mountains. In Texas, the limits have been set rather more arbitrarily at the Cross Timbers on the east and in central Texas on the south, and including the Llano Estacado to the west. The Pecos Valley bordering the Llano Estacado on the west may be taken as the western limit.

Geographically, there are no sharp breaks between this section and the Central Plains, except perhaps where the Raton Mesa and the Mesa de Maya extend eastward along the Colorado–New Mexico boundary from Trinidad nearly to the northwest corner of Texas.[1] The western portion is mainly in the High Plains, here known as the Llano Estacado, which comprises some sixty thousand square miles in Texas and New Mexico. This vast treeless short-grass tableland stretches from the Canadian Valley southward for three hundred miles to the Pecos, surrounded on all sides by high escarpments and unbroken by any through-flowing streams. Lower plains, usually rolling and sometimes hilly or interrupted by escarpments or mountains, lie to the east. These originally suported a tall-grass prairie, with extensive tracts of mes-

[1] R. T. Hill, "Physical Geography of the Texas Region," U. S. Geological Survey *Topographic Folio 3* (1899); Fenneman, *Physiography of Western United States, op. cit.,* 37–47.

quite and desert-grass savanna in Texas; and the streams that rise along the deeply indented margin of the High Plains to flow eastward across the prairies run in timbered, terrace-lined valleys.

In northeastern New Mexico and extending into southeastern Colorado, an uplift of the land surface followed by extensive outpourings of lava and these in turn by erosion has resulted in a rugged terrain with broad plateaus, basalt-capped mesas, and buttes; and the streams which drain the area often run in deep, narrow canyons. Unlike the Plains to the east, the slopes and higher parts of this section support stands of juniper and pinyon, as well as forests of yellow pine and other trees. Summer rainfall tends to be somewhat greater than on the High Plains generally, averaging around the eight inches sometimes regarded as the minimum for corn-growing.

In historic times, the principal tribes of the Southern Plains were the bison-hunting Apaches, Comanches, and Kiowas in the west, and the semihorticultural Caddoan peoples in the better watered, agriculturally favored prairies to the east. The Apaches were already present at the dawn of the white-contact period, having been met by Coronado in eastern New Mexico in 1541 and by Oñate in northern Oklahoma in 1601. According to Kroeber, they "were mountain tribes, marginally Southwestern, fronting on the plains and hunting bison"; but the contemporary Spanish accounts describe them as full-fledged plainsmen, as dog-nomads rather than horse-nomads.[2] In the eighteenth century, they were driven farther south and west into eastern New Mexico by the Comanches expanding from the Colorado Rockies; and the Comanches dominated the Southern Plains until their power was broken in the nineteenth century.

The Caddoans of the Southern Plains appear to have been principally the various groups collectively identified as the Wichitas, and including the Taovayas, Tawakonis, Wacos, and others. Some of these were living in the Arkansas Valley of central Kansas in

[2] Kroeber, "Cultural and Natural Areas of Native North America," *loc. cit.*, 79; Hammond and Rey, *loc. cit.*, 186, 235, 261–62, 292–93, 300, 310–11; D. A. Gunnerson, *loc. cit.*

the mid-sixteenth century, where they can be identified with the natives of Quivira who were met by Coronado in 1541. There may have been other related groups farther south in Oklahoma at that period, and there certainly were during the eighteenth century when heavy pressure from the Plains Apaches on the west and the Osages on the east were forcing the northernmost Wichita peoples southward, down the Arkansas Valley and into the Red River drainage. There appears to be no clear record of Wichita groups in Texas, south of the Red River, before the eighteenth century.[3]

Turning now to the archaeological record, we may note first that from the Southern Plains section has come much of our most important information bearing on the early big-game hunters. In northeastern New Mexico, for example, is the type station of the Folsom complex, where the distinctive fluted points were first recognized in unquestioned association with skeletons of fossil bison. Other bone beds containing the remains of extinct bison and possibly representing additional kills by the early hunters are said to occur in the region south of the Mesa de Maya.[4] South of the Canadian River, on the rim of the Llano Estacado, is the San Jon site, with a cultural sequence running from the early hunters to the recent Indians.[5] Farther south is the extensively worked and well-known Clovis-Portales or Blackwater Draw locality, of especial significance for its stratigraphic evidence that Clovis Fluted points and associated mammoth remains are older than Folsom Fluted points and the fossil bison that occur with them.

Farther east on the Llano Estacado have come other notable finds, most of which have been briefly described in an earlier chapter, and need only be noted again here. These include the Miami site, where Clovis Fluted points and a scraper were found

[3] A. D. Krieger, "Culture Complexes and Chronology in Northern Texas, With Extension of Puebloan Datings to the Mississippi Valley," University of Texas *Publication No. 4640* (October 22, 1946), 144–50.

[4] F. Wendorf, personal communication, January 19, 1960.

[5] Roberts, "Archeological and Geological Investigations in the San Jon District, Eastern New Mexico," Smithsonian *Miscellaneous Collections*, Vol. CIII, No. 4 (1942).

in association with mammoth bones; the Lipscomb site, where eighteen Folsom points and other artifacts occurred with extinct bison; the Lubbock site, where bones of extinct bison and four Folsom Fluted points were taken from a layer dated by radiocarbon at 9,883, plus or minus 350 years ago; the Plainview site, type station of the Plainview point, eighteen of which were taken from a bone bed estimated to contain more than one hundred individuals of extinct bison; and the Colorado City site, where three Plainview points were collected with fossil bison. Mention should also be made here of the Scharbauer site, near Midland, where a fragmentary human skull was found under geological circumstances that suggest a pre-Folsom dating.

Most of these early sites represent former lake beds, water holes, and stream courses where the now extinct elephants, bison, horses, and other large game animals sought water or grazing, and where their remains and the artifacts left with their skeletons by the hunters who slew them have long since been covered by wind-blown deposits now undergoing extensive erosion by wind and water. Most date from a period probably 7,000 years ago and earlier. No sites pertaining to this period have yet been excavated in Oklahoma, though early types of weapon points are known from that state.

Not much evidence is yet available regarding the pre-pottery peoples who inhabited the Southern Plains after the early big-game hunters and who drew their sustenance from game animals of modern types. Camp sites and bison kills in the Texas Panhandle and adjacent New Mexico, from which have come notched and shouldered projectile points, various kinds of knives, scrapers, choppers, drills, and other chipped stone tools, and also milling stones, are thought to represent this later stage, when the people combined hunting with the gathering of plant foods, and included in their hunting small game as well as large.[6]

[6] Hughes, "Little Sunday: An Archaic Site in the Texas Panhandle," *Bulletin* of the Texas Archeological Society, Vol. XXVI (1955), 55–74; C. D. Tunnell and J. T. Hughes, "An Archaic Bison Bill in the Texas Panhandle," *Panhandle-Plains Historical Review*, Vol. XXVIII (1955), 63–70; Wendorf, "The Archaeology of Northeastern New Mexico," *El Palacio*, Vol. LXVII, No. 2 (1960), 57.

In the Cimarron Valley of northeastern New Mexico and the Oklahoma Panhandle, caves and rock shelters have yielded other traces of simple seminomadic hunting and gathering peoples, some of whom also grew corn.[7] Owing to more favorable conditions of preservation, the remains here include perishable items as well as artifacts of stone. In caves south of Kenton, Oklahoma, the bones of the bison, deer, antelope, rabbit, and other forms are fairly plentiful in the refuse left by these people. Wild seeds, acorns, and other vegetal items are also present, and there is direct evidence of maize and squash. From one cave came ears of corn stored in a bag made of prairie-dog skin; shelled corn was found inside two bundles of grass. In another cave were found corncobs with sticks inserted in the butts; in several instances, two cobs were coupled by such sticks. Circular, flattened cakes made of acorns mixed with wild plums or cherries had been perforated for stringing, the more easily to be stored until they were used. Yucca-leaf sandals, coiled basketry fragments, rabbit-fur and skin bags, wooden drills for kindling fire, sharpened sticks, and triangular snares were among the normally perishable items recovered. Of weapons, the spear thrower and the foreshaft of a dart were directly indicated, but there was no evidence of the bow and arrow. Bone objects included awls for piercing and basket-making, and also short tubular beads. There were also crude flaked-stone implements and milling stones. Figures painted in red on cave walls included human representations, and others of unrecognized forms. No pottery, grooved axes, or other polished-stone artifacts have yet been reported from these cave deposits. A possible antiquity of some thousands of years has been estimated for the materials.

Less well known are the scanty remains described from extreme northeastern New Mexico under the term Fumarole culture.[8] These occur in natural "pipes" resulting from former hydro-

---

[7] Renaud, "Prehistoric Cultures of the Cimarron Valley, Northeastern New Mexico and Western Oklahoma," Colorado Scientific Society *Proceedings*, Vol. XII, No. 5 (1930), 122–35.

[8] Renaud, "Prehistoric Cultures of the Cimarron Valley, Northeastern New Mexico and Western Oklahoma," *loc. cit.*, 117–22.

thermal activity, the larger openings thus left having been utilized by man for residence and camping purposes. Here were found fireplaces, milling slabs with oval-shaped grinding depressions, animal bones, and many percussion-flaked quartzite scrapers, knives, borers, and projectile points. Deer, elk, and rabbit bones outnumbered those of bison. Tubular beads, whistles, and a few other artifacts of bone were found. There was no evidence of corn or squash, and the milling stones were presumably used for grinding wild vegetal products. It has been suggested that these remains may represent a nomadic hunting and gathering people who perhaps preceded the corn-growing peoples of the Kenton caves.

Along the southern and eastern margins of the area with which we are here primarily concerned there is rather more evidence bearing on these hunting and gathering folk. In central Texas, for example, there are large accumulations of fire-cracked stones mixed with ashes and cultural material. These, the burned-rock middens, have been found on stream terraces, in caves, and in rock shelters, and the deposits sometimes reach a depth of five or six feet. In them are found dart points of various kinds, chipped knives, scrapers, axes, choppers, and quantities of scrap, as well as milling stones and handstones. There are some polished stone pendants, occasionally incised, crude boat-shaped weights for spear throwers, bone awls, antler flaking tools, and perforated shell hoes; but arrowpoints, pottery remains, or traces of domestic crops or agriculture are absent. The size of these accumulations indicates that some of the localities were used over long periods of time, perhaps representing the central settlement for small groups of hunters and gatherers who wandered for much of the year over surrounding tracts of territory in search of animal and plant foods. Among the animal bones, those of the deer are especially plentiful. The grinding tools were presumably associated with the collecting of wild vegetal products—seeds, roots, and the like. A simple, long-lived, hunting-gathering culture is indicated, and one which may have persisted here for hundreds, or even thousands, of years. Its beginning has been estimated at perhaps four or five thousand years B.C. and it may have continued well into the Christian Era.

There are local differences in the artifact assemblage, but all are included in the general term Edwards Plateau aspect.[9]

Along the eastern margin of the area, there are still other remains that probably date largely from this intermediate period—after the time of the early big-game hunters but mostly before the arrival of pottery-making peoples. Along the streams and in caves and rock shelters in northeastern Oklahoma there are small, deep sites, some with as much as ten or twelve feet of accumulated debris from human occupation.[10] From these have been taken large stemmed and notched projectile points, drills, knives, scrapers and chopping tools. There are also grooved axes, grinding stones, anvil stones, and small mortars. Designated the Grove focus, these sites are believed to represent the long-used stations of small groups of hunters and gatherers who subsisted on the abundant game and wild vegetal products of the forested hills and valleys. The time of their residence here is still undetermined.

Farther south, along the the Poteau River and Fourche Maline Creek, and perhaps more widely spread in eastern central Oklahoma, are prepottery middens which also show long occupation during which appreciable changes in the artifacts took place.[11] The streamside refuse accumulations consist of dark soil through which are scattered animal bones, stones, ashes, artifacts, human and dog burials, and other remains. Chipped-stone artifacts, particularly projectile points, are plentiful in these deposits. Most of the points are stemmed and of large size; and there are also knives, scrapers, drills, double-bitted axes, and miscellaneous forms. Bone objects include antler-tip and splinter projectile points, long bone pins with flattened, carved, or otherwise elaborated ends, atlatl hooks, flaking tools, fishhooks, bird-bone whistles, cylindrical beads, and perforated animal teeth. Pottery appears in the upper levels of some of the deposits.

[9] D. A. Suhm, A. D. Krieger, and E. B. Jelks, "An Introductory Handbook of Texas Archeology," *Bulletin,* Texas Archeological Society, Vol. XXV (1954), 102–12.

[10] R. E. Bell and D. A. Baerreis, "A Survey of Oklahoma Archeology," *Bulletin,* Texas Archeological and Paleontological Society, Vol. XXII (1951), 10–14.

[11] Bell and Baerreis, *loc. cit.,* 19–27.

How widely the remains of the Grove focus and Fourche Maline people are distributed in Oklahoma has not yet been established, since most of the systematic and sustained excavations in the State have been made in the eastern section. The Grove focus is thought to be related to the Ozark Bluff Dweller remains of Missouri and Arkansas; and all three are evidently rooted in the Archaic (pre-pottery and pre-agricultural) cultures of the eastern United States. It seems likely that during the centuries or millennia represented by these occupations, some of the practices indicated and artifact types revealed by archaeology must have spread west and northwest into the Plains; but up to the present, no convincing evidence of such a spread has come to light.[12]

As we have noted, pottery occurs in the later stages of some of the Fourche Maline sites. At perhaps roughly the same time, other pottery-making peoples closely related to the Woodland and Hopewellian peoples of eastern Kansas and Missouri resided in northeastern Oklahoma.[13] They were followed perhaps as early as A.D. 500, by a series of sedentary, village-dwelling people whose populous communities were often centered around temples or ceremonial structures on platform mounds, and who left large, well-stocked burial mounds and cemeteries, made elaborate pottery in great variety of shapes and decorative styles, and were highly competent craftsmen and artists in many other lines of endeavor. A high point of this occupation is the well-known Spiro Mound group. The various local manifestations of these people are grouped by archaeologists under the common rubric of Gibson aspect.[14] In the main, their occupation lay east of the Plains, in-

[12] The Afton Spring materials from Ottawa County, Oklahoma (see W. H. Holmes, "Flint Implements and Fossil Remains from a Sulphur Spring at Afton, Indian Territory," U. S. National Museum *Annual Report for 1901* [1903], 237–52), have not yet been firmly placed in time; but recent stratigraphic evidence from Pomme de Terre Reservoir in western Missouri suggests that the curious angular-bladed corner-notched points date at least in part from pre-pottery times (Wood, "The Pomme de Terre Reservoir in Western Missouri Prehistory," MS [1960]).

[13] Bell and Baerreis, *loc. cit.*, 27–33.

[14] Bell and Baerreis, *loc. cit.*, 33 ff., 96–97; Krieger, "The Eastward Extension of Puebloan Datings Toward Cultures of the Mississippi Valley," *American Antiquity*, Vol. XII, No. 3 (1947), 145–48; Suhm, Krieger, and Jelks, *loc. cit.*, 151–55.

cluding a wide area in Arkansas, Louisiana, and northeast Texas; but there is some evidence in the form of trade pottery, pipes, and perhaps other items that they were in contact with the prehistoric rectangular-house dwellers of east central Kansas and perhaps even farther northwest.[15]

In late prehistoric and early historic times, after perhaps A.D. 1200 and continuing into early white-contact days, somewhat simpler cultures collectively known as the Fulton aspect succeeded the Gibson aspect occupation. Here again there are local and chronological variants, of which about one dozen have been named and defined by archaeologists. One characteristic feature of the Fulton aspect remains is the frequency of shell-tempered pottery, which also predominates in several late prehistoric cultures farther west and to the north. According to Bell and Baerreis, there was a marked shrinkage of territory occupied in Fulton aspect times in Oklahoma, during which other peoples with a shell-tempered pottery tradition resided in the area.[16] One of these, represented by the Neosho focus, shows marked resemblances to some of the Plains materials from southern Kansas, as does the Fort Coffee focus in east central Oklahoma. It seems possible that some of the putatively Wichita remains in southern Kansas have roots in the Fulton aspect or in immediately following cultures of eastern Oklahoma; and Chapman has recently suggested that the material culture of the Osage in western and southwestern Missouri may have evolved in that locality from one of the post-Fulton, shell-tempered pottery complexes distributed around the flanks of the Ozark plateau.[17] The need for further work in this important section on the border of the Plains, where the high and complex cultures of the old "Caddoan" area came into contact with less advanced peoples from the Plains to the west and north, is evident.

To return to the people of the Plains and prairies, probably the

[15] Wedel, "An Introduction to Kansas Archeology," *loc. cit.,* 515, 519–20, 619.
[16] *Loc. cit.,* 97.
[17] Chapman, "The Origin of the Osage Indian Tribe, an Ethnographical, Historical, and Archeological Study," unpublished Ph. D. dissertation, University of Michigan (1959).

best known archaeological materials in the Southern Plains are those left by the pottery-making, semihorticultural village Indians who seem to have overspread much of the prairie land by the twelfth century or a little earlier, and who in one form or another dominated the region for some three to five centuries. They are represented by numerous and varied occupational sites which show many similarities to the prehistoric village dwellers of the Central Plains during the comparable period of *circa* A.D. 1000 to 1450, plus some basic relationships to the higher cultures of the Caddoan area. In contrast to the older sites we have been considering, where there are generally no habitation remains or other evidences of fairly fixed and continuous residence, the late prehistoric cultures of the Texas-Oklahoma region have usually left fairly well-defined traces for archaeological study.

In central Oklahoma we may note first the Washita River focus, best known from sites in Garvin and Grady counties.[18] The village sites of the Washita River people are situated on stream terraces and upland promontories conveniently near potable water. They consist of remains of square houses with four center posts, an extended, covered entranceway, a prepared clay floor and fire basin; and the presence of burned clay with grass impressions suggests the structures were daubed with clay, if not earth-covered as in the Central Plains. Cache pits used secondarily for refuse disposal, and flexed and semiflexed burials, with or without offerings, are also found on these sites, but there is no indication that the communities were fortified. Refuse bone includes bison, deer, antelope, turkey, rabbit, and other forms, betokening a heavy reliance on the chase. Turtle, fish, and mussels were apparently used. There is direct evidence of corn and beans; and agriculture was carried on with the use of the bison scapula hoe with a socket for hafting, the bison frontal hoe with a horn-core handle, and the digging stick equipped with a point fashioned from

---

[18] Bell and Baerreis, *loc. cit.*, 75–81; K. Schmitt, "The Lee Site, Gv3, of Garvin County, Oklahoma," *Bulletin*, Texas Archeological and Paleontological Society, Vol. XXI (1950), 69–89; Schmitt and R. Toldan, "The Brown Site, Gd1, Grady County, Oklahoma," *Bulletin*, Texas Archeological and Paleontological Society, Vol. XXIV (1953), 141–76.

the cannon bone of the bison. Metates and manos were used in food preparation.

Various cutting and scraping jobs were performed with triangular, oval, lanceolate, and diamond-shaped chipped-stone knives and scrapers, polished celts, and shell scrapers. For skin-working there were rib and deer metapodial beaming tools, stone drills and bone awls, needles, etc. Arrow-shaft wrenches were fashioned from deer leg bones. Ornaments included bone and snail-shell beads. Stone pipes and deer-antler headdresses indicate ceremonial or ritual practices. Miscellaneous tools include sandstone awl sharpeners, whetstones, arrow-shaft smoothers, hammerstones, and curved bone squash knives. Pottery was fairly plentiful and surprisingly varied, usually tempered with shell, or with sand, crushed sherds, or bone. Vessels were mostly plain-surfaced jars, with flat bases and occasional handles; and some pieces were cord-roughened. Disks, figurines, and elbow pipes were also made of clay. Chipped stone included Kay County flint as well as Alibates dolomite from the Texas Panhandle quarries.

A closely related culture is represented by several sites in Custer County, farther up the Washita River, to which the name Custer focus has been assigned.[19] Much is still to be learned about the Custer focus people, their communities, and their distribution. Both the Washita River and Custer focus remains are apparently late prehistoric in time, but neither has yielded any evidence of white contact. The time period of 1300–1600 has been suggested as a likely time span for these remains. There are strong indications that the general culture here represented may extend northward onto other westerly tributaries of the Arkansas and perhaps into southern Kansas.

Another late prehistoric culture is the Henrietta focus, represented by numerous sites in north central Texas on the upper Brazos and Red rivers and their tributaries.[20] Sites cover from one to five or more acres, and include refuse deposits up to five feet

[19] Bell and Baerreis, *loc. cit.*, 81–83.
[20] Krieger, "Culture Complexes and Chronology in Northern Texas, With Extension of Puebloan Datings to the Mississippi Valley," *loc. cit.*, 87–159; Suhm, Krieger, and Jelks, *loc. cit.*, 80–87.

or more in depth. The house type is unknown. The people's livelihood was obtained from hunting with bow and arrow, the taking
of fish with bone hooks, and the growing of maize. As in the
central Oklahoma sites just noted, the Henrietta sites have hoes
made either of socketed or unsocketed bison scapulae or of bison
frontals with the horn core attached; and bone digging-stick
points are present. Perforated musselshell hoes have also been
found. Simple pits were used for storage, but the undercut Plains
cache pit is apparently unreported. Flat sandstone metates with
one- and two-hand manos were used with a to-and-fro grinding
motion. Most of the chipped- and ground-stone artifacts were
like those of the Washita River peoples. Pottery included jars and
deep bowls, characteristically shell-tempered and plain-surfaced,
and some of the jars had flat disk bases. The impressions of coiled
basketry have been noted on some of the sherds.

The Henrietta focus communities are believed to have flourished about the same time period as has been suggested above for
the Washita River and Custer focus peoples. Although no detailed comparative analysis of these several cultures has been made,
the available data on their way of life and on the arts and industries of the various peoples strongly suggest a widespread culture
analogous to the Central Plains phase, which includes the Upper
Republican, Nebraska aspect, and related prehistoric peoples of
Kansas and Nebraska. Krieger has argued strongly against the
identification of Henrietta focus with the Wichita tribes; but it
will not be surprising if it or one of the related late prehistoric
Oklahoma-Texas cultures turn out to be the base from which the
Great Bend aspect of central Kansas largely developed, in which
case we may perhaps legitimately consider them the remains of a
Caddoan or ancestral Wichita people.

In and east of the Cross Timbers in north central Texas, on the
Upper Trinity drainage, are the sites of the Wylie focus.[21] A conspicuous but still unexplained feature of many of these sites is a

[21] R. L. Stephenson, "The Hogge Bridge Site and the Wylie Focus," *American
Antiquity*, Vol. XVII, No. 4 (1952), 299–312; Suhm, Krieger, and Jelks, *loc. cit.*,
87–92.

single large, saucerlike pit from ninety to one hundred feet in diameter and up to ten feet deep at the center, with a built-up earthen rim. Some single and multiple flexed burials, usually without accompanying artifacts, have been found. There is some evidence of small wattle and daub houses. Agriculture is inferred from charred corn, bison-scapula hoes, and milling stones; and hunting, fishing, and gathering are also indicated. Most of the pottery apparently represents wares that were more characteristic of contemporary peoples to the west and east, and may not be of local manufacture. Sharing material culture traits both with the Henrietta focus people beyond the Cross Timbers and the Caddoan people to the east, the Wylie focus remains are estimated to date somewhere between A.D. 1300 and 1600.

Along the Canadian River and its short tributary creeks in the northern panhandle of Texas are a number of village sites that differ markedly from the prairie sites we have been considering. Many of the artifacts found here are rather similar to those of the prairie peoples, and the time period is roughly the same. The Canadian River sites are of particular interest because they appear to represent the remains of Plains Indians who were strongly influenced in at least one respect—their architecture—by contemporary Pueblo people to the west. Archaeologists who have worked with these materials have assigned to them the designation Antelope Creek focus. Similar materials in the Oklahoma Panhandle are known as the Optima focus; and the broader term Panhandle aspect has been proposed by Krieger to include all of these closely related variants.[22]

The Antelope Creek people lived in villages of widely varying size, usually situated on terraces and upland promontories overlooking the Canadian River or one of its tributary streams. The houses were sometimes single-room affairs; more often, perhaps, they consisted of a number of adjoining rooms, pueblo fashion,

[22] Krieger, "Culture Complexes and Chronology in Northern Texas, With Extension of Puebloan Datings to the Mississippi Valley," *loc. cit.*, 17–74; Suhm, Krieger, and Jelks, *loc. cit.*, 66–73; V. Watson, "The Optima Focus of the Panhandle Aspect: Description and Analysis," *Bulletin*, Texas Archeological and Paleontological society, Vol. XXI (1950), 7–68.

PLATE IX. *Upper:* Aerial view of Buffalo Pasture (lower center), site of a late eighteenth century fortified Arikara village in Stanley County, South Dakota. *Lower:* Aerial view of Sully Village, site of an unfortified Arikara village in Sully County, South Dakota. The dark spots along the bluff top indicate location of former earth-covered lodges.

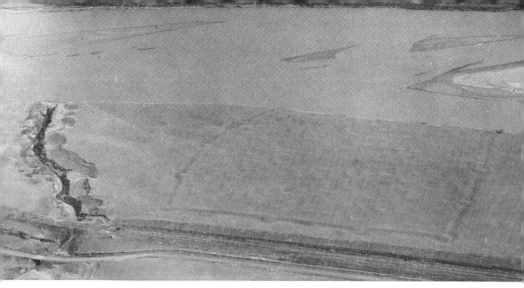

PLATE X. Aerial views of the fortified Huff village site, dated about A.D. 1500, in Morton County, North Dakota. (North Dakota Historical Society). *Upper:* Oblique view from west, showing enclosing ditch and house pits; Missouri River in background. *Lower:* Vertical view, showing excavated and unexcavated long-rectangular-house sites enclosed by ditch with ten bastions.

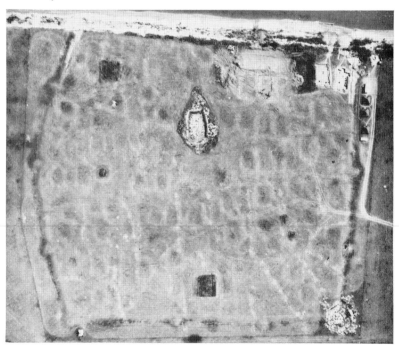

PLATE XI. House sites on the Middle Missouri. (River Basin Surveys, Smithsonian Institution). *Upper:* Circular house floor of the Arikara Indians in Stanley County, South Dakota. *Lower:* Superimposed house floors at the Dodd site, Stanley County, South Dakota, with later circular house partly removed by excavation of earlier long-rectangular house with entrance ramp in foreground.

PLATE XII. Some common bone tools of the Plains Village Indians. *Upper:* Agricultural tools, including left to right, unsocketed and socketed bison shoulder-blade hoes; hoe made of bison frontal with a horn-core handle; and digging-stick tip. *Lower:* Skinworking tools, including left to right, serrate-edge fleshing tool; cannon-bone beamer or dehairing tool; deer pelvis beamer; two paint applicators; and L-shaped elkhorn scraper handle fitted on short arm with stone or iron blade when in use.

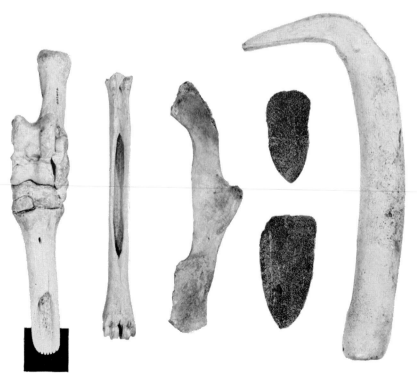

PLATE XIII. *Upper:* Miscellaneous bone tools, including left to right, whistles; incised and plain "snow snake" heads; decorated tubes; quill flattener; combs; decorated knife handle (bottom). *Lower:* Bone knife handles set with stone and iron blades; fishhooks; and toggle harpoon head.

PLATE XIV. *Upper:* Shell and bone ornaments from Middle Missouri village sites. *Lower:* Stone pipes from Arikara sites, about A.D. 1750, at left, and from long-rectangular-house sites, about A.D. 1300, at right.

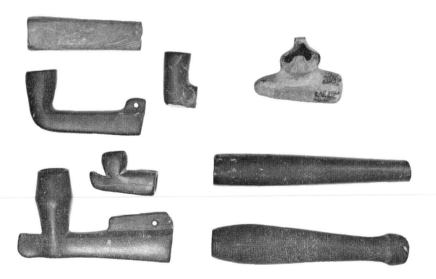

PLATE XV. Miscellaneous bone, stone, and glass objects from Middle Missouri village sites. *Top row:* native-made Arikara glass ornaments, about A.D. 1800–30, from Leavenworth site, South Dakota. *Middle:* bone and stone gaming chips from Mandan sites, North Dakota. (North Dakota Historical Society). *Bottom:* four bird-headed bone objects, Mandan. (North Dakota Historical Society).

PLATE XVI. Arikara burials, about 1750–90, Stanley County, South Dakota. (River Basin Surveys, Smithsonian Institution). *Upper:* Two pole covered graves. *Lower:* Burial of arrow maker, with tools beside skeleton.

with smaller, variously-shaped cells and cubicles that may have served for storage or other special uses. The rooms are from twelve to twenty-five feet across, usually square, with a central fireplace around which are four postholes in which the primary roof supports once stood. Walls are of stone and adobe. There is no evidence that any of these structures was more than one story in height, or of defensive works connected with the communities.

The subsistence of these people was based on maize agriculture, carried on in subirrigated patches in the nearby creek bottoms; on the hunting of bison, deer, antelope, smaller mammals, and birds; and presumably also on the gathering of seeds, fruits, and other wild vegetal products as they became available. The bison-scapula hoe and the bone digging-stick tip were the principal farming tools, while the metate and mano were used for grinding and preparation of vegetal foods. There is no indication of fishing.

The stone, bone, antler, and other artifacts used by these people in carrying on their domestic activities differed little from those of their contemporaries to the east. They included numerous chipped knives of various shapes, as well as scrapers, drills, choppers, unshaped sandstone blocks with short grooves from the sharpening of bone or wooden objects, awls of turkey and mammal bone, occasional eyed needles, flaking tools of bone and antler, grooved ribs that have been variously termed rasps, tallies, and pottery markers, and simple bone, stone, and shell ornaments. Many of the chipped implements were made of stone from the famous Alibates dolomite quarries north of Amarillo. Obsidian was doubtless carried in from the west, as was the turquoise which sometimes appears. A single utility pottery ware, characterized by globular jars with over-all cord-roughened exterior surfaces, is associated with the Antelope Creek and Optima focus remains.

Once regarded by some as evidence of an eastward extension of Puebloan peoples shortly after the beginning of the Christian Era, excavation has shown that the Antelope Creek sites are actually from a relatively late period, though certainly pre-white-contact. Probably few informed scholars today would quarrel with Krieger's view that

Antelope Creek focus represents a Plains bison-hunting and agricultural population basically very similar to Upper Republican, which wandered into the Canadian Valley and there came into contact with Puebloan civilization as it was expanding eastward toward the end of the classic or Pueblo III period . . . [The] relationship seems to have been rather one of trade plus the borrowing of an architectural style, without affecting the remainder of the Antelope Creek culture.[23]

Except in the kind of houses used, the material culture and inferred way of life of the Antelope Creek people parallels closely that of the Upper Republican people of the Central Plains, as we have outlined it in another chapter. There are less close similarities to the Custer, Washita River, and Henrietta peoples of Oklahoma and north central Texas, again excepting architecture and with notable differences in the pottery wares as well.

From the presence of datable Puebloan potsherds in some of the excavated sites, the Antelope Creek culture has been dated at around 1300–1450, with the possibility recognized that other sites may prove to belong to a time one century or two earlier. It is not likely that they were occupied much later, since Coronado reported no fixed settlements of agricultural Indians when he passed through the Texas Panhandle in 1541 enroute to Quivira. The thesis has been advanced that the panhandle sites were abandoned as a result of an extended drought in the Upper Republican territory to the north. It has been suggested also that the abandonment of the villages may have resulted from enemy raids, perhaps by the Apaches newly arrived in the Southern Plains. A few workers have entertained the view that these villages may, indeed, have been partly of Apache origin, but there is no present evidence in support of this. Further work in this intriguing district is urgently needed, including particularly detailed analyses of the material culture of additional excavated sites, further data on the chronological position, and studies on the wider relationships of the remains.

[23] "Culture Complexes and Chronology in Northern Texas, With Extension of Puebloan Datings to the Mississippi Valley," *loc. cit.,* 142.

South of the Canadian Valley, the archaeological remains assume a somewhat different character.[24] Here, on the flat, unbroken sod lands of the Llano Estacado, agriculture with hand tools was impossible, and the Indians found the region useful chiefly for hunting purposes. The ponds and lakes offered camping sites for the hunting parties that utilized the area; and around some of the ancient dry lake beds there were springs and seeps to which the parties returned again and again over the years. More important, perhaps, were the sandy areas of the southern Llano Estacado, where Pueblo pottery has been gathered at numerous sites. Krieger has called attention to the agricultural potentialities of a sizable block of sandy lands "extending from the vicinity of Muleshoe, Texas, and Clovis, N.M., southward along both sides of the State line nearly to the Pecos River in Texas." Here the native vegetation consisted of low-growing shin oak associated with bluestem bunch grass and assigned to the tall-grass formation or prairie grassland. The soils are light and tend to blow when broken out; but they freely absorb and retain the rainfall which later becomes available to growing vegetation. Unlike the short-grass sod, which became useable for agriculturists only with introduction of sod-breaking machinery, these sandy lands could be managed with hand tools. The majority of artifacts recovered in this region by collectors indicate occupation by Pueblo peoples, and these materials occur "either in dune areas or near the small widely scattered springs and seeps." In addition to pottery, the materials include manos and metates, evidently used in Pueblo fashion with a back-and-forth motion, projectile points, and miscellaneous cutting and scraping tools. Whether these materials represent repeated seasonal movements into the southern Llano Estacado by Pueblo peoples or result from permanent occupation by peoples moving eastward from the Pueblo area of New Mexico is undetermined. Most appear to predate the fourteenth and fifteenth centuries.

[24] Krieger, "Culture Complexes and Chronology in Northern Texas, With Extension of Puebloan Datings to the Mississippi Valley," *loc. cit.*, 75–82; J. B. Wheat, "Two Archeological Sites Near Lubbock, Texas," *Panhandle-Plains Historical Review*, Vol. XXVIII (1955), 71–77.

Archaeological remains on the historic time level in the Southern Plains are not yet very well known. Excavations in sites dating after approximately the year 1700 are still to be made. Probably the eighteenth century saw the disappearance of the semisedentary way of life among the Indians here, with the Plains proper largely taken over by Athabascan, Shoshonean, and other migratory hunting peoples by whom the village dwellers were forced eastward into the timber-fringed borders of the prairies.

There are, nevertheless, certain sites that promise interesting and important information if and when systematic investigations are undertaken. Two of these are situated on the west bank of the Arkansas River near Newkirk, Oklahoma.[25] The larger is just below the mouth of Deer Creek. Here, prior to modern farming activities, there were once numerous mounds—forty or more by report, ranging in height from one to three feet, and in diameter from thirty to fifty feet. Where plowed, these show a high ash content, with much bison bone and lesser quantities of flints, scrapers, potsherds, and other occupational debris. Shell-tempered pottery, clay pipes, and bone hoes and awls constitute most of the items found on the surface. In addition, quantities of iron axes, hoes, knives, gun parts, and other white-contact items are present, including much brass and many glass beads. Metate fragments and many manos suggest a semihorticultural subsistence basis. In the unplowed section, there were visible in 1940 traces of several small mounds as well as what appeared to have been an earthwork or enclosure flanked by an interrupted ditch. The trade materials have been identified as of French origin, dating from the period 1725–50. The native materials, so far as the small sample in the national collections is indicative, suggest relationships to the Great Bend materials in Kansas, but they are by no means identical. Thorough excavation and intensive analysis of these materials are urgently needed.

Some two hundred miles to the south, on the Oklahoma-Texas

[25] Bell and Baerreis, *loc. cit.*, 91; C. R. Steen, "Two Early Historic Sites on the Southern Plains," *Bulletin,* Texas Archeological and Paleontological Society, Vol. XXIV (1953), 177–88.

boundary line, is the Spanish Fort site—actually two large sites on opposite banks of the Red River.[26] Much material has been gathered here, but mostly from the surface, and the exact nature of the local culture complex is somewhat uncertain. Plain, shell-tempered pottery; numerous stone and clay elbow pipes; clay figurine fragments representing animals, humans, and in one case a horse head with an incised bridle; metapodial digging-stick points; and numerous large and small arrow points, scrapers, and other stone artifacts are present. With these native materials have been found many iron axes, hoes, knives, gun parts, and other items; brass bracelets, rings, and pot fragments; and glass beads. There is a possibility that some of the native items actually belong to earlier peoples who resided in this locality, and had no connection with the Indians who received the white-trade goods. Interestingly enough, among the Indian-made materials are Tewa Polychrome sherds that originated in the Upper Río Grande Valley as well as others identified as Natchitoches Engraved, a historic Caddo pottery native to extreme northeast Texas and adjacent Arkansas.

These sites have been identified as the Taovayas (Wichita) villages where the confederated Wichitas, Comanches, and other tribes repelled an attack by a large Spanish force under Colonel Parilla in 1759. At that time the village was strongly defended by a stockade and ditches, and flew the French flag. There were also French traders in residence, who furnished the natives with guns, ammunition, and other manufactured goods in return for buffalo robes, meat, Apache slaves, and horses and mules stolen from the Spanish settlements by the Comanches. Evidently an important Indian-White trading center, it is not known how long the village or villages had been established, though E. A. Harper suggests they were perhaps the site to which the Panipiquets, or Taovayas, moved from the Kay County sites sometime in the early 1750's.[27] The twin villages at Spanish Fort were the residence

[26] Krieger, "Culture Complexes and Chronology in Northern Texas, With Extension of Puebloan Datings to the Mississippi Valley," *loc. cit.*, 161–64; Suhm, Krieger, and Jelks, *loc. cit.*, 92–98.
[27] "The Taovayas Indians in Frontier Trade and Diplomacy, 1719–1768," *Chronicles of Oklahoma*, Vol. XXXI, No. 3 (1953), 271–72.

of the Taovayas until about 1811, when the tribe, greatly reduced in numbers and prestige, finally dispersed.

Since the two village sites in Kay County, Oklahoma, and the Spanish Fort sites were important outposts of French trade in the mid-eighteenth century, they would seem to offer an exceptional opportunity for the study of relationships between the French and the Taovayas Indians. The documentary material bearing on the Taovayas villages has been organized by Harper, and soundly based archaeological information derived from systematic investigations at the sites should give us a remarkably full picture of the rise to prominence and the subsequent decline of an important eighteenth-century tribe of the Southern Plains.

At the southern extremity of the region with which we are here concerned there are many small camp sites and rock-shelter locations that evidently represent, in part, a historic occupancy. The hunting of deer, bison, and other animals, the gathering of vegetal products, and some fishing are indicated, but there is no evidence of agriculture. A plain pottery ware, bone tempered and featuring some jars with handles, occurs at these sites, along with small arrow points, scrapers, knives, drills, choppers, grinding stones, and fishhooks. These sites have been designated by archeologists as the Austin focus, and they have been tentatively attributed to the Tonkawas who lived in central Texas during the eighteenth and nineteenth centuries.[28]

In the plains and plateau area of northeastern New Mexico, the archaeological situation, as it concerns late prehistoric and early historic Indian occupations, has been materially clarified by several recent studies.[29] Here, as in southeastern Colorado, there appear to be a few sites on which cord-roughened pottery has been collected, suggesting former residence by prehistoric Plains Indians. Except in small quantities and as presumed trade items,

[28] Krieger, "Culture Complexes and Chronology in Northern Texas, With Extension of Puebloan Datings to the Mississippi Valley," *loc, cit.,* 165–68.

[29] R. H. Lister, "Notes on the Archeology of the Watrous Valley, New Mexico," *El Palacio,* Vol. LV, No. 2 (1948), 35–41; J. H. Gunnerson, "Archaeological Survey in Northeastern New Mexico," *El Palacio,* Vol. LXVI, No. 5 (1959), 1–10.

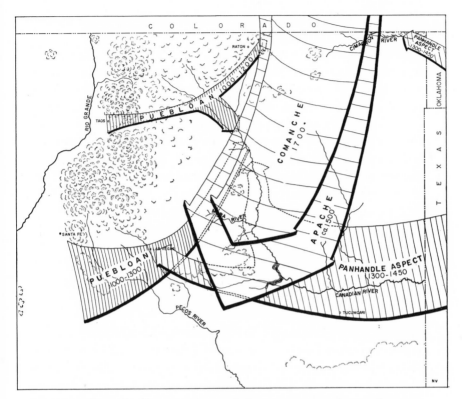

Fig. 11. *Schematic diagram of population movements in northeastern New Mexico in late prehistoric and early historic times, according to Wendorf.*

El Palacio

Pueblo pottery and other materials apparently extend only a short distance eastward from the base of the Sangre de Cristo Range and along the stream valleys issuing from their eastern slopes. Slab-walled ruins of single unit houses, reminiscent of some of the Texas Panhandle sites, have been reported as far west as the vicinity of Las Vegas. Farther north, on Ponil Creek, the Cimarron, and other westerly tributaries of the Canadian, small sites have yielded stone artifacts and micaceous pottery, sometimes associated with white-trade materials, and believed to date from

149

the eighteenth and nineteenth centuries. Stone tipi rings are also reported from this section.

Some of the interrelationships of Plains and Puebloan peoples in northeastern New Mexico have been further considered by Wendorf.[30] He sees Puebloan influences or actual intrusions of people from the Upper Río Grande communities as reaching at least as far eastward as the Canadian Valley via two main routes. One route was from Taos across the mountains to the headwater tributaries of the Canadian, and on to the Raton-Trinidad locale; the other was around the southern terminus of the Sangre de Cristo to the Pecos River and thence north to the Mora and Canadian. The latter movement "apparently occurred as an actual immigration of Puebloan people," whereas the northern one possibly represents a spread of Puebloan influences to local populations who remain otherwise unidentified. These eastward thrusts of Pueblo people and/or cultural influences are dated from the associated pottery between approximately A.D. 1000 and 1300.

Following abandonment of the Puebloan and Pueblo-like communities east of the Sangre de Cristo, semisedentary Plains people representing the Panhandle aspect of Texas and Oklahoma appear to have moved into northeastern New Mexico. This intrusion extended west to the Las Vegas district, up the Canadian beyond the Mora, and along the Dry Cimarron in the extreme northeastern corner of New Mexico. Dated Puebloan pottery associated with these materials from the east falls between 1325 and 1450, suggesting that the sites were abandoned during the fifteenth century.

For the canyon-cut and mesa-studded country in southeastern Colorado, there is as yet little published information other than that gleaned through short survey trips.[31] There are a good many

[30] "The Archaeology of Northeastern New Mexico," *loc. cit.* 55–65.

[31] Renaud, "Archaeological Survey of Eastern Colorado," *Archaeological Survey Series*, University of Denver (1931); N. W. Dondelinger and R. M. Tatum, "Preliminary Survey of Sites in Las Animas County, Colorado," *Southwestern Lore*, Vol. VIII, No. 1 (1942); Wedel, "Archeological Reconnaissance in Southeastern Colorado," *Explorations and Field-Work of the Smithsonian Institution in 1938* (1939), 91–94.

camp sites marked by chipped-stone artifacts, rejectage, and occasional fireplaces. Pottery-bearing sites are not common; they include multi-roomed pueblo ruins in the vicinity of Trinidad, and other scattered materials, chiefly non-Puebloan, elsewhere to the east and northeast. Along the Apishapa, the Purgatoire, and other deeply intrenched lesser streams, there are caves and rock shelters from which have been taken small projectile points and other chipped-stone artifacts, bone and shell beads, grinding stones, and occasional burials; in others, such items as corncobs, pumpkin seeds, wooden foreshafts, nocked arrow fragments, painted and sinew-wrapped sticks, and bedrock grinding basins have been noted. Especially intriguing are numerous rude boulder constructions, which include tipi rings from eight to fifteen feet in diameter, as well as hilltop enclosures and walls up to three feet high or more which are locally termed "Indian forts." Canyon walls, large boulders, and rock ledges, where of suitable nature, frequently bear petroglyphs. Most are made by pecking; a few are painted, usually in red. There are many representations of animals, especially of small two-horned, goat-like or antelope-like creatures. Other animals, birds, horses and horsemen, human figures, and geometric, spiral, circular, and linear designs also occur.

Although we cannot yet be certain, it seems likely that much of the unpainted pottery and Plains-like stonework in northeastern New Mexico and southeastern Colorado reflects the occupancy of this region by the Plains Apaches during the sixteenth, seventeenth, and early eighteenth centuries. Unpainted micaceous pottery was manufactured in historic times at the pueblos of Taos and Picuris, where in fact it has been the principal ware since the Pueblo Revolt in 1680; and it was made also by the Jicarilla Apaches, by whom it was very likely carried northward into the Plains of eastern Colorado, western Kansas, and Nebraska. Among the late archaeological materials of the Upper Canadian and Upper Arkansas drainage, then, we may have archaeological confirmation of the seventeenth- and eighteenth-century Spanish documents which tell us that some of the contemporary Apaches were living in semipermanent villages of flat-topped houses and were growing corn under irrigation.[32] The corn and pumpkin remains from rock shelters on the Purgatoire possibly represent crops grown in the nearby canyon bottoms by Apaches.

The cord-roughened pottery that also occurs scatteringly in the region doubtless belongs to an earlier occupation, or occupations. Most of it is probably related to the Panhandle aspect peoples of the Texas-Oklahoma region or to the Upper Republican people of the Central Plains; but there are also traces of an older Woodland pottery horizon in the region. Pointed-bottom vessels with cord-roughened surfaces, much like those found in Woodland sites in Nebraska and Kansas before about A.D. 600, have been reported along the mountain-plains border zone south of the Arkansas River; and the somewhat similarly shaped utility pots of the Largo–Gallina–Governador section in northern New Mexico, apparently associated in part with stockaded settlements dating from about A.D. 1000, are regarded as evidence of intrusions or influences from the Plains on an earlier time level than the Panhandle-Pueblo contacts farther east in the Canadian drainage.[33]

The limitations set for this book do not permit extended discussion of the intriguing problem of Plains-Puebloan relationships as these are reflected in the growing archaeological record; but we may consider briefly certain other suggestions of former contacts between the peoples of the two regions. In sites in the Chama Valley of north central New Mexico, a locally-made pottery with incised decoration of a distinctly non-Puebloan kind known as *Potsuwi'i Incised* appeared after A.D. 1400.[34] In style and technique, this decoration has much in common with that on late prehistoric pottery in the Mississippi, Ohio, and Missouri valleys and

[32] A. B. Thomas, *After Coronado: Spanish Exploration Northeast of New Mexico, 1696–1727*, 64, 112–15.

[33] H. P. Mera, "Some Aspects of the Largo Cultural Phase, Northern New Mexico," *American Antiquity*, Vol. III, No. 3 (1938), 236–43; F. C. Hibben, "The Gallina Phase," *American Antiquity*, Vol. IV, No. 2 (1938), 131–36; E. T. Hall, Jr., "Early Stockaded Settlements in the Governador, New Mexico," *Columbia Studies in Archaeology and Ethnology*, Vol. II, Pt. 1 (1944).

[34] J. A. Jeancon, "Excavations in the Chama Valley, New Mexico," Bureau of American Ethnology *Bulletin 81* (1923), 54–57; Wendorf, "Salvage Archeology in the Chama Valley, New Mexico," School of American Research *Monograph No. 17* (1953), 55, 98.

on early historic vessels from eastern Nebraska and the Missouri Valley in South Dakota. More puzzling is a small, high-necked vase or water bottle from an early white-contact site on the Loup River in east central Nebraska on which the details of decoration are strikingly reminiscent of the incised patterns on the large jars from the Chama Valley, although here a time difference of perhaps a century or more supposedly intervenes between the time levels represented.[35]

Associated with the Potsuwi'i Incised pottery in the Chama sites are certain hide-dressing tools that also seem to have their closest counterparts archaeologically in the Central Plains of Nebraska and eastern Kansas. These include the beamer or dehairing tool, made of the leg bone of a deer or other mammal, and a drawknife-like hide scraper fashioned from the ilium, or pelvic bone, of the deer or another large animal. The first of these types also occurs, as we have noted elsewhere, in Upper Republican sites in Nebraska, which are in part contemporaneous with the Chama sites; the second is reported so far only from Hopewellian sites near Kansas City, dated at about A.D. 400 or earlier, where the preceding beamer type also is found.

It is not clear at the moment how these similarities in pottery decoration and bone tools are to be explained, beyond the fact that they almost certainly indicate some sort of contact between the people; but it can be suggested that, with the constantly improving controls over the time factor that are developing as our archaeological knowledge increases, the day may not be far distant when a thorough re-examination of Plains-Puebloan relationships on the pre-white contact level can be assayed with promise of more illuminating results than have been attained thus far.

In closing this review of the principal archaeological materials in the Southern Plains, we must take note of certain mineral resources that were clearly of considerable importance to the aboriginal populations. Best known, perhaps, is the Alibates flint

---

[35] Nebraska State Historical Society Museum, Cat. No. N1-4129 from the Burkett Site, Nance County, Nebraska (information from M. F. Kivett); compare with Jeancon, *loc. cit.*, figs. 25–26.

quarry, situated on the south side of the Canadian River about thirty-five miles north of Amarillo in Potter County, Texas.[36] Here there are many old pits of varying sizes and depths, most of them nearly filled with soil. Around them, the ground surface is littered with flint chips, cores, flakes, hammerstones, quarry blanks, and chipped artifacts, which in places have accumulated to considerable depth. The stone sought by the ancient quarrymen was an agatized dolomite of Upper Permian age which is said to occur also, but perhaps in inferior quality, in a number of other localities along the Canadian and elsewhere in the panhandle region. The stone varies widely in color, including reds, browns, grays, and white, which are often present in alternating bands and sometimes imparting a strikingly variegated effect to the artifacts into which they were fashioned. Alibates dolomite was evidently widely sought throughout a very long period of time, having been recognized in artifacts from many sites in Texas, Oklahoma, southern Kansas, Colorado, and New Mexico, with a range in time that extends from Folsom, Clovis, and Plainview to the early historic period.

Elsewhere in the panhandle plains area, quartzite, cherts, chalcedony, silicified woods, and various other hard, crystalline rocks suitable for heavy-duty tools were fairly readily available in many localities. Of particular interest, perhaps, is the report that the Canadian River terraces contain large numbers of "small relatively flattish boulders of schistose fibrolite," an exceedingly tough stone especially well suited to the making of axes. A good many axes of this material were found at the Pecos ruin; and Witte suggests the Canadian Valley as the likely source of the stone there used.[37]

There is no evidence, so far as I am aware, as to whether or to what extent the prehistoric Indians of the Southern and Central Plains used salt. In historic days, however, two large salines in northern Oklahoma were frequently visited by the Plains and

[36] A. H. Witte, "Certain Archeological Notes on the High Plains of Texas," *Bulletin,* Texas Archeological and Paleontological Society, Vol. XVIII (1947), 79–80; J. B. Shaeffer, "The Alibates Flint Quarry, Texas," *American Antiquity,* Vol. XXIV, No. 2 (1958), 189–91.
[37] *Loc. cit.,* 78–79.

Prairie tribes. These were the Great Saline on the Salt Fork of the Arkansas, about four miles east of Cherokee, now commonly known as the Alfalfa County Salt Plain, and the Rock Saline, or Little and Big Salt Plains, on the Cimarron, beginning just south of the Kansas line.[38] Several contemporary accounts from the nineteenth century describe these features and the Indian visits to them. When Tixier accompanied the Osages to the Great Saline in 1840, he spoke of the bison "which are always found near the salines," and thus suggested an additional attraction which may have brought distant Indians to the salt deposits whether or not they wished to utilize the salt itself.

[38] C. N. Gould, "The Oklahoma Salt Plains," *Transactions*, Kansas Academy of Science, Vol. XVII (1901), 181–84; L. C. Snider, "The Gypsum and Salt of Oklahoma," Oklahoma Geological Survey *Bulletin 11* (1913), 203–205; J. F. McDermott, ed., *Tixier's Travels on the Osage Prairies*, 224, n. 8, 240, 249–51.

CHAPTER SIX

THE MIDDLE MISSOURI

NORTH OF THE NIOBRARA, which empties into the Missouri about nine hundred miles above St. Louis, is the Middle Missouri area. Its core is an eight-hundred-mile segment of the Missouri River, roughly from the mouth of the Yellowstone, in western North Dakota, to the southern boundary of South Dakota, five or six miles below Fort Randall Dam. Throughout much of this section, the Missouri follows a course set by the later ice sheets, which deflected southward to the Mississippi an older drainage system that emptied into Hudson Bay. In the millennia since that shift, the river has entrenched itself hundreds of feet below the general surface of the Missouri Plateau. In an often dry and thirsty land, it became the life line of a belt in which various features of topography, climate, natural vegetation, and soils were combined in a setting that permitted the establishment of a large, concentrated native population following a sedentary way of life based upon cultivation of the soil.

In the nineteenth century, the valley of the Missouri was a main artery of travel for fur traders, explorers, and others. Many of these left us a notable legacy of travel narratives, including accounts of the Indians then to be seen in the area. In addition, within the narrow confines of its trench, the Middle Missouri holds an amazing wealth of archaeological data.[1] From White River to the

[1] Will, "Archeology of the Missouri Valley," *Anthropological Papers*, American Museum of Natural History, Vol. XXII, Pt. 6 (1924); Strong, "From History to Prehistory in the Northern Great Plains," Smithsonian *Miscellaneous*

Little Missouri, the ruins of old villages, camp sites, burial grounds, and associated remains are strewn along both banks in extraordinary numbers. Especially conspicuous are the traces of former earth-lodge villages, which include some of the largest, best preserved, and most impressive sites in the entire Plains region. Above the Knife, village ruins are comparatively scarce and usually of late date; and clusters of stone tipi rings occur in increasing numbers. From the variety of materials seen, it is clear that different peoples over a long period of time have had their habitat here.

After approximately 1750, various bands of the Dakotas, the Assiniboines, and other wandering bison-hunters ranged widely across this territory. These, however, established no fixed towns and little of the archaeology is attributable to their passage. But along the main stem, in what is now South Dakota, the village-dwelling, corn-growing Arikaras resided at various times in a series of fortified and unfortified communities. Upstream, above the Grand, were the towns of the Mandans. Historically, these stood in the vicinity of the Heart River and above, but in earlier periods they were evidently located farther downstream. Beyond, still on or close to the banks of the Missouri, were the Hidatsas, long resident about the confluence of the Knife with the main river. The Cheyennes, on their historic (late eighteenth century) movement westward from the Red River drainage to the Black Hills, and in the process of changing from a partially gardening to a primarily hunting economy, are thought to have sojourned for a time on the Missouri. It is likely, too, that still other semi-sedentary groups, of whom few or no records are now known, at various times considered the Middle Missouri region their home.

Today, this stretch of the Missouri includes the location of three huge multipurpose dams—the Garrison, Oahe, and Fort Randall—whose impounded waters will ultimately submerge more than 550 miles of the valley floor and its adjacent terraces, together with hundreds of Indian villages and camp sites. More dams and

Collections, Vol. C (1940), 353–94; Will and T. C. Hecker, "The Upper Missouri River Valley Aboriginal Culture in North Dakota," North Dakota Historical *Quarterly*, Vol. XI, Nos. 1 and 2 (1944), 5–126.

further flooding are in prospect. The interagency archaeological salvage operations stemming from these great water-control projects have made the Middle Missouri a focus of intensive surveys and excavations on a scale never before attempted in the Plains region.[2] A very considerable body of specimens and supporting data has accumulated from this work in the years since the second world war; but the great bulk of this information remains still unpublished. When and as this eventually appears in print, it will greatly illuminate the still dimly perceived story of man's activities in the region. At present we can do little more than suggest the direction in which the evidence points, and recognize the fact that such interpretations as are here attempted are subject to revision, perhaps even to abandonment, as newer information becomes generally available.

Let us first look more closely at the environmental setting as it was before the damming of the Missouri. In the new trench cut by the southward spilling of the ice-blocked streams, the melt waters of the pre-Wisconsin glacier deposited a thick bed of silt, clay, sand, and gravel.[3] On this valley fill, the present Missouri follows a winding course between bluffs several hundred feet high, and from one to six miles apart. The sediments laid down by the river in recent times form low-lying flood plains, islands, and bars. Above the flood plains, which vary up to two or three miles in width, terrace remnants rise like benches at various elevations from 20 to 150 feet, or more, above the stream. Where the river swings against the foot of the bluff on one side, it leaves on the opposite bank a broad flat or "bottom," portions of which may be reclaimed by the stream when the channel shifts in time of high water. The

[2] Wedel, "Prehistory and the Missouri Valley Development Program . . . in 1947," Smithsonian *Miscellaneous Collections*, Vol. CXI, No. 2 (1948) 21-24; Cooper, "Recent Investigations in Fort Randall and Oahe Reservoirs, South Dakota," *American Antiquity*, Vol. XIV, No. 4, Pt. 1 (April, 1949), 300-10; Wedel, "Prehistory and the Missouri Valley Development Program . . . in 1948," Bureau of American Ethnology *Bulletin 154*, River Basin Surveys Papers No. 1 (1953), 24-29; Cooper, "The Archeological and Paleontological Salvage Program in the Missouri Basin, 1950-51," Smithsonian *Miscellaneous Collections*, Vol. CXXVI, No. 2 (1955), 51-69.

[3] Flint, "Pleistocene Geology of Eastern South Dakota," U. S. Geological Survey *Professional Paper 262* (1955), 140-43.

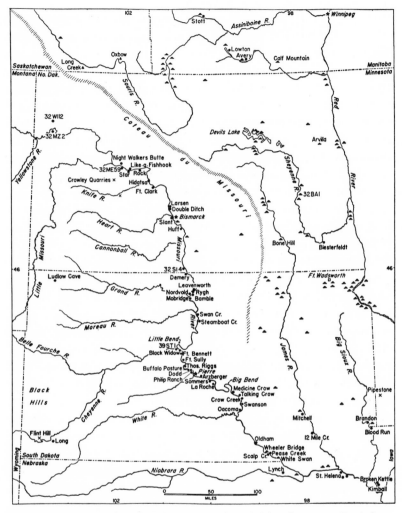

FIG. 12. *Map of the Middle Missouri and Northeastern Periphery, showing the location of certain archaeological sites and other features.*

banks, thus, are characteristically a succession of bottomlands and terraces alternating with rough hilly sections fronting directly on the river. Native settlement usually took place on the terraces, above reach of the tremendous floods that occasionally sweep the valley. The nearby bottom lands, cleared of their lush natural vegetation, provided excellent garden sites, as well as sheltered locations for the winter villages.

The principal tributaries rise in the short-grass plains and badlands to the west, and join the main stem from valleys cut several hundred feet below the upland. They, too, have extensive flood plains into which the present streams have lowered themselves. These valleys have so far disclosed surprisingly few evidences of fixed towns or villages; but scattered camp sites suggest that they furnished routes of travel for small groups engaged in hunting, trading, raiding, and other sporadic short-term activities.[4] By these routes the Missouri River villages had access to various useful or desirable materials, among them the plate chalcedony of the Badlands on White River, the gypsum and cave onyx of the Black Hills on the Cheyenne, and the ever-popular dark translucent or molasses-colored chalcedony quarried in large quantities along the Knife in Mercer County, North Dakota.

The timber that grew naturally in the valley was another important resource for its human inhabitants, furnishing fuel, winter shelter, building supplies, and cover for a variety of game animals. It consisted of groves of mixed deciduous trees, chiefly the cottonwood, ash, elm, box elder, hackberry, and oak, all growing on the valley bottoms and the older islands. Here, too, the chokecherry, buffalo berry, wild plum, and grape supplied edible fruits. Along the unstable stream banks and on newly formed bars and islands, willows predominated. Stands of tall, straight-growing juniper, especially prized by the Indians for house-building, occurred on some of the islands and streamside bottoms, and, usually in more scrubby form, on many of the north-facing valley slopes.

The Middle Missouri lies mostly outside what we know today as the Corn Belt. Above White River, the normal June to August rainfall averages under eight inches annually, and large-scale corn agriculture is unprofitable. Here, limited and uncertain precipi-

[4] Cooper, "Archeological Investigations in the Heart Butte Reservoir Area, North Dakota," Bureau of American Ethnology *Bulletin 169*, River Basin Survey Papers No. 9 (1958), 32–34.

tation, a short growing season, and occasional early-fall frosts pose a serious handicap to the commercial grower. Yet, despite the harshness of the climate, the native people whose villages dotted the valley from half a millennium before Columbus' landfall, drew a large part of their subsistence from the cultivation of corn, along with beans, squash, and sunflower. From a lush warm-weather plant requiring high day and night temperatures during a growing season of 150 days or more, the Missouri River Indians transformed corn into a tough, compact plant three or four feet high, maturing in 60 to 70 days, and possessing marked resistance to drought, wind, cold, and frost. How much time was required for this transformation, we do not know; but its outcome ranks high indeed as an achievement in plant-breeding. At the beginning of the white-contact period less than 250 years ago, the northern limit of native maize agriculture was at the Hidatsa villages on the Knife River.[5] In earlier times, it may well have lain farther north.

The historic tribes whose archaeological antecedents are of foremost interest in this section are the Mandans, Arikaras, and Hidatsas. Other semisedentary groups may have been present, but if so, their traces are obscure or unrecognized and their influence on native cultural development remains uncertain. Of the tribes named, the Mandans were evidently the earliest to arrive. Tradition says that they first reached the Missouri, from an easterly direction, near the mouth of the White, whence they moved gradually up the main stem.[6] When first seen by white men in the mid-eighteenth century, they were a prosperous and important people whose stockaded, orderly towns dominated the locality around the junction of the Heart with the Missouri. The striking differences between their way of life and that of the wandering hunters by whom they were surrounded gave them an aura of mystery; and about their alleged light skin, fair hair, and other "non-Indian" attributes, both cultural and physical, was written a good deal of nonsense to "prove" their descent from the Welsh

[5] Will and G. E. Hyde, *Corn Among the Indians of the Upper Missouri*.
[6] A. W. Bowers, "Mandan Social and Ceremonial Organization," University of Chicago *Publications in Anthropology* (1950), 8-19.

or, later, from the Norse.[7] Many of their sites have been surveyed, a few partially excavated, and attempts made to organize the resulting archaeological data.[8] Several periods in their development have been tentatively outlined, but the sustained work needed to support and amplify these schemes is yet to be done. Probably, however, few students would quarrel with Strong's appraisal that "Viewed as a whole, the material manifestations of Mandan culture apparently represent a climax for the northern Plains."

The Arikaras, northernmost of the Caddoan-speaking peoples and cultural rivals of the Mandans, dominated the Missouri Valley in South Dakota during most of the historic period. Traditionally derived from the Pawnees of Nebraska, they were present in southern South Dakota in considerable numbers early in the eighteenth century, when the French first contacted them. Their earlier history has long been unclear; but owing to the location of the older sites in areas scheduled for early inundation by the federal water-control program, they promise soon to be probably the best-known tribe, in archaeological terms, of the Middle and Upper Missouri areas.

The Hidatsas were comparatively late arrivals, probably entering the region from eastern North Dakota. All of the sites which can be certainly, or probably, attributed to them lie well upstream, at or above the Knife. Some of their sites have been sampled by archaeologists, and studies have been made on their ceramic history; but very little of this information has been published, and none of it in the desired detail.

Of the hundreds of village and camp sites whose locations have been established along the Middle Missouri, most were inhabited during the last thousand years and evidently represent the remains of fixed communities whose residents made pottery and depended, in varying degree, on the cultivation of maize and other crops. Of the earlier hunting groups who may be presumed to have

[7] M. T. Newman, "The Blond Mandans: A Critical Review of an Old Problem," *Southwestern Journal of Anthropology*, Vol. VI, No. 3 (1950), 255–72.

[8] Will and H. J. Spinden, "The Mandans," *Papers*, Peabody Museum American Archeology and Ethnology, Harvard University, Vol. III, No. 4 (1906); Will and Hecker, *loc. cit.*

roamed the region for many hundreds of years previously, there is surprisingly little evidence at present. From the uplands of Tripp, Hyde, and a few other counties in South Dakota have come fluted points that suggest the passage of Folsom or other Paleo-Indian peoples; for North Dakota, the evidence is even scantier. There are no known camp sites, game kills, or butchering grounds that can be identified with the early big-game hunters. Since artifacts attributed to Folsom and other early hunting cultures have been found in some quantities in Wyoming, Montana, and the Canadian Prairie Provinces to the west and north, and early types of material are also known from Minnesota and Iowa to the east, it may confidently be expected that similar finds dating from five to ten thousand years ago will eventually come to light in the area traversed by the Middle Missouri. Perhaps, as in other sections of the Plains, these ancient remains will turn up less frequently in the main valley than along the lesser tributaries, on the eroded upland margins, and in the badland areas of the smaller waterways.

If Paleo-Indian remains are scantily represented, the intensified and widespread archaeological surveys of recent years have nevertheless brought to light a number of localities along the Middle Missouri where occupations by non-pottery peoples are indicated. This is in line with what might be expected, since local collections have long been known to include artifact types that pretty certainly antedate the known pottery cultures of the area. Non-pottery materials are exposed in cut banks, along eroded terrace edges, in freshly graded roadside ditches, and in other locations where sections of the subsurface soils may be examined. They are found at various depths in or on old soil surfaces, from a few inches to many feet beneath the present ground surface. Here the close observer may find splintered and broken animal bone, worked flint and chips, occasionally a hearth or an unbroken projectile point or scraper, and other signs of former human activity. These things indicate, of course, that men were camping at these spots at a time when the ground surface was lower than at present, and that wind or water have since deposited soils to varying depths on top of the old living level.

It does not necessarily follow, of course, that all sites without pottery are the remains of people on a pre-pottery level of culture. Some probably mark camping locations of the eighteenth- and nineteenth-century Dakotas or other nomadic tribes. Others may be hunting camps of earlier peoples who dwelt normally in settled villages, but chose not to encumber themselves with such bulky and breakable furniture as pots when in quest of game. On the other hand, the considerable depth at which some of these exposures occur strongly suggests a respectable antiquity, an antiquity that may be measured in terms of thousands, rather than hundreds, of years. Some of the artifacts found also point to an antiquity greater than that of any of the pottery-making people of the area.[9] There is, in short, good reason to believe that some of the non-pottery exposures on old land surfaces are indeed the remains of hunting and gathering people who had not yet learned the art of pottery-making, or bound themselves to a settled home through cultivation.

Non-pottery sites are not easily found, and their identification as *pre-pottery* is seldom possible from survey alone. The artifact yield is ordinarily very low as compared with that from later village sites, and the often considerable overburden makes extensive excavation a costly and time-consuming operation. On the other hand, there are considerations that weigh heavily in favor of their further investigation. The simple hunting and gathering peoples doubtless occupied the area for a longer period of time than did the later farmers, and we know much less of their way of life and of the people themselves. They may have witnessed marked changes in the natural environment, climatically and otherwise, that did not take place during the later, and shorter, Village Indian period. Painstaking work will be needed to clarify the picture here; and the task will require not alone archaeological know-how, but also the special knowledge and skills of the geologist, the botanist, and others outside the field of archaeology.

[9] A. H. Coogan and W. N. Irving, "Late Pleistocene and Recent Missouri River Terraces in the Big Bend Reservoir, South Dakota," Iowa Academy of Science *Proceedings*, Vol. LXVI (1959), 317–27.

As in the Central Plains, so on the Middle Missouri the oldest remains of pottery-making peoples are believed to be those attributable to the Woodland culture. Their traces in the Dakotas are inconspicuous and widely scattered. Sites are usually small and poorly defined; they are sometimes deeply buried and they seldom promise more than a scanty return for the excavator. The consequence is that we still know very little about these people, their handicrafts, and their way of life. In the Garrison Reservoir area and above, there are instances where thick, cord-roughened potsherds and medium to large-stemmed or corner-notched projectile points occur in buried strata *below* the remains of later people who made simple-stamped pottery and small, triangular, side-notched points. Some of these sites are on buttes and other high points, from which considerable areas could be kept under surveillance for game or hostiles. Near Whitlock's Crossing, in the Oahe Reservoir area, thin occupational strata containing Woodland sherds have been reported. North of Chamberlain, Woodland pottery was found in a dark-soil zone three feet or more below the surface of the river terrace; and at Oacoma a Woodland zone underlies round houses. Several sites in the Big Bend district near Fort Thompson have yielded similar remains, and other occurrences are suspected. Again, as in the Central Plains where the Woodland materials on the Middle Missouri occur in a stratigraphic succession, they appear consistently as the earliest of the pottery-bearing zones.[10]

For the most part, these remains are thought to correlate with the Middle Woodland materials to the south and east, and probably date from before A.D. 500 or 800. They suggest the presence of small bands or family groups, probably without maize horticulture, living in simple, impermanent lodges, and deriving their livelihood by valley-bottom hunting and the gathering of fruits, seeds, roots, and other wild vegetable products. Further investigation of such sites as have not been destroyed by flooding or con-

[10] Wedel, "Prehistory and the Missouri Valley Development Program . . . in 1947," *loc. cit.*, 50.

struction activities may amplify this interpretation in some measure.

What appears to be a later variant of Woodland culture, with relationships to the south in Nebraska, is also known from the Fort Randall Reservoir area. This has been investigated by the University of South Dakota at two sites—Scalp Creek and Ellis Creek —situated on the right bank of the Missouri about twelve miles west of the town of Lake Andes.[11] Here there was evidence of repeated occupation over a fairly long period. Small, shallow pits, burned areas that probably indicate hearths, and scattered post molds were found, but no patterns of holes that could be taken as indications of house structures. The pottery was uniformly cordroughened. Rims included several types, some with raised bosses around the rim, others with the imprint of single cords running horizontally about the vessel rim or forming triangular patterns. Projectile points include triangular, side-notched forms; and there was a considerable variety of chipped-stone knives, scrapers, choppers, and other implements. A boat-shaped stone, with an encircling groove around each end, was probably a weight for the atlatl or spear thrower. There were also simple clamshell ornaments of several kinds. Few bone or antler tools were found. There was no direct evidence of corn growing, although the buffalo shoulder-blade digging tool was present. A low mound near the Scalp Creek site yielded the partly flexed remains of six individuals, all without accompanying artifacts, but suspected of association with the nearby residence area. In many respects, this assemblage reminds one of the Loseke Creek focus remains in east central Nebraska, where charred grains of corn suggest at least an incipient horticulture. The Loseke Creek materials, as we have noted elsewhere, are regarded as a late Woodland manifestation; and the two South Dakota sites just described suggest that here there may have been actual fusion of such a Woodland culture with later peoples having a different cultural inventory.

[11] W. R. Hurt, Jr., "Report of the Investigation of the Scalp Creek Site, 39GR1, and the Ellis Creek Site, 39GR2, Gregory County, South Dakota, South Dakota Archeological Commission *Archeological Studies, Circular No. 4* (1952).

Still other Woodland peoples are suggested by several mounds and mound groups situated at various points along the Middle Missouri. Mounds are much less common here than farther east, particularly so above the Big Bend; but they occur to some extent throughout practically the entire length of the Missouri Valley in the Dakotas. Small, inconspicuous mounds may be found on the bluffs above Chamberlain, on a high terrace a few hundred yards below the mouth of the Cheyenne River, at the point where the North Dakota–South Dakota state line crosses the Missouri, and upstream. Groups that include larger structures, up to three or four feet high and as much as fifty to sixty feet across, are known in the Big Bend–Fort Thompson district, where recent investigations have not yet been described in print.

Of interest are the findings at two mound sites excavated in Fort Randall Reservoir area by the River Basin Surveys in 1947 and 1948. On a terrace below Wheeler Bridge, two mounds were opened. Each covered a rectangular pit containing secondary burials. At the base of one mound was a carefully prepared clay floor; and traces of wood suggest that the pit below the mound was originally covered with poles or logs. On the pit floor were two bundle burials and the carelessly deposited remains of at least three other individuals. The larger long bones in one bundle had been carefully drilled before interment. There were no associated artifacts; but thick, cord-roughened potsherds and a few washer-like objects of shell came from the fill of one mound, and part of a large-stemmed projectile point lay in a fragmentary skull in the second.[12]

The second site investigated was a large mound in the spillway of Fort Randall dam. Here, again, there was evidence of a rectangular pit with traces of timbers in association. Burials occurred, however, only in the mound fill and at its base, and these were secondary in character. There were no artifacts in direct association with the human bones, but several occurred in the fill and in the many rodent burrows traversing the mound. They included

[12] Wedel, "Prehistory and the Missouri Valley Development Program . . . in 1947," *loc. cit.*, 19–20, pl. 1.

parts of two small, vertically-elongate pottery vessels, somewhat reminiscent of pottery from Sterns Creek in eastern Nebraska; several washer-like shell objects; a few tubular and disk beads of shell; two projectile points; and numerous canine teeth of wolf or large dog, each with a perforation neatly cut through the flattened root of the tooth. Many of the traits exhibited in these mounds recall certain archaeological materials from western Minnesota.

No village or camp sites have yet been correlated with the burial mounds found along the Missouri River, so that our picture in this regard concerns only one aspect—the burial practices—of the people involved. It is unfortunately true, too, that the waters of the reservoirs will eventually submerge just those portions of the valley in which the builders of the mounds presumably had their homes and carried on their daily life.

It is not yet possible to say just when the Woodland occupancy of the Middle Missouri ended, or how that ending took place. It seems highly probable, however, that by the eleventh century of the Christian Era, and perhaps even as early as the ninth or tenth century, settlements of quite another character were being established on the Missouri in southern South Dakota, and possibly also farther up the river into North Dakota. These suggest a much more stable occupancy than that inferred from the camp sites of the Woodland peoples, and one that was based in much larger measure on the cultivation of maize and other domestic plants. They mark the beginning of what has been appropriately termed the Plains Village pattern[13] and they reflect a way of life which, with many variations in time and space, was to persist into the nineteenth century.

The earlier stages of this new way of life are manifested at an increasing number of recorded village sites scattered along the Missouri from the mouth of White River to, approximately, the Knife. Where the sites have not been deeply mantled by wind-

[13] D. J. Lehmer, "Archeological Investigations in the Oahe Dam Area, South Dakota, 1950–51," Bureau of American Ethnology *Bulletin 158*, River Basin Survey Papers No. 7 (1954), 139–40.

deposited soils or covered by later village remains, the sodded surface is commonly pitted with circular to oblong depressions and shows marked variations in the nature or luxuriance of the natural vegetation. In cultivated or broken ground, or where erosion has cut into the edges of the terraces on which the sites lie, potsherds, articles of chipped and ground stone, bone or shell, refuse animal bone, and other detritus resulting from human activity may be found, and sometimes traces of storage pits or other man-made structures may be detected by the experienced eye. Excavations have been made in a number of these sites in South Dakota, notably between Chamberlain and the Big Bend, and between Pierre and the Cheyenne River; and in North Dakota, at the Paul Brave (32S14), Huff, and a few other sites. This work, which has been only partly reported in print, abundantly demonstrates the distinctiveness of this early Village Indian way of life as compared to the preceding Woodland pattern; and the notably richer and more varied artifact yield provides a much better insight into the life habits and practices of the people represented.[14]

Perhaps the most distinctive single feature of these early Village Indian locations is the house form. Since no white man ever saw these structures in use, their nature must be inferred entirely from the buried ruins which remain. Characteristically, the house was a long-rectangular affair, erected in and over a straight-walled pit from two and one-half to five feet deep, and from thirty to sixty-five feet long. In some cases, the house pit was nearly as wide as it was long; but usually the length was one and one-half to nearly two times the width. The long axis ordinarily lay in an approximately north to south direction, with the entrance at the south end. This was a sloping trench descending from the ground level eight to fifteen feet beyond the pit, over which was a sort of vestibule built against the house wall; at the edge of the pit, the trench continued as a ramp raised above the earth floor of the house and terminating in a step five to eight feet inside the house. There was often a post on either side of the inner end of the entrance ramp,

[14] Lehmer, "The Sedentary Horizon of the Northern Plains," *Southwestern Journal of Anthropology*, Vol. X, No. 2 (1954), 143–47.

and the step was sometimes protected by short, steplike cross logs. The main fireplace was a large basin located off center on the midline of the house, and usually within a few feet of the inner end of the entry ramp. Storage pits were dug into the floor along the walls and in the alcoves on either side of the doorway.

The superstructure, to judge from the distribution of postholes in the pit floor, was supported by a row of posts set vertically just inside each of the longer walls, and by a row of widely-spaced larger posts running down the midline of the pit. Sometimes this single row was replaced by two lines of posts a few feet apart, one line on either side of the midline. There is some evidence that in the earlier houses, the front and back walls consisted of closely set posts, like the side walls, whereas in later houses there were fewer, smaller, or no posts in the end walls except for the large rearmost members of the midline row.

As to the exact nature and appearance of the finished houses, we can only speculate. A hip roof, carried by rafters sloping in two directions from a central ridge beam, is suggested where the center row consists of a single line of posts. Where the center posts formed two rows, the summit of the roof may have been flat, with a sloping section on each side to the eaves. It is possible that the pole framework was covered with willows, grass, and finally earth; but, unlike the prehistoric rectangular houses of the Central Plains, the house pits of the Middle Missouri very rarely yield any traces of grass-impressed wattling clay or burned earth. A heavy thatch of grass may, therefore, have been the final covering, perhaps with earth banked against the sidewalls.

The arrangement of houses and other features within the village community varied considerably. At some sites, the houses appear to have been laid out in fairly regular rows separated by open lanes; and the entire settlement, as at the Huff site, was sometimes protected by a ditch within which was a palisade with regularly placed bastions. In others, placement was without recognizable order or was adapted to the irregularities of the site chosen. Where villages occupied a terrace point or promontory, a ditch was sometimes cut across the neck of the point and it might be augmented

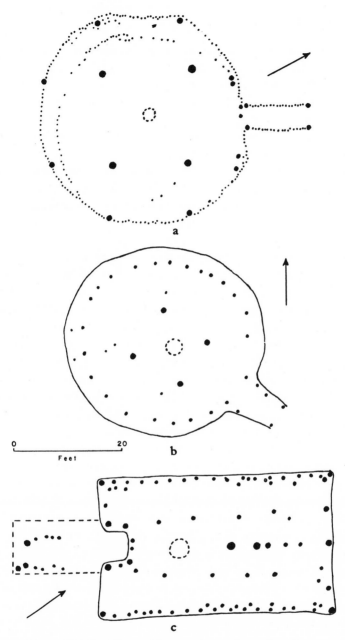

FIG. 13. *Some Middle Missouri house floor plans, showing character-istic shapes and posthole patterns, but with subfloor cache pits omitted.* a. *Arikara, about* 1700–50; b. *La Roche focus, about* 1500–1650; c. *Thomas Riggs focus, about* 1200–1300. *Arrows point north.*

by a stockade or a pole and brush fence. Storage pits were scattered about among the houses and along the better-drained terrace edges. The villages consisted of less than half a dozen to twenty or more house units, not all of which were necessarily occupied at the same time. Depending on their size, the lodges probably accommodated from seven to fifteen persons each, perhaps more in the larger structures. It seems doubtful that any of the known settlements included more than two or three hundred people, and most were probably considerably smaller. In any case, whatever the exact figure may have been, it is probable that the communities included larger numbers of people than customarily occupied the earlier Woodland camp sites.

It is generally presumed that the subsistence economy of the long-rectangular-house people on the Middle Missouri was based on both hunting and gardening. This we know was true of the approximately contemporary rectangular-house people of the Central Plains, as also of the later Village Indians of the Middle Missouri. Of hunting, there is ample evidence in the quantities of animal bone—bison, deer, elk, and smaller forms—found at each village site. Of cultivation, there is no direct evidence, such as charred corn, beans, squash, or other items. There is indirect evidence, however, in the form of numerous carefully dug pits substantially identical with the underground corn caches seen in use among the later Indians of the region, and in the bone digging tools or hoes, which also have their counterpart in the artifact inventory of the horticultural Indians of historic times. Finally, the very presence of fixed communities of several dozen to scores of individuals, residing in large substantial dwellings, partially protected by ditches and palisades, and manufacturing quantities of pottery, implies a way of life feasible only with an assured and ample food supply. It would have been impossible for people depending entirely, or even primarily, on the pursuit of moving game herds, on the gathering of wild plant products, or on such fishing as the Missouri offered. The Village Indian way of life was the outgrowth of a successfully developing food-producing economy, in contrast to the primarily food-collecting subsistence pattern of the earlier Woodland peoples.

We conclude, then, that hunting and gardening were important basic occupations of these people. Hunting was undoubtedly the work of the men. It was done with the bow and arrow, the latter provided with small triangular side-notched stone points. The principal source of meat was the bison, with deer, antelope, elk, smaller mammals, and birds of decreasing importance. Since horses were unknown, much of the hunting was probably done in the bottoms and along the broken valley margins within a few miles of the villages. Whether there were prolonged seasonal bison hunts in which most of the community took part, as was customary in later prehorse and horse days, we do not know. Probably many bison were salvaged from the river, when breakup of the ice in spring brought death to the crossing herds, and carried the carcasses within reach of the communities living on the river banks.

Gardening was carried on by the women, who tilled their little patches of corn, beans, and squash on the nearby cleared bottom lands with bone-bladed hoes and sticks. The shoulder blade of the bison usually furnished the hoe blade; but there are also digging or hoeing implements cut from the top of the bison skull, with a part of the horn core left attached as a handle. The diagonally-cut chisel-like leg bones of large mammals, with a hole for hafting drilled through the remaining joint end in a plane parallel to the long axis of the bone, may have been wear-resisting tips for digging sticks, planters, or root diggers. Such garden produce as was not eaten fresh was dried and stored for later consumption in underground storage pits in or among the houses.

Fishing, of which there is as yet no good evidence from the earlier Woodland sites, was also practiced by the Village Indians. This is indicated by frequent finds of catfish and other bones, and by curved bone hooks, unbarbed, but with notches along the shank for attachment to a line. There is evidence that the toggle harpoon head of antler or bone was known to these people, probably as a fishing device. Weirs and traps may also have been used, as they were by some of the historic Village Indians; but of these there is no archaeological indication. Fresh-water clamshells occur at practically all sites, suggesting another probable source of food.

From the house floors, cache pits, and refuse deposits of this period have been taken many artifacts that offer some clues to the domestic and other activities of the people. Unfortunately, not all parts of the period are equally well known, and many important sites still remain unexcavated or undescribed in print. It is not always possible, therefore, to say that a specific implement type was in use at the beginning of the long-rectangular-house period, and some of the types seem, from present evidence, to have appeared in the later sites only. In any case, in the remarks that follow, it must be recognized that further information may show that some of the implements and other items mentioned did not make their appearance until the long-rectangular-house peoples had been established for a time on the Middle Missouri.

The various food products obtained by the hunters and from the garden patches were prepared, of course, in different ways. Dried corn may have been reduced to meal by grinding; and since milling stones that might have been so used are rare or absent, we may infer that the upright wooden mortar was used with a wooden billet for a pestle. Bone knives cut from the bison shoulder blade, and sometimes including a curved form somewhat similar to the modern banana knife, were probably used in cutting up squashes, melons, and other soft foodstuffs. Grooved stone mauls and hammers were employed in breaking up marrow bones, and for pounding meat and vegetable products. Of spoons and other eating or culinary utensils, other than pottery vessels to be noted later, there is no evidence at present.

As with later groups in the region, the dressing of animal skins and their conversion into clothing and perhaps containers, must have been an important activity. For this, there were various kinds of chipped-stone knives, including especially an asymmetrical form with rounded ends and one curved edge, the other straight. Sections of bison rib, with one edge slotted near the end, were

174

probably handles into which the chipped-stone blades were set. Such knives could have been used, and doubtless were, for cutting other materials besides hides and meat. Small, triangular stone scrapers, with one surface flat and the other steeply chipped, may have been used in hide-dressing, and these were often set into the hollowed-out ends of bison ribs and perhaps into wooden handles. Chisel-shaped tools fashioned from bison or elk leg bones, and often provided with fine teeth at the working end, were used in removing surplus flesh and fat from the hides. There is some evidence, too, that the L-shaped elkhorn scraper, with a stone blade secured to the short arm, was known at this early period. Final rubbing down of the skin was done with blocks of pumice salvaged from the river, or with roughly hemispherical bone implements cut from the end of a bison femur. The flat surface of open-textured bone produced in the removal of these pieces provided the same sort of abrading surface as the pumice.

Sewing of the skins was done with the aid of bone awls, which included wide, flat forms split from a bison rib and also more slender types formed either from a splinter or from a deer leg bone split so that the joint end provided a convenient butt. Slender eyed needles of bone are present at some sites. A very common tool is a piece of heavy bone three to seven inches long, with one or both ends rounded, which has been tentatively identified as a "quill flattener," but whose real use is not known. It may have been used for smoothing pottery, for flint knapping, or for other purposes.

Of woodworking, there is almost no direct evidence; but the cutting and trimming of sizable logs and poles in house construction must have entailed a great deal of time and labor. The butts of some of the surviving house posts show charring, suggesting that trees were sometimes felled with fire. Ground-stone celts with polished blades that are sometimes badly nicked from hard usage doubtless served as axes, these having been provided with wooden or withe handles when in use. Probably some of the larger, heavier, chipped-stone implements were also used as chopping or cutting tools. For lighter woodworking, smaller chipped knives and scrapers may have served as cutting, trimming, or shaping tools. The making of arrow shafts required special tools, including oblong sandstone blocks with a shallow groove worn lengthwise in one face; whether these were used in pairs, with the shafts rotated as they were drawn between the two blocks, as was done by the historic Indians, we do not know. Sections of bison rib, pierced with one or more holes that show wear, served as wrenches for straightening arrow shafts.

For adornment of costume or the person there were a few small disk beads, larger circular pieces with central perforation, and simple, oblong pendants pierced at the end or one side, all made of fresh-water clamshell. Animal effigies of bone, pierced for suspension are also known; and there are thin, flat objects of scraped bone or antler, sometimes bearing incised decoration, that were probably armlets or bow guards. Red pigment was obtained from hematite.

Even scarcer are objects that suggest ceremonial or ritual uses. Well-made, tubular, catlinite pipes have been found in houses of the later period. Bone whistles, in the form of simple bird-bone tubes with a triangular opening near one end, can perhaps be included here. Shell or bone effigies, carved in the form of birds, with the bill, wings, and tail accentuated by incised lines, may have had a ritual significance as representing the thunderbird, or they may have been ornaments.

There are, of course, other artifacts concerning the use of which we know even less than we do about those mentioned above. Rounded, water-worn cobblestones with battered areas are commonly termed hammerstones, and these occur in considerable numbers at virtually all sites. Blunt-tipped bone pieces may have been punches or flint-knappers. From at least one rectangular house have come "balls" made of short sections of elk antler; these may be rejectage from the manufacture of some still unidentified tool, or they may have been especially made for purposes unknown. Mallet-like objects of elk antler, with a tine forming the handle and a short segment of the main shaft providing the pounding surface, have also been found.

There is virtually no evidence either of the methods of disposing of the dead. Few burials have been found, and it has been suggested that scaffold or tree burial was practiced, as by many of the later Plains Indians. At the Thomas Riggs site was found a single tightly-flexed burial in a cache pit; and further work may show that primary burial was an established custom.

The handicrafts of these people undoubtedly involved the manufacture of much leatherwork, probably the production of basketry and simple matting, and perhaps the preparation of bison-hair and vegetable-fiber cordage and other items, but of these perishable materials there is little or no archaeological evidence. There is abundant proof, however, that pottery-making was an important activity in all of the villages. The products of the potters varied considerably in their characteristics from place to place, and also from time to time within the same district. Generally speaking, the potter mixed her clay with crushed or burned granite, so that the tempering matter usually included angular particles of quartz, feldspar, and mica. There is no indication of coils in any of the pottery, and the vessels were presumably modeled by hand, or with paddle and anvil, from a lump of clay. Most of the vessels were evidently intended for domestic use, and their range in form was comparatively limited. The most common shape was a more or less globular or full-bodied jar with rounding shoulders and base, a constricted neck, and a vertical or out-turned rim. At some sites, the vessel surfaces were characteristically roughened by beating the soft clay with a cord-wrapped paddle. The rims, often simple and out-turned, were sometimes wedgelike or S-shaped in cross section, and carried incised horizontal lines, crisscross patterns, or triangular motifs. There are interesting resemblances here to the rectangular-house pottery of the Central Plains. On some vessels, the incised decoration was replaced with single-cord impressions. At other sites, and particularly above the Cheyenne River, cord-roughening as a surface treatment disappears; and vessel exteriors were either smoothed off or else show the parellel ridging produced by a grooved or thong-wrapped paddle. The smoothed shoulder areas sometimes carried simple incised or trailed straight-line decoration; and commonly a finger-notched fillet of clay encircled the rim an inch or so below the lip of the vessel. Handles or small pierced lugs were sometimes placed on the rim, but these were not common.

The variations in the products of the potters are of great importance to the archaeologist. The consistent presence or absence of certain features, and the changes in their character or treatment, furnish the specialist with a primary basis for determining the relationships between sites and for arranging them on a time scale. For example, the earlier long-rectangular houses below the Cheyenne River appear to show a higher proportion of cord-roughened vessel surfaces as we go back in time and down the river, whereas the later sites have an increasing percentage of smoothed and simple stamped (ridged) pottery. North of the Cheyenne, on the other hand, cord-roughening is virtually absent, and smoothed and simple stamped pottery is characteristic. Some of these pottery differences are paralleled by variations in details of house form and construction. Present evidence indicates, moreover, that certain kinds of stone, bone, shell, and other artifacts were absent or scarce in earlier times, but became very common in later times, or else changed their form measurably. The order in which these changes in house form, pottery, and associated artifacts took place is not always easy to determine in the absence of a reliable chronology based on tree rings or radiocarbon studies; but stratigraphic and seriational methods often help to determine which sites are earlier or later than others, and so suggest which group may have borrowed ideas or techniques from another.

Since the classification of sites and the ordering of groups of closely related sites on the Middle Missouri is still in a state of flux, it would be most unwise to burden the general reader here with details that too often frustrate even the specialist. It is already evident, however, that several groupings will eventually be established; and these will emerge more clearly when analysis and publication of field studies has progressed further. At the moment, the earliest level of occupation at the Dodd site, on the west bank of the Missouri about six miles above Pierre, appears to represent an early stage in the long-rectangular-house tradition.[15] Here, the oldest house sites generally had posts evenly spaced around the house pit; the pottery included a high proportion of cord-roughened potsherds and none with simple stamping; a number of the artifact types enumerated above were either not present or were doubtfully so; and there are no radiocarbon, tree-ring, or other "absolute" dates. To this assemblage, the term Monroe focus has been assigned. Later houses at the same site, which have yielded somewhat different kinds and proportions of pottery and other artifacts, have been distinguished as the Anderson focus.

Other village sites with cord-roughened pottery that may be closely related to, or on approximately the same time level as, the Monroe and Anderson cultural complexes, occur just below Oahe Dam, and apparently upstream to a point near the Cheyenne River. There are doubtless others downstream, but here we are hampered by insufficient information from the Big Bend Reservoir area. Such sites as Swanson and Crow Creek also show some similarities, but in both the pottery shows an influence from contacts with the prehistoric peoples of the Central Plains and is apparently related also to the Over focus, elsewhere represented by several village sites in southeastern South Dakota.[16]

Surveys of the Big Bend Reservoir area below Pierre indicate that there are large and complex village sites, many with indications of more than one occupation. Long-rectangular houses apparently underlie circular houses here, as they do upriver from Pierre. Cord-roughened pottery, presumably associated with these long houses, occurs commonly, as do other wares. Also, there are many examples of fortified sites, including rectangular enclosures with bastions, recalling the well laid out Huff site; oval enclosures, with bastions; and enclosures without visible bastions. Because of repeated occupation, careful excavation will be required to determine the true associations between the various features found at these sites.

[15] Lehmer, "Archeological Investigations in the Oahe Dam Area, South Dakota, 1950–51," *loc. cit.*, 118–34.
[16] Hurt, "Report of the Investigation of the Swanson Site, 39BR16, Brule County, South Dakota," South Dakota Archeological Commission *Archeological Studies, Circular No. 3* (1951).

What is generally thought to be a later horizon is represented by the Thomas Riggs site, about twenty miles northwest of Pierre on the east bank of the Missouri.[17] Here there are long-rectangular houses with lightly built or "open" end walls, the pottery is all smoothed or simple stamped with some incised decoration but no cord-roughening, and most of the artifact types we have named in preceding pages are present. Closely related sites across the river near and above old Fort Bennett, including the early levels at the Lower Cheyenne River site, 39ST1, and on the Black Widow Ridge at site 39ST203 (see fig. 12), further illuminate this period. A radiocarbon determination from a house post at Thomas Riggs yielded a date of A.D. 1228 plus or minus 200 years, which is considerably earlier than has generally been supposed. Remains that should probably be included in the Thomas Riggs focus are known, or suspected, to occur both upstream and down from the Pierre–Cheyenne River district; and there are interesting similarities between Thomas Riggs focus remains and those from recently worked long-rectangular-house sites in the Fort Yates district in North Dakota.

Still further upstream, from unexcavated sites running in some numbers as far as the Knife River, surface collections of pottery samples assigned to an "Archaic Mandan" level also recall the wares of the early long-rectangular-house sites of the Pierre–Cheyenne River district. There is good reason to believe that the "Archaic Mandan" used long-rectangular dwellings. Somewhat later in time, apparently, are the even more numerous "Middle Mandan" sites, thought to represent the period during which rectangular houses gave way to circular forms, and in which a characteristic feature is decoration of vessel rims with single-cord impressions in various patterns. Especially common here are bands of horizontal lines, frequently in combination with sets of upward-arched cord impressions forming the well-known "Mandan rainbow" motif. Until a great deal more systematic excavation has

---

[17] Hurt, "Report of the Investigation of the Thomas Riggs Site, 39HU1, Hughes County, South Dakota," *South Dakota Archeological Commission Archeological Studies, Circular No. 5* (1953).

been done in these northern materials, and detailed reports become available, the nature of the resemblance to more southerly remains and their general significance must remain obscure.[18]

It should be borne in mind that the variations we have noted from one group to another among the long-rectangular-house cultures on the Middle Missouri in South Dakota are counter-balanced by important basic similarities that distinguish all of these groups from the archaeological remains of later peoples in the same region, as well as from the prehistoric rectangular-house cultures of Nebraska and Kansas. In recognition of these underlying relationships, it has been suggested that the Monroe, Anderson, and Thomas Riggs cultural complexes, or foci, be combined into one larger unit of classification; and for this unit, the designation of Middle Missouri tradition, or phase, has been generally adopted by workers in the Plains region.[19]

We do not know either the beginning or the ending dates of the period during which the long-rectangular-house peoples resided on the Middle Missouri. The few radiocarbon dates available indicate that some of the communities were in existence as early as the eleventh century, that is, before A.D. 1100. Indeed, other dates for the Swanson and Breeden sites would put these as early as the eighth or ninth centuries, much earlier than any date we have for the Central Plains rectangular-house peoples.[20] At the other end of the scale, tree-ring counts on eleven oak timbers from the Huff site in Morton County, North Dakota, gave cutting dates ranging from 1485 to 1543.[21] The Huff site, with its neatly arranged rows of rectangular houses and a well-marked defensive ditch with ten regularly spaced bastions, has been assigned to the "Middle Mandan" period, and is fairly certainly not one of the older rectangular-house communities of the North Dakota Village Indians. It is

[18] Will and Hecker, *loc. cit.,* 54–69; Will, "Tree-Ring Studies in North Dakota," *loc. cit.,* 13–14.

[19] Lehmer, "Archeological Investigations in the Oahe Dam Area, South Dakota, 1950–51," *loc. cit.,* 140–43; Hurt, "Report of the Investigation of the Thomas Riggs Site, 39HU1, Hughes County, South Dakota," *loc. cit.,* 56–57.

[20] *Missouri Basin Chronology Program,* Statement No. 2, June 15, 1951.

[21] Will, "Tree-Ring Studies in North Dakota," *loc. cit.,* 15–16.

only fair to note that some doubt has been cast on the reliability of the North Dakota tree-ring dates, and that they have not been independently verified or corrected by other methods, such as radiocarbon offers. If further observations verify such dates as are currently at hand, both from radiocarbon and from tree-rings, the long-rectangular-house period on the Middle Missouri would appear to have spanned from five to eight centuries of time.

In any case, the findings of archaeology indicate that some time before the arrival of white men, the long-rectangular-house villages were superseded by settlements of circular houses markedly unlike the earlier structures in virtually every particular. In these villages, moreover, were made pottery wares that were quite distinct from the earlier ones. Some of the everyday tools and other artifacts of the long-rectangular-house peoples were taken over, but occasionally with modifications in various details; and several new kinds of artifacts make their appearance. Some of these are thought to be innovations from the south, perhaps brought from the Central Plains by migrants. Possibly the marked cultural changes that we know took place after about A.D. 1500 reflect the arrival of new peoples or "tribes," but of this we cannot yet be certain.

Of particular interest in this connection is the fortified hilltop village known as the Arzberger site, seven miles east of Pierre.[22] The fortification, a palisaded ditch nearly 1 ½ miles long, enclosing 44 acres, and including 24 bastions, is reminiscent of that at the Middle Mandan Huff site some 250 miles upriver, with which it may be approximately contemporaneous. The houses, however, are altogether unlike the long-rectangular structures we have been considering. Instead, they show a floor plan basically like that in prehistoric Central Plains lodges—a central hearth surrounded by four equidistant main postholes, and these, in turn surrounded by an outer series in circular or perhaps subrectangular pattern.

[22] A. C. Spaulding, "The Arzberger Site, Hughes County, South Dakota," *Occasional Contributions, No. 16,* Museum of Anthropology, University of Michigan (1956).

The artifacts are surprisingly diversified. Pottery includes smoothed, cord-roughened, simple stamped, and incised or trailed ware; and the gamut of rim shapes and treatments is much wider than that in older villages of the area. Like the stone, bone, and other non-ceramic materials, the pottery apparently includes a number of types carried over from earlier Middle Missouri cultures, plus others that seem as certainly to be new to the area and which persisted into subsequent cultures.

While unanimity of interpretation is lacking, the implications of the site have been lucidly discussed by Spaulding. He views the culture represented as "basically of Central Plains Upper Republican type," strongly influenced by "Oneota" (Upper Mississippi) and also by Middle Mandan cultures from upriver. He suggests further that it may represent "an early stage in the separation of the Arikara tribe from the parent Pawnee," that this separation occurred "prior to the Lower Loup phase of culture development in Nebraska," and that the Arzberger site may be dated "approximately on the boundary between the 15th and 16th centuries." These conclusions have significant implications in Plains prehistory, and they certainly call for further investigation. There is evidence, as we have noted elsewhere, that the Upper Republican peoples abandoned their range in western Nebraska perhaps not long after a drought that has been dated by tree rings at 1439–68; and if these displaced agriculturists moved eastward or northeastward in search of more dependable lands, Arzberger may have been one of the points at which they finally settled and found themselves faced with a new set of social problems.

Dissenting voices have argued that Arzberger represents not necessarily a single culture, but rather two distinct occupations that followed each other so closely that their respective traces were not separable in excavation, or in the subsequent analysis. Further research will doubtless settle this important point. Meanwhile, it is perhaps worth pointing out that the northeast Nebraska–southeast South Dakota area in late prehistoric times seems to have been one of intense human activity and an avenue through which both populational and cultural movements passed up the Missouri and between the prairies and plains. Its complexity may well resist convincing interpretation for some time to come.

That the later peoples of the Middle Missouri included as part of their material culture inventory certain traits from the prehistoric Central Plains seems likely. Lehmer has developed this thought in plausible fashion and has suggested for the following period the term Coalescent.[23]

Most of what we know about the circular-house peoples of the earlier period, that is, before the appearance of any traces of white contact, comes from excavations at the Myers and Black Widow sites, on the west bank of the Missouri between old Fort Bennett and the Cheyenne River; at the La Roche site, about twenty miles downstream from Pierre, in extreme southeastern Stanley County; and at the Scalp Creek site, twelve miles west of Lake Andes.[24] Surveys indicate that there are many other sites, especially in the Big Bend Reservoir area and upstream to or beyond the Cheyenne River. Some appear to be of impressive size and well worthy of extended investigation. Frequently, they overlie older sites that presumably or demonstrably have long-rectangular-house ruins; and here the broken pottery and other materials scattered about over the ground surface are intermixed with the remains of the earlier occupations. At such sites, of course, there is a challenging opportunity to determine from direct stratigraphic evidence the order in which successive peoples resided in the locality; but the mixing of materials that so often took place sometimes raises thorny problems for the investigator. The hard fact is that a great deal more painstaking work is in prospect here before we can

[23] "Archeological Investigations in the Oahe Dam Area, South Dakota, 1950–51," *loc. cit.*, 147–54.

[24] L. J. Hoard, "Report of the Investigation of the Meyer Site, Stanley County, South Dakota," South Dakota Archeological Commission *Archeological Studies, Circular No. 2* (1949); E. E. Meleen, "Report of an Investigation of the La Roche Site, Stanley County, South Dakota," South Dakota Archeological Commission *Archeological Studies, Circular No. 5* (1948); Hurt, "Report of the Investigation of the Scalp Creek Site, 39GR1, and the Ellis Creek Site, 39GR2, Gregory County, South Dakota," *loc. cit.*, 3–15.

speak with confidence about archaeological matters other than the general course of events.

The earliest circular-house village sites apparently represent loosely arranged rambling communities, with lodge rings scattered more or less irregularly over several to many acres of ground. There is usually no visible evidence of fortification, but the Scalp Creek site was enclosed by a stockade and a ditch. The wide dispersal of houses in many of the communities would have made the construction of defensive works extremely difficult, if not impossible. There may be as few as one dozen lodge rings, or as many as one hundred or more. In unbroken or recently broken ground, the locations of the former houses are usually conspicuously marked by circular depressions or by raised rings with sunken centers. At some sites, there is a small refuse dump twenty to thirty feet in diameter and up to one or two feet in depth, situated within a few yards to the south or southeast of each of the house rings. La Roche and other sites in the Big Bend district are situated on the broad, open river terraces. Myers and Black Widow, on the other hand, are on lofty, flat-topped ridges open to every breeze or gale, several hundred yards distant from any apparent supply of surface water or building material, and accessible from the river only by a climb that must have taxed the patience and stamina of any aboriginal housekeeper or builder.

Basically, the circular houses of the Middle Missouri were much like those in the Central Plains, whose construction we have already noted in an earlier section. Practically without exception, they included the following features: (a) An excavated, often saucerlike area twenty to fifty feet in diameter and varying in depth from a few inches to three feet, within which (b) four primary roof supports were planted in a square or quadrilateral around (c) a simple basin-shaped fireplace about three feet in diameter; (d) a floor that was seldom more than the tramped bottom of the house pit; (e) a secondary system of posts planted around the perimeter of the floor to support the top of the side wall and the base of the roof; (f) one or more storage pits dug beneath the floor; (g) a narrow, post-lined entrance passage opening generally southward from the main structure; and *(h)* a covering of poles, willows, joint grass, and finally earth or sod, which left only a smoke vent at the peak of the dome-shaped roof.

Since each house erected by the Indians was the product of non-professionals working without detailed plans and specifications, a good many variations of the basic pattern are encountered by the excavator. Some of these probably resulted from shortages of suitable building materials, as for example, when one of the four primary supports was actually made up of two or more lighter members set close together. Others may reflect changing tastes or customs as time passed, or the varying standards of workmanship toward which different builders strove. Whatever their basis, it appears likely that some of the variations occur more frequently at one period than at another, and so they may in time be shown to have real chronological significance.

With respect to the principal architectural features—central fireplace, four primary supports, excavated floor, and presumed lodge covering—the earlier circular houses conform more closely to the basic pattern. The posts in the outer series appear to have been usually widely spaced, that is, from two to ten feet apart; and there is usually no evidence of the leaning wall posts which were presumably set with their bases on the lip of the house pit. Sometimes the outer series is poorly defined and incomplete, either because postholes were missed by the excavator, or because of uneven spacing by the builders. Frequently, even where the outer series is more or less complete and regular, there is a scattering of additional postholes in a seemingly planless manner between the four primary supports and the outer series. These may represent the installation of props beneath sagging rafters or the replacement of decayed posts in the basic series. The vestibule-like entrance passage is often poorly defined, with only a few scattered posts or widely spaced pairs of posts to indicate its direction and approximate dimensions. Many of the later people, as we shall see presently, handled these matters in a different, and seemingly more effective, manner.

For their sustenance, the circular-house people relied, as had their predecessors, principally on hunting and gardening. Bison was the chief game sought, with deer, antelope, elk, and smaller mammals of secondary importance. The usual weapon of the hunters, pedestrian still, was the bow and arrow tipped with a small, triangular flint point. Turtle bones, clamshells, and fish remains form only a small percentage of the food refuse; and curved bone hooks show the manner of obtaining the fish.

Charred corncobs of eight- and ten-rowed varieties, and occasional squash or pumpkin seeds, are direct evidence of at least two important domestic food plants. Probably beans were also grown. How productive the tillage methods were we do not know, but the pits in which surplus crops were presumably stored are neither plentiful nor large. Bison scapula hoes are commonly found; beyond removal of the spine and sharpening of the broader end, they show little modification. Bone digging-stick tips and the curious scooplike hoes or spades (or trowels?) fashioned from part of the frontal bone and attached horn core of the bison seem to have been rare or absent; but since the latter, at least, is a fairly common tool at both earlier and later sites in the region, further investigation or evidence not yet reported in print may show that it should be included here.

Charred cherry pits suggest that the chokecherry may have been as popular at this time as it was among the later Indians; and this popularity was probably true also of the wild plum, buffalo berry, and grape, and of various starchy roots and tubers, such as the Indian breadroot, or tipsin, of which no archaeological evidence has yet been reported.

The artifacts of stone, bone, and other materials from these sites represent mainly utilitarian forms required in the everyday domestic activities of their owners. In the preparation of food, the grinding of dried corn and the crushing of berries was done on flattened stone slabs with which were used smaller round or oblong handstones. If there were also wooden mills, no trace of them has come down to us. Such vegetable products as squash, pumpkins, and wild tubers could have been cut up with the rectangular to oblong bone knives made from thin sections of bison scapulae. For the dressing out of game, but suitable for other cutting jobs as well, there was a variety of chipped-stone knives. These included leaf-shaped and oblong forms sharpened on all edges, and others of rectangular outline made from plate chalcedony and chipped on two edges.

In the processing of skins and their manufacture into clothing and other articles, there was need for various cutting, scraping, rubbing, and piercing tools. In addition to the stone knives, there were small, triangular end scrapers, side scrapers with one or two long edges sharpened from one face, lumps of pumice with the surfaces worn flat or rounding, and numbers of bone awls. Among the latter, the wide, flat type made from one-half of a split animal rib is much scarcer than it was among the older long-rectangular-house people. More common are well-made forms fashioned by grinding down a split deer leg bone, with part of the joint end left at the butt; slender, irregularly shaped specimens made by smoothing and sharpening fortuitous slivers of bone; and especially the so-called "rib-edge" type, made actually from a long, stout splinter cut from the edge of the long spine of a bison neck vertebra, and ground down to a more or less triangular cross section. This last type has not been reported from the long-rectangular houses, but becomes more plentiful in later times. Some of these awls, in addition to service as skin perforators, may have been used in stitching basketry, but of this industry there is at present no evidence.

There were several kinds of grinding and polishing devices. For smoothing arrow shafts and similar rodlike objects, the oblong sandstone buffer with a lengthwise central groove was employed, probably in pairs. Broken buffers and irregularly shaped pieces of pumice frequently bear short, deep, irregular grooves on one or more surfaces, presumably from the sharpening of awls or for shaping tips on other bone or wooden objects. Pumice is, in fact, a common find in these sites, and was evidently in much demand for its abrasive qualities.

Among other tools, we may note presence of the ungrooved ax, or celt, made from tough granite or diorite by pecking and grinding; and possible presence of the full-grooved maul or hammer. Short heavy sections of elk antler, with both ends somewhat battered, may also have been hafted and used as mallets. Bone artifacts include the bison rib arrow-shaft straightener or "thong dresser," commonly with two or more slightly elongate holes; undecorated tubes that may have been beads; occasional whistles from the wing bones of the pelican, swan, or eagle, with a single triangular hole near one end; and bison ribs bearing numerous transverse cuts across the outer face, which have been variously labeled as musical rasps or resonators, tally bones, and pottery-paddles for producing the familiar ridged or "simple stamped" surface on vessel exteriors. There are also curious curved fragments of narrow, dressed strips of bone or antler, whose original length and purpose remain unknown, but of which there are increasing numbers in some later sites. Small spatulate objects of bone also await identification. Finally, it should be noted that the "quill flattener" of the preceding long-rectangular-house people occurs much less commonly in the circular-house sites.

There is very little work in shell. At some sites have been found fresh-water clamshells that show considerable wear on the edge opposite the hinge, as though from scraping hides, wood, or pottery. Even rarer are small pendants, sometimes clawlike in shape, and pierced at one end for suspension or attachment.

Practically nothing yet found throws any light on ceremonial and ritual practices. The methods used in disposing of the dead are unknown. Pipes were made of catlinite and also of pumice. Unlike the earlier tubular forms, these usually had a bulbous upright bowl set at right angles to the stem and having a short prow-like knob or projection beyond the bowl.

Pottery-making was an important household activity, and the broken products of this industry form the largest proportion of finds at virtually all known sites. Much of the pottery was well made and some of it was tastefully decorated, but its principal uses must have been utilitarian. Virtually the only form yet recognized is the jar, suitable for cooking, storage, water-carrying, and similar humble but essential domestic services. Vessel surfaces, never cord-marked, were usually either left smooth or treated with a grooved or thong-wrapped paddle; and in the latter case, the ridged shoulder area was commonly smoothed to receive the incised decoration that characterized the greater proportion of the pottery. Rims were customarily straight, of uniform thickness from neck to lip, and the lip usually bears diagonal incisions or other ornamentation. Sometimes the outer rim surface was left plain or ridged; but much more frequently it bears from five to fifteen horizontal incised or trailed lines.

On the vessel shoulder, straight-line incising was characteristic. The most common design was a series of triangular areas, each filled with parallel lines, and with the lines in adjoining triangles slanting in different directions. Occasionally, alternate triangles were filled with small punch marks, chevrons, or herringbone patterns; or the shoulder was covered with rows of short diagonal lines, those in each row slanting in opposite direction from those in the rows immediately above and below. Handles were very seldom placed on the vessels, but rims sometimes have small tabs or unpierced vertical lugs affixed just below the lip.

The horizontally incised rims and heavily decorated vessel shoulders are perhaps the outstanding pottery characteristics of the prehistoric circular-house peoples of the lower Oahe–Big Bend district. Below the Cheyenne River, they mark the sites of what has been termed the Bennett focus; but the rims, at least, also occur in significant proportions upstream to or beyond the Grand River. They are found also at sites grouped in the La Roche focus below Pierre, and at intermediate levels at the Talking Crow and Oldham sites in Fort Randall Reservoir. Rims and incised vessel fragments that are practically indistinguishable from Bennett focus pieces have been found as far west as the Black Hills, in what may have been hunting camps of the Village Indians. On smaller and thinner vessels, the same rim and shoulder decoration occurs widely up the Niobrara in northern Nebraska.[25]

In terms of the several tribes we know inhabited the Middle

[25] Cooper, "Recent Investigations in Fort Randall and Oahe Reservoirs, South Dakota," *loc. cit.,* 304.

Missouri in historic times, we can only speculate regarding the identity of the prehistoric circular-house people that have been considered to this point. Among them, in the long stretch of river valley northward from Pierre, were probably groups whose descendants are known to history as the Mandans, whose traditions indicate two general movements up the Missouri.[26] The older long-rectangular houses may have been left by an earlier group of Mandans and related peoples. Farther south, it is tempting to suggest that some of the La Roche focus sites were the home of ancestral Arikara peoples. Between the known Arikara villages of later times and some of the great La Roche communities, there are many striking resemblances in artifact types, architecture, and probably other aspects of material culture; and it seems a safe guess that the roots of the Arikaras lay partially in some of the prewhite communities below Pierre. In no case, however, is it yet possible to trace satisfactorily either the Arikaras or the Mandans back in time from their historic locations to the prewhite-contact sites from which their forebears may have come. Neither can we be certain that there were not other groups involved, perhaps speaking unrelated languages but sharing in the more or less uniform way of life that characterized the inhabitants of the area at this period.

The recent surveys of the Big Bend reservoir area, as we have already noted, have disclosed an extraordinary number of village sites here, including some of great size. It is not yet clear whether this evidence reflects a widespread growth in the local Middle Missouri population, that may have resulted in a notable increase in the number and size of native communities, or is to be attributed to other factors, such as an unusual concentration of peoples from formerly more widely scattered settlements. The phenomenon is of more than passing interest, however, since it gives promise of furnishing important linkages between preceding and following groups, and thus may permit eventual definition of the threads that may be supposed to connect the prehistoric with the fully historic native occupations here.

[26] Bowers, "Mandan Social and Ceremonial Organization," *loc. cit.*, 15–18.

There is another intriguing facet to the matter. When the
Arikaras, designated by Bourgmond as "Aricara" and "Caricara,"
first emerge into written history early in the eighteenth century,
they were reportedly settled in forty-three villages located on
both banks of the Missouri above the "Smoking River."[27] They
were characterized as a very numerous people, who had already
seen the French. We have, unfortunately, no way of estimating
the margin of error in the number of villages given, and the figure
was probably based on hearsay rather than first-hand observation.
It suggests, nevertheless, that the Arikaras were at that period a
populous tribe, possibly residing not in the few fortified towns
in which white visitors found them fifty years later, but in many
more communities. This view is consistent with the assertions of
Lewis and Clark, Brackenridge, and other early nineteenth-century observers, who were told that the few Arikara towns then
existing held the survivors of nine, ten, seventeen, thirty-two or
more earlier settlements. It may be suggested that a visitor to the
Big Bend–Pierre–Cheyenne River district in Bennett–La Roche
times would perhaps have found good reason to accent Bourgmond's figures. In the absence of white-contact materials from
these sites, we must suppose either that they were mostly too early
in time, or else that the first estimates of the French refer to settlements in the final phases of this period and the very beginning of
the following contact period.

Of the villages that grew out of the La Roche communities, we
do not yet know very much. They should be broadly distinguishable from the earlier ones by the appearance in them of traces of
white contact, particularly by small and variable amounts of metal

[27] Marc de Villiers, *La Decouverte du Missouri et l'Histoire du Fort Orleans*
(1673–1728), 62, takes this to be the Niobrara, more commonly known to the
French as *L'eau qui court*. However, on maps resulting from Capt. W. F. Ray-
nolds' 1859–60 explorations of the Yellowstone and Missouri rivers, the White
River carries two additional designations: *Makisi-ta Wakpa*, and Smoking Earth
River. The original Raynolds map is in National Archives, Cartographic Branch,
RG 77, Q 106 and Q 106, No. 1. It appears, with geology added, in F. V. Hayden's
Geological Report of the Exploration of the Yellowstone and Missouri Rivers,
Under the Direction of Captain W. F. Raynolds, Corps of Engineers, 1859–60.

and glass. Where such materials are fairly plentiful, we may infer that they resulted from commercial ventures set up by French, Spanish, or English traders after the middle of the eighteenth century. Other sites which yield more limited quantities of contact goods presumably date from an earlier period. It may be supposed that intertribal trade brought an occasional trinket or small tool to the Missouri River natives from other Indians in contact with Frenchmen bartering for furs westward from the Upper Great Lakes. This, however, must have been only a dribble; and it is unlikely from any present documentary evidence that metal or glass goods were reaching the Middle Missouri much before the final decade or two or the seventeenth century, or that they were arriving in significant quantity before the second quarter of the following century. At the same time, it should be recognized that some of the villages in which small amounts of European goods occur, may have been inhabited for some or many years prior to the arrival of these items.

Concerning the earlier postwhite villages in the South Dakota section of the Missouri Valley, then, we can say little. There are a good many sites on the east bank which, to judge from their surface remains, probably belong to late prehistoric or early historic peoples, whereas practically all of the Arikara towns mentioned in the later documents, if identifiable at all, were evidently on the west (right) bank. Circular-house villages with small quantities of white trade-goods and having pottery that appears to be in the Arikara tradition, have been excavated at the Talking Crow, Oacoma, and Oldham sites in the Fort Randall Reservoir area; and at the Oldham site they were associated with bastioned fortifications. Unfortified hamlets on the west bank in the Fort Bennett district may also pertain to this period, since the pottery is less like the earlier Bennett focus incised wares and more like that on later eighteenth century Arikara sites. What seems to be implied is a gradual movement northward from the Fort Randall–Big Bend locale, the breakup of the large prehistoric settlements into many smaller communities, and eventually a withdrawal of the east-bank people to the west bank of the Missouri in the face of growing pressure from the Dakotas, newly arrived from the east shortly after the middle of the eighteenth century.

That some large settlements continued into the contact period on the Missouri below the Cheyenne River is suggested by such sites as Sully village, on Telegraph Flat near New Fort Sully. Here house sites number between three and four hundred, with at least three large ceremonial structures, and considerable quantities of refuse, but without visible indication of fortifications. It seems likely that several interludes of occupation are represented, rather than that the site was fully occupied at any one time. Sully Village site has been the locus of the largest single excavation project yet undertaken on the Missouri; and the analysis and full reporting of its character should add greatly to our picture of native community life in the late seventeenth and eighteenth centuries.

Before the middle of the eighteenth century, significant changes had taken place in that region. This featured the gathering together of native population into a number of compact, strongly fortified villages, mostly situated on the west bank of the river. As early as 1743, when the elder La Vérendrye visited the Mandans, he found them in six or seven well-fortified villages said to contain from one to two hundred houses each. Downriver were other groups—the "Panaux" and "Panani," both of whom had forts and lodges like those of the Mandans, and who, in addition, were provided with horses. Five years later, La Vérendrye's sons visited the "fort" of the Gens de la Petite Cerise, or Little Cherry People, possibly a band of the Arikaras, near present Pierre. Later, on their way northward to the Mandan towns, they noted a camp of Prairie People, who may have been among the advance guard of the expanding Dakotas.[28]

The populous and strongly fortified towns of La Vérendrye's time and during the next few decades represent, I think, the heyday of Village Indian culture on the Middle Missouri. They consisted of large well-constructed houses, and are marked today by

[28] L. J. Burpee's *Journals and Letters of Pierre Gaultier de Varennes de la Verendrye and His Sons.*

deep extensive refuse deposits and a rich and varied artifact inventory. We may infer that the maize-bean-squash agriculture with which Indians had been experimenting here for several hundred years had developed into a productive and dependable basis for settled community life. The surplus crops and stored food resources of these flourishing communities were perennial attractions to the wandering bison-hunters to the east and west, whether for trade or for plunder. Through these contacts, the Village Indians acquired guns from the east and horses from the south and west, in exchange for corn, hides, and other items. In later days, they became foci of the white trade—French, Spanish, and English. Until well into the nineteenth century, in fact long after their days of relative greatness were gone, the stockaded villages along the Missouri continued to function as trading centers.[29] Thus, they participated deeply in the main currents of Plains cultural development; and like other middlemen before and since, rose to pre-eminence and prosperity. There was a price on this pre-eminence, however, and part of it is reflected in the defensive works with which the communities found it necessary to surround themselves.

To this period, centering in the eighteenth century but doubtless with roots in the seventeenth, belong some of the better-known village sites of the region. Philip Ranch, Buffalo Pasture, Lower Cheyenne Village, Swan Creek, and Bamble are among these; and the unfortified, but impressively extensive Sully Village probably belongs, at least in part, in this group. Farther north, the Rygh site with its deep middens, and the Mobridge site, should be included; and, in the Mandan area, we may note Slant Village at the mouth of the Heart, Double Ditch, and others of the group sometimes classed as the Later Heart River group. The chronological position of many of these sites is far from clear, as are their interrelationships with other sites. At some of these locations, there are also earlier occupations without evidence of white contact. Many other sites doubtless await investigation and description, or will soon be lost beneath the rising waters of the reservoirs.

[29] J. C. Ewers, "The Indian Trade of the Upper Missouri Before Lewis and Clark: An Interpretation," Missouri Historical Society *Bulletin*, Vol. X, No. 4 (1954), 430-32.

The village sites generally consist of twenty to fifty, or more, house sites. These are closely spaced, often with only very narrow walkways between the adjacent structures. Surrounding the houses is a deep ditch, which in some instances must have been as much as eight or ten feet deep when freshly dug. On the inner edge of the ditch there was a stockade, constructed of upright logs or of poles which were presumably interlaced with horizontal poles and brush. These were the forts of the eighteenth-century French visitors. In plan, the fortified area was usually more or less circular or oblong, and lacked the rectangular bastions that are a common feature of the prehistoric fortified villages such as Arzberger and Huff. Cache pits are abundant in these sites, and occur both within and outside the houses.

The houses themselves retain the basic circular form with four primary center supports; but there are details in which they differ notably from the earlier structures. For one thing, they are commonly larger, ranging in diameter from thirty to nearly fifty feet. The outer circle of postholes usually consists of numerous small, closely-set units which often must have virtually touched one another; and at intervals of eight to fifteen feet, heavier posts were interspersed among these. Against the close-set poles were placed the willow, grass, and earth covering. The pits in which the houses were erected varied in depth; but in many cases were probably not more than one foot or so in depth when originally dug.

Garbage disposal seems to have been mainly between the dwellings, against the inner face of the encircling stockade, and sometimes in the dry ditch beyond. In the rigidly restricted space so utilized, there may be up to three or four feet of refuse, including large quantities of animal bone, ashes, broken pottery, floor sweepings, and discarded household materials. La Vérendrye described the towns of the Mandans in 1743 as "very clean" and orderly; but one suspects that in wet weather the inhabitants of these crowded communities carried on their daily life in a malodorous environment. By contrast, the widely-dispersed open communities of earlier times were models of sanitary planning.

The archaeologist, probing these garbage dumps two centuries

196

after they were laid down, is grateful for the wealth of cultural material they contain. The period represented, roughly from the second quarter to the final quarter of the eighteenth century, may well have been the climax of native culture in the region, judged by the abundance and variety of its material leavings. The pottery, it is true, is more certainly a utilitarian ware, and lacks much of the pleasing incised decoration found on earlier products in the region. But in other respects, the material remains are gratifyingly abundant and well made. Certain of the sites have long drawn collectors to their lush and easily worked middens.

The pottery, which occurs in great abundance, consists usually of simple stamped ware; and the incised designs that so commonly covered the shoulders and upper bodies of earlier vessels are much less common. Also characteristic of the vessels of this period is a sort of brushed effect on the neck and adjacent rim, as if the soft clay had been stroked with a handful of grass stems. Thickened rims which have been pinched into an undulating or "wavy" form are common. Decorative use of single cord impressions is found on many rims and on the handles. Farther north, cord impressions on the exteriors of S-shaped rims are relatively much more common than in the South Dakota section. The presence of small, well-made vessels, usually with two handles, and decorated with cord impressions on the rim and fine-line incising on the shoulders, is to be noted. Such vessels have been found several times with burials, suggesting that the older incised pottery type survived into this later period as a funerary ware.

With respect to the artifact inventory, one of the outstanding features of this period is the abundance of well-made bone objects. These include a varied assortment of utilitarian forms, such as the ubiquitous hoes made of bison shoulder blade and, at some sites, considerable numbers of bison frontal "scoops" with horn core handles; curved bone fishhooks in various sizes, along with the open-center blanks from which they were fashioned; two-, three-, and four-hole arrow-shaft wrenches of bison rib; the familiar chisel-like hide fleshers made of bison or elk cannon bones, with finely toothed blade; knife handles of deer rib, slotted along one edge to receive a metal blade; wedge-shaped objects of cancellous bone, for applying pigment to such leather articles as tipi covers, parfleches, and garments; various forms of awls split from ribs, from deer or antelope leg bones, and from the fore edge of the spine from the hump vertebrae of the bison; and long flat needles (?) fashioned from bison rib.

Nonutilitarian bone objects include whistles of bird bone, sometimes with incised decoration; polished mammal bone tubes, with incised lines encircling the ends or spiraling around the middle or otherwise placed; rare bone combs, with teeth deeply and irregularly cut with metal tools; snow "snakes" with rounded head, socketed at the butt to receive two diverging sticks with feathered ends, and often ornamented on one surface and the edges; and other lesser objects. Many of the bone items bear unmistakable marks of metal tools, and were probably cut with steel axes or heavy knives. At some sites, there are numbers of bison horn cores still carrying the deep, straight cuts left by these tools.

Objects of antler included many deerhorn tips, perhaps used in flint-knapping or intended for modification into projectile points or as implement handles; long, narrow curving strips that were probably armlets; and occasional thin scraped sections whose purpose is uncertain. The large L-shaped elkhorn hide-scraper, with stone or metal blade lashed to the shorter arm, is also indicated.

Work in chipped stone included a limited number of triangular and stemmed arrow points, these being gradually replaced by brass and iron points; and also small numbers of drills, scrapers, and knives of various shapes and sizes. Grooved mauls are plentiful, as are hammerstones that have been subjected to heavy use in pecking, variously shaped sandstone blocks with worn surfaces, along with occasional longitudinally grooved arrow-shaft smoothers used in pairs.

There are a few catlinite ornaments, and pipes made of this stone occur in fair numbers. Some of them are straight tubes; more are elbow-shaped, often with a projecting prow beyond the upright bowl and with a perforated keel or loop at the inner end of the stem. These resemble forms found widely in early historic times throughout the Plains, and often denominated the "Siouan" type.

Associated with these villages in the South Dakota sector are cemeteries, some of which have yielded important information on burial customs of the eighteenth-century Arikaras. The bodies were placed, usually flexed, in individually dug grave pits from three to six feet deep. Over the corpse were placed slanting cedar poles or wood slabs, one end resting on the grave floor, the other leaning against the grave wall above the corpse. Sometimes, perhaps characteristically, the poles were further covered with coarse matting, and above this, the grave was filled with dirt. With the deceased were deposited items such as pottery vessels, stone pipes, bone tools, metal knife blades, glass beads, and other objects. Excepting the smaller items, such as beads, the grave accompaniments were seldom numerous—a pot, a pipe, a wooden bowl, and no more.

Now and then, a more richly stocked burial is encountered, or one whose contents apparently reflect the special abilities or tastes of the deceased. Thus, in the grave of a presumed arrow maker at Lower Cheyenne Village (39ST1), were an arrow-shaft gauge, three shaft wrenches, a bone flint-knapping tool, broken remnants of worked wood suggesting a "killed" bow, and masses of red, yellow, white, black, and purple pigment. With another male, buried six feet underground, were six polished-bone tubes on a fiber cord, two small, rectangular bone dice, six small, marble-like catlinite balls, the long, slender beaks of two water birds, the skulls and mandible fragments of several rodents, and several conical copper jingles that had been sewn to a leather garment or belt. A child of about six years had evidently been clad in a leather garment to which were sewed some fifty copper cones; around the neck had been a string of white paste beads; and in the grave was a small, flat-bottomed wooden bowl and a small pottery vessel.

Other graves included two individuals, sometimes deposited one above the other but both below the customary pole covering; or, one individual, usually a small child, lay above the poles. In still others, the bones of a very small infant shared the grave of a male, both burials evidently made at the same time.

Still other variations, which may reflect older practices, involved the burial of two to five or more individuals in a single large pit. Whether these were the unfortunate victims of a smallpox epidemic, of a hard winter or food shortage, or of enemy action is, of course, impossible to determine. Occasional bone bundles suggest a reburial; or they may reflect survival of the practices of an earlier period, when secondary interment may have been customary.

We still know much too little about how the interesting pattern of small, compact fortified villages originated, developed, and spread throughout the Middle Missouri region. That it was a general development seems clear from the fact that large circular houses and simple stamped pottery were characteristic of these sites practically everywhere. The recurring finds of European goods wherever extended excavation is undertaken, at any rate north of Bad River, is further evidence of the lateness of the communities. That such strongly fortified villages were in existence by 1740 is clear from the observations of the La Vérendryes, father and sons. The great majority of the known sites, however, were notably smaller than the populous and powerful villages of 130 or more lodges reported for the Mandans in 1748. South of the Grand River, at least, there were seldom more than a score or two of houses within the fortifications, sometimes with additional units outside. There is no way of determining whether the "Aricara" and "Caricara" at the time of Bourgmond's 1714 writing were protecting themselves in similar fashion.

It should be noted, too, that the eighteenth-century defensive works are usually much less elaborate than were the fortifications of the prehistoric sites, such as Huff and Arzberger. Whereas the earlier villages were laid out in a rectangular or rectilinear pattern, with regular spaced bastions, the early historic communities were laid out in more or less circular or rounded oblong fashion and neither the visible ditches nor such stockade lines as have been dug offer any evidence of bastions.

Still unclear, too, is the relationship of these "forts" to the great rambling unfortified communities of the earlier circular-house peoples in the Bennett-LaRoche focus tradition. The latter are clearly the older, but are they directly ancestral, or are there intervening stages? Are we to infer a gradual movement of proto-Arikara (and other?) peoples northward from the general Big Bend locale, and the breakup of the large prewhite settlements into a number of smaller, closely circumscribed villages situated mostly along the west bank of the Missouri? If so, what were the motivations for these demographic changes?

Possible explanations suggest themselves. The withdrawal of village-dwelling peoples from the east bank of the Missouri may reflect the growing might of the Dakotas. Perhaps present in small numbers as early as 1740, these people presumably poured into and across the Missouri Valley in ever increasing numbers from the Minnesota prairies and woodlands during the following decades. That the fortifications at Buffalo Pasture, Philip Ranch, Lower Cheyenne Village, Double Ditch, and other contemporaneous sites were designed for security against alien peoples of some numbers and prowess seems most probable; and the "Drang nach Westen" of the Siouans, if it did not cause the concentration of corn-growing populations into fortified towns, was certainly a potent factor in keeping the people so protected.

A second factor, it may be suspected, was the smallpox. There is little information on this problem prior to the devastating epidemic of 1780–81, which swept the upper Missouri and regions to the north and west with deadly effect.[30] There may well have been earlier visitations among the Village tribes, of which no documentation has come down to us. Early travelers on the Missouri make repeated mention of the smallpox as the agent of extensive depopulation, and the results of enemy action against a Village group weakened in numbers and dispirited by epidemics must have been far-reaching. Writing in 1795, Trudeau credited the Arikara with a former strength of four thousand warriors and thirty-two "populous villages, now depopulated and almost entirely destroyed by the smallpox which broke out among them

[30] E. W. Stearn and A. E. Stearn, *The Effect of Smallpox on the Destiny of the Amerindian*, 46–48.

three different times." In his day, the survivors of these scourges had been reduced to three villages with "about 500 fighting men" near the mouth of the Cheyenne River.[31] Unfortunately, the data are not at hand from which we might judge the effect of recurring and widespread epidemics on redistribution of populations and changes in settlement patterns; but it may be suggested that a community of many hundred inhabitants, such perhaps as Sully Village in its heyday, might well have seen its citizens scattered widely and permanently in their frantic efforts to escape disfigurement and death when smallpox struck.

Wooden walls and dry ditches stayed for a time, but did not halt, the decline of the Village Indians. By Lewis and Clark's time, the six (or nine?) former Mandan towns in the Heart River locale had dwindled to two poorly fortified villages, of forty or fifty lodges each, some twenty miles below the Knife. The Hidatsas were still in their villages on the Knife, just above its mouth. The Arikaras occupied three villages, which had become two in 1811, a few miles above the Grand River, with a string of recently abandoned sites scattered down the Missouri to present Chantier Creek. In these villages, the remnants of the three tribes still clung stubbornly to what was left to them from the more prosperous days of fifty or one hundred years earlier; but by 1830–40, the end was near.

In this critical twilight period, we no longer need to rely solely, or even mainly, on the findings of archaeology alone. For we have narratives of a host of competent observers who traveled through the region or sojourned for various purposes among its inhabitants. Beginning in the 1790's, Trudeau, Evans, D'Eglise, and other representatives of the Missouri Company recorded their firsthand observations in varying degrees of completeness and accuracy.[32] After the turn of the century came Tabeau in 1803–1805, Lewis and Clark in 1804–1806, Bradbury and Brackenridge in 1811,

[31] Mrs. H. T. Beauregard's "Journal of Jean Baptiste Trudeau Among the Arikara Indians in 1795," Missouri Historical Society *Collections*, Vol. IV, No. 1 (1912), 28–31.

[32] A. P. Nasatir, *Before Lewis and Clark, Documents Illustrating the History of the Missouri, 1785–1804.*

Catlin in 1832, Maximilian in 1833–34, Chardon in 1834–39, and Culbertson in 1850, plus various Indian agents, army officers, missionaries, and others thereafter.[33] Not the least important part of this record are the paintings left us by such artists as Catlin and Bodmer.

The archaeologist finds these narratives and pictorial records invaluable, not only for what they tell of the Indians of this period, but also for the clues they furnish toward the identification and interpretation of other materials found in older sites. They pertain most directly, of course, to the materials originating in a series of archaeological investigations, still largely unreported in print, at several of the nineteenth-century village sites. These include the Leavenworth Arikara site, occupied *circa* 1803–32; Rock Village (Hidatsa, c.1830); Star Village (Arikara, 1862); Night Walker's Butte (Hidatsa, c.1750–1800?); and Like-a-Fishhook (Arikara-Mandan-Hidatsa, after c.1845).

In direct response to the ever-present menace of the Sioux, the post-1800 villages were nearly all fortified; but more than one traveler noted that the stockades were haphazardly constructed or in dilapidated condition, partly because the villagers were utilizing the timbers for firewood. Some of the communities were of considerable size, since they represented the drawing together of most or all of the remaining members of the once populous tribes. The Leavenworth site, for example, included two nearly contiguous groups of 60 or 80 large lodges each, with a combined population probably in the neighborhood of 1,500 or 1,800 souls.[34]

[33] A. H. Abel, *Tabeau's Narrative of Loisel's Expedition to the Upper Missouri;* R. G. Thwaites, *Original Journals of the Lewis and Clark Expedition, 1804–1806;* J. Bradbury, "Travels in the Interior of America, 1809–1811," in Vol. V of Thwaites' *Early Western Travels;* H. M. Brackenridge, "Journal of a Voyage up River Missouri in 1811," in Vol. VI of Thwaites' *Early Western Travels;* G. Catlin, *North American Indians, Being Letters and Notes on Their Manners, Customs, and Conditions;* Prince Maximilian, "Travels in the Interior of North America," in Vol. XXIII of Thwaites' *Early Western Travels;* T. A. Culbertson, "Journal of an Expedition to the Mauvaises Terres and the Upper Missouri in 1850," Bureau of American Ethnology *Bulletin 147.*

[34] Strong, "From History to Prehistory in the Northern Great Plains," *loc. cit.,* 366–70; Wedel, "Archeological Materials from the Vicinity of Mobridge, South Dakota," Bureau of American Ethnology *Bulletin 157,* Anthropological Papers, No. 45 (1955), 69–188.

At Fort Clark, where Maximilian reported 65 huts and 150 warriors in 1833, Culbertson was told that there were 200 lodges of Arikaras in 1850. Other villages, such as the stockaded hilltop fortress known as Night Walker's Butte, consisted of 40 or 50 small lodges.

Essentially, the large circular lodges of this period resembled those of the contemporary Pawnees and other earth-lodge-using tribes throughout the Plains. Like those in other sections, too, they were generally closely crowded into the fortified area without order or plan, except that the Mandans still retained from earlier times the open central plaza in which stood the sacrosanct "ark of the first man." White visitors sometimes spoke well of the commodious and comfortable lodges, but dissenting opinions were also made. Tabeau, who shared one with an Arikara chief and his household, observed sourly that they "should be inhabited only by Ricaras, dogs, and bears"; and Brackenridge, in 1811, found the Leavenworth village "excessively filthy, the villainous smells, which everywhere assailed me, compelled me at length to seek refuge in the open plain."

Archaeology indicates that these late houses frequently differed structurally from those at the earlier fortified villages, though they nearly always retained the four central posts. At Leavenworth and Rock Village, for example, the outer series of roof-wall supports were set well within the pit; and the butts of the leaning wall members rested on the ground four feet or more outside, with space for sleeping quarters between. This is in contrast to the earlier situation at Lower Cheyenne Village and Buffalo Pasture, where the outer series of posts was interspersed among the closely set leaners, whose lower ends were let into the floor just within the wall of the pit. Other details may reflect tribal idiosyncrasies; for example, the Hidatsa practice of lining fireplaces with stone slabs set on edge, and of digging trenches to accommodate the wall posts along the vestibule entrance.

Agriculture was still the hub of the subsistence economy; and early travelers were impressed with the flourishing gardens of corn, beans, melons, tobacco, and other produce near the villages.

Bradbury termed the Arikara women "excellent cultivators," in spite of the prevalence of bone hoes over iron; and he observed further that he had not seen, "even in the United States, any crop of Indian corn in finer order, or better managed, than the corn about these villages." Equally revealing is his report that the Arikaras had no corn to trade at this time because excessive rains had penetrated their underground caches and spoiled the stored food stocks.

Hunting was important, too, as would be expected at a time when horses were becoming increasingly plentiful; but enthusiasm for the chase on the part of the Village Indians seems to have been tempered by the Sioux war parties hovering about the settlements. The Sioux, like other nonsedentary Indians to the west and southwest, were drawn to the sedentary villages not only by the lure of booty but also by the opportunities for trading. The same considerations were undoubtedly operating in earlier days, when the Sioux brought guns from the east and other tribes brought horses from the west for exchange at the Missouri River villages.

There is no need to dwell here on the everyday life of the Village Indians of this time, since it has been vividly recorded by contemporary observers in works that are readily available, and the archaeological materials still to be collated with the written record have not yet been detailed. We note only that many of the characteristic bone, stone, and other manufactures of the Indians continued the tools and implements found in the earlier fortified towns, as we have described these, but they are present in lesser numbers and are often less carefully made and finished. The potter's art shows a progressive decline, with simple stamped utilitarian wares the rule, and brushed necks characteristic. Even as late as the 1860's, at Like-a-Fishhook Village, some pottery was being made; and occasional details of treatment and ornamentation clearly recall the earlier and better wares.[35]

In the increasing amount of iron axes, gun parts, steel traps,

[35] Wedel, "Observations on Some Nineteenth Century Pottery Vessels from the Upper Missouri," Bureau of American Ethnology *Bulletin 164*, Anthropological Papers, No. 51 (1957), 87–114.

brass kettles, and other heavy items, we see the growing dependence of the Indians on the white traders settled among them. An interesting development of this period is the Indian practice of grinding up the glass beads received in trade, and recasting them into ornaments of their own design, an art said to have been learned from a Spanish captive.[36]

The increasing volume of white trade is strikingly manifested in the burials of this period, at the same time that they show the persistence of some of the earlier native practices. In the cemeteries investigated at the Leavenworth site, for example, inhumation and flexing of the corpse were still customary,[37] as they were at Lower Cheyenne Village and Swan Creek; but pole or slab coverings were no longer used. With a high proportion of the dead were found glass and metal objects. These included large numbers of white and blue glass beads; tubular and conical ornaments, hawk bells, bracelets, and buttons, of brass; iron arrowheads, fire steels, a straight-edge razor, and other items; a wooden-backed mirror; double-armed crosses of white metal; cotton and metal "lace"; woollen and cotton trade fabrics; and a bottle which, if we may trust the legend blown into the glass, once yielded to its owner a few drafts of that popular and widely traveled early-day nostrum—Turlington's Balsam of Life.[38]

Along with these trade materials were found small clay pots, usually cruder and less competently decorated than the earlier funerary vessels; catlinite ornaments and pipes; occasional chipped- and ground-stone objects; perforated animal teeth and bird claws; bone tubes and whistles; wooden clubs and vessel fragments; and traces of native leatherwork ornamented with porcupine quills.

[36] M. W. Stirling, "Arikara Glassworking," *Journal*, Washington Academy of Sciences, Vol. XXXVII, No. 8 (1947), 257–63; Wedel, "Archeological Materials from the Vicinity of Mobridge, South Dakota," *loc. cit.*, 152–53.

[37] Wedel, "Archeological Materials From the Vicinity of Mobridge, South Dakota," *loc. cit.*, 96–102.

[38] Wedel and G. B. Griffenhagen, "An English Balsam Among the Dakota Aborigines," *American Journal of Pharmacy*, Vol. CXXVI, No. 12 (1954), 409–15; Griffenhagen and J. H. Harvey, "Old English Patent Medicines in America," U. S. National Museum *Bulletin 218*," Contributions from the Museum of History and Technology, Paper 10 (1959), 155–83.

Interestingly enough, some of the lesser odds and ends dug up here, unidentifiable in themselves, can be recognized in Catlin's paintings and their function thereby established.

At some of these late sites, there are evidences of trade contacts other than those with whites. Worked steatite at Rock Village, including vessels, probably originated somewhere in the Wyoming region. Dentalium and other marine shells support the observations of early-day travelers regarding intertribal trade between the upper Missouri Indians and tribes west of the Rockies. Catlinite was obtained, as it evidently had been for centuries previously, from the famous pipestone quarries in southwestern Minnesota.

The movements of the Arikaras, Mandans, and Hidatsas during these final decades of their prereservation life should perhaps be noted briefly. The principal Mandan town after 1800 was at the Fort Clark site about twenty miles below the Knife River, with a smaller village nearby on the north (left) bank. Here the smallpox epidemic of 1837, touched off by a case on the steamboat *Assiniboin*, all but wiped out the tribe while the trader Chardon recorded its ravages.[39] The handful of survivors were dispossessed by the Arikaras in 1838, and drifted upriver to settle, between 1854 and 1858, near the Hidatsas. These had removed about 1845 from their old Knife River villages to the vicinity of Fort Berthold, an American Fur Company post on the north (left) bank of the Missouri about twenty miles below Elbowoods.

The Arikaras left their fortified village at the Leavenworth site, ten miles north of present Mobridge, South Dakota, after its shelling by United States troops under Colonel Henry Leavenworth in August, 1823. After a brief stay upriver near the Mandans, they returned to their old village where they remained until 1832. Then followed a very incompletely documented wandering in the Plains which included a winter's stay with the Skidi Pawnees on the Loup River in Nebraska. In 1838, back on the Missouri, the Arikaras took over the old Fort Clark Mandan village, but moved upstream after the destruction of Fort Clark in 1861. Their attempt to found a new town, Star Village, opposite Fort Berthold,

[39] Abel, *Chardon's Journal at Fort Clark, 1834–1839.*

was frustrated by the Sioux; and in 1862, they crossed the river to join the Mandans and Hidatsas at Like-a-Fishhook, the last earth-lodge town on the Missouri. In this locality, the heart of which has but recently disappeared beneath the waters of Garrison Reservoir, the survivors and descendants of the Three Affiliated Tribes have since resided.

In the perspective of archaeology, as from the data of history, it is clear that the Village Indian way of life was possible, in last analysis, for one principal reason—corn. On the successful development of corn agriculture and on the assured food supply it provided, the natives of the Middle Missouri based their complex culture with its fixed villages, substantial populations, and an elaborate social, political, and ceremonial organization. And all of this activity, we may note again, took place in a difficult region that lies near or at the northern margin of corn growing in North America.[40]

The white settlers who pushed into the region and tried farming quickly learned the scope of that Indian achievement. Unsuccessful with the eastern corn they brought along, they turned to the Indians. Here they found flint, flour, and sweet corn in surprising variety, all remarkably acclimated to the rigors of the north country. Among these, white seedsmen in the 1880's obtained basic strains characterized by extreme hardiness, earliness, and drought resistance. From these, in turn, were developed a series of varieties which have since become well established in the regional farm economy.

Corn was but one of the Village Indian gifts which have been of basic importance and lasting value to Northern Plains agriculture. Another came in the form of a handful of seeds presented by a Hidatsa, Son of Star, to the pioneer Bismarck seedsman, Oscar H. Will, in payment for some small favor. Out of that handful came the Great Northern bean, now one of the leading commercial field beans of the United States. It is a great pity that, while

---

[40] Will, "Indian Agriculture at its Northern Limits in the Great Plains Region of North America," *Twentieth International Congress of Americanists,* Vol. 1 (1924), 203–205; Will and Hyde, *op. cit.*

we have two or three classic accounts of native agriculture on the Middle Missouri, the full story of the white man's borrowing from the Indian was never recorded by the men most intimately concerned.

CHAPTER SEVEN

THE NORTHEASTERN PERIPHERY

EAST AND NORTH FROM THE TRENCH of the Missouri, the surface of the Missouri Plateau slopes gently upward for some fifty or sixty miles to the hills of glacial debris that mark the Coteau du Missouri. Beyond this belt, the steppe and mixed grasses give way to a prairie landscape increasingly dotted with lakes, marshes, and patches of deciduous timber. The James, Vermillion, and Big Sioux rivers, flowing southward into the Missouri, and the Sheyenne–Red River system emptying northward into Lake Winnipeg, provide most of the surface drainage. Beyond the forty-ninth parallel, the prairies merge into the aspen grove or park belt running north and west across Manitoba, Saskatchewan, and Alberta.

In historic times, these prairies were controlled by the Dakotas and Assiniboines, who can be traced back into their Minnesota homeland of late prehistoric and early historic times. The principal archaeological remains now known from this region also resemble those of Minnesota and northern Iowa more closely than they do those of the Middle Missouri–Great Plains area; and their roots clearly lie toward the east rather than the west. In terms of Plains Indian culture, as well as geographically, the region is marginal to the greater culture area with which we are primarily concerned. Accordingly, its designation here as the Northeastern Periphery seems appropriate.

From the earliest days of white contact here until after the middle of the last century, this region was dominated by various tribes of the Dakota Sioux.[1] Earlier, the "seven council fires" of the

Dakotas burned in central Minnesota, along the lakes and streams feeding the Mississippi. Here, in the early seventeenth century, the French first encountered the Nadouessioux, describing them as people who hunted, rather than planted, and who also made pottery. These were the Eastern Sioux, or Santees, residing in the Mille Lacs district with its abundant village sites and mounds. They were distinguished on the early eighteenth-century maps of Delisle and others, from the Western Sioux beyond the Mississippi, and the "Tinton" (Teton) around Big Stone and/or Traverse Lake.[2] How long these tribes had occupied the localities so attributed to them, we do not know; but in the ensuing decades, perhaps lured by the game herds and pushed by better armed people on the east, they shifted westward. Between 1700 and 1750, the Tetons moved on toward the Missouri, eventually to cross that stream, acquire horses, and establish their dominance over a vast tract to the west. Their eastern kindred also moved, but not so far, choosing to remain in the prairies and along the woodland margin. By the nineteenth century, the "spirited and warlike" Yanktonais ranged from the James to the Missouri and north to Devils Lake; the Yanktons were between the James and the Big Sioux, thence southward; and the Sissetons and other Santees occupied the country about Big Stone and Traverse lakes, the upper Coteau des Prairies, and northward. The Assiniboines, by tradition an offshoot of the Yanktonais, seem to have spearheaded the Dakota advance to the north and west, supposedly in the seventeenth century, but perhaps even earlier.

There is no traditional or other evidence, apparently, that the Dakotas met with resistance from alien peoples as they overran the prairies of eastern North and South Dakota. Probably this belt,

[1] S. R. Riggs, "Dakota Grammar, Texts, and Ethnography," 53 Cong., 2 sess., *House Misc. Doc. 173*, (1893), 155–88; G. K. Warren, "Explorations in the Dacota County, in the Year 1855," 34 Cong., 1 sess., *Sen. Exec. Doc.* 76 (1856; ser. 822).

[2] N. H. Winchell, "The Aborigines of Minnesota," Minnesota Historical Society (1911), 25–62, 437 ff.; S. W. Pond, "The Dakotas or Sioux in Minnesota as They Were in 1834," Minnesota Historical Society *Collections*, Vol. XII (1908), 319–501.

which had already been the home of several other groups, had been abandoned by those who left the archaeological remains that are so characteristic of the region. There are a few village sites with pottery that were apparently occupied in postcontact times. There are many others, particularly in the present corn-growing area of southeastern South Dakota, that are older, but which mark the sites of former semisedentary towns whose inhabitants grew corn and made pottery. No less interesting are the hundreds of mounds with which the prairie belt is besprinkled.

These sites, moreover, include several that apparently stand intermediate culturally between the Village Indians of the Middle Missouri and the easterly districts from which their forebears, in part, are believed to have come. Among these are the Brandon site, on the Big Sioux near Sioux Falls, and the Mitchell and Twelve-Mile Creek sites on the lower James. To these and other less fully known sites, the term Over focus has been assigned by archaeologists.[3]

The village sites of the Over focus consist of twenty-five to fifty houses each, situated on streamside terraces, and partially protected by ditches. The houses have a long-rectangular floor plan, recalling in their main features those of the Thomas Riggs focus in the Pierre–Cheyenne River district. Although direct evidence of domestic plants is wanting, the shoulder-blade hoe and underground storage pit are regular features of the sites, and agriculture was doubtless practiced.

Pottery is rather varied. It consists of full-bodied jars with a constricted orifice, as well as a few bowls. Vessel surfaces include smoothed, cord-roughened, and incised or trailed wares, with plain, incised, and cord-impressed rims. Handles are present, and they sometimes include representations of animal forms. These,

[3] E. E. Meleen, "A Preliminary Report of the Mitchell Indian Village Site and Burial Mounds," South Dakota Archaeological Commission *Archeological Studies, Circular No. 2* (1938); W. H. Over and E. E. Meleen, "A Report on an Investigation of the Brandon Village Site and the Split Rock Creek Mounds," South Dakota Archeological Commission *Archeological Studies, Circular No. 3* (1941); Hurt, "Report of the Investigation of the Swanson Site, 39BR16, Brule County, South Dakota," *loc. cit.*

like the angular shoulders and broad-trailed designs on some of the pottery, point to connections with Middle Mississippi sites to the east, such as the well-known Aztalan site in southern Wisconsin.

Artifacts of chipped stone include triangular and side-notched arrow points, asymmetrical knives with one curved and one straight edge, plate chalcedony knives, end and side scrapers, drill points, and occasional diamond-shaped knives with beveled edges. Grooved mauls, diorite celts, sandstone arrow-shaft smoothers, and catlinite are present. Bone awls split from deer legbones, knives, cannon-bone fleshing tools that may have either a smooth or toothed edge, fishhooks, arrowheads, and knife handles set with stone blades also occur, as does the scoop made of bison frontal bone with a horn-core handle. Animal bone refuse indicates that the bison was much used.

The people who left these sites had trade relations or other contacts in various directions. In addition to the Middle Mississippi elements present in the remains, there are pottery and other traits that recall the Mill Creek culture of northwestern Iowa, which has been described in an earlier chapter. The notable resemblances between these sites and some of the early long-rectangular-house communities on the Middle Missouri has led some to suggest that these may mark the, or a, migration route of peoples of an ancestral Mandan stock on their way out of the Minnesota-Iowa area toward the Middle Missouri.[4]

Farther to the north, other village sites have been found in the river valleys of the Northeastern Periphery. Surveys in the Jamestown district have disclosed sites in which small circular houses with four center posts occur, calling to mind the circular earthlodges of the Village Indians. Some of the pottery in the district is also remindful of that manufactured by the Village Indians along the Missouri in North Dakota. There are white-trade goods, and the period is probably in the middle or latter eighteenth century. How close these similarities are and what they mean in terms of possible population movements from east to west may be appre-

[4] Hurt, "Report of the Investigation of the Swanson Site, 39BR16, Brule County, South Dakota," *loc. cit.*, *21.*

ciably clearer when the results of recent investigations by the River Basin Surveys appear in print.[5]

Still another important village site is that on the Sheyenne River about twelve miles below Lisbon, North Dakota. This has been identified as a Cheyenne village of about 1750, burned by the Chippewas.[6] It consists of about seventy house rings, protected on all sides except the river bank by a deep unbastioned ditch, without evidence of stockade posts. The houses are circular in plan, with four central posts, and in four instances, exhibit a secondary circle of outer posts. All houses excavated to date, seven in number, show evidence of having been burned. Cache pits are plentiful outside the houses, but not within.

Pottery is mainly simple stamped, with vertical brushing on the necks, conforming closely in these particulars to the historic wares of the Middle Missouri. Vessel rims are characteristically thickened slightly and bear ornamentation made by impressions with a cord-wrapped stick. Plain cord impressions, incising, and punctating are less common. The decorative treatment recalls that on Minnesota pottery rather than that characteristic of the Middle Missouri or Plains ware.

With respect to other material remains, the site has yielded stone and bone artifacts paralleling those from the contemporary Middle Missouri village sites. Bone implements are plentiful and varied; they include many bison scapula hoes, elk cannon-bone toothed fleshers, edge-slotted bone knife handles, rib-shaft wrenches, cancellous bone paint brushes, whistles, beads, and an incised bracelet or bow guard. Also present are catlinite elbow pipes, grooved shaft polishers, grooved mauls, grinding stones, stemmed arrow points, scrapers, triangular knife blades, crescentic shell knives or scrapers, seeds, and birch bark. Much refuse animal bone attests the importance of hunting. White-contact materials consist of some glass, an eighteenth-century trigger guard drilled

[5] Roberts, "River Basin Surveys," *Seventieth Annual Report,* Bureau of American Ethnology (1952–53) 16.

[6] Strong, "From History to Prehistory in the Northern Great Plains," *loc. cit.,* 370–76.

for use as an ornament, lance, arrow, and knife blades of iron and brass, and glass beads used as decorative insets in pottery.

The site is of especial interest for several reasons. For one thing, it indicates that as late as the mid-eighteenth century, and doubtless some time after the arrival of white men, the Cheyennes were still an agricultural as well as a hunting people, whereas by the time of Lewis and Clark fifty years later, they were full-fledged tipi-using bison hunters without traces of agriculture or fixed villages. In most respects, their material culture and settlement pattern were much like those of the Arikaras, Mandans, and Hidatsas, but with some traits clearly linking them with the Minnesota Woodland peoples. No sites showing their transition from agriculture to purely hunting have as yet been recognized or studied between the Sheyenne site and their historic habitat about the Black Hills and southward.

An important, but still imperfectly understood, feature of the archaeology of the Dakotas is the presence of considerable numbers of mounds in their eastern portions.[7] They are most plentiful in the region adjoining Minnesota and Iowa, and occur in diminishing numbers to the west. Groups of varying sizes are to be found along the Big Sioux River, in the vicinity of Big Stone and Traverse lakes, and down the Red River at various localities northward to a point below Winnipeg. Other groups were scattered along the Sheyenne and James rivers, on many of their tributaries, and about the shores of Devils Lake. Northward, they occur throughout much of southern Manitoba, especially in the Pembina River drainage, on the Assiniboine River, and notably on the Souris River above and below its junction with Antler Creek in the southwestern corner of the province. West of a line running from the former Wheeler Bridge through Wessington

[7] T. H. Lewis, "Mounds on the Red River of the North," *American Antiquarian*, Vol. VIII, No. 6 (1886), 369–71; C. Thomas, "Report on the Mound Explorations of the Bureau of Ethnology," Bureau of American Ethnology *Twelfth Annual Report* (1894), 35–39; Will, "A Resume of North Dakota Archeology," North Dakota Historical *Quarterly*, Vol. VII, Nos. 2 and 3 (1933), 154–57; Will, "An Unusual Group of Mounds in North Dakota," *American Anthropologist*, Vol. XXIII, No. 2 (1921), 175–79.

and Faulkton, South Dakota, thence along the margin of the Missouri Coteau, mounds are much less common and the groups are usually smaller. There are a few localities of occurrence along the Missouri, as we have already noted. West of the Missouri they have apparently not been reported; north of that stream in Saskatchewan, the Coteau may be thought of as defining their approximate limit on the south.

The mounds of this northern region are usually larger, more numerous, and probably more productive of archaeological materials than those south of the Niobrara in the Central Plains. They are found principally on the bluffs overlooking the stream valleys and on eminences near lakes or creeks, much less commonly on river terraces. The villages and camp sites in which the erstwhile builders of the mounds carried on their everyday activities remain for the most part undiscovered—or, if their locations are known, they have not been carefully investigated and their connections with the mounds established.

Such evidence as is available suggests that several kinds of structures are represented by these mounds, and that they may have

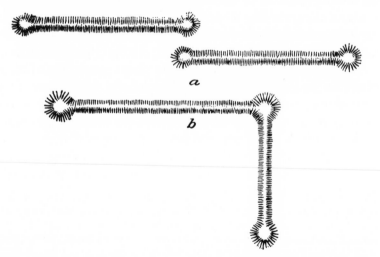

FIG. 14. *Linear mounds on Souris River, Manitoba.* (After Thomas, 1894).

been intended to serve more than one purpose. Most common are round-topped burial mounds of earth, or of earth and stones. These vary widely in size, ranging from small elevations fifteen or twenty feet in diameter and one foot or less high to large circular or oblong constructions sixty to ninety feet across and up to ten or twelve feet high. Sometimes they occur singly, but more often they are in groups numbering from two or three to fifty. According to one early account, there were more than forty mounds, in groups of four to ten each, on the hills within a few miles of old Fort Wadsworth, near the head of the Coteau des Prairies; and within ten miles of Sioux Falls, South Dakota, some 275 mounds were reported, including one group of about fifty.[8]

Linear or elongate mounds are much less common. They were a feature of some of the groups in the Souris-Antler and Devils Lake–Walsh County districts, and are known also from the Upper James River drainage in North Dakota.[9] Some were simple platform-like affairs two hundred feet or more long, twenty to thirty feet wide, and two feet or less high. Others were essentially low embankments running in straight lines for hundreds of feet, terminating sometimes in rounded expansions at one or both ends, or else connecting a large mound with one or more lesser satellite structures. One Walsh County embankment is said to have been over twenty-six hundred feet long. In some instances, the embankments with enlarged or mounded ends assumed two or more sides of a rectangle, or were arranged in echelon. Early-day observers, some of whom searched the linears in vain for graves, noted that these structures were not situated in defensible spots, and would have been of no value as fortifications.

The nature and origin of the mounds have whetted the curiosity of white men almost from the first days of permanent settlement here. As early as 1858, Professor Henry Youle Hind, in charge of the Assiniboine and Saskatchewan exploring expedition, observed

[8] A. J. Comfort, "Indian Mounds Near Fort Wadsworth, Dakota Territory," *Smithsonian Institution Annual Report for 1871* (1873), 389–98; C. Thomas, "Report on the Mound Explorations of the Bureau of Ethnology," *loc. cit.*, 38–39.
[9] H. W. Montgomery, "Remains of Prehistoric Man in the Dakotas," *American Anthropologist*, Vol. VIII, No. 4 (1906), 640–51.

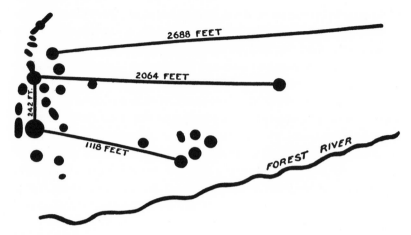

2688 FEET

2064 FEET

242 FT.

1118 FEET

FOREST RIVER

FIG. 15. *Mounds and connecting embankments, Walsh County, North Dakota.*

American Anthropologist

"a number of conical mounds, and the remains of an intrench-ment" on the Souris near the forty-ninth parallel. Informed by a half-blood that these marked "an old Mandan village," Hind opened one of the mounds and "penetrated six feet without find-ing anything to indicate that the mounds were the remains of Mandan lodges."[10] A few years later, in 1867, Gunn described the opening of a mound on Red River below Winnipeg, wherein sev-eral human skulls, an "earthen kettle," stone pipes, turtle-shell ornaments, and shell beads were found, and decayed oak timbers placed horizontally.[11]

Farther south, in the Dakotas, mound explorations seem to have begun in the vicinity of some of the army forts established after the Civil War. In 1871, for example, Surgeon A. I. Comfort[12] opened several mounds near Fort Wadsworth (later Sisseton). Most he regarded as sepulchral, since they contained human bones

[10] H. Y. Hind, *Northwest Territory. Reports of Progress,* 44.
[11] D. Gunn, "Indian Remains Near Red River Settlement, Hudson's Bay Ter-ritory," *Smithsonian Institution Annual Report for 1867* (1868), 399.
[12] Although his name has been persistently given as A. *J.* Comfort in archae-ological records for approximately eighty years, his middle name was Ivins.

and evidences of intense fires. Others had clay floors, but no signs of burning; and these he termed domiciliary. At about the same time, Cyrus Thomas of the Hayden Survey, aided by soldiers and Sioux scouts from a nearby military post, partially trenched a mound on Pipestone Creek two miles southeast of Jamestown. This, the largest of three mounds connected by low earth ridges, yielded the remains of several human skeletons, but no artifacts. Another mound in the vicinity was opened by one Captain H. G. Thomas, who found "two bushel bags full of bones," eight skulls, many shells, but little else. Thomas the entomologist hazarded no guesses about the builders of the mounds; but Thomas the army officer thought they were an offshoot of the Ohio mound builders who "deteriorated in this barren land" and were "so poor that a flint-headed weapon, a shell necklace, and a stone for grinding their food, were all their starving, surviving relatives could afford them on their sorrowful journey to the spirit land."[13]

These early and incidental probings into the mounds were followed in due course by more extended and sustained investigations; but again it must be observed that not all of this has been published. In the eastern portion of the Dakotas, mound distributions were mapped by the Hill-Lewis survey, but if any excavation was done, no published account seems to have come of it. In the summer of 1889, Reynolds visited a number of mounds in the eastern Dakotas and as far northwest as the Souris-Antler district, in the interests of the Bureau of American Ethnology; and he seems to have done a little test excavating. The most extended operations, however, were those by Montgomery in the early part of the nineteenth century, conducted partly with team and scraper, and reported in three papers between 1908 and 1912.[14] Much more meritorious and painstaking was the work of W. B. Nickerson,

13 Comfort, loc. cit.; C. Thomas, "Ancient Mounds of Dakota," Sixth Annual Report, U. S. Geological and Geographical Survey of the Territories . . . for the Year 1872 (1873), 655–58.
14 Montgomery, "Remains of Prehistoric Man in the Dakotas," loc. cit.; Montgomery, "Prehistoric Man in Manitoba and Saskatchewan," American Anthropologist, Vol. X, No. 1 (1908), 33–40; Montgomery, " 'Calf Mountain' Mound in Manitoba," American Anthropologist, Vol. XII, No. 1 (1910), 49–57.

who surveyed and excavated a number of mounds in southern Manitoba in 1912–14. Nickerson's field methods and recording were remarkably advanced for his time; and it is pleasant to record that the field report he compiled has recently been prepared for publication by Miss Katherine Capes of the National Museum of Canada.[15]

In summary, then, a great many Dakota and Manitoba mounds have been explored in one fashion or another, during the past eighty or ninety years. Unfortunately, much of this work was never published; and what has been published, except in the past decade or two,[16] provides a very incomplete picture of the situation as measured by present-day standards of archaeological reporting. It seems clear, however, that the great majority of the mounds were directly connected with disposal of the dead, and that the methods employed varied widely in details.

In or under most of the mounds which have been opened there were found one or more circular-to-oblong pits which contained the remains of one or several skeletons. Commonly, traces of decayed wood are found over these submound pits, indicating that they were originally covered with poles, logs, or slabs. Many of the individuals were buried in the flesh, the bodies usually being more or less doubled up, or flexed, and the bones lying in proper anatomical relationship. Others were as certainly secondary burials, interment in or under the mound having been preceded by exposure of the corpse until the softer tissues had disappeared, after which the bones were gathered up for final deposition underground. Some graves have yielded the dismembered parts of many skeletons, which suggests that the members of the community concerned may have buried only at intervals. In some mounds, no pits or traces of wood coverings were reported, and there were

[15] K. Capes, "The W. B. Nickerson Survey and Excavations, 1912–1915, of Southern Manitoba Mounds Region," unpublished manuscript in the National Museum of Canada.

[16] See, for example, G. W. Hewes, "Burial Mounds in the Baldhill Area, North Dakota," *American Antiquity*, Vol. XIV, No. 4, Pt. 1 (April, 1949), 322–28; R. S. MacNeish, "An Introduction to the Archaeology of Southeast Manitoba," National Museum of Canada *Bulletin 157*, Anthropological Series No. 44 (1958).

only broken bones scattered through the mound fill. An especially interesting feature of some of the Manitoba mounds opened by Montgomery is the prominence given the bison, as shown by the finding of complete skeletons of this animal, and also of skulls in direct and recurrent association with the grave pits.

Although Thomas' 1871 explorations in a mound-embankment complex near Jamestown revealed nothing of consequence in the embankment, it should be noted that Nickerson found burials beneath such an embankment and in both terminal mounds at the Sims Mound near Snowflake in the Pembina drainage of southern Manitoba. Those beneath the embankment were in a bottle-shaped pit dug five and one-half feet below the sod line. Here, originally "seated about the edge of the pit, with legs extended into the pit bottom," were the remains of a number of individuals of all ages. There were traces of a pole and boulder covering in the pit, as well as articulated buffalo vertebrae which probably represented a meat offering made at the time of burial.

Associated with many of these mound burials were artifacts of various kinds. They include articles of pottery, stone, bone, shell, and other materials. Though never present in quantity, they are of much significance for the light they throw on the relationships of the builders of these mounds.

Of particular interest are the small mortuary vessels of pottery which have been found in widely scattered localities in the Dakotas and Manitoba. These are small pots, globular in shape, with a constricted neck and an outflaring rim that may have four slightly-raised points equally spaced around its circumference. Usually, they are decorated with a groove that starts at the bottom and spirals upward around and around the body. Less commonly, there are vertical or horizontal lines, or alternating blocks of such lines. Vessels or fragments with this spiral grooving have been found in mounds near Big Stone Lake, near Jamestown, North Dakota, around Devils Lake, in the Souris district, and as far to the northwest as Kyle, Saskatchewan, far beyond the principal area of occurrence of mounds in the Northeastern Periphery. So far as I can determine, however, no similar pieces have been found in the village and camp sites of the region, and it may be suggested that the pottery was made primarily for mortuary use.

Among the non-pottery materials present, there are occasional items of chipped stone, such as arrow points, spearheads, and knives. Ground and polished stone includes tubular catlinite pipes, some slender and thin-walled, others heavier and shaped like a modern cigar holder; small catlinite tablets incised with animal designs; and occasional disks and other objects.

Articles of bone include sturdy spear points, or "harpoons," barbed along one edge; whistles with triangular openings; and small tubes that may have been beads. Thinly scraped bone or antler plates, curved, incised, and provided with edge perforations, have been identified variously as armlets, anklets, or head ornaments. At Calf Mountain Mound, Montgomery found one of these "in position around the radius and ulna of the forearm," suggesting the manner of use in that instance, at any rate. Perforated antler tines, sometimes knobbed at the tip, possibly represent handles for tools of unknown use, or perhaps were intended for insertion of beaver incisors.

Shell is represented chiefly by small pieces apparently intended for adornment of the person or costume: flat, washer-like objects with a large center opening; thick, cylindrical beads fashioned from the columella of a marine shell; Marginella shells pierced for stringing; and small, tubular or disc-shaped beads. There are also occasional spoonlike pieces, with a short extension at one side and edge notches, and larger circular gorgets with two holes for suspension.

Iron, glass beads, or other items showing contact with white men are not normally found in these mounds, except where associated with later burials made intrusively into the structures. There is evidence, though, that the natives were acquainted with copper. In one of the Souris mounds, Montgomery found a skull "having a flat band of native copper around it." Other observers have reported scraps or small sheets of this material, as well as occasional beads made by rolling strips of metal into simple tubes.

Little of a perishable nature seems to have survived, though there is occasional mention of beaver fur, leather scraps, or wooden objects that appear to have been shaped by man. A hint of recency for the mounds is given in the repeated finding of birch bark with the burials, usually as scraps or small rolls, but also in the form of sewn parts of baskets or containers.

There is a special interest to the large marine shell gorgets that have turned up in a number of widely separated localities. The circumstances of their discovery are not always matters of record; but some were certainly taken from burial mounds. Montgomery reported two from Manitoba, including one from Calf Mountain; and additional examples have recently been described by Howard from North Dakota.[17] Most are pear-shaped in outline, from six to eight inches long and have the convex surface fashioned into the representation of a human face. Near the broad end two holes represent the eyes, with the nose in low relief indicated between. Around the eyes are incised circles, forked designs, or zigzag lines that run downward. Some of these pieces are virtually identical with mask gorgets from Ohio, Tennessee, and elsewhere in the Ohio Valley; and all represent a late prehistoric ceremonially inspired art style that once flourished over much of the southeastern United States. The same may be said of the circular shell gorget found by Montgomery at Calf Mountain which has a spider-like design on the reverse, and also of the scalloped Doerr gorget with a conventionalized rattlesnake from Logan County, North Dakota. None of these striking objects has yet been found, as far as I know, in the village sites of the Middle Missouri, with possible exception of a still undescribed gorget said to have been found near Fort Bennett.

Several of the North Dakota mask gorgets bear incised designs on their reverse, including the horse, the elk, and the bear. These are done in a style similar to that on the incised catlinite tablet found by Montgomery in the Devils Lake district, and were presumably made by natives to whom these gorgets were a recognized part of their culture. Since the horse was unknown on the

[17] J. H. Howard, "The Southern Cult in the Northern Plains," *American Antiquity*, Vol. XIX, No. 2 (October, 1953), 130–38.

eastern Dakota plains before 1725–50, it would appear probable that some of these gorgets were still in use at a comparatively late date and, conceivably, might even have been seen by some of the earliest whites in the region.

Although it can probably be concluded safely that most of the mounds were built for burial of the dead, the time of their construction and the identity of their builders remain uncertain. None has yet been dated by tree rings, or radiocarbon, or other "absolute" method. The general absence of iron, brass, and glass beads signifies that the burials beneath the mounds were placed there before contacts with white men had been established; that is, before A.D. 1650–1700. Certain features of the burials, such as use of log coverings, are remindful of practices in early burial mounds of the Ohio Valley; but it is entirely possible that early customs survived into much later periods among mound-burying people in a peripheral area such as this was. A few items—birch-bark containers, catlinite, and shell mask gorgets—seemingly point to a late period, but none of these can give us a very precise dating. In view of the varied character of the mounds, of the burials in them, and of the associated artifacts from locality to locality, it may be suspected that mound-building was probably carried on for a period of some length. Quite possibly some of the structures were already old and their origin forgotten when others were being erected.

As to the people who built them, we can say little more than that they were apparently quite closely related to prehistoric residents of the Minnesota region. None of the mounds can be linked with any of the Village Indians whose earth lodges stood on the upper James and Sheyenne rivers in the eighteenth century, and whose archaeological remains resemble much more closely those of the Mandans, Hidatsas, and Arikaras of the Middle Missouri. There is nothing to show that any of these tribes normally buried their dead in or under mounds.

It has long been suspected that the spread of mound-building peoples into the eastern Dakota plains was perhaps correlated with the diffusion of Siouan tribes from the Upper Mississippi region.

In Manitoba, some of the mounds are believed to be directly associated with nearby village sites wherein the pottery and other remains show strong resemblances to the Blackduck focus of northern Minnesota. This, in turn, has been tentatively, but plausibly, attributed to the Assiniboines, who, as recently as 1775, were burying their dead in dug pits covered with logs over which the earth was then heaped.[18] At least one mound in southern Manitoba has yielded a copper piece said to be of European origin; and the fact that this locality was Assiniboine in early white-contact times lends some support to the identification.[19] Moreover, the village and camp sites thus regarded as probably Assiniboine are believed to date back some centuries before arrival of the whites; and this would presumably cover the span of time in which the Assiniboines were moving from the Minnesota woodlands westward and northward into the prairie-park belt and on to the plains.

It does not necessarily follow, however, that all mounds in the Northeastern Periphery must be laid at the door of the Assiniboines, even if some can be so explained. The placing of bison skulls with the dead appears to have been practiced not only by the Assiniboines, but also by other historic Siouan tribes of the upper Missouri and Northern Plains region. Side by side with such widespread practices as log covers on submound burial pits and the placing of spirally incised pots with the dead, there are wide variations in many details of mound construction and furnishings. As long ago as 1908, for example, Montgomery noted in his Souris explorations that spirally grooved pottery and catlinite pipes were absent from burials in the mounds associated with linear embankments, though they occurred repeatedly in nearby mounds which lacked embankments. How consistently these and other differences would stand up under critical re-exam-

18 C. Vickers and Ralph Bird, "A Copper Trade Object from the Headwaters Lakes Aspect in Manitoba," *American Antiquity*, Vol. 15, No. 2 (1949), 157–60; MacNeish, "The Stott Mound and Village, Near Brandon, Manitoba," *Annual Report*, National Museum of Canada, 1952–53, *Bulletin 132* (1954), 45–52.

19 Vickers, "Burial Traits of the Headwaters Lakes Aspect in Manitoba," *American Antiquity*, Vol. XIII, No. 2 (1947), 109–14.

ination of the evidence today or under further carefully controlled field investigations, it is impossible to say. And, in any case, it is exceedingly difficult to see how we could determine whether they reflect tribal, cultural, or time differences, or are to be attributed to other factors. Since the same group of mounds, and sometimes even the same mound, may exhibit widely varying types of burials, it is evident that the people responsible for them were by no means bound to follow a rigidly set procedure, but could exercise some flexibility of choice in the disposal of their dead.

In addition to the suggested Blackduck (Assiniboine) connections in Manitoba, there are also interesting similarities between some of the Dakota mound materials and another prehistoric mound-building culture in northwestern Minnesota. This is the Red River aspect of the archaeologist, perhaps more familiarly known through the Arvilla Gravel Pit culture or the Arvilla focus.[20] Practically all known sites occur on the gravel beaches marking the east and west shorelines of glacial Lake Agassiz, now the Red River Valley. Although most of the investigations to date have been on the Minnesota side of the valley, the first site discovered was near Arvilla, in eastern North Dakota.[21]

Discovered in 1908 during gravel-quarrying operations for the Great Northern Railway, the site has been entirely destroyed and little detailed information survives. It is reported to have included approximately 100 graves strung in an irregular line fifteen hundred feet long atop a gravel ridge, apparently without any trace of mounds. The grave pits averaged about eight feet in diameter, eight feet in depth, and were filled with black humus that set them off sharply from the light-colored gravel into which they had been dug. Most of the pits were destroyed by steam shovel, and their contents scattered and lost. Of the few that were dug by hand, each contained from four to eight human skeletons, placed in "flexed upright sitting position all facing toward the center of the grave." It was the belief of the diggers that all burials in

[20] L. A. Wilford, "A Revised Classification of the Prehistoric Cultures of Minnesota," *American Antiquity*, Vol. XXI, No. 2 (1955), 137–38.
[21] A. E. Jenks, "The Problem of the Culture from the Arvilla Gravel Pit," *American Anthropologist*, new ser., Vol. XXXIV, No. 3 (1932), 455–66.

each grave had been made at the same time, and that there was no evidence of reopening of the pits to deposit additional bodies later. The few artifacts said to have come from the burials included two heavy bone spear points or "harpoons," strongly barbed along one edge; a triangular toothed ivory knife; an elk cannon-bone flesher with a toothed blade; several thick cylindrical marine-shell beads; and a grooved sandstone smoothing block.

The Minnesota sites are nearly all mounds, either circular and varying widely in height and diameter, or else low-rectangular structures from one hundred to two hundred feet long, fifteen to twenty-five feet wide, and not more than one foot high. Beneath the mounds are found one or more deep pits, in which are flexed or, less commonly, extended burials. Occasionally the pits contain disorderly masses of disarticulated bones. Artifacts are not uncommon in these burials; and they include pottery, clay pipes, chipped- and ground-stone objects, and a wide range of artifacts in bone, antler, teeth, and shell.

Among these grave offerings, there are a number of items which particularly recall the eastern Dakota mound materials. Thus, in bone, there are flat, unilaterally-barbed spear points or "harpoons," bird bone whistles, and edge-perforated arm bands; in antler, perforated tine sections, probably designed for insertion of beaver-teeth chisels; in shell, thick cylindrical marine-shell beads, flat, washer-like ornaments, trapezoidal and other pendants, and other forms. There are also objects of native copper, though these are not common.

Unfortunately, as far as may be judged from the readily available surveys of Minnesota archaeology, most of these items are listed for both Blackduck and Arvilla. The principal distinction, aside from pottery differences which are of little help in the classification of Dakota mounds, seems to be that Arvilla (Red River aspect) is "the richest of all Minnesota aspects in objects of bone, antler, teeth, and shell."[22] Both Blackduck and Arvilla burials yield some small pottery vessels; those in Blackduck mounds differ from

[22] Wilford, "A Tentative Classification of the Prehistoric Cultures of Minnesota," *American Antiquity*, Vol. VI, No. 3 (1941), 243–46.

the pieces found in the nearby associated village sites; and in neither have spirally grooved vessels, like those in the Dakota mounds, been found. To the nonspecialist who has not viewed the entire assemblage on which the Blackduck and Arvilla complexes have been set up, it appears that the distinctions between the two are not marked, or else that a particular site can be safely assigned to one or the other only on the basis of much larger quantities of material and data than are usually available from the Dakota mounds.

The problem of the Dakota mounds is still a challenging and important one. That all, or even a significant proportion, of the structures will ever be acceptably identified with a historic tribe or its forebears is perhaps expecting too much. Failing this, it is still highly desirable that the relationships of the mounds in one locality or of one type to those in other localities or of other types be clearly formulated, so that a measure of order can be brought into the present tangle. Systematic field work of the sort done in recent years under the river basin salvage program, but on a sustained and continuing basis, is urgently needed. So also is a thoroughgoing analysis of previous work, including re-examination of the scattered notes and collections resulting therefrom. This would undoubtedly be a frustrating and difficult task. Many of the mounds were dug without any sense of scientific problem, and the specimens collected have been irretrievably lost. With the notable exception of the astonishingly meticulous records kept by Nickerson in his southern Manitoba investigations, now being readied for publication by Katherine Capes, little or none of the excavating done before 1930 can be characterized as truly systematic or scientific. I believe, however, that such a study should be tried; a dedicated and persevering scholar would surely earn the lasting gratitude of his colleagues and of a host of interested nonprofessionals by bringing such a work to fruition.

Boulder outlines are, or were, another interesting feature of the region. T. H. Lewis wrote in 1886 that they occurred from southern Iowa and Nebraska northward to Manitoba, and from the Mississippi through the Dakotas to Montana.[23] Over much of this

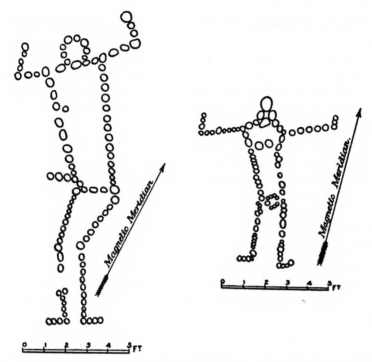

FIG. 16. *Boulder outlines on Punished Woman's Hill, Coddington County, South Dakota.*

American Anthropologist

great tract, agricultural development has long since effaced them; but interesting examples are still to be seen in the eastern Dakotas. They were said to have been particularly plentiful in the Ree and Wessington hills and the intermediate district.

The method of construction was simple. From the boulder-strewn slopes and nearby hilltops, the natives gathered up stones of suitable size and shape and arranged them upon the ground in order to outline whatever geometric form or other figure they had in mind. Circles seem to have been by far the most common, with

[23] Lewis, "Stone Monuments in Southern Dakota," *American Anthropologist*, Vol. II, No. 2 (1889), 159–64; Lewis, "Bowlder Outline Figures in the Dakotas, Surveyed in the Summer of 1890," *American Anthropologist*, Vol. IV, No. 1 (1891), 19–24.

rectangles, parallelograms, animal and human figures of less frequent occurrence.

Among the circular outlines, the great majority were of the simple sort called tipi rings, the stones presumably having been used to hold down the edges of the tipi covers. These seem to have occurred usually without any mounds; and the type extends, of course, far beyond the mound area. Others were more complex. Some consisted of several rows of closely laid stones, pavement fashion, with an unpaved area inside; or they had openings, or smaller circles attached at one side, or perhaps short single rows of stones extending outward in several directions from the main circle. In other examples, circles were bisected, quartered, or otherwise divided; and these, too, were constructed with and without openings. Commonly, these outlines occurred in groups, or were associated with cairns, mounds, or other features.

Some of the effigies have been described, and are more or less well known. Lewis describes two human figures on Punished

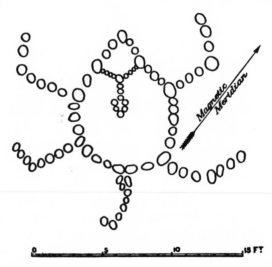

Fig. 17. *Boulder outline on Snake Butte, Hughes County, South Dakota.*

American Anthropologist

Woman's Hill, in northeastern Coddington County, South Dakota. One figure, 13 ½ feet long and made of 104 boulders, he
identifies as a male with upraised arms; the other is a female, 8 feet

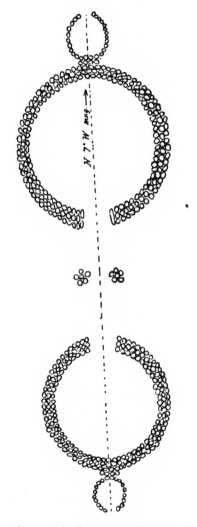

FIG. 18. *Boulder enclosures in Stutsman County, North Dakota.*

American Anthropologist

long and made of 92 boulders. From the first of these two a boulder trail ran toward a stone cairn; and nearby were other cairns and another boulder trail. On a lofty knob north of Wessington, known as Turtle Peak, were the outlines of a 15-foot woman and an 18-foot turtle, again with other outlines scattered nearby. One of the largest boulder effigies is on Medicine Butte northeast of Pierre. Here two rows of boulders delineate a snake measuring 360 feet along the undulations and made up of 825 boulders. Many tipi circles, a few squares, some other outlines, and cairns are scattered over the hilltop. Still another example is the turtle outline and other figures—squares, circles, parallelograms included—on Snake Butte north of Pierre. In one of the circles, digging disclosed ashes at the center, but none of the other circles here or at Medicine Butte showed such traces.

The age of the boulder outlines and effigies, as well as the identity of their creators, has not been established. There are no associated artifacts that would provide a clue to their builders or users. The Dakota identified the simple circles in groups as tipi rings, for which no great antiquity is necessarily involved; and there is good reason to accept this as valid. Some of the historic Indians, as Lewis noted long ago, "have a way of accounting for these outline figures"; but he was convinced that they were very ancient and long

FIG. 19. *Boulder outline in Stutsman County, North Dakota.*

American Anthropologist

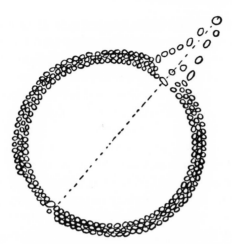

FIG. 20. *Boulder outline in Jerauld County, South Dakota.*

American Anthropologist

antedated the arrival in the region of the Dakota tribes. They may
have originated at different times and for various purposes. Other
than Indian tradition or legend, there seems to be nothing that
would convincingly link them with any known historic tribe of
the area.

Still another type of remains, and one which seems certainly to
represent the work of recent Indians, includes the bone paths and
pavements that formerly existed in the James River drainage.[24]
On the Elm River near present Westport, South Dakota, two or
three mounds were said to have been connected by pathways
made of bison leg bones. One such path, 500 paces long, had 492
counted bones in 50 measured feet, "each bone being broken
apart in the middle, evidently to obtain the marrow. The bones
in the pathway were only partially buried in the ground, and the
glistening white line could be distinctly seen for 2 or 3 miles . . . ."
Another report, possibly referring to the same location, states that
the bones were set up in the ground "like stakes."

[24] W. McAdams, "Exploration of Apparent Recent Mounds in Dacotah,"
American Antiquarian, Vol. VIII, No. 3 (1886), 156–58; J. E. Todd, "Boulder
Mosaics in Dakota," *American Naturalist*, Vol. XX, No. 1 (1886), 1–4.

Farther down the valley, in a larger group of mounds, near Ordway, four mounds were thus connected with bone paths. Tests in some of the mounds disclosed near the center of each, at the base, a "mass of human bones, both male and female . . . in a good state of preservation . . . so close together and somewhat in confusion that I was inclined to believe they might have been denuded of flesh before burial . . . ." There were no signs of metal or glass in any of these mounds; and it is probably safe to suppose that the burial and covering mounds antedated the bone paths.

Some eighty miles northwest of old Fort Wadsworth, on the road to Fort Stevenson, Comfort described a conical hill which was "paved with bones of a certain kind obtained from the legs of buffaloes. Walks leading in different directions to the distance of several hundred feet are paved with the same bones placed end to end and two courses in width." The hill was used as a lookout by the Cheyennes, and was known to the Dakotas as Bone Hill. This feature was described briefly in 1839 by Nicollet, who says it was "called by the voyageurs *Butte-aux-Os,* (or bone hillock, bone hill), in consequence of a large heap of bones of animals that the Indians have gathered up and arranged in a certain order." The *Butte-aux-Os* is shown on Major General G. K. Warren's 1867 map of Nebraska and Dakota, and portions of the states and territories bordering thereon.[25]

As we have already noted, the mounds of the eastern Dakotas continue northward beyond the forty-ninth parallel into southern Manitoba, to and beyond the Assiniboine River. There are also village and camp sites in the Manitoba region, including several that contain a succession of occupation levels running back several thousand years into the past. Recent excavations, combined with a critical reanalysis of earlier explorations, have given us a good beginning toward the understanding of the prehistory of the region.[26]

No sites assignable to a Paleo-Indian period have been found.

[25] Comfort, *loc. cit.,* 398.

[26] Vickers, "Archeology in the Rock and Pelican Lake Area of South-Central Manitoba," *American Antiquity,* Vol. XI, No. 2 (1945), 88–94; MacNeish, "An Introduction to the Archaeology of Southeast Manitoba," *loc. cit.*

That the early big-game hunters were probably present, however, is indicated by surface finds of projectile points identified with the Folsom, Plainview, Angostura, Scottsbluff, and Eden types. These finds have been made mainly west of the Red River Valley. They suggest the eventual discovery of camp or kill sites belonging to the hunters of extinct forms of bison and other large game.

The principal stratified sites from which carefully controlled data are available are Lockport, on the east bank of Red River, ten miles below Winnipeg, and Cemetery Point, at the mouth of Whiteshell River, some seventy miles east and north of Winnipeg. Neither can be considered, at present, a Plains location; but there is some reason to suppose they may once have been in a grassland setting. Lockport lies near the eastern edge of the aspen park belt, and Cemetery Point is in the coniferous forest.

The earliest levels at both sites represent the camps of hunting peoples. Chipped-stone artifacts predominate, and they consist mainly of projectile points, cutting implements, large choppers, and scrapers—in other words, the tools for killing game, dressing it, and preparing the meat and hides for human use. Projectile points include a lanceolate form with a concave or indented base, remindful of the McKean point of Wyoming. Later, corner- and side-notched forms were added. The prevalence of bison bone in the camp refuse suggests that the area may have been a grassland when these people occupied the sites. A few fishbones were found at Lockport; and from Cemetery Point came a large moose (?) antler spearhead, barbed along one edge, that may have been used for spearing large fish such as sturgeon. These levels have been tentatively dated at 5,000 to 2,500 years ago. They include two subdivisions, designated by archaeologists as the Whiteshell focus (estimated 5,000–3,500 years ago) and the Larter focus (estimated 3,500–2,500 years ago). Materials closely similar to those from Whiteshell have been found also at Rock Lake, in the Pembina drainage.

In a later level, at Lockport, dated tentatively at about 2,500–1,500 years ago, the refuse includes bones of birds and of forest animals (elk, hare, and deer), mixed with those of fish and bison.

235

Chipped stone includes numerous thin, retouched flakes, blade fragments, and corner-notched dart or spear points; and some of the stone used is the brown chalcedony like that from the Knife River drainage of North Dakota. Pottery appears for the first time at this level. The usual vessel form seems to have been more or less coconut-shaped or vertically elongated. Surfaces were generally plain, but a few bear the marks of a cord-wrapped paddle. Decoration was achieved by impressing into the soft clay a toothed implement or a thin-edged tool wrapped with cords, or by use of a pointed stylus to produce a series of overlapping punctates. The nature of the material used for cordage is unknown; but the presence of twisted string perhaps permits the inference that it was also used for bags and perhaps other woven items. Termed the Anderson focus, these materials are thought to correspond in time to the Hopewellian (Middle Woodland) period of the eastern United States.

Out of the Anderson focus presumably developed the next stage, or Nutimik focus, assigned to the period 1,500–1,000 years ago. Fishbones are plentiful; and since the pottery sometimes shows net imprints, it is possible that nets were also used in taking fish. Bison bones are outnumbered by those of deer, elk, beaver, bear, and other forms; and musselshells suggest another food source. The pottery and stone tools differ from earlier forms mainly in details; and bone awls appear. There are strong resemblances to materials excavated along Rock Lake, but the distribution of the culture is not very well known as yet.

Overlying the Nutimik materials and probably dating within the last one thousand years are the remains designated as the Manitoba focus. These evidently have a strong distribution toward the southwest, having been recognized at the Stott site near Brandon, in the upper levels of the Avery site on Rock Lake, and elsewhere. At Lockport, the dominant bone refuse is fish, suggesting that this was a fishing station; and unilaterally barbed spearheads are present. Farther west, bison bones predominate and an economy oriented toward big-game hunting is indicated. Small triangular and sidenotched points indicate the use of the bow and arrow; and there are scrapers, cutting tools, and other tools useful in a hunting culture. Bone awls and whistles are present, as are scrapers made from leg bones of the deer, with rounded ends. Steatite tubes that were possibly pipes, and full-grooved mauls occur; and Knife River chalcedony was among the materials used in fashioning chipped-stone objects. The pottery was characteristically decorated about the rim with a cord-wound edged tool or with deep, circular punch marks. Many of the burial mounds west of Red River and south of the Assiniboine are regarded as evidence of the mortuary complex of the Manitoba focus. The pottery shows strong resemblances to that of the Blackduck focus in northern Minnesota, and the material is believed to be assignable, at least in large part, to the Assiniboines. At Lockport, the remains are beneath silt layers thought to represent a wet period between A.D. 1350 and 1400. Thus, if correctly identified with the Assiniboines, this would imply that people representing this group were spread throughout southern Manitoba long before the seventeenth century, which is generally regarded by ethnologists as the time of their push from Minnesota into Canada.[27]

The last archaeological manifestation recognized in the Lower Red River region is the Selkirk focus. This is absent from south central and southwestern Manitoba, but appears to have a wide distribution in northern Manitoba and northern Saskatchewan. The sites occur along waterways, and the deposits are usually thin. Hunting and fishing are indicated. The pottery includes many pieces treated with a fabric-wrapped tool. The materials show many similarities to the Manitoba focus, but lack cylindrical marine-shell beads, bird-bone whistles, and tubular pipes; and on the other hand include scapula hoes or shovels, antler celts, storage pits, large, triangular lance heads, and other items not known from Manitoba focus sites. MacNeish suggests that the Selkirk focus represents the remains of the Cree, whose habitat long bordered that of the Assiniboines on the north.

No recent investigations have been made on the mounds of the

[27] MacNeish, "An Introduction to the Archaeology of Southeast Manitoba," *loc. cit.*, 53, 64, 83.

Souris-Antler district in southwestern Manitoba; but they have been collectively designated as the Melita focus. That they, like those around Devils Lake and the burials at Arvilla, are somehow related to the Blackduck and Manitoba focus complexes, is generally recognized. The exact nature of that relationship, however, must await further research.

As far as present evidence goes, the mounds of the Northeastern Periphery and the village or camp sites thought to be associated with some of them, represent entirely the remains of people who lived by hunting, fishing, and gathering. In none of the archaeological excavations yet made has any indication of corn been found, or any indirect evidence that it may have been grown. Still, the people of the early historic circular-house villages in the Sheyenne and Upper James river valleys must have been, in considerable degree, cultivators of the soil and they thus offer an argument in favor of the practicability of a community life based partly on corn-growing.

The region lies, of course, beyond what is generally considered the safe limit of aboriginal agriculture with native American food plants.[28] At the same time, we should not overlook the fact that corn has been grown by Indians on the Fort Totten and Turtle Mountain reservations in North Dakota, by the Assiniboines of the Wood Mountain and Pipestone reserves in Canada, and elsewhere in these northern sections. Moreover, in September, 1857, Dr. Hector and Captain Palliser reported that Indian corn ("which will not succeed in England or Ireland") was ripening in the mission garden at Qu'Appelle Lakes;[29] and in the following year, Professor Hind again mentions Indian corn at Qu'Appelle Lakes and also at Fort à la Corne, below the junction of the North and South Saskatchewan rivers. At Nepoween Mission, across the river from Fort à la Corne, Hind saw more Indian corn, "from

[28] Will, "Indian Agriculture at its Northern Limits in the Great Plains Region of North America," *loc. cit.;* Kroeber, "Cultural and Natural Areas of Native North America," *loc. cit.,* 212.

[29] J. Palliser, *The Journals, Detailed Reports, and Observations Relative to Captain Palliser's Exploration of a Portion of British North America, 1857–1860,* 13, 51.

PLATE XVII. Some Middle Missouri pottery vessels. Arikara domestic (*Upper left*) and mortuary (*Upper right*) pottery, about A.D. 1750–
1800; *Middle row:* Bennett focus incised vessels, sixteenth or seventeenth century; *Bottom:* Thomas Riggs focus vessel, about A.D. 1300.

PLATE XVIII. Burial mounds of the Northeastern Periphery and Middle Missouri. (River Basin Surveys, Smithsonian Institution). *Upper:* Burial mound near Devils Lake, North Dakota. *Lower:* Disarticulated or bundle burials in grave pit beneath mound, with traces of log cover visible on edges of pit; Wheeler Bottom, South Dakota.

PLATE XIX. Four pottery vessels and incised catlinite tablet from burial mounds of the Northeastern Periphery. (Royal Ontario Museum and Smithsonian Institution).

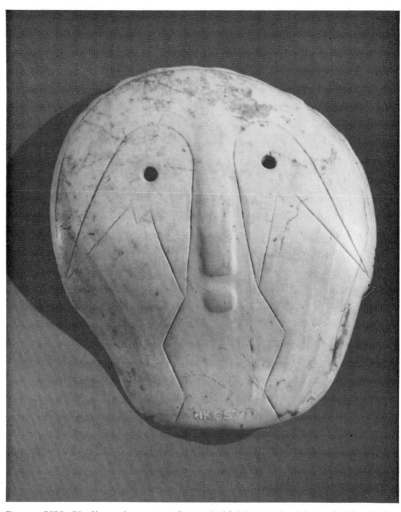

PLATE XX. Shell mask gorget from Calf Mountain Mound, Manitoba. (Royal Ontario Museum).

PLATE XXI. Miscellaneous artifacts from the plains. *Upper:* Five prehistoric pipes from Nebraska. *Lower left:* Prehistoric bone or antler bowguard from Nebraska. *Lower right:* Projectile point and tubular stone pipes from burial mounds of the Northeastern Periphery. (Nebraska State Historical Society and Smithsonian Institution).

PLATE XXII. *Upper:* Excavating a Middle Prehistoric camp site in Boysen Reservoir area, Wyoming. (River Basin Surveys, Smithsonian Institution). *Lower:* Stone tipi rings on the Marias River uplands near head of Tiber Reservoir, Montana. (River Basin Surveys, Smithsonian Institution).

PLATE XXIII. *Upper:* Petroglyphs in Boysen Reservoir, Fremont County, Wyoming. (River Basin Surveys, Smithsonian Institution). *Lower:* Ridges of stone refuse beside aboriginal quartzite quarry pits on Flint Hill near head of Angostura Reservoir, South Dakota. (River Basin Surveys, Smithsonian Institution).

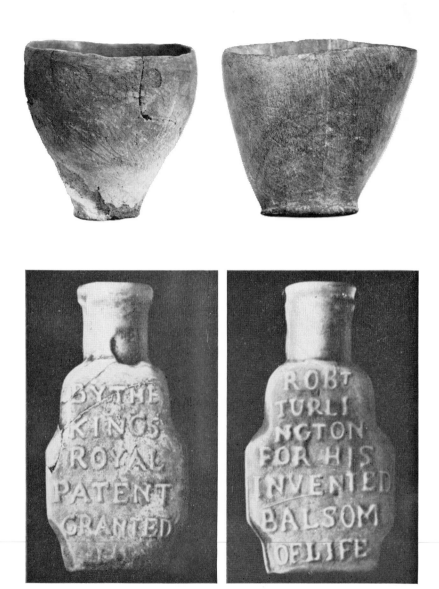

PLATE XXIV. *Upper:* Flat-bottomed vessels from northwestern Wyoming. (Smithsonian Institution). *Left,* clay pottery from Goff Creek, Park County, Wyoming. *Right,* soapstone vessel from Yellowstone National Park. *Lower:* Turlington's Balsam of Life bottle from Fort Atkinson trading post, North Dakota.

seed grown on the spot last year." It was Hind's belief that Indian corn and melons in the valley of Lake Winnipeg "would ripen with certainty, if ordinary care is taken in selecting soil and in planting seed."[30]

From this, it would appear that as a supplement to a native hunting-gathering economy, it would perhaps have been feasible to grow corn in favored spots throughout portions of the Dakota-Manitoba mound area in prehistoric times. It is possible, of course, that the people who spread from Minnesota into North Dakota and Manitoba and there raised mounds over their dead, were not "long and deeply addicted' to corn-growing, as were the Village Indians who resided for centuries in the Middle Missouri Valley. It would be interesting to know, nevertheless, whether cultivation of corn was ever tried by these prehistoric prairie dwellers beyond the Knife River Hidatsa villages that represented the northernmost Indian farming communities since white contacts began.

[30] Hind, *op. cit.*, 34, 49, 127.

CHAPTER EIGHT

THE NORTHWESTERN PLAINS

BEYOND THE MISSOURI, in the western Dakotas, Wyoming, Montana, and northward, are the Northwestern Plains. They include, south of the forty-ninth parallel, the drainage basins of the Yellowstone and the Upper Missouri, as well as much of the North Platte drainage. Beyond the International Boundary, they sweep northward for another 150 miles to or a little beyond the fifty-second parallel, taking in most of the Palliser Triangle and the drainage of the South Saskatchewan. They terminate on the west where the short grass reaches the pine-clad slopes of the Rocky Mountains, except in Wyoming. Here, for present purposes, they extend to the Continental Divide, and include the Bighorn, Wind River, Laramie, and other basins partially enclosed by the easternmost ranges of the Rockies.[1]

The region includes some of the most arid lands in the entire Great Plains. Only in its easternmost portions, around the northern edge, along the front of the Rockies, and on some of the isolated mountain masses, does the annual precipitation normally exceed fifteen inches. Along the International Boundary, the average is usually ten inches or less; and in the Bighorn basin, the figure drops to six inches.

The native vegetation is dominated by blue grama and other

[1] W. Mulloy, "A Preliminary Historical Outline for the Northwestern Plains," University of Wyoming *Publications*, Vol. XXII, Nos. 1 and 2 (1958), 8–21; W. A. Mackintosh, "Prairie Settlement: The Geographical Setting," *Canadian Frontiers of Settlement*, Vol. I (1934), 89–135 and Fig. 23; W. G. Kendrew and B. W. Currie, *The Climate of Central Canada*, 149–72 and Figs. 1 and 3.

short grasses. Elevated tracts, like the Black Hills and the Cypress Hills, that rise two thousand feet or more above the surrounding plains, are well forested and often deeply grassed. Large areas in Wyoming and Montana, as well as extensive sandy stretches along the South Saskatchewan, are covered with sage and other desert shrubs. Particularly is this true of central Wyoming, where the mountain barrier along the west is interrupted by a series of inter-connected basins collectively known as the Wyoming Basin. Here, many thousands of acres east of the Continental Divide have been taken over by sagebrush, which has pushed from the west far into the plains grassland along the Yellowstone, Big Horn, and North Platte drainages. The typical landscape in these sections is much more reminiscent of the Great Basin than of the Great Plains. It is evident that through the great natural gateway that centers about historic South Pass, men and animals, like the natural vegetation, have passed back and forth between the Great Basin and the Great Plains for some thousands of years.

The low rainfall and a short growing season make this a region in which an agricultural economy based on maize or other native American domesticates was not possible. Even today, a high pro-portion of the land is devoted to stock-raising, and agriculture is practiced only in favored spots or with the aid of irrigation.

In historic times, as during the nineteenth century, the North-western Plains were the home of a number of tribes whose liveli-hood was derived principally from the chase. North of the Mis-souri, in western Montana and ranging to the Bow and Red Deer valleys, were the Blackfeet. Farther east, where the short grass merges into the park belt in Saskatchewan, were the Plains Crees, whose hunting forays along the South Saskatchewan frequently brought them into conflict with the Blackfeet. To the south were the Gros Ventres of the Missouri, a branch of the Arapaho, and the Assiniboin, the latter ranging between the Missouri and Qu'Appelle rivers. In the Yellowstone basin were the Crow, and to the east and south, the Teton Dakota. Around the Black Hills and southward through eastern Wyoming and western Nebraska, were the Arapahoes and Cheyennes. The Shoshones occupied the

Wind River and other basins in west central Wyoming. Other groups from the west occasionally hunted along the eastern front of the Rockies, but usually by sufferance or in defiance of one or another of the tribes named above.

The way of life followed by these peoples is so well known that we need only outline it briefly here. Generally considered the "typical" Plains tribes, all were nomadic in the sense that they could move readily from place to place without loss of homes or other belongings. All possessed horses, made frequent or exclusive use of the skin tipi, the travois, and the parfleche, and were skilled in skin-working. During the spring, summer, and fall, they ranged widely over the Plains, transporting themselves and their baggage by horse and dog, sustaining themselves on the flesh of the bison, and drying large quantities of meat for winter use. Hunting practices included such co-operative devices as the surround, the pound, and the use of falls or "jumps." With the approach of cold weather, they retired to the protection of wooded valley bottoms, or to broken, hilly, or mountainous localities where shelter, wood, water, and forage for their horses were available. Since agriculture was absent, pottery-making of negligible importance, and residence changed frequently, there is little or nothing at their former camp sites from which the archaeologist can hope to learn much about the people.

There is evidence that most of these horse-nomads were comparatively recent arrivals in their historic Plains habitat, and practically all have been so regarded for many years. In the north, the Blackfeet, Plains Crees, and Assiniboines, when first met by white men, were apparently still largely based on the partially timbered grasslands of the Canadian park belt. As late as the middle of the eighteenth century, as we have noted in an earlier chapter, the Cheyennes were still semisedentary agriculturists in eastern North Dakota; the Dakota Sioux had just begun to drift westward across the Missouri; and the Crows had been west of the Missouri for perhaps less than one century. For the Arapahoes, the evidence of their time of arrival is less satisfactory; and it has been suggested that they and the Blackfeet may have been "ancient occupants of the northern true plains, or rather of the foothills of the Rockies and the plains tributary thereto."[2] The Shoshones in historic times were rather less whole-heartedly committed to the Plains bison-hunter way of life than most of the other groups; and there is still disagreement among scholars whether, or to what extent, they may once have occupied a substantial area of the Plains in Montana and Alberta before the Blackfeet established their domination over the region. At least one archaeologist has recently suggested that the late prehistoric and early historic remains in southern Alberta reflect the former presence of the Blackfeet here, rather than the Shoshones.[3]

What, then, was the nature of the earlier human occupations of the northwestern short-grass and sagebrush plains? Half a century ago, Wissler observed that the area yielded few artifacts "that can be assigned to a culture other than that of the historic period" and noted further the possibility of a "prehistoric uninhabited region" in its western portions. Fifty years earlier, Professor Hind had written that Indian antiquities "are rarely found in the valley of the Saskatchewan south of the North Branch," although in the Qu'Appelle Valley he had noted the "remains of ancient encampments, where the Plains Cree, in the day of their power and pride had erected large skin tents, and strengthened them with rings of stones placed around the base." And as recently as 1936, it was suggested by another scholar that in prehorse days, the Plains were only "nibbled at" here and there by venturesome representatives of hunting groups based on the mountains to the west or of semi-agricultural peoples in the river valleys to the east.[4]

In the past twenty-five or thirty years, since the beginning of systematic archaeological work in the region, these older views have been found unacceptable. It has become abundantly clear that the Northwestern Plains, while they lacked large or numerous

---

[2] Kroeber, "Cultural and Natural Areas of Native North America," *loc. cit.*, 82.
[3] R. G. Forbis, "Some Late Sites in the Oldman River Region, Alberta," National Museum of Canada *Bulletin 162* (1960), 158–64.
[4] C. Wissler, "Ethnographical Problems of the Missouri Saskatchewan Area," *American Anthropologist*, new ser., Vol. X, No. 2 (1908), 201; Hind, *op. cit.*, 53, 109; Kroeber, *Anthropology*, 823.

village remains like those along the Middle Missouri or burial mounds such as those on the Northeastern Periphery, nevertheless contained many evidences of a long occupation by man. The story that is being pieced together from these traces is still very imperfectly known; but each passing year sees additional bits fitted into the narrative that is emerging.

The archaeological features here are of various kinds. They include large numbers of camp sites, sometimes situated on the wind-whipped surface of the land or, again, buried at varying depths in stream terraces; hearth areas, both with and without burned and fire-fractured stones; groups of tipi rings, cairns, boulder alignments, and enclosures; quarries from which stone for weapons and utensils was obtained; and workshop stations of various kinds, some of them situated far from present water or otherwise favored stopping points. Game traps or kills, where bison were stampeded over cliffs or steep slopes to be butchered below, are a widespread feature of the region, and have only recently become the subject of sustained investigation. Where suitable geological conditions exist, there are caves and rock shelters which were occupied by man, as well as rock carvings and paintings of many kinds and of varying antiquity.

On these sites may be found chipped-stone projectile points, scrapers, knives, and choppers, along with the rejectage left in their manufacture. Ground stonework is less common; but grinding implements are found at many locations. Soapstone vessels, with flat bottoms and bulging sides, are known from a number of places in Wyoming and Montana. Pottery is relatively rare; but, contrary to anthropological teaching of thirty years ago, it has been found in small amounts over almost the entire Northwestern Plains region. It is most common, apparently, along the eastern margin, where there is also some evidence of more permanent settlements than are characteristic of the region farther west.

Most of the camp sites so far recorded, unlike the semiagricultural villages and their associated refuse deposits along the Middle Missouri, show no great depth of occupational debris and so were presumably inhabited for relatively short periods of time. On the

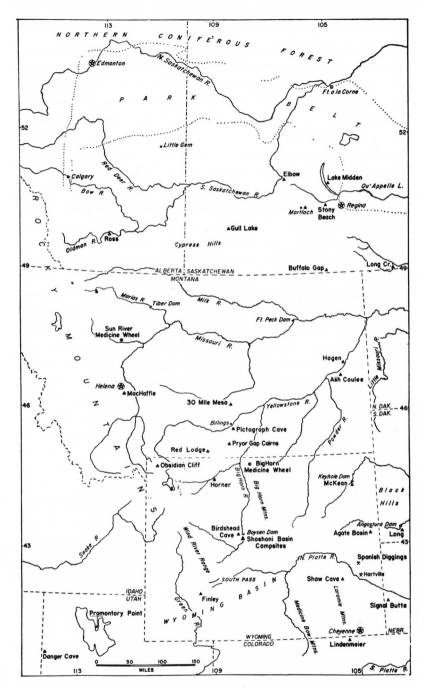

NORTHERN CONIFEROUS FOREST

113   109   105

⊗ Edmonton

N. Saskatchewan R.

P A R K

B E L T

Ft. a la Corne

52   52

• Little Gem

Red Deer R.

• Calgary

Bow R.

S. Saskatchewan R.

Elbow

Lake Midden

Qu'Appelle L.

Mortlach Stony Beach ⊗ Regina

R O C K Y

Oldman R. Ross

▲Gull Lake

Cypress Hills

49 ---   ALBERTA SASKATCHEWAN   Buffalo Gap▲   Long Cr.▲   49
MONTANA

Marias R. Tiber Dam   Milk R.

Sun River
Medicine Wheel

Ft. Peck Dam

M O U N T A I N S

Missouri R.

Hagen

Ash Coulee

Little Missouri R.

Helena ⊗   ▲MacHaffie

30 Mile Mesa ▲   Yellowstone R.

N. DAK.   46
S. DAK.

46

Billings • ▲ Pictograph Cave

Powder R.

Red Lodge▲   ▲ Pryor Gap Cairns

▲ Obsidian Cliff   • BigHorn
Medicine Wheel

Keyhole Dam
McKean▲

Black
Hills

Horner

Big Horn R.

Big Horn Mtns.

Birdshead
Cave ▲   • Boysen Dam
▲ Shoshoni Basin
Campsites

Angostura Dam
Agate Basin ▲   Long

43   Snake R.   43

Wind River Range

N. Platte R.

Spanish Diggings
⚹

SOUTH PASS

Shaw Cave ▲   ⚹ Hartville

Laramie Mtns.

G R E E N   R I V E R   B A S I N

IDAHO
UTAH   ▲ Finley

Signal Butte

Promontory Point

W Y O M I N G

Medicine Bow Mtns.

Cheyenne ⊗   NEBR.

Green R.

WYOMING
COLORADO   Lindenmeier

• Danger Cave

0   50   100   150
MILES

113   109   105   S. Platte R.

F IG. 2 1. *Map of the Northwestern Plains, showing location of certain archaeological sites.*

other hand, it must be noted that at an increasing number of these locations, there is clear evidence of repeated residence in the form of successive refuse- and artifact-bearing levels separated from one another by wind- or water-laid soil deposits. These stratified sites include both terrace locations and rock shelters; and their successive strata, in which the artifact inventory and the way of life inferred from it often changes from level to level, are the clues for chronological arrangement of the varied remains now known to exist in the region.

Since pottery is scarce and late here, and lacks the variety found in the wares of more easterly sections, other types of artifacts serve as guides to chronology. Projectile points are most satisfactory in this respect, since they show perceptible changes in form, size, and other particulars through time.[5] Other categories of artifacts, such as milling stones, are absent or much less common in some levels or at some sites than at others. Later sites often yield greater numbers and a wider variety of artifacts than do earlier ones.

In establishing the time relationships and succession of cultures in the Northwestern Plains, the most important sites are, of course, those in which stratification in some depth is manifested. Among these are several of particular significance. Pictograph and Ghost caves, a few miles southeast of Billings, Montana, have provided an unusually long sequence, a relatively large and varied series of artifacts, and a number of perishable items not usually found at open camp sites or in buried terrace strata.[6] In the fill of these caves, which reached a maximum depth of twenty-three feet at Pictograph Cave, three prehistoric periods and one historic period have been recognized. Birdshead Cave, in the Owl Creek Range of western Wyoming, is another notable site; but here the deposits are shallower, the cultural strata thinner and much less productive, and the inferences are consequently less convincing than at the Billings caves.[7]

[5] Mulloy, "A Preliminary Historical Outline for the Northwestern Plains," *loc. cit.*, 143.
[6] *Ibid.*, 22–118.
[7] W. L. Bliss, "Birdshead Cave, a Stratified Site in Wind River Basin, Wyoming," *American Antiquity*, Vol. XV, No. 3 (January, 1950), 187–96.

The archaeological salvage operations in recent years at Boysen, Keyhole, Angostura, and other reservoir areas have turned up several stratified sites, and for some of these excellent reports are available.[8] On the southeastern margin of the area, Signal Butte and Ash Hollow Cave in western Nebraska have contributed important information on the time relations between the western potteryless hunting cultures and the better known pottery-making peoples of the Central Plains.[9] Other stratified sites that merit mention because their record spans a long period of time include the MacHaffie site near Helena, Montana, the Mortlach site twenty miles west of Moose Jaw, Saskatchewan, and the Long Creek site in extreme southeastern Saskatchewan.[10]

Far from having been an uninhabited area in prehorse days, the Northwestern Plains have revealed indisputable evidence of human activity running back several thousand years into the past. The oldest traces so far recognized belong to the period of the early big-game hunters, between five and ten thousand years ago. They consist chiefly of numerous surface finds of dart or spear points, including several kinds of fluted, stemmed, and unfluted leaf-shaped forms. Unfortunately, these early kinds of points have not often been found in this region in subsurface situations where the associated artifacts could be identified, or in stratified sites where their temporal position could be accurately established. Much of the information bearing on these early hunter-folk comes, in fact, from sites in adjacent regions, where the associations have been more clearly determined.

[8] Mulloy, "The McKean Site in Northeastern Wyoming," *Southwestern Journal of Anthropology*, Vol. X, No. 4 (1954), 432–60; Mulloy, "Archeological Investigations in the Shoshone Basin of Wyoming," University of Wyoming *Publications*, Vol. XVIII, No. 1 (1954), 1–70; Bliss, "Early Man in the Northwestern Plains," *Proceedings*, Fifth Plains Conference of Archeology (1949), 121–26.

[9] Strong, "An Introduction to Nebraska Archeology," *loc. cit.*, 224–39; Champe, "Ash Hollow Cave," *loc. cit.*, 5–57; Bliss, "Early and Late Lithic Horizons in the Plains," *Proceedings*, Sixth Plains Conference for Archeology (1950), 108–16.

[10] Forbis and Sperry, *loc. cit.*; B. Wettlaufer, "The Mortlach Site in the Besant Valley of Central Saskatchewan," *Anthropological Series No. 1* (1955), Department of Natural Resources, Regina; Wettlaufer, "The Long Creek Site," *The Blue Jay*, Vol. XV, No. 4 (1957), 167–69.

Fluted point fragments regarded as of Folsom origin have been found at the MacHaffie site near Helena, Montana, in the deepest of three cultural strata. Along with the points occurred scrapers, choppers, knives, and chips left in the fashioning of artifacts, together with the bones of deer, rabbit, wolf, and a bison of larger size than the living species. A fluted point was also found in the lowest level of Pictograph Cave, but here it was associated with other points of generally later types. As surface finds, fluted points have been found also in the Lower Yellowstone Valley, and at many other locations from Wyoming through Montana to Saskatchewan and Alberta. Their occurrence at the Lindenmeier site, near the southern end of the area herein classed as the Northwestern Plains, has already been noted in an earlier chapter.

Other records of the early big-game hunters include the Angostura complex, as found at the Long site just south of the Black Hills; and the gracefully shaped blades found in some numbers at an ancient bison kill in Agate Basin in northeastern Wyoming. Radiocarbon dates of 7430 and 5766 B.C. for the Long site suggest a later period than that in which the Folsom people are believed to have flourished; and the earlier date, at least, is regarded as referring to a culture mainly oriented toward big-game hunting. As we have indicated elsewhere, points identified as of Angostura type, sometimes on dubious grounds, have been reported from widely scattered localities in and beyond the Northwestern Plains.

Still another stage, and apparently a somewhat later one, is represented by the Finley site near Eden and the Horner site near Cody. From both have come excellent examples of the exquisitely fashioned Eden points, as well as specimens of the less carefully finished and more strongly shouldered Scottsbluff points. The Horner site has supplied, in addition, scrapers, knives, choppers, gravers, and other artifacts. Both sites evidently represent game kills, where bison in some numbers were slain and butchered. Radiocarbon determinations for the Horner site indicate a date of about 5000 B.C.; and geological estimates for the Finley site place it in the same time range, about 7000 years ago.

Neither of these sites showed any cultural stratification; but it should be noted that at the MacHaffie site, Scottsbluff points were found in a stratum overlying that from which the fluted Folsom fragments were taken. Since this sequence parallels that at the Lindenmeier site, the younger age of the Scottsbluff points as compared to Folsom seems clear. There is still difference of opinion as to whether these showings apply to the Plains region generally.

As to the people who left these remains, the excavated sites give us little or no information on the size, composition, and organization of the human communities they represent. As elsewhere on this time level, there are no traces of the dwellings or of other features of camp life, except perhaps a few fireplaces which seldom give indication of prolonged or intensive use. The artifacts include almost entirely implements primarily adapted to the chase and to processing of the kill—knives, scrapers, chopping tools, and weapon points. Grinding tools that might have served for processing vegetal foods, such as seeds and berries, are scarce or absent. At none of the sites yet studied is there any evidence of the domestic dog.

The period in which the early big-game hunters dominated the Northwestern Plains has been designated by archaeologists in the area as the Early Prehistoric Period. From the available evidence, we infer the presence of small groups of wandering hunters who relied principally on the large, gregarious game animals for their sustenance. The earlier groups evidently took animals of species now extinct; the later ones possibly drew on modern forms of bison and other animals. None of the known sites gives evidence of long residence or of frequent returns to the same spot. One suspects that even the Horner site, where the remains of two hundred or more bison were found, may have been used for a relatively short period, since there is little evidence of man's domestic activities here beyond the artifacts and a few small lightly-fired hearths. That the total population of the region was small and sparse seems certain; but since the typical artifacts have been found widely dispersed throughout the region, it must be assumed that the people traveled over considerable distances in their search

249

for the herds. It is also likely that during the severe winters that characterize the region, the camps, like those of the later horse-nomads, were moved to localities where fuel, water, shelter, and game could be obtained.

Much more abundant than the sites of the early big-game hunters are others evidently representing a later period, broadly categorized as the Middle Prehistoric Period.[11] Most of these probably date after about 3000 or 2500 B.C. These, too, occur in a variety of locations—as open camp sites on stream terraces and in dune areas, as charcoal-stained occupation levels in terraces, caves, and rock shelters, and in association with mass kills of bison of recent species. There are hearths of several kinds, and at some locations these are present in considerable numbers. Some are little more than fire-darkened spots; others may be basin-like, of varying sizes and shapes, and lined or floored with stones. Occasional small cylindrical pits suggest storage devices, but whether for food, household articles, or for other purposes is unclear. Again there are no posthole patterns or other satisfactory evidences of habitations. The deposits are sometimes of considerable depth and strongly suggest repeated occupations of the same spot.

The great majority of the artifacts recovered consist of stone-work. This includes butchering and skin-dressing tools, such as knives, scrapers, chopping tools, drills, and perhaps gravers. Finds at sheltered locations, such as Pictograph Cave, suggest that bird and mammal bone awls, oblong bone objects with incised lines that may be gaming counters, rib wrenches, and perhaps soap-stone ornaments may also belong to this time level. The projectile points usually differ sharply from the earlier forms. A characteristic form is more or less leaf-shaped with a concave, or indented, base to which the designation of *McKean* point has been given by workers in the area. Other points have shoulders that tend to mark off the blade from the stem; and there are also a few with side notches.

[11] Mulloy, "A Preliminary Historical Outline for the Northwestern Plains," *loc. cit.*, 209–13, 221–22; Mulloy, "The McKean Site in Northeastern Wyoming," *loc. cit.*, 453–57; Mulloy, "Archeological Investigations in the Shoshone Basin of Wyoming," *loc. cit.*, 52–65.

The artifact assemblage suggests, of course, considerable reliance on the hunt; but in contrast to the bone refuse from earlier sites, those we are now considering reveal a larger proportion of small mammal species along with the remains of antelope, deer, and bison. The remains of birds and reptiles also appear in some sites; and these, like the musselshells noted in some localities, suggest other food resources not known to have been utilized by the early big-game hunters.

Another notable difference from the early period remains is the frequent occurrence of flat grinding slabs and handstones. Most of the slabs have an elliptical grinding surface, and the handstone was probably used with a rotary motion rather than in a to-and-fro movement like that of the Pueblo Indians. These devices are usually regarded as evidence of a changing subsistence economy featuring the crushing of seeds, roots, and other vegetal products; and they appear to be rather more plentiful in the later sites which date, by radiocarbon, from about 1500 B.C. and later.

The increased abundance of bones of small animals, birds, frogs, and the like, togther with the frequent presence of milling stones,

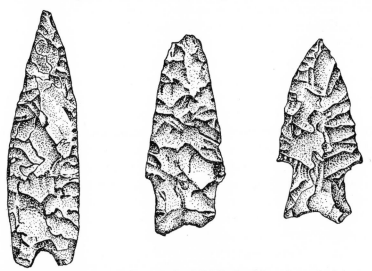

FIG. 22. *Some weapon points of the Middle Prehistoric period (c.1500* B.C.). Left to right: *McKean, Duncan, and Hanna points.*

point to a way of life not usually associated with the Plains Indians and their primary reliance on bison-hunting. They suggest, in fact, food-getting practices more like those of the non-horse Shoshoneans—the "Shoshokos" or "Walkers," for example, and the Gosiute, who dwelt in the barren wastes of the Great Basin from southern Idaho through Utah to Nevada. Among these people, the search for food was a never-ending one. Lacking great herds of bison, or rivers of salmon, or groves of oaks, men sustained themselves by the gathering of wild seeds, roots, berries, and other edible vegetal items, plus the taking of whatever small or large game chance and ceaseless foraging offered. Seldom did this foraging produce a surplus to be stored for tomorrow's needs; and most of the limited natural resources were in forms that made individual effort, or search by small groups, more productive than community efforts.

Even in recent years, seeds were extensively eaten by these Basin Shoshoneans; and the grinding slab on which seeds were reduced to meal was a regular item of household furniture. Seeds were sometimes boiled as mush in basketry vessels, or they could be eaten uncooked. Chokecherries and other berries were pounded up and dried, but were not, as among the Plains tribes, mixed with meat.

Among nonvegetal foods, rabbits were a prominent item. They were taken in nets, by clubbing, and occasionally in fire drives where there was sufficient vegetation to support a fire. In addition to meat, they furnished material for that highly important Shoshonean product—rabbit fur cordage from which cold weather robes and blankets were fashioned. Antelope, deer, bison, and mountain sheep were used, of course, whenever they could be obtained. Ground squirrels, marmots, and other small rodents, as well as lizards, snakes, and the like were gathered. Among the Shoshokos, grasshoppers were taken in drives, to be roasted or spitted before the fire, boiled in soup, dried in the sun, or crushed into a paste which was then dried.

Such a way of life, with the limited food resources available, was possible only with small groups—independent families, perhaps, or an extended family group, seldom more than a dozen to a score of persons, who moved from place to place as different foods became seasonally or otherwise available, and who were prepared to move to another locality as the resources within reach of one camp were exhausted. A sort of cyclical nomadism, or limited wandering, was thus customary, each family or band presumably returning intermittently to one of its previous camp sites when its resources had replenished themselves.

This collecting of food by roving search, with an inventory of tools limited to the minimum required for food-getting and the manufacture of simple clothing, baskets, and other portable household equipment, seems to explain most satisfactorily the kind of sites that represent the Middle Prehistoric period in Wyoming—and most notably, in the Wyoming Basin and adjacent localities. Its pursuit over many hundreds of years, without significant change in the food resources of the region, would result in the scores of simple, meager archaeological sites with which the region abounds. If the natives—sometimes termed the Foragers—contented themselves with simple brush shelters, such as were customary among the historic seed-gatherers and foragers of the Great Basin, the absence of recognizable dwelling remains is understandable. Conceivably, a single group would have visited several sites in a single year; and such sites would probably be scattered in a variety of locations, depending upon the foods available from time to time. It is not a way of life that would leave rich or well-marked stations, unless perhaps in caves or rock shelters where basketry, fur and skin articles, and wooden objects might be preserved; nor would it produce the varied artifacts of stone, bone, pottery, shell, and other categories that are found on the village sites of the semiagricultural peoples farther to the east.

It is not yet clear how widespread the Forager way of life was in the prehistoric Northwestern Plains. It was strongly developed, apparently, in and around the Wyoming Basin in the second millennium before Christ, where the ecological setting strongly resembled that in the nearby Great Basin. Farther east, such sites as Signal Butte I indicate that big-game hunters rather than foragers

253

and millers were flourishing at this time; and there is some reason to believe that to the north also, in Montana and the Canadian Prairie Provinces, game was a more constant and important food resource than were the items for which the natives of the Wyoming Basin used their milling equipment. It has been suggested that climatic or other conditions perhaps made the Northwestern Plains unsuited to bison and other large game during this period, thus forcing the human inhabitants to reorient their subsistence economy along different lines.[12]

Although radiocarbon dates for the earliest Middle Prehistoric hunters are not at hand, it is likely that they were considerably later in time than were any of the early big-game hunters. It is not impossible, therefore, that the intervening gap of some thousands of years for which there is at present little or no evidence of human occupancy in the region, represents the hot, dry Altithermal period we have noted elsewhere. We do not know what the native vegetation of the region was during this interval, but the higher temperatures and diminished precipitation in Altithermal times may well have reduced the short-grass country to a near desert and expelled from it the large game herds that drew the early big-game hunters into its grasslands. With displacement of the major game animals toward the east or north, man would presumably have found a primarily hunting way of life impossible, and therefore either betook himself to other regions as well, or was reduced to the status of a forager where edible vegetal products, plus anything that walked, crawled, or flew, was levied upon for sustenance.

Some of the characteristic projectile points of the Middle Prehistoric period in the Wyoming area are much like those found in prehistoric levels in the caves of the Intermontane region. Radiocarbon dates suggest that these types are somewhat older in the Great Salt Lake region, as at Danger Cave. It may be, therefore, that with the amelioration of desert conditions following termination of the Altithermal, repopulation of the Wyoming-Montana

[12] Mulloy, "Archeological Investigations in the Shoshone Basin of Wyoming," *loc. cit.*, 63.

region was accomplished in considerable part by Desert Culture immigrants from the west, who followed the Great Basin flora through the Wyoming Basin into the sagebrush and short-grass country lying along the eastern slope of the Rockies. Such an immigration, perhaps going on for a long time, would account for certain other Great Basin features which appear in still later culture horizons east of the Continental Divide.

In summary, then, the Middle Prehistoric period in the southern portions of the Northwestern Plains seems to be characterized, first, by a series of hunting peoples not primarily concerned with large game, but instead utilizing whatever animal forms were at hand in a presumably desert or semidesert environment, and second, by another series of hunters and gatherers to whom vegetal foods were of increased importance. In much of the region, particularly in the Wyoming basin and elsewhere in the sagebrush country, the way of life may have been much like that of the Great Basin foragers; but as the early levels at Signal Butte and elsewhere indicate, there were apparently still areas around the fringes of the region, to the east and north, where large game continued to be a mainstay of native life. That the Great Basin forager way of life, or Desert Culture, dominated the Plains as a whole "at the height of the Altithermal"[13] or at any other time has not yet been established.

Still other camp sites may be assigned to a later time level, after perhaps A.D. 500, for which the designation Late Prehistoric period has been employed.[14] The terrace sites, rock shelters, caves, and other locations so categorized still yield mostly stone tools, including weapon points, butchering and skin-dressing tools, and some grinding implements. Among the points, there are several kinds of small side-notched, stemmed, and triangular forms that usually differ markedly from those of the Middle Prehistoric period, but are remindful of those found on prehistoric pottery-bearing sites in the Eastern Plains. Presumably, they mark the

[13] J. D. Jennings, "Danger Cave," Society for American Archaeology *Memoir No. 14* (1957), 284.

[14] Mulloy, "A Preliminary Historical Outline for the Northwestern Plains," *loc. cit.*, 222.

appearance of the bow and arrow, superseding the dart or spear of earlier times. They indicate, too, that as the semiagricultural peoples from the Mississippi-Missouri Valley were spreading westward across the grasslands, nomadic hunters and gatherers were still residing along the stream valleys and among the "breaks" of the Northwestern Plains. They leave no room for the view that the area was uninhabited in prehistoric times.

Cave deposits, such as the upper levels in Pictograph Cave and those in nearby Ghost Cave, have materially extended the range of traits assignable to this period, although they possibly relate to the later portion not long before the historic period. Here appear such items as the following: grooved mauls; sandstone arrow-shaft smoothers, with a longitudinal groove; chipped knives set into slotted-rib or bent-stick handles; straight and expanded-base drills; bone awls of various kinds; bison toe bones, with a hole broken into one face; cannon-bone fleshers with a serrate blade; rib wrenches; circular to oblong bone game counters; bird-bone whistles; pierced teeth; unilaterally-barbed bone spearheads; incised antler bracelets; wooden arrow shafts; fore-shafted cane arrows; fire drills and hearths; split and painted or scored gaming sticks; spire-lopped Olivella and Dentalium shell beads; coiled basketry; and remains of bison hide and hair. All of this suggests a richer material culture; and while it may be due in part to vastly more favorable conditions of preservation, it is also possible that it reflects a better living based on successful bison hunting, rather than on foraging, and on the resulting greater leisure from the ceaseless food quest where bison and large game, rather than seeds and rabbits, furnished the main basis of the subsistence economy.

The Late Prehistoric period also saw the appearance of pottery, previously present only sporadically, if at all, along the eastern margin of the Northwestern Plains. Thick cord-roughened sherds that recall Woodland pottery from Nebraska have been found at Keyhole and Angostura reservoirs on the flanks of the Black Hills; and these may date from the later stage of the Middle Prehistoric period. From at least two sites at Angostura Reservoir have come thinner cord-roughened sherds that suggest Upper Republican ware of the thirteenth to fifteenth century; and other sites have yielded similar pieces in eastern Wyoming. At Angostura, the pottery was accompanied by bone awls, knifelike bone objects, tubular beads, and other items reminiscent of some of the Eastern Plains pottery cultures. These, like the trailed or incised potsherds of a well-known late prehistoric Middle Missouri pottery ware found at Angostura, suggest that the semisedentary Village Indians sometimes hunted, traded, or sojourned for other reasons in and around the Black Hills.

Other kinds of pottery are more widespread and probably more characteristic of the Northwestern Plains, and indicate that some of the pottery makers were not chance or seasonal visitors to the Northwestern Plains. Near Glendive, Montana, the Hagen site has revealed evidence of semipermanent habitations and other materials resembling the products of the Mandan and Hidatsa Village Indians along the Middle Missouri.[15] Toothed cannon-bone fleshers, bone knife handles, and other items, including the pottery, have also been found at Ash Coulee site, a few miles to the south. It has been suggested that these sites may represent the Crows on their way westward into the Plains, to take up a bison-hunting way of life after their split from the Hidatsa village dwellers following a semihorticultural way of life. Other sites, such as Ludlow Cave, again may be either frequently used hunting stations for parties from the Middle Missouri villages, or else further traces of once horticultural Indians in a transitional stage from cultivators on the Missouri to full-fledged year-round bison hunters on the Western Plains.[16]

The upper levels at Birdshead Cave have also yielded pottery fragments, but not of kinds identifiable with the easterly wares represented around the Black Hills. This pottery, like the soapstone vessel fragments found with it, is quite likely of Shoshone origin and fairly recent in time. Rabbit-hair cordage from a slightly earlier level in the cave also points toward the Great Basin

[15] Mulloy, "The Hagen Site, a Prehistoric Village on the Lower Yellowstone," *loc. cit.*
[16] Mulloy, "A Preliminary Historical Outline for the Northwestern Plains," *loc. cit.*, 195.

and a probable Shoshone origin. Not identified at Birdshead Cave, but found at a number of sites in the Yellowstone Valley and elsewhere along the eastern front of the Rockies, are sherds from flat-bottomed pottery vessels which have somewhat the form of a flower pot, and often remind one of the soapstone jars from the area. These, too, have their counterpart in the northern Great Basin; and their occurrence in the Northwestern Plains may reflect a former wide distribution of the Shoshones in the Yellowstone drainage, whence their pottery ware became dispersed, along with soapstone vessels, over an even wider range of territory.[17]

The general recency of pottery in the Wyoming region, except for the occasional earlier Woodland-like pieces in the east, seems to be indicated for the region to the northward, as well. It is usually associated with small projectile points of late prehistoric and early historic types, and seldom is found at much depth underground.[18] Fabric-marked sherds in the Marias drainage have been found with metal scrap, suggesting that they date after the arrival of white man's goods.[19] In the stratified sites that have been tested in Canada, as at Long Creek and at Mortlach, pottery occurs only in the uppermost levels. Other sites, such as the "middens" at the Elbow of the South Saskatchewan, at Gull Lake, at Stony Beach, and elsewhere in the Plains region, similarly produce pottery only in their upper and later deposits.[20] Much of this pottery includes pieces marked with a cord-wrapped instrument, reminiscent of Blackduck and other late Woodland wares in Minnesota. Other pieces are fabric-marked, and seem to be related to

[17] Mulloy, "A Preliminary Historical Outline for the Northwestern Plains," *loc. cit.*, 196–202; Wedel, "Earthenware and Steatite Vessels from Northwestern Wyoming," *American Antiquity*, Vol. XIX, No. 4 (1954), 403–409.

[18] A. B. Kehoe, "Ceramic Affiliations in the Northwestern Plains," *American Antiquity*, Vol. XXV, No. 2 (1959), 237–46.

[19] Wedel, "Notes on Aboriginal Pottery from Montana," *Journal*, Washington Academy of Sciences, Vol. XLI, No. 4 (1951), 130–38.

[20] Wettlaufer, "The Mortlach Site in the Besant Valley of Central Saskatchewan," *loc. cit.*, 20, 26; Wettlaufer, "An Archeological Survey of Saskatchewan," unpublished manuscript, The National Museum of Canada and Provincial Museum of Saskatchewan, No. 1 (1951).

pottery of the park belt. It appears likely that practically all this pottery is on a late prehistoric time level, and was perhaps brought into the Western Plains with some of the Algonquian and other tribes as they moved out of the Eastern Woodlands across the park belt into the Plains to become fulltime bison-hunting peoples.

What seems to be indicated for this Late Prehistoric time level is a continuation of the combined hunting-gathering way of life that characterized the previous period, but apparently with increasing use of larger game such as bison and antelope. In the east, as around the Black Hills, the presence of pottery apparently representing several different traditions from the Eastern Plains indicates either that the pottery-making groups were occasionally venturing westward on long distance hunting trips, or else that some representatives of these groups were on their way from a semisedentary, partly agricultural economy toward a full-fledged hunting-gathering way of life. The varied eastern pottery wares to which these westerly sherds are related—Woodland, Upper Republican, Middle Missouri, and Blackduck, among others— indicate that the contacts with the western hunter-gatherers were a continuing thing over centuries of time, not merely sporadic adventures.

The Historic period, as it is known from ethnology and history, has already been discussed. Generally speaking, this is the time of the mounted bison-hunters, the equestrian groups who were to develop to the full the conventional Plains Indian way of life. There is not much that can be added to the picture from archaeology, since the transient camps of the nomadic hunters, even if they can be found or recognized, seldom offer much inducement to the archaeologist.

The last occupation represented at Pictograph Cave—thinly in the cave itself, but more adequately on the canyon floor below— evidently belongs to the time when metal was known to the natives. In addition to pottery, which includes both Hagen-like wares and pieces of flat-bottomed Shoshone pottery, there are arrow points, knives, and scrapers; wood cut with metal tools; rare brass and iron fragments; and there were also postholes around a well-packed earth floor, suggesting some sort of pole house frame, perhaps covered with hides or thatch.

Also belonging to the historic period are the curious log, and log and rock, structures which have been reported from various points along the Yellowstone drainage.[21] These are of several kinds; some are conical, of vertically placed poles with stone slabs outside; others may be hemiconical and built against a rock cliff; still others are of horizontal logs, sometimes with a tree incorporated into the structure, or with slabs added to the outside, or with one wall of the structure formed by a cliff wall. They have been found singly and in small clusters; and among the few associated artifacts there are potsherds, stone implements such as points, knives, and scrapers, and homemade and commercial gunflints. The structures recall the war lodges and "forts" said to have been erected by war parties in historic times and occasionally described by white travelers.[22]

Rock cairns and lines consisting of piles of stones are another common feature of the archaeology of this area, particularly in the section near the mountains. Norris described some of these constructions, with heaps of stones three to five feet high and eight to twelve feet in diameter, in Trail Pass between Fort Ellis [near present Bozeman] and the Upper Yellowstone, between Emigrant Gulch and Dome Mountain, and elsewhere; but beyond charcoal and a few arrowheads and other stone tools, he was unable to find anything in them.[23] More recently, cairns at Pryor Gap, some forty miles south of Billings, yielded stone tools, bone and shell ornaments, pierced elk incisors and coyote canines, Olivella and Dentalia, and glass beads, along with potsherds. These

---

[21] Mulloy, "A Preliminary Historical Outline for the Northwestern Plains," *loc. cit.* 169–78; Mulloy, "The Northern Plains," in J. B. Griffin's *Archeology of Eastern United States* (1952), 132.

[22] Ewers, "The Blackfoot War Lodge: Its Construction and Use," *American Anthropologist*, Vol. XLVI, No. 2, Pt. 1 (1944), 182–92; H. M. Fuller and L. R. Hafen, *The Journal of Captain John R. Bell*, 135–37; Maximilian, *loc. cit.*, 42, 55, 183.

[23] P. W. Norris, "Prehistoric Remains in Montana, Between Fort Ellis and the Yellowstone River," Smithsonian Institution *Annual Report for 1879*, (1880), 327–28.

remains were in historic Crow territory, but it cannot be demonstrated that they were left by this tribe, rather than by the Shoshones, or by some other group.[24]

There has been so little systematic excavation in the Canadian Prairie Provinces that the outline of prehistoric cultures there still remains to be set up. It is likely, however, that it will parallel that now evidenced for the Wyoming-Montana region. As surface finds, there is evidence of the early big-game hunters at least as far north as the North Saskatchewan drainage. No artifacts have yet been reported *in situ*. At such stratified sites as Mortlach, however, there is indication of a long series of hunting and gathering cultures comparable to those of the Middle Prehistoric period south of the International Boundary. On the basis of projectile point similarities, it is likely that the Thunder Creek culture, oldest in the Mortlach series and radiocarbon-dated at 1445 B.C., may correlate with the Middle Prehistoric period. Neither this nor any of the subsequent cultural strata yielded any grinding tools, suggesting that the various people who lived at this particular spot at any rate were primarily hunters. Elsewhere in this region, milling stones have been found; but it has not yet been shown that seed- and root-gathering or a foraging way of life ever achieved the prevalence inferred for the Wyoming Basin and contiguous districts. On the ceramic level, the significance of the fortified pit-house village near Cluny, Alberta, investigated by Forbis in 1959, remains a matter of great interest pending full publication of details.

The archaeological record, then, suggests that the Northwestern Plains have been characterized throughout the time of their human occupancy by hunting peoples primarily. In the Early Prehistoric period, they hunted almost exclusively large game animals—particularly the bison—of forms now extinct in the earlier period, of modern form in the later. Hunting may have been the principal subsistence device throughout the north. In the south,

[24] N. C. Nelson, "Camping on Ancient Trails," *Natural History*, Vol. XLIX, No. 5 (1942), 262–67; Mulloy, "A Preliminary Historical Outline for the Northwestern Plains," *loc. cit.*, 178–80.

there seems to have been a period, perhaps of several thousand years duration, when the gathering and grinding of vegetal foods was important, and small game had to be drawn upon. In Late Prehistoric times, large game again became of primary importance, as we know it was in the historic period.

TIPI RINGS

Among the most abundant and widespread antiquities of the Northwestern Plains are those commonly known as tipi rings. These are found in limited numbers in northern Colorado and extreme western Nebraska, and more frequently in the Dakotas eastward approximately to the Missouri River from Fort Randall northward; but the greatest numbers appear to be in Wyoming and Montana, with many additional occurrences in southern Alberta and Saskatchewan.[25] They are found on river bottoms, on stream terraces at varying heights, on the upland margins, and on elevated ridges and spurs, sometimes at considerable distances from visible existing sources of water and wood. Characteristically, they consist of boulders and field stones, from a few inches to a foot or more in diameter, placed at intervals to form circles from five to over forty feet in diameter. Often these boulders are embedded in the sod and give the impression of considerable antiquity. Some rings have a small cluster of stones near the center suggesting a fireplace, and similar clusters sometimes occur just outside the circles. The rings often occur singly, but may be found in groups of almost any number up to two hundred or more. Artifacts and camp rubbish are usually extremely scarce in and around the rings, so that their assignment to any specific time period, tribe, or culture is not easy.

These circles have been commonly designated tipi rings on the supposition that they were used around the edges of the tipis to weigh down the skin covers, functioning thus in place of, or in addition to, the wooden pegs. This interpretation has been ques-

[25] Bliss, "Archeological Reconnaissance in Wyoming and Montana, 1946-1947," *Proceedings*, Fifth Plains Conference for Archeology (1949), 7-12.

tioned by some, however, and there has been a good deal of discussion regarding their meaning. Mulloy has argued against their use as weights for tipi covers or otherwise in connection with ordinary habitations, and has included them under the rubric "Manifestations of unknown relationships." He points out that many of those along the Rocky Mountain front include far more stones than would seem to be needed for such use, that nearly all lack discernible fireplaces or packed floors, that they are often in locations poorly suited for camping from the standpoint of wood and protection, and that they generally lack the debris that would be expected if domestic pursuits had been carried out in or near them.[26]

More recently, T. F. Kehoe has approached the question through a detailed analysis of tipi rings on the Blackfeet Reservation in western Montana and in adjacent Alberta, with which he combined a comprehensive review of ethnological data and early historical documents.[27] Kehoe was shown typical rings marking the locations of tipis whose owners and builders were known to, and named by, his Indian informants; and he demonstrates convincingly that the use of boulders, or in their absence, of blocks of sod, to hold down tipi covers among such tribes as the Blackfeet, Crees, Crows, and Dakotas was common practice rather than an occasional incident. Blackfoot traditions assert that stones were extensively so used in the old days before the horse (and the iron ax) had reached them and when tipis were commonly of smaller dimensions. The usual range in size of boulder circles in the Blackfoot country coincides with the size range of Blackfoot tipis, and the averages likewise show close agreement. The apparent absence of fireplace remains in many rings can be

[26] Mulloy, "The Northern Plains," *loc. cit.*, 137; Mulloy, "A Preliminary Historical Outline for the Northwestern Plains," *loc. cit.*, 211-13; Mulloy, "Archeological Investigations in the Shoshone Basin of Wyoming," *loc. cit.*, 53-55.
[27] T. F. Kehoe, "Tipi Rings: The 'Direct Ethnological' Approach Applied to an Archeological Problem," *American Anthropologist*, Vol. LX, No. 5 (1958), 861-73; T. F. Kehoe, "Stone Tipi Rings in North-Central Montana and the Adjacent Portion of Alberta, Canada: Their Historical, Ethnological, and Archeological Aspects," Bureau of American Ethnology *Bulletin 173*, Anthropological Paper No. 62 (1960), 417-73.

explained on various grounds—scattering of the ashes by wind on removal of the protecting lodge, and the frequent Indian custom of cooking outdoors in pleasant weather. The observed absence of domestic refuse is what would be expected in camps of short duration made by hunting peoples with few possessions and seldom or never occupying the same spot a second time. The wide range in size is also expectable: small circles may be attributed to children's play tents or to those of widows or aged persons, unusually large ones to special ceremonial functions. Finally, Kehoe suggests that the size and arrangement of ring groups reflects the changing needs of the subsistence cycle and the ceremonial observances which, in summer, brought large numbers of people together for a brief period. Most of the rings in the Blackfoot country he regards as dating from the eighteenth and early nineteenth centuries.

Since much of Kehoe's evidence includes eyewitness accounts and explanations, it cannot be lightly dismissed; and his arguments inspire confidence. Probably many of the considerations he advances are applicable over a much wider area than that with which the Blackfeet were intimately concerned. At the same time, it appears improbable that *all* boulder rings wherever found in the Northwestern Plains can be so easily explained. Mulloy presents physiographical and other evidence suggesting that some of the rings may be much older, perhaps long antedating the introduction of the horse to the Northern Plains Indians. It is quite likely, therefore, that the rock circles, so freely designated tipi rings wherever they occur, include structures or alignments that served different purposes and perhaps at widely differing periods of time despite their general similarity.

The boulder rings so far considered, for which the term tipi ring seems apt, are for the most part simple circles detached from one another. Many others depart more or less widely from a circular form; they may be eccentric, elliptical, somewhat D-shaped, or vaguely square or quadrilateral. Sometimes the "rings" intersect each other in bewildering fashion; or they may adjoin one or more neighboring rings with which they share a common dividing line of stones. I have seen such conjoined units or cells on lofty wind-swept flats at elevations of 9,500 feet or more in the Bighorn Mountains, the wall lines here usually consisting of large numbers of small to medium angular stones. In the same vicinity are small groups of stone circles, 4 to 12 in number, with traces of short rows of stones sometimes connecting 2 circles. These are usually situated near "sinkholes" from whose broken margins came the limestone slabs and blocks that form the circles. With rare exceptions, no stones or traces of fire can be found in the circles. Jasper, chert, and other chips, and an occasional small, well-made, corner-notched projectile point, were the only other evidence of human activity. None of the locations seem especially desirable for human habitation—all are open to cold winds and at a distance from wood and water. Their purpose, like their age, remains undetermined.

Other rock constructions in the Missouri Plateau have a more restricted distribution than the tipi rings. On elevated places in the western Dakotas, Wyoming, and Montana may be found cairns —piles of rock that sometimes mark, or are locally thought to mark, Indian graves, boundary lines, or other features, but which seem more often to have been erected for reasons that still elude us. One of these cairns, a "mixed earth and boulder deposit" on the floor of Pryor Canyon, southern Montana, was found to include "the usual stone objects, glass beads and animal bones. More abundant were bone and shell ornamental items, chiefly beads and pendants. The surprise was the collection of some 200 potsherds." This does not sound very much like a burial mound; but the structure was not completely excavated, and the burials, if any existed, may have escaped detection.[28]

Of another sort is a group of interesting stone structures I saw on a memorable Sunday trip into the Pryor Mountains with members of the Powell Rock Club in 1952. Our first stop was a lofty, wind-swept plateau affording a magnificent panorama across Montana and Wyoming. Eastward, across the great canyon of

[28] Nelson, "Contribution to Montana Archeology," *American Antiquity*, Vol. IX, No. 2 (1943), 162–69.

the Bighorn River were the Bighorn Mountains; northward, the broken plains rolled away into the haze of the Yellowstone Valley; and seventy miles to the west, the snow banks of the Bear Tooth Range shimmered in the June sun. Along the rim of the plateau, irregularly spaced at intervals of twenty-five to seventy-five yards, were rudely laid structures of slabs. Each was in an elliptical, oblong, or horseshoe shape, open at the center and without a cover. Where one end was left open, as was the case with at least five of the structures, the open end was to the east. One had a slab floor; several held dry, well-seasoned sticks of wood. The enclosures were roughly four to five feet wide, five to eight feet long, and eighteen to twenty-four inches high. Similar structures were reported to occur on McCullough Peak east of Cody, on Heart Mountain, and on some of the higher points northwest of Cody.

Local tradition avers that these structures once sheltered beacon fires used in signaling the Indian bands who were wont to cross the Bighorn Valley within sight of the plateau rim. I noted no evidence of burning, however, nor were there any artifacts in association. It is perhaps significant that in most of the structures, the open space was large enough to hold a man lying down and the walls were high enough to have given some protection from the wind. It seems possible that these were fasting shelters used by young men in quest of visions. Considering the isolated and difficult location of these constructions in the Pryors and apparently elsewhere, and the solitude required by vision-seekers, this would seem to me a more plausible explanation than the view that they housed beacon fires.

MEDICINE WHEELS

Much less common than tipi rings are wheel-shaped stone monuments or "medicine wheels" scattered sparingly from northwestern Wyoming to southern Alberta. Basically, they consist of a central circle or cairn from which lines of stones radiate outward, sometimes to an enclosing circle. Their meaning has given rise to much speculation, and controversy about their origin and purpose still continues. Probably the largest and most elaborate of these, and certainly the best known, is that in the northern Bighorn Mountains some 25 airline miles east of Lovell, Wyoming. It stands above the timber line on a rocky shoulder of Medicine Mountain at an elevation of about 8,700 feet, and commands an impressive view of the Bighorn Basin and the Rockies beyond. It has been described in some detail by Simms, who visited it in 1902, and by Grinnell. The descriptions differ in several particulars, perhaps partly because of disturbance of the stones by visitors and livestock in the intervening period; and the ground-plan

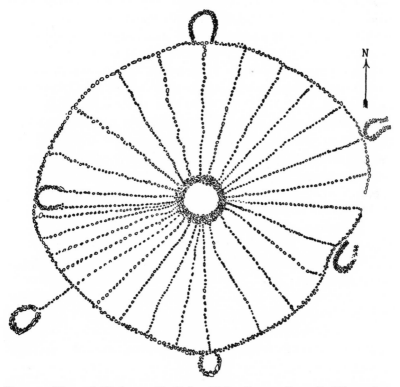

Fig. 23. *Plan of Bighorn Medicine Wheel, near Lovell, Wyoming.*

American Anthropologist

sketches they provide are by no means identical.[29] The plan shown here is based on a sketch by T. M. Galey in Grinnell's report.

Broadly speaking, the Bighorn medicine wheel consisted of large stones and slabs forming an irregular circle seventy-five to eighty feet in diameter, with a two-and-one-half-foot gap on the east. At the center was a smaller circle of piled slabs, twelve feet in outside diameter and three feet high, from which twenty-seven or twenty-eight lines of closely set stones radiated spoke-fashion to the outer ring. Within the larger circle and adjoining it on the west side, Grinnell recognized a stone-walled U-shaped structure nine feet long by five feet wide, opening toward the center with which its sides were connected by two spokes. Four or more low, oval or circular constructions, with walls fifteen to eighteen inches high, were spaced irregularly around the perimeter and in contact with it. About twelve feet southwest of the wheel, joined to it by an extension of one of the spokes, was a closed oval structure, "nearly long enough for a man to lie down in." The easternmost structure was a covered squarish or boxlike affair which could be entered by crawling through a low opening on its east side. On projecting slabs at the east side of the inner circle, according to Simms, "rested a perfectly bleached buffalo skull which had been placed so that it had the appearance of looking toward the rising sun," and other bison bones lay on nearby rocks. Grinnell says that two fifteenth-century Venetian beads and two specimens of wampum were found under one of the spokes.

Simms wrote that the Crows knew about the wheel, but could say nothing about its builders except that "it was made by people who had no iron." Two Sioux visitors among the Crows connected the Arapahoes and Cheyennes with it. Grinnell reported that an old and well-traveled travois trail across Medicine Mountain passed near the wheel, but thought that the antiquity of the wheel could not be doubted even though the beads indicated sacrifices

[29] S. C. Simms, "A Wheel-Shaped Stone Monument in Wyoming," *American Anthropologist*, Vol. V, No. 1 (1903), 107–10; G. B. Grinnell, "The Medicine Wheel," *American Anthropologist*, Vol. XXIV, No. 3 (July-September, 1922), 299–310.

made here within recent years. Other explanations vaguely attribute the wheel to the "little people" and to the Sheep Eater band of Shoshones. Grinnell calls attention to parallels between various details of the wheel and the plan of the Cheyenne Medicine Lodge —the outer circle corresponding to the wall of the lodge, the inner circle to the center pole, the spokes to the twenty-eight rafters, and

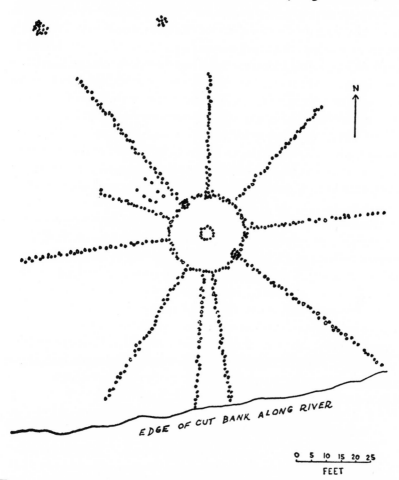

FIG. 24. *Plan of Sun River Medicine Wheel, near Lowry, Montana.*

Journal of Washington Academy of Sciences

269

the U-shaped affair on the west to the altar. Others would assign to the wheel a greater antiquity and an undetermined authorship, along with many of the tipi rings in the same general region.[30]

In the general vicinity, according to Grinnell, there were at least two similar wheels—one in southern Montana on the Bighorn River below old Fort C. F. Smith, the other in northern Wyoming near a trail traveled by the Tongue River Cheyennes from Montana on their visits to the Shoshones near Fort Washakie. As far as I know, there are no descriptions of these. Of less elaborate construction is another wheel on the north bank of Sun River near Lowry, Montana.[31] Its hub is a stone circle four feet across, surrounded by a second circle twenty-one feet in diameter. From this, eleven lines of rocks radiate outward at irregular intervals and to distances varying from twenty-one to forty feet. There is no enclosing circle. No signs of burning were noted in the inner ring; and it is not clear whether there were cairns or walled structures attached. Total diameter approximates one hundred feet.

Still simpler forms of medicine wheels were apparently used by the Blackfeet within the past century or two to mark the residence or grave of an outstanding war chief. Indeed, one of these is reported to have been constructed near Spring Coulee, Alberta, as recently as 1940. It includes a twenty-seven-foot circle, with a three-foot opening on the east flanked by two larger stones. Four lines of stones, each thirty feet long, run outward from the circle, one in each of the cardinal directions. Inside the circle, on its east-west diameter, lay two three-foot-stone-circled fireplaces. Other examples consist of simple circles, as small as twelve feet across and containing no hearth stones, but with four short lines extending outward along the cardinal directions.[32]

---

[30] Mulloy, "The Northern Plains," *loc. cit.*, 137; Mulloy, "A Preliminary Historical Outline for the Northwestern Plains," *loc. cit.*, 212–13.

[31] T. F. Kehoe, "Stone 'Medicine Wheels' in Southern Alberta and the Adjacent Portion of Montana," *Journal*, Washington Academy of Science, Vol. XLIV, No. 5 (1954), 135.

[32] H. A. Dempsey, "Stone 'Medicine Wheels'—Memorials to Blackfoot War Chiefs," *Journal*, Washington Academy of Sciences, Vol. XLVI, No. 6 (1956), 177–82.

PLATE XXV. Chain mail from the Paint Creek site in McPherson County, Kansas, probably of sixteenth-century Spanish origin.

PLATE XXVI. Peace medals from Pawnee graves at the Hill site, Webster County, Nebraska, occupied about A.D. 1800. (Nebraska State Historical Society). *Upper:* British medal bearing likeness of George III and dated 1762. *Lower:* Spanish medal bearing likeness of Charles IV and dated 1797.

OTHER ANTIQUITIES

The quarrying of stone for tools and utensils, and in lesser degree, the digging or mining of hematite and other materials, were additional activities of the prewhite contact peoples that have left their traces in the Northwestern Plains. The exact sources of the raw materials used at a given village or camp site can rarely be established; but some of the localities from which such stones as quartzite and obsidian, or hematite for pigment were certainly obtainable, are well established. In some instances, these localities still form an interesting, if inadequately studied, feature of the prehistory of the region.

The best-known and most extensive aboriginal quarries here are unquestionably the so-called Spanish Diggings in eastern Wyoming, with which the Spanish had nothing to do.[33] They consist of innumerable groups of pits scattered over the hills and ridges of the Muddy Creek drainage in northeastern Platte County and adjacent Niobrara County; and the name has been extended to include similar features found over an area of several hundred square miles from the Platte River eastward to Rawhide Butte, and extending into Goshen and Converse counties. Other quarries of similar character have been reported from northern Niobrara County near the junction of Hat Creek and Old Woman Creek.

The groups number from a dozen or so to scores of pits, and range from five or ten to forty or fifty acres, or more, in extent. In the aggregate, they represent a truly prodigious amount of labor, which must have involved many people over a long period of time.

The material so assiduously sought by the ancient quarrymen was a fine-grained quartzite aptly described by Dorsey as "of variegated color, passing from yellowish brown to violet gray, varied with shades of pink, violet, yellow, purple, etc." In addition nodular masses of jasper, chalcedony, and agatized material were available in the quartzite beds. To reach the stone desired, pits were

[33] G. A. Dorsey, "An Aboriginal Quartzite Quarry in Eastern Wyoming," Field Columbian Museum *Anthropological Series*, Vol. II, No. 4, Pub. No. 51 (1900), 233–43; Holmes, "Handbook of Aboriginal American Antiquities," Bureau of American Ethnology *Bulletin 60*, Pt. 1 (1919), 210–13.

dug through the overlying soil and rock strata until stone of workable quality was accessible. The pits vary widely in size and appearance. Some are now comparatively small and shallow, and the fill supports a sparse stand of grass and small herbs; others are up to forty or fifty feet in diameter, from six to fifteen feet, or more, in depth, and have a remarkably recent look. Among the pits, and often covering their walls and floors, are immense quantities of broken stone and refuse.

Surprisingly few tools that might have been used in the quarrying operations have been found. They include a few rough hammerstones with battered edges, but seemingly no mauls or sledges such as would seem to have been required to break up the masses of stone for handling or for later artifact manufacture. Worked flakes and large, coarsely chipped blanks and rejects also occur.

On the hillsides and in the valleys among the groups of quarry pits are found vast numbers of stone circles, or tipi rings. In and around these have been picked up scrapers, worked flakes, and scraps evidently left in the secondary working of the materials obtained from the diggings. In addition, there are numerous workshop areas, where the native flintsmiths reduced the masses of raw stone to smaller pieces that were more easily transported. Final chipping and finishing were apparently done in the distant camps and villages to which the roughed-out blanks were carried.

Material thought to have originated in the Spanish Diggings has been found as far east as the Missouri River near Omaha, and perhaps even farther away, in sites that antedate the coming of white men by several centuries. It is impossible to say, however, at what early date in the prehistoric past the excavating was begun by the aboriginal workmen.

Another important quarry area occurs at the southern edge of the Black Hills, around Edgemont and Hot Springs, South Dakota. Perhaps the largest of the ancient workings is on Flint Hill, six and one-half miles due south of Minnekahta. Here, as Darton and Smith reported more than forty years ago,[34]

[34] "Description of the Edgemont Quadrangle," U. S. Geological Survey Geo-

In the ridges on either side of Chilson Canyon, the [Dakota sandstone] formation is largely represented by a hard, gray to purplish-gray quartzite, . . . and there are extensive excavations made by the Indians for material for arrowheads and other implements . . . .

The old diggings, occupying nearly a half-section of land, are on a high tableland, at an elevation of about 4,500 feet. They consist of scores of large and small craterlike pits and adjacent piles of rough workshop debris. Large quarry blanks are present in great profusion; all are of quartzite, but varying in color from gray and purple, through red and brown, to yellow. Tipi rings are abundant in the neighborhood, and are said to extend northward for some miles toward the Black Hills proper. The site is strikingly reminiscent of the pitted areas at the Spanish Diggings, but covers a much smaller area.

Similar workings which I have not visited are reported on Parker Peak, 4 miles north of Flint Hill, at an elevation of over 4,800 feet. Other native workings have been noted on Battle Mountain, northeast of Hot Springs, where there are extensive ledges of quartzite. The stone found at all these quarries is represented at many archaeological sites in the nearby Angostura Reservoir, and at other localities in the general area.

From the mountains of Wyoming and Montana came other raw materials that were carried far to the east across the Great Plains. Soapstone for the manufacture of pots, pipes, and other articles was one of these. The exact location of the quarries used by the Indians has never been satisfactorily established, but there are some leads that might be worth following up. Thus, Samuel Aughey, territorial geologist, many years ago reported a deposit on the "north side of Rattlesnake Mountain, on the headwaters of the South Powder River," in present Fremont County; and another small occurrence of "massive soapstone and fibrous talc" is said to be on Badger Creek, on the west side of the Teton

logic Atlas of the United States, *Folio No. 108* (1904); see also Hughes, "Investigations in Western South Dakota and Northeastern Wyoming," *loc. cit.*, 270 n. 3.

Range.[35] This may be the same locality, northeast of Driggs, Idaho, where an old prospector once told a Washington geologist that there was "an exposed face on which lie partially cut away blocks of soapstone, with fragments of broken pots at the foot of the exposure." As far as I am aware, none of these locations has been visited or studied by archaeologists.

Farther to the north, between Mammoth Hot Springs and Norris Geyser Basin in the Yellowstone National Park, is the well-known Obsidian Cliff[36] or canyon, from which considerable quantities of stone were evidently taken by the Indians until comparatively recent times. Despite its easily worked character, however, obsidian was much less popular among the native Plains flintsmiths than was the more abundant and readily available quartzite. That some of the obsidian found in the prehistoric sites of the Central and Northern Plains, as among the Hopewellian peoples of A. D. 200–400, came from this locality appears probable, though that in the later sites from the Republican Valley southward is more likely from New Mexico or Colorado deposits.

Not far south of the Spanish Diggings is the famous Hartville uplift with its important iron-ore deposits. Here, in the Frederick-Sunrise district, hematite occurs in both hard and soft varieties, the latter being light red in color and readily staining the fingers. There is good evidence that before the white man developed these deposits, the soft varieties of hematite were being sought by the Indians. In the early days of prospecting and mining, ancient drifts running as far as forty feet into the mountain and extending to depths of twenty feet or more were encountered. In these old diggings and around their openings were found quantities of stone implements and refuse such as hammers and sledges.[37] How widely and by whom these materials were carried and traded, we have

[35] F. W. Osterwald and D. B. Osterwald, "Wyoming Mineral Resources," Geological Survey of Wyoming *Bulletin 45* (1952), 159–60.

[36] Holmes, "Notes on an Extensive Deposit of Obsidian in the Yellowstone National Park," *American Naturalist*, Vol. XIII (April, 1879), 247–50.

[37] E. P. Snow, "The Hartville Iron Ore Deposits in Wyoming," *Engineering and Mining Journal*, Vol. LX (October 5, 1895), 320–21; R. F. Gilder, "Indian Sites Near Frederick, Wyoming," *Records of the Past*, Vol. VII, Pt. 4 (July-August, 1908), 179–82.

no way of knowing; but it seems clear that these deposits were an important resource for the Indians in the days before better paint materials were obtainable from the traders.

Gypsum in crystalline form, soft and easily fashioned into ornaments, was obtained by some of the Plains Indians in the northwestern part of the Black Hills. In the summer of 1874, during Lieutenant Colonel G. A. Custer's Black Hills reconnaissance, Captain William Ludlow, engineer officer of the expedition, reported that, on July 22, "the course led southward up the Redwater valley, which is from four to ten miles in width, and bounded by high hills heavily timbered with pine. The gypsum appeared in enormous quantities. One of the guides took me off to the right to see a huge mass of it, crystallized and shining beautifully in the sun. The Indians, for generations, have, in passing, split off pieces for ornaments, and by degrees cut a shoulder several feet deep on it at the level of the ground. Inyan Kara was in sight all day to the southward . . . ." A scientist member of the expedition, George Bird Grinnell, describes this feature as "a large mass of pure gypsum which rose from the plain 8 feet high, 8 feet wide, and about 20 feet long. We could see that it had once been much larger, and the Sioux scouts with us stated that the Indians had for centuries been in the habit of visiting it and carrying away fragments from which to make ornaments."[38]

On the canyon walls and rock ledges widely scattered throughout the Northwestern Plains, particularly in and around the broken and mountainous areas, there are to be found many petroglyphs and pictographs. There is a wide variety of designs, ranging from simple to highly complex, and probably representing a greater range of motifs than is to be seen in any other section of the Plains area. Notable "galleries" of this aboriginal art include Pictograph Cave in southern Montana; Dinwoody Canyon in Fremont County, Wyoming; Castle Gardens south of Moneta, in Natrona County, Wyoming; Whoop-Up Canyon near Newcastle in northeastern Wyoming; the Red Canyon district in the

---

[38] W. Ludlow, "Report of a Reconnaissance of the Black Hills of Dakota, Made in the Summer of 1874," Engineer Department, U. S. Army (1875), 12, 76.

southern Black Hills; and Writing-on-Stone on the Milk River in southern Alberta.[39]

Most of the figures were made by pecking, grinding, or rubbing, in all likelihood with stone tools; a few are in a fine-line incising technique. Where these include rows of human figures associated with fire arms, as in the southern Black Hills, they are evidently of recent origin and were perhaps made with metal tools. Less common are the painted pictographs, usually done in red, black, or white, rarely in green or other colors.

Geometric designs include straight and wavy lines, dots, circles, crosses, squares, triangles, "ladders," zigzags, crisscross or screen-like motifs, and various combinations, elaborations, or modifications of these and other elements. Among the life forms are antlered creatures that may be deer or elk; two-horned goat- or antelope-like animals; bison; rare turtles; birds with outspread wings and turned head that remind one of the shell "thunderbird" carvings occasionally found in village sites in the eastern Plains; horses and equestrian figures; and many others. Humans are represented in various ways, from simple sticklike figures to relatively complicated ones. In one widespread style, the shoulders are sharply angular with the neck and head rising from a deep V, the arms outspread with open hands, and perhaps with lines hanging from the arms like fringes or plumes, or with other features that suggest attempts to depict details of dress, adornment, or body painting.

Particularly interesting are the circular or oblong shieldlike designs, often bisected or quartered by vertical and/or horizontal lines, sometimes with short pendant lines that suggest fringes, and not uncommonly embellished with geometric or life-form motifs.

[39] Mulloy, "A Preliminary Historical Outline for the Northwestern Plains," *loc. cit.*, 118–39; D. S. Gebhard and H. A. Cahn, "The Petroglyphs of Dinwoody, Wyoming," *American Antiquity*, Vol. XV, No. 3 (1950), 219–28; Renaud, "Pictographs and Petroglyphs of the High Western Plains," *Eighth Report* of the Archeological Survey of the High Western Plains (1936), 9–24; H. I. Smith, "An Album of Prehistoric Canadian Art," Canada Department of Mines *Bulletin* 37, Anthropological Series, No. 8 (1923), 102–107; K. G. Secrist, "Pictographs in Central Montana," Montana State University *Anthropology and Sociology Papers, No. 20* (1960).

That these are intended to depict shields is strongly suggested by the fact that many show the bearer's head above and his feet below. Sometimes a spear- or arrowlike object also occurs in association. None, as far as I know, is shown as carried by a horseman, though small circular objects that may well be shields sometimes occur on equestrian figures. These shields or shield-bearing pedestrians have been reported in a number of localities from Wyoming, through central Montana, to southern Alberta, and are thought to date from a late prehistoric period. They are similar to others found farther south in the Utah-Colorado region, which have been attributed to the Fremont culture and probably date from before A.D. 1200.[40]

As in other sections of the Plains region, the rock carvings and drawings of the Northwestern Plains are for the most part still undated, and the identity of their makers is undetermined. In the absence of representations of guns, horses, and other elements known to have been introduced by Europeans and Americans, it is seldom possible to make convincing correlations of these materials with other antiquities that may occur nearby. Attempts have been made to establish sequences of types on the basis of style or superposition of elements or on other grounds; but the validity of sequences so made and their wider applicability throughout the region remains to be proved.

[40] Wormington, "A Reappraisal of the Fremont Culture," *Proceedings*, Denver Museum of Natural History, No. 1 (1955), 160.

CHAPTER NINE

✋ THROUGH A GLASS, DARKLY—

". . . THE VAST TRACT of untimbered country which lies between the waters of the Missouri, Mississippi, and the western Ocean . . . may become in time equally celebrated as the sandy deserts of Africa. . . . our citizens will through necessity . . . leave the prairies incapable of cultivation to the wandering and uncivilized aborigines . . . ."

So wrote Captain Zebulon M. Pike in 1808, after two years of exploration in the Great Plains.[1] Like many who followed him, he could not foresee that within the next century these same prairies and plains would yield an untold wealth of grains, minerals, livestock, and manufactures; that they would support many times the sparse and scattered population he found there. Nor had he any way of knowing that, in earlier days, the aboriginal population had not always or everywhere been so "wandering and uncivilized" as were the Indians he met.

New Jersey–born and eastern bred, Pike in his disdain for the western prairies and plains reflected the point of view that was to dominate the easterner's thinking about the grasslands for many years to come. Until the 1930's, for example, the usual approach to the problems of human prehistory in the Plains was essentially a negative one. Anthropological dogma held that the prairies and plains offered no inducements to men without horses or to would-be farmers without the plow. In 1859, Lewis H. Morgan flatly

---

[1] *An Account of Expeditions to the Sources of the Mississippi During the Years 1805, 1806, and 1807*, Appendix to Part II, 8.

stated that "the prairie is not congenial to the Indian, and is only made tolerable to him by possession of the horse and the rifle."[2] Within the past half-century, as we have previously noted, professional anthropologists have variously suggested the possibility of "a prehistoric uninhabited area" in the Western Plains; that the Great Plains were "rather bare of archeology"; that the region was essentially a transient hunting ground visited seasonally by peoples whose principal residence was either in the mountains to the west or in the woodlands to the east; and that the occupation of the Plains by a hunting people without horses is "incredible . . . to many students of the Plains area."

In light of the archaeological surveys and excavations of the past thirty years, there is no longer any question about whether or not the Plains were inhabited by man in prehorse days. We can be quite sure they were. Our questions are rather, in what way and by what groups did their peopling come about, and how did these groups adjust their ways of living to the varying opportunities and limitations of the Plains environment? In previous chapters we have seen that, as hunters, as foragers, or, in later times when and where circumstances permitted, as semisedentary tillers of the soil, men have resided in the region—in the prairie as well as in what is now the steppe—for a very long time.

We do not yet know at what date the first men set foot on the North American Plains, whence they came, or the exact nature of their culture and way of life. Beyond question, however, man was present here before the final extinction of some of the larger mammals characteristic of the Pleistocene epoch, including notably the mammoth, the native horse, and a large form of bison now extinct. It is clear, too, that from his earliest demonstrable presence here, man's subsistence was closely linked with the larger game animals that thronged the grasslands. Most of our evidence comes, in fact, from his game kills and butchering grounds, and from the transient camps out of which he operated.

Among these early big-game hunters, the oldest of whom we now have archaeological record are those who tipped their hunt-

[2] L. A. White, ed., *Lewis Henry Morgan, The Indian Journals, 1859–60*, 42.

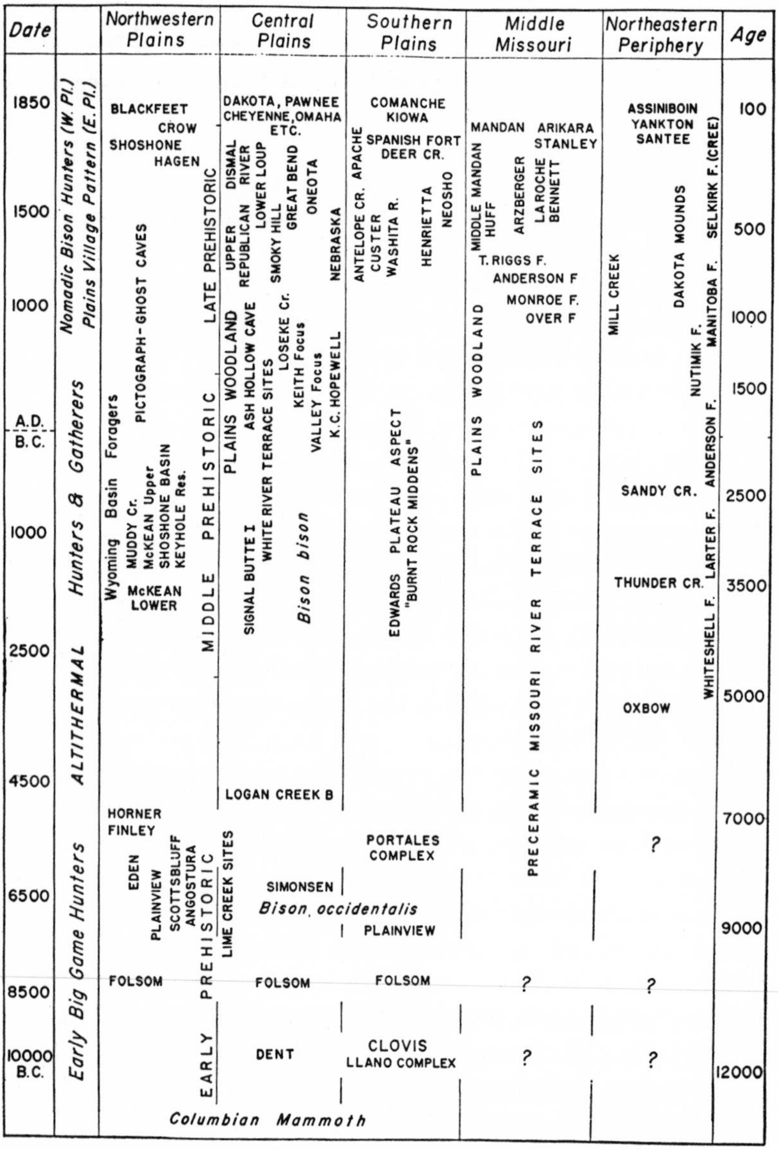

Date			Northwestern Plains	Central Plains	Southern Plains	Middle Missouri	Northeastern Periphery		Age
1850	Nomadic Bison Hunters (W.Pl.)		BLACKFEET CROW SHOSHONE HAGEN	DAKOTA, PAWNEE CHEYENNE, OMAHA ETC.	COMANCHE KIOWA	MANDAN ARIKARA STANLEY	ASSINIBOIN YANKTON SANTEE		100
		Plains Village Pattern (E.Pl.)		DISMAL RIVER LOWER LOUP GREAT BEND ONEOTA	SPANISH FORT DEER CR.	MIDDLE MANDAN HUFF ARZBERGER LAROCHE BENNETT		SELKIRK F. (CREE)	
1500			PICTOGRAPH-GHOST CAVES	UPPER REPUBLICAN SMOKY HILL NEBRASKA	ANTELOPE CR. APACHE CUSTER WASHITA R. HENRIETTA NEOSHO		MILL CREEK	MANITOBA F.	500
1000	Hunters & Gatherers	Foragers		PLAINS WOODLAND ASH HOLLOW CAVE WHITE RIVER TERRACE SITES LOSEKE Cr. KEITH Focus VALLEY Focus K.C. HOPEWELL		T. RIGGS F. ANDERSON F MONROE F. OVER F		NUTIMIK F. ANDERSON F.	1000
A.D. B.C.		Wyoming Basin		SIGNAL BUTTE I	EDWARDS PLATEAU ASPECT "BURNT ROCK MIDDENS"	PLAINS WOODLAND	SANDY CR.	LARTER F.	1500
1000	ALTITHERMAL		MUDDY Cr. McKEAN Upper SHOSHONE BASIN KEYHOLE Res. McKEAN LOWER	*Bison bison*			THUNDER CR.	WHITESHELL F.	2500
2500						PRECERAMIC MISSOURI RIVER TERRACE SITES			3500
							OXBOW		5000
4500				LOGAN CREEK B					
	Early Big Game Hunters		HORNER FINLEY EDEN PLAINVIEW SCOTTSBLUFF ANGOSTURA	LIME CREEK SITES	PORTALES COMPLEX		?		7000
6500				SIMONSEN *Bison occidentalis*	PLAINVIEW				9000
8500			FOLSOM	FOLSOM	FOLSOM	?	?		
10000 B.C.				DENT	CLOVIS LLANO COMPLEX	?	?		12000

Columbian Mammoth

FIG. 25. *Provisional chart showing approximate time relationships of certain archaeological sites and complexes in the Plains area.*

ing spears with the large fluted heads known as Clovis points, and who before 11,000 years ago pursued the mammoth in the lush grasslands and around the water holes of what is now the High Plains steppe. In later sites, bones of the mammoth are not present, and the animal remains are principally those of bison of the now extinct form described variously as *Bison taylori, Bison antiquus,* and *Bison occidentalis.* With these are associated the well-known Folsom Fluted points and the unfluted Plainview points, probably dating mostly after about 10,000 years ago. Recently investigated mass kills of *Bison occidentalis* in northwestern Iowa, with which were found side-notched points of types characteristic of the eastern United States, indicate that big-game hunters were present in the Eastern Plains at least as early as 8,400 years ago. Still later, around 7,000 years ago, came the people who left the Eden and Scottsbluff weapon points and associated materials, and those represented by the Portales complex in the Southern Plains. It is possible that some of these later groups were taking bison of essentially modern species.

Beyond the fact of their existence, and some understanding of the sort of hunting and butchering equipment they possessed and of the animals upon which they largely subsisted, we still know little about these early hunters. They were probably present only in comparatively small numbers and in scattered groups; but the wide dispersal of their characteristic weapon points and other tools indicates that the people, though limited to travel on foot and not known to have had dogs as possible beasts of burden, may have roamed over considerable distances in search or pursuit of their quarry. Most of the artifacts that have survived from this remote period are of stone, and consist of knives, scrapers, choppers, and other implements primarily designed for the chase and for processing the products of the chase. Their weapon points were of several distinctive kinds, and often show high competence in flint working. Grinding stones are rare or absent at most of these early sites; but it seems likely that some use must have been made of roots, berries, and seeds in season, and perhaps of small game when the larger animals were for any reason not readily obtainable.

Most of the archaeological sites in the Southern and Western Plains for which radiocarbon age determinations are available appear to be either older than about 5000 B.C., and so may be assigned to the early-big-game-hunter period, or else are later than about 2500 B.C. The intervening gap for which we still have few or no dates corresponds to the estimated time of the Thermal Maximum or Altithermal period, during which temperatures in the western United States are believed to have risen while the rainfall decreased. In what way these changed climatic conditions may have affected the hunters in the Western Plains we do not yet know from any direct evidence; but it is widely believed that the increasing warmth and aridity may have reduced the natural vegetative cover from a prairie to a desert or semidesert one, thereby forcing the larger game animals and the men who depended upon them to follow the shifting grasslands to other regions in the east or north where there was heavier precipitation. Some of the early hunters may have followed the eastward-spreading grasslands into the prairie peninsula; others perhaps moved northward into the Prairie Provinces of southern Canada.

The next people of whom we have evidence in the Western Plains, then, appear to date mainly from a time after about 2500 B.C., when the moister and cooler Medithermal climate was succeeding the waning Altithermal drought. Their traces have been found in numerous camp sites, workshops, and rock shelters throughout the Northwestern Plains, and have been most intensively investigated in the Wyoming-Montana region. The archaeological deposits, though not usually very productive, are sometimes of considerable depth, and suggest repeated occupations over lengthy periods of time. Cutting, scraping, and chopping tools are present; and the weapon points are usually markedly unlike those of the early hunters in form and workmanship, and show much less skill in flint-working. Bone refuse, especially at sites in the Wyoming region, often includes a high proportion of small animal remains and a notable scarcity of bison. That the gathering and processing of seeds and other vegetal substances was an increasingly important part of the subsistence economy is suggested by the appearance of grinding stones.

For these post-Altithermal small-game hunters and gatherers in the Northwestern Plains the term Foragers has commonly been used. It indicates a belief that the wider range of foods represented may reflect a sharply diminished supply of bison as an aftermath of the climatic adversities of the Altithermal period, with a resulting need on man's part for piecing out his diet with whatever edible items could be wrung from the limited resources of a harsh and difficult natural environment. While this interpretation appears to be valid for the Wyoming region, where a Forager way of life apparently persisted until the coming of the white man, the relative abundance of bison bone and of hunting tools at such sites as Signal Butte I and Logan Creek in Nebraska, at Pictograph Cave and in the bison kills of Montana, and at other locations from southern Canada to Texas and New Mexico suggests that throughout a large part of the Great Plains bison were still an important feature of the subsistence economy, even though gathering may have played a larger role during this period than among the early big-game hunters.

None of the peoples we have considered to this point were acquainted with the art of pottery-making nor, with exception of the Kenton cave-dwellers of the Upper Cimarron drainage, are any of them known to have practiced agriculture. Their artifacts, as revealed by archaeology, consisted principally of articles of chipped stone, occasionally with some bone tools, and in the later stages with grinding implements. On the Southeastern Periphery, where influences from early people of the eastern United States are strongly manifested, ground- and polished-stone items were also present. The term *Lithic* period has sometimes been used to categorize these remains, and to distinguish them broadly from those of the later pottery-making, or Ceramic, peoples of the Plains region.

At a date still undetermined but possibly before the beginning of the Christian Era, the potter's art came to the people of the

Plains. The earliest pottery of which we have evidence shows many similarities to some of the widespread Woodland wares of the Upper Mississippi–Ohio region. It has been found most often in the Eastern Plains from the Dakotas southward to Oklahoma; and where it occurs in stratified sites, it underlies all other pottery horizons. Though usually coarse and heavy by comparison with later wares, it does not suggest a local invention; and its distribution bears out the view that it was introduced into the trans-Missouri Plains from the east by people possessing a Woodland culture.

The Plains Woodland people are best known from investigations in the Central Plains, particularly in Nebraska and northern Kansas; but it seems clear that the area which they once occupied included also parts of the Middle Missouri region to the north, much of Oklahoma to the south, and probably extended west to the Colorado Rockies. On the basis of differences in pottery styles, projectile-point forms, and in other particulars, several variants have been recognized. They include the relatively advanced Hopewellian village sites and stone-chambered burial mounds of the Kansas City–Kansas River–eastern Oklahoma district, and also a number of simpler cultures represented in many small, inconspicuous sites widely scattered throughout the Plains. The Hopewellian sites, with their plentiful storage pits, accumulations of village debris, and varied artifact inventories in stone, bone, and other materials, suggest a fairly stable and fixed community life. It was based in part on hunting and gathering, with bison evidently less important than deer; and from these sites, assigned on the basis of radiocarbon determinations to the first two or three centuries of the Christian Era, have come the earliest dated remains of corn and beans found so far in the Plains. Otherwise, most Woodland sites seem to be those of people practicing mainly a creek-valley hunting and gathering subsistence economy and apparently having little or no agriculture except in the later period of their stay here. The time span of their presence is still uncertain, with radiocarbon dates ranging from about 1900 B.C. to the seventh or eighth century A.D.

The period during which the Woodland peoples occupied the Plains is still very inadequately known. It is an important one, however, for several reasons. For one thing, it witnessed the first appearance of pottery. Much more significant is the fact that it marks the stage during which the people of the region took up the cultivation of crops, thereby beginning the change-over from simple food-collecting to a food-producing subsistence economy, and thus preparing the way for a far more secure hold on the land than any of their predecessors had.

In much of the region west of the Missouri River and southward through the Eastern Plains, the Woodland peoples were followed in late prehistoric times by others whose archaeological remains give indication of a more firmly established occupancy of the land. Although their settlements were concentrated chiefly along the streams in the eastern sections, in what is actually the tall-grass prairie, it is clear that some of these groups, who were certainly crop growers, also ventured far to the west and for a time followed their semisedentary way of life in the creek valleys along the margins of the High Plains. Their subsistence economy was a dual one, in which the people exploited alike the agricultural potential of the fertile bottom lands and the abundant game resources of the wooded stream valleys and the adjacent grassy uplands. These were the Plains Village Indians; and their basic way of life, but with variations in detail, endured in the Eastern Plains for perhaps one thousand years or more. Its beginning, once estimated at about A.D. 1200, now appears to date back as much as three or four centuries earlier if radiocarbon findings may be relied upon.

Common to the way of life of practically all the Village Indians were certain practices that also serve to distinguish their remains from those of the simpler peoples who preceded them in the region. These included the use of permanent multi-family habitations, usually larger and more substantially constructed than anything of which we have record from the Woodland period; residence in fixed villages, which were sometimes or in some localities protected by ditches and stockades, and with which

285

numbers of underground pits for food storage were normally associated; abundant pottery of distinctive character; and a much greater range of artifacts in stone, bone, horn, and shell. The bone hoe, varying in form but generally fashioned from a bison shoulder blade and unknown from the Woodland sites, can be considered a hallmark of this period. Curved bone hooks, toggle harpoon heads, and fish bones are direct evidence of fishing, of which there is no indication from the preceding Woodland sites.

The Village Indian period may be conveniently thought of as consisting of two stages. In the earlier, where there is no evidence of contact with white men, the villages were usually fairly small; houses were square or rectangular in floor plan, and were either earth-covered or mud-plastered in the Central and Southern Plains; and the associated pottery was plain surfaced or cord roughened. From the Niobrara southward, many of the settlements stood along the lesser streams rather than on the major watercourses. The picture in general, from the Dakotas to Texas. seems to be one of innumerable small, widely scattered communities, probably not often exceeding a few score inhabitants, the women tilling their gardens in the nearby creek bottoms and the men hunting along the valley margins and on the adjacent uplands. Many of the basic elements of the culture of these small-town peoples, such as their pottery, their agriculture, and their community life, were rooted ultimately in the east; but the way of life had a much stronger Plains flavor than did that of the earlier Woodland groups. North of the Niobrara, the ancestral Mandans may have been among the people represented; farther south, the Pawnees and other Caddoan groups were possibly among these early-day farmers in the Plains.

In late prehistoric times, perhaps not more than a century or so before the first white men reached the Plains in the mid-sixteenth century, there appear to have been major shifts in the distribution of the native population and notable changes in the community patterns. The small earth-lodge settlements on the westerly streams were apparently abandoned, whether because of drought or for other reasons we do not yet know for certain.

Villages became fewer in number and larger in size, and were commonly situated on the larger streams; the houses assumed a circular floor plan, and were typically earth covered; and the pottery included simple stamped, incised, and plain, but no cord-roughened wares. These characteristics persisted into the historic period among the sedentary tribes of the Middle Missouri, notably the Mandans, Arikaras, and Hidatsas, and among the Eastern Plains tribes farther south, such as the Pawnees, Omahas, Otos, and Kansas. On the Middle Arkansas and southward, the grass-house villages of the Wichitas and other Caddoan-speaking groups had superseded the earlier settlements of wattle-and-daub and earth-lodge habitations. Some of these historic tribes were very likely lineal descendants of the early farmers of the prehistoric small-town communities; others seem to have been later arrivals who adopted the way of life of the people they found residing in the region.

In terms of material abundance, the early historic period between perhaps 1500 and 1700 in the Southern and Central Plains, and between 1600 and 1750 on the Middle Missouri, probably represented the high tide of the Village Indians in the Eastern Plains. The greater stability of residence and the marked concentration of tribal populations in a smaller number of larger towns undoubtedly sparked a notable flowering of culture and a richer and more abundant life by comparison with the earlier days. One wonders whether the great intervillage and tribal rituals and institutions for which such people as the Pawnees, for example, were so widely known in later days, and the numerous societies which formed such an important part of their community life had their real development and growth in this period. The way of life of these historic groups is, of course, well recorded in the travel narratives and other writings of many European and American explorers from the sixteenth to the nineteenth centuries.

While such Village Indians as the Mandans, Arikaras, and Pawnees were working out their destiny along the river valleys from the Missouri westward to the edge of the High Plains, other groups from the east were pressing into the prairie lands. In the eastern

Dakotas and southern Manitoba, a people or peoples about whom we still know all too little, were erecting various kinds of burial mounds and linear earthworks. Some of their artifacts were like those of the prehistoric rectangular-house dwellers along the Middle Missouri, with whom they may have been in direct contact. Among these groups may have been the ancestral Assiniboines, slowly working their way northwestward out of the Minnesota lake country; and one wonders whether they may also have included the forerunners of some of the historically marginal Western Plains Algonkian groups, such as the Blackfeet. It seems possible that some of the mounds along the Middle Missouri may mark an early wave of Dakotan peoples, pushing westward from the Minnesota area even before they had become the proud equestrian buffalo-hunters and raiders of history.

Farther south, along the eastern margin of the Central Plains, a string of Oneota sites is thought to represent an influx of Siouan-speaking peoples adjusting their basic economy and way of life to the Plains Village Indian pattern. Their shell-tempered and trailed or incised pottery is readily distinguishable from practically all other Plains wares, but most of the other artifacts are similar to those of the late prehistoric and early historic Village Indians. A subsistence economy based partly on horticulture and partly on bison and deer hunting is indicated. Such marginal tribes as the Iowas and Missouris were certainly carriers of Oneota culture, and it is possible the Kansas were also. The Osages are thought to have developed out of late prehistoric cultures widely distributed around the flanks of the Ozark Plateau, being influenced in early historic times by contact with Oneota groups to the north; but the available archaeological evidence makes them look less like a Plains group than like a marginal Prairie people who acquired Plains hunting practices and other traits in comparatively late times.

As for the steppe belt fronting the Rockies from Alberta to Texas, we still know relatively little regarding their inhabitants in late prehistoric days, following the indicated occupations by the Woodland and the later earth-lodge Village peoples. It has long been thought likely, on the basis of historical and traditional data, that the Shoshones at one time held the plains of Alberta and Montana, from which they were dispossessed in the eighteenth century by the Blackfeet and possibly other tribes; but dissenting views have been expressed on this point. Archaeological evidence suggests that hunters and gatherers who may well have been Shoshoneans lived in the Wyoming Basin, carrying on a Forager way of life that had been characteristic of the area for some thousands of years before. The Plains Apaches, as full-fledged pedestrian bison-hunters whom the Spanish called the *Querecho*, were certainly in the southern High Plains shortly after 1500; before that, they were quite likely in the plains north of the Arkansas, but no convincing archaeological evidence of their passage has yet come to light here. The Apaches are known to have practiced some horticulture in western Kansas, Nebraska, and elsewhere in the High Plains during the seventeenth and early eighteenth centuries, perhaps under stimulus from Pueblo fugitives or through frequent trade and other contacts with the Pueblo towns on the Upper Río Grande. Shortly after 1700, the Comanches moved out of the Rockies into the adjacent Southern Plains, took over the horse from the Río Grande settlements, and turned on the Apaches. During the second quarter of the eighteenth century, after some two hundred years of recorded residence in the Plains—first as pedestrian bison-hunters, then as part-time farmers and hunters— the Apaches were finally driven from the Plains by the Comanches.

The distribution of tribes throughout the Plains in historic times has been briefly and incidentally noted from time to time in earlier chapters in this book. Broadly speaking, the Village Indians north of the Niobrara were largely limited to the immediate valley of the Missouri; to the south, they dwelt mainly east of the ninety-ninth meridian. Farther west, the pedestrian hunters of pre-horse days became, or were supplanted by, the mounted bison-hunters of historic days. From the Spanish settlements in Mexico and the southwestern United States, the horse spread rapidly northward and eastward, transforming and greatly enriching the life of the nomadic hunter groups. This interesting and highly important

289

phenomenon has been discussed often, but new data and interpretations may still be anticipated. As early as 1640, the Indians of western Kansas are thought to have been partly mounted; and within one hundred years, the horse had reached the Blackfeet in Alberta. By 1800, practically all of the Plains tribes were supplied with horses; but it was the roving warriors and hunters of the Western Plains—the Blackfeet, Crows, Dakotas, Cheyennes, Arapahoes, Comanches, and their contemporaries who held the balance of power and dominated the region. Penned up in their walled towns by the mounted and foot-loose warriors and plunderers from the west, and scourged periodically by the smallpox and other introduced diseases, the Village Indians along the eastern edge of the Plains, carriers of a cultural tradition and dual way of life that had persisted for one thousand years or more, were in final and irreversible eclipse.

THE INDIAN AND THE PLAINS

Incomplete though the archaeological record admittedly is, it has already brought about notable modifications in long-held preconceptions regarding man's way of living in the Plains environment. We can no longer think of the Plains Indians solely in terms of the mounted and war-bonneted bands that faced the invading white man with increasing determination in the three and one-half centuries after Coronado and before Wounded Knee. It is doubtlessly true that in historic times, during the days of greatness of the horse Indians, the "richest [Plains Indian] cultures were found where the bison herds were thickest, and the herds thickest where the grass and climatic conditions were the most favorable."[3] During this period a distinctive and colorful type of culture flourished here, and it was clearly correlated with the distribution of the buffalo and of the open grassland plains. But the bison range and the grassland extended beyond the homelands of the "typical" Plains tribes; and in terms of this greater Plains area it is *not* true that migratory nomadism was the only kind of culture or way of

[3] Wissler, *The Relation of Nature to Man in Aboriginal America*, 218.

life that could or ever did flourish in the region. The often argued case for the Plains Indian as a product of the natural environment, a product whose outstanding feature a sociologist has asserted was mobility and for which a recent beginning and development has been proposed by some, overlooks the fact that the final period of Plains Indian supremacy was a product of both the natural environment and of historic accident. The historical accident, of course, was the arrival of the white man and introduction of the horse, for whose use the open plains and their countless bison—along with the pedestrian hunters—were made to order. Thus, the Plains environment did not predetermine the direction in which native culture would have to go; rather, it offered certain options which at different times and places, and in varying degree, were accepted and developed in different ways by the native populations.

In historic times, the greater Plains area was characterized by two markedly dissimilar subsistence economies or ways of life. Along the stream valleys of the prairies in the eastern part, where fertile bottom lands, adequate rainfall, and the growing season permitted, the native economy was based upon the cultivation of domestic crops, with hunting as an important supplement. The tribes residing here dwelt in large permanent villages situated near timbered streams where wood, water, and arable ground were close at hand. Dwellings consisted of circular earth-covered or grass-thatched structures, with some use of bark coverings among the more recently arrived groups. The livelihood was based largely on cultivation of maize, beans, squash, and sunflowers, supplemented by the gathering of numerous wild berries, fruits, and tubers. The products of the chase were of almost equal importance, particularly after acquisition of the horse. All of the larger game animals were drawn upon, but bison were the principal objective. To obtain them, one or two carefully organized hunting trips were made annually toward the western sections. On these occasions, the entire population of the villages with exception of the very young, the senile, and the decrepit moved en masse, living in portable skin tipis and hauling their baggage on horseback or by travois, and behaving in general like the nomadic hunting tribes of the Western Plains. These great tribal hunts were reported for the Kansas as early as 1723; how much earlier they were practiced we cannot say. At the temporarily deserted villages, the possessions which could not be carried along were concealed in underground storage pits. In aboriginal times all these village groups made pottery, and possessed, in addition, well-developed industries in bone, stone, horn, shell, and other materials. Unlike the briefly occupied camp sites of the western hunters, the abandoned house sites, cache pits, and refuse accumulations of the village dwellers usually yield a rich harvest for the archaeologist.

In the Western Plains, where the white man's experience with corn-growing has generally been less successful for climatic reasons, the historic Indians depended primarily upon hunting, with the bison as the cornerstone of their subsistence economy. Throughout the spring, summer, and fall organized bands of these Indians lurked about the fringes of the herds, subsisting chiefly on the flesh of the bison and drying large quantities of meat to be stored for winter use. In winter the roving camp units usually retired to sheltered stream valleys or broken areas which, because of water, wood, and forage for the horses, were sometimes used year after year. In such localities, too, the bison were more likely to be found during inclement weather. Large herds of horses were to be seen around every camp. The skin tipi was in universal use. Skin-working was highly developed; but otherwise the implements, utensils, and industries were limited to essentials which could be easily and conveniently carried on horseback from camp to camp. Surplus foods were stored in skin containers. Except for the limited cultivation of tobacco, agriculture was nonexistent; so was pottery-making, though many of these tribes had some tradition of the art in earlier times. The gathering of wild fruits, berries, and starchy roots and tubers augmented the products of the chase; maize was obtained by trade or theft from the settled agricultural tribes. An elaborate militaristic system had been built up, and much of the time not occupied in food-getting was given over to raiding and horse-stealing. No definite tribal boundaries were recognized by these people, and the distances traveled by them during their hunting trips and in war forays frequently totaled many hundreds of miles.

In part, the historic distribution of these two ways of life reflects, of course, native man's ways of adapting his habits to the limitations and opportunities of the natural environment. In the west, where climatic limitations—insufficient rainfall and a short, uncertain growing season—made corn-growing precarious, man found in the immense bison herds a more secure food source and adjusted his way of living to the requirements of a constantly moving food supply. In the east, where climate was a less restrictive factor, he added a food-producing economy to the pre-existing food-collecting (hunting and gathering) economy and thus was able to develop a more stable community life with larger population aggregates and a richer and more complex social and religious life.[4]

The interactions between the Plains Indian and his environment, as is hinted in the foregoing paragraphs, were many and varied, but unfortunately they have never been the subject of a detailed ecological study. None can be attempted here. Such a study should involve not only the effect of the environment upon the Indian, to which some attention has been paid by a number of workers, but also the effect of the Indian upon the environment.[5]

[4] Possibly, as John C. Ewers has suggested to me, the dissimilarities between these two ways of life, as judged from the archaeological findings and from the respective material culture inventories, would be much less striking if the total cultural assemblages, including social organization, ceremonialism, and other nonmaterial traits, were considered. It is certain that the transformation from a semiagricultural Village life to all-out nomadic bison-hunting could be made in a relatively short time, as is illustrated by the Cheyennes, probably by the Crows, and perhaps by such other tribes as the Arapahoes and Gros Ventres. I know of no convincing historic examples of the reverse shift, from roving bison-hunters to semiagricultural Village Indians, except on very rare and transitory occasions, as long as the bison were available and plentiful.

[5] Gilmore, "Uses of Plants by the Indians of the Missouri River Region," *loc. cit.*, esp. 56–61; F. E. Clements and R. W. Chaney, "Environment and Life in the Great Plains," Carnegie Institution of Washington *Supplementary Publications*, No. 24 (rev. ed.) (1937); Kroeber, "Cultural and Natural Areas of Native North America," *loc. cit.*, 76–88; Wedel, "Environment and Native Subsistence Economies in the Central Great Plains," *loc. cit.;* Wedel, "Some Aspects of Human Ecology in the Central Plains," *loc. cit.*

It may be doubted that the roving hunters of the Western Plains materially affected the plant and animal resources upon which they levied for their sustenance. Their hunting involved primarily the bison, though antelope, elk, deer, and smaller forms were by no means ignored when circumstances favored or necessitated their utilization. That their hunting was sometimes prodigal and resulted in the killing of far more animals than could possibly be utilized for meat or hides is undoubtedly true. Yet it may fairly be questioned whether the native Indian alone could have eliminated the herds, even with the horse and gun. The near extinction of the bison in the 1880's resulted from a variety of factors, notably such immediate ones as the building of the transcontinental railroads and the coming of the commercial hide-hunter, but no less from the heavy inroads by transplanted eastern Indians moved to reservations west of the Mississippi, and the steadily increased pressure of white populations on the trans-Mississippi lands.

In addition to the game animals, the Indian utilized numerous plant species for a wide variety of purposes—for food, for fibers, for medicine, for dyestuffs, and otherwise. As Clements and Chaney have noted, however, the relatively sparse and scattered nature of the human population makes it seem "improbable that these uses produced any significant effect on the composition of the prairie as a whole, though the harvesting of underground parts of the pomme blanche *(Psoralea esculenta)*, onion, water chinquapin *(Nelumbo lutea)*, Indian potato *(Apios tuberosa)*, and others must have reduced greatly the abundance of these, at least locally." Such local effects would have been much more pronounced, of course, in the vicinity of the settled villages in the east than around the transient and frequently moved camps of the western hunters.

Among the Village Indians, too, the needs for plant materials used in constructing the large, substantial earth-covered lodges and grass houses may have altered temporarily and in some degree the local plant communities. The relatively limited stands of hardwood timber in the bottom lands along the Missouri and Platte rivers, for example, very likely had some influence on selection of

294

locations for the Indian towns; and the late George F. Will, of Bismarck, expressed the opinion that the scarcity of oak along the Missouri in North Dakota probably reflected the popularity of this durable and highly prized wood among the Mandan and Arikara house-builders. Also in much demand for its durability in building was the juniper; and in some places the stands of this species were probably considerably depleted by village construction. In some of the larger towns of historic times, there were from one to two hundred or more lodges, which required the cutting of many hundreds of trees, and the drain upon the available supply in the bottom-land pockets may well have been such that the most sought after species were severely reduced in abundance. In the prehistoric Central Plains, where earth-lodge-building peoples spread far toward the west into country whose creek valleys were sparsely wooded, the shortage of good building materials undoubtedly affected the size and location of the house clusters and the quality of construction. The big bluestem and slough grass used in thatching houses and as a foundation for the earth covering of the lodges, on the other hand, was presumably never in short supply for very long.

Among the western Indians the needs for structural wood were much less taxing. For tipi poles, these people preferred the lodgepole pine; and the great stands of this species nearest the Plains, as in the Black Hills, the Cypress Hills, in the Laramie Range at the head of Lodgepole Creek, and on the eastern slopes of the Bighorn Mountains, were frequently resorted to by the historic tribes. Here it may be doubted that these inroads were severe enough to deplete appreciably the available stands of this pine.

The influence of the Indian on the local composition of the plant communities is especially well demonstrated around the village sites of the Eastern Plains. Here, where man removed or broke the sod to erect his houses and fortifications, plant his gardens, and dump his trash, the disturbances were often of sufficient magnitude to leave scars hundreds of years after abandonment of the living sites. Thus, many of the village sites of the past three to six centuries, where there are extensive accumulations of ashes, animal bone, and other organic debris of former human occupation, are marked by exuberant growths of ragweed and other ruderal plants; and their locations on aerial photographs can often be unmistakably determined and delimited by the marked color differences between their vegetative cover and that on the surrounding prairie.

To what extent the Indian may have been instrumental in introducing wild species into the Plains, or in extending the distribution of local species, is not clear. It is entirely possible, however, that edible or otherwise desirable fruits, seeds to be used for beads or other purposes, and even living roots with medicinal or other wanted qualities were sometimes carried for considerable distances by the Indians and then, unwittingly or by design, were dropped or emplaced where they would grow and reproduce. Gilmore was of the opinion that the crab apple, normally restricted in northeastern Nebraska to "one creek which flows into the Niobrara River from the south at about the line between Holt and Knox Counties, 150 to 200 miles from any other localities where trees of this species grow," was introduced to this locality by Indians. The distribution of the sweet flag, or calamus, highly regarded by the Pawnees and found in "certain restricted areas within the old Pawnee domain" in Nebraska, he thought was perhaps another example of a plant whose natural occurrence had been altered by Indian activity. But these were, after all, relatively minor items, with little effect on the general composition of the prairie. The major introductions of the Indians were the domestic crop plants, none of them of native origin unless it was the sunflower, and none significantly altering the native vegetation. The periodic burning of the tall-grass prairies by the Indians, mainly along the eastern and northern margins, was doubtless of some importance in determining floral distributions and the location of the tree line, but the actual extent of this factor is still undetermined. I do not agree with the views of those who hold that the Indian custom of hunting by fire drives created the grasslands of central North America.[6] Certainly, in comparison with the vegetational changes brought about by the white man and his plow, his overgrazing of the native sod, and other large-scale disturbances of the soil, the Indian cannot be said to have materially altered the native vegetation of the plains and prairies.

THE PLAINS IN PREHISTORY

The native culture of the Plains has long intrigued scholar and layman alike, and there have been numerous views regarding the origin and development of the aboriginal societies that flourished here in prewhite and early-white days. As we have noted from time to time, anthropologists, historians, sociologists, and others have speculated on these matters, usually taking as their point of departure the colorful life of the historic horse-nomads and attempting to show how such a way of life was a more or less "logical" outgrowth of the environmental peculiarities of the region. To many, unaware of the richness and depth of the archaeological background, the character of the historic culture was such that they concluded this was the only one practicable—that without the horse and gun, the Indian would never have attempted seriously or successfully a life on the Plains.

One of the first American scholars to speculate seriously on the nature and antecedents of the historic Plains Indian culture was Wissler.[7] He regarded eleven tribes as "typical," including the Assiniboines, Arapahoes, Blackfeet, Crows, Cheyennes, Comanches, Gros Ventres, Kiowas, Kiowa Apaches, Sarsis, and Teton Dakotas. Characteristic of these were the following traits: Primary dependence upon the buffalo and very limited use of roots and berries; absence of fishing, agriculture, pottery, bas-

[6] Wedel, "The Central North American Grassland: Man-made or Natural?" loc. cit.

[7] See, for example, the following papers by Wissler: "Diffusion of Culture in the Plains of North America," *Proceedings*, Fifteenth International Congress of Americanists, Vol. II (1907), 39–40; "Ethnographical Problems of the Missouri Saskatchewan Area," *loc. cit.*, 197–207; "Material Cultures of the North American Indians," *American Anthropologist*, Vol. XVI, No. 3 (1914), 449–51.

ketry, and true weaving; the tipi as a movable dwelling; transportation by land only, with the dog and travois (in historic times with the horse); clothing of buffalo and deer skins; high development of work in skins; special rawhide work (parfleche, cylindrical bags, etc.); use of a circular buffalo-hide shield; weak development of work in wood, stone, and bone; geometric art, mostly confined to painting on rawhide and quill or bead embroidery; a simple band organization; the camp circle; a series of graded men's societies; the sun dance ceremony; and sweat-house observances, scalp dances, etc.

As long ago as 1908, admitting that "our knowledge of the archeology of this area is so vague that an assumption of any sort seems scarcely justifiable," Wissler noted traces of Pueblo influence on the southwestern border of the Plains, and the existence of "earthworks and other remains seemingly related to those east of the Mississippi" in the eastern Prairie Plains. From this he was led to suspect "an older center of population near the eastern border," and to suggest the probability of "a prehistoric uninhabited region" farther west, where "the ground roamed over by the Kiowa, Shoshoni, Arapaho, Cheyenne, and Tetons seems to yield few artifacts that can be assigned to a culture other than that of the historic period." In a later paper, he "localized the center of Plains culture between the Teton, Arapaho, Cheyenne, and Crow, with the odds in favor of the first"; but he suggested, too, that the "non-agricultural dog-using rovers after buffalo" met by Coronado in 1541 represented the "outlying fringe of the older Plains culture . . ." prior to the adoption of the horse. The peopling of the Plains, he finally concluded, "was a recent phenomenon due in part to the introduction of the horse."

The theory that the peopling of the Plains was a comparatively recent event has had wide acceptance among scholars, most of whom seem to have had fewer reservations than did Wissler about what archaeological research might reveal. Kroeber, for example, has vigorously argued for this point of view in several papers.[8]

---

[8] See especially the following papers by Kroeber: "Native Culture of the Southwest," University of California *Publications in American Archaeology and*

Thus, in 1928, he observed that "the largely negative results of archeology indicate the Plains as only sparsely or intermittently inhabited for a long time. The population was probably in the main a Woodland one along the eastern margin . . . ." In the west, he held, the people "probably clung in the main to the foot of the Rockies, where wood, water, and shelter were more abundant, fauna and flora more variegated, a less specialized subsistence mechanism sufficient; and from there they made incursions into the plains to hunt their big game . . . ." To Kroeber, it looked "as if the foot-traveling Indians could not have made a year-round living off the migratory bison . . . ." As recently as 1948, disregarding or discounting the Coronado data, he asserted that "the tepee or conical skin tent dragged on poles; the ordered camp circle of tepees; the bedding, clothing, and even receptacles of skins and rawhide . . ." were of late origin, and "had no counter-part in the region even as late as 1600. As a culture area the Plains had a late brilliance, with its war bonnets and ponies; but it had no historical depth."

As a few ethnologists have realized in recent years, these older views of the Plains as a "series of vanishing peripheries around a cultural vacuum" are no longer tenable, but need to be drastically revised.[9] In the perspectives of archaeology, it can no longer be contended that the Western Plains were largely an uninhabited tract before the introduction of the horse; and the view that its prehorse inhabitants were merely occasional would-be agricul-turists straying out of the eastern woodlands or occasional hunt-ing parties venturing hesitantly forth from the security of the western foothills is also inadequate. On the contrary, it is fairly clear that man has existed in these grasslands for some thousands of years. It is perhaps true that his earliest remains—those of the

Ethnology, Vol. XXIII, No. 9 (1928), 394–95; "Cultural and Natural Areas of Native North America," loc. cit., 76–88; Anthropology, 823.

[9] F. Eggan, "The Ethnological Cultures and Their Archeological Back-grounds," in J. B. Griffin's Archeology of Eastern United States (1952), 39–40; Lowie, "Reflections on the Plains Indians," Anthropological Quarterly (formerly Primitive Man), Vol. XXVIII (new ser., Vol. III), No. 2 (April, 1955), 63–86; Ewers, "The Horse in Blackfoot Indian Culture," Bureau of American Ethnology Bulletin 159 (1955), 336–38.

early big-game hunters—have been found most often near the mountain front; but archaeological findings in eastern Colorado, in western Kansas and Nebraska, in Texas, and elsewhere in the High Plains indicate that hunting groups were operating far out on the Plains thousands of years ago. The widespread occurrence of these early remains and sites suggests that these hunter-folk were crossing and recrossing the Plains on a considerable scale.

As to the inhabitants of the Western Plains between the time of the early big-game hunters and that of the historic hunters, we still know all too little. That the region was not uninhabited is indicated by such finds as Signal Butte, those in the White River terraces, and by innumerable other small and often obscure sites which have come to light through the widespread surveys and excavations of recent years. That the record of prehistoric man in the western short-grass plains will be materially augmented and amplified in the years to come is most probable. To the knowing traveler and hunter, even on foot, these steppes were not the uninviting and forbidding landscape they may seem to the modern-day observer, once the locations of the springs and water holes, the sheltered creek-side camping spots and rocky overhangs, and the better game and berrying localities became known.

Before the arrival of the horse, subsistence on the herds plus the harvesting of wild vegetal products where necessary undoubtedly meant a less colorful, more austere, and somewhat more uncertain existence than that of the mounted bison-hunters of historic times. Nevertheless, the Coronado documents make it abundantly clear that when the first white men set foot on the Plains, roving peoples "who lived like Arabs" and "whose sustenance comes entirely from the cows because they neither sow nor reap corn" were already living in the Southern Plains in considerable numbers and apparently in sizable communities early in the sixteenth century. I do not get the impression that these were a "miserably poor and almost chronically hungry" rabble, despite their lack of horses. Their reported habits of wintering near the settlements of the sedentary peoples, and the documented trade relationships with the Pueblos to the west and with other maize-

300

growing tribes to the east, remind us of the later historic inter-actions between hunters and agriculturists. Dog traction, portable skin tipis, extensive skin-working, pemmican, sign language, and other culture traits mentioned suggest a mode of life basically like that of the later Plains hunting peoples.

All of this seems to me to indicate that, long before the coming of Europeans and the horse, man had devised basic subsistence techniques that enabled him to survive and function in the creek valleys and around the water holes of the short-grass plains. With respect to the intermittently and sparsely watered upland areas of the High Plains, it is not contended that the indicated occupa-tions were on a year-round basis if the contemporary climatic conditions were substantially like those of the present. Undoubt-edly, there were cold-weather and dry-season movements by the people to valley bottoms and to broken, hilly, or mountainous tracts which offered shelter, water, and wood, just as was custom-ary among the historic mounted bison-hunters of the region. At such times the bison were given to movement out of the open storm-swept or drought-ridden plains, and with the cornerstone of their subsistence economy gone, the Indians would have moved also.

That bison-hunting as a prime basis for human subsistence is far older in the Plains than Coronado's time we know from the ancient kills at Folsom, Lindenmeier, Olson-Chubbuck, Agate Basin, and elsewhere. But what sort of culture did these early hunters possess otherwise? That skin-working was also practiced can be inferred from the scraping, cutting, and piercing tools of flint, and the occasional bone awls and needles found at some of these early sites. These implements of six to ten thousand years ago do not differ significantly in type from the knives, scrapers, choppers, and awls found at historic sites in the Plains. It is en-tirely possible, though not directly provable, that the skins taken by the early hunters were used for manufacture of shelters, as well as for clothing and receptacles. Is it unlikely that techniques for drying, pulverizing, and storing surplus meat from these kills were unknown in the ten thousand years between Folsom man and the Querechos of the sixteenth century?

A review of the traits listed by Wissler as characteristic of the historic Plains tribes reminds us of the fact that, practically without exception, the traits are such as would not survive the passage of hundreds or thousands of years of time. This holds, too, for the material culture described by the Spaniards for the Querechos. Here, it will be recalled, were noted the primary reliance on the bison for food, shelter, and clothing, and there is clear and unmistakable mention of dog traction, the travois, the conical skin tent, extensive skin working, dried meat and pemmican, sign language, and other typical Plains culture traits. There is virtually nothing in this list which would leave traces to be uncovered by the archaeologist in the old camp sites. To be sure, we do not know how old the techniques and traits noted by the Spaniards among the pedestrian bison-hunters were; but must we therefore assume they were original and recent inventions of the Querechos and Teyas, who by some are thought to have been no older in their sixteenth-century habitat than perhaps 1500? If, as most students now believe, the Querechos were Plains Apaches who originated in the Athabascan homeland far to the north in Canada, it seems likely that they adopted or perfected many of their Plains subsistence techniques during their long trek southward along the mountain front or via the High Plains corridor to the Plains of Texas and New Mexico.

That the prehorse bison-hunters of the Western Plains were not necessarily intermittent or part-time plainsmen based primarily on the mountains or foothills, as has sometimes been contended, is indicated by the widespread nature of the archaeological finds of hunting sites hundreds of miles from the mountain front. There is no documentary or other evidence that the Querechos in the Southern and Central Plains were mountain based; and in the far Northern Plains, where the Blackfeet have been regarded as the most likely representatives of the prehorse Plains population, Ewers has shown that the earliest indicated home of these people was in the Eagle Hills, four hundred miles or more from the mountains. With one important stipulation—the availability of dogs suitable for traction and burden-bearing purposes—I see

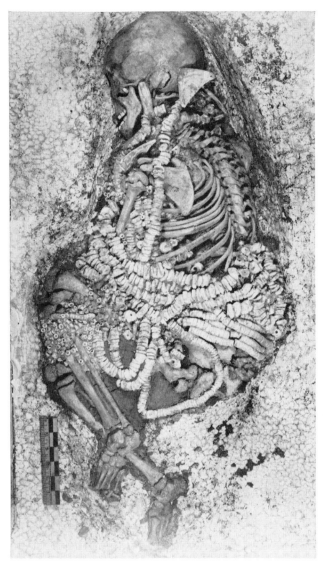

PLATE XXVII. Child burial with shell beads and ornaments, from Woodruff ossuary, in Phillips County, Kansas, dated about A.D. 600. Laboratory photo of very unusual find. (River Basin Surveys, Smithsonian Institution).

PLATE XXVIII. *Upper:* Brush shelters of the Great Basin foragers, probably Paiute, in 1873. (Smithsonian Institution). *Lower:* Earthlodge village of the Pawnees, a typical semihorticultural tribe of the Eastern Plains, on the Loup River near Genoa, Nebraska, in 1871. (Smithsonian Institution).

no reason why the Querecho-Teya way of life could not have been practiced in the Western Plains from Texas to Alberta for many hundreds, even thousands, of years before Coronado met the Apache dog-nomads in the Southern Plains. Without dogs to help move their belongings, the prehistoric dwellers on the margins of the Plains may possibly have been the timorous hillmen visualized by some students as the prehorse plainsmen; with draft animals, on the other hand, they could have ranged far and wide over the grasslands, so long as they did not lose contact with the herds.

The influence of the horse in enriching the material culture of the tribes who acquired it has been discussed many times, most recently and perhaps in fullest detail by Ewers.[10] I am in complete accord with two points made by him:

> I am of the opinion that *the* reason European explorers failed to find a pedestrian buffalo-hunting people on the northern High Plains was that horses had already been introduced to that region before white men reached it.
>
> It is my contention that the horse complex was adapted to a pre-existing pedestrian buffalo-hunting economy the bearers of which readily recognized that horses would be of great advantage to their way of life. The culture of the pedestrian hunters may have included most if not all of the traits Wissler has ascribed to it as well as other traits which survived with little modification in the Horse Culture Period . . . .

So far as basic subsistence techniques were concerned, the striking parallels between the sixteenth-century dog-nomads in the Southern Plains and the later horse-using tribes from there northward has been clearly set forth in contemporary eyewitness accounts. Thus, according to the *Relación postrera de Cíbola*,

> Traveling many days over these plains, the Spaniards came to an

[10] "The Horse in Blackfoot Indian Culture," *loc. cit.*, 299–340; see also Wissler, "The Influence of the Horse in the Development of Plains Culture," *American Anthropologist*, Vol. XVI, No. 1 (1914), 1–25, and Kroeber, "Cultural and Natural Areas of Native North America," *loc. cit.*, 76–79, 87–88.

inhabited rancheria with about 200 houses. The houses were made of tanned cattle skins, white, and built like pavilions or tents. These Indians live or sustain themselves entirely from the cattle, for they neither grow nor harvest maize. With the skins they build their houses; with the skins they clothe and shoe themselves; from the skins they make ropes and also obtain wool. With the sinews they make thread, with which they sew their clothes and also their tents. From the bones they shape awls. The dung they use for firewood, since there is no other fuel in that land. The bladders they use as jugs and drinking containers. They sustain themselves on their meat, eating it slightly roasted and heated over the dung. Some they eat raw; taking it in their teeth, they pull with one hand, and in the other they hold a large flint knife and cut off mouthfuls. Thus they swallow it, half chewed, like birds. They eat raw fat without warming it. They drink the blood just as it comes out of the cattle. Sometimes they drink it later, raw and cold. They have no other food.

These people have dogs similar to those of this land, except that they are somewhat larger. They load these dogs like beasts of burden and make light pack saddles for them like our pack saddles, cinching them with leather straps. The dogs go about with sores on their backs like pack animals. When the Indians go hunting they load them with provisions. When these Indians move—for they have no permanent residence anywhere, since they follow the cattle to find food—these dogs carry their homes for them. In addition to what they carry on their backs, they carry the poles for the tents, dragging them fastened to their saddles. The load may be from 35 to 50 pounds, depending on the dog.

Castañeda adds the following significant details:

They dry their meat in the sun, slicing it in thin sheets. When it is dry, they grind it, like flour, for storage and for making mash to eat. When they put a handful in an olla it soon fills it, as the mash swells a great deal. They cook it with fat which they always try to have with them.[11]

Three hundred years later, in 1857, Professor Hind wrote of

[11] Hammond and Rey, *loc. cit.,* 262, 310–11.

the Plains Crees and their neighbors in the Saskatchewan-Alberta plains:

> The bison or buffalo, the horse and the dog are to the Prairie Indians what domestic animals and the production of the farm and the forest are to civilized races. During the greater part of the year the Prairie Indians follow the buffalo, and not only subsist on the flesh of this animal, but from its skin and sinews they make their tents, clothing, saddles, bowstrings and dog harness. The hide cut into strips serves them for cordage, the sinews split into threads for twine. The dried dung is often their only fuel for weeks together in the treeless plains between the Assiniboine and the Grand Coteau, and on the south Branch of the Saskatchewan. Dried meat, pemican, marrow, soft fat, sinews, dressed skins and robes, all from the buffalo, form their articles of commerce, in exchange for which they demand tea, which is now becoming a most coveted luxury, tobacco, powder and shot, and if possible, rum. It may truly be said that they exist on the buffalo, and their knowledge of the habits of this animal is consequently essential to their existence.[12]

The historical record unfortunately tells us nothing of the social and ceremonial life of the dog-nomads; but as Lowie has cogently observed, this "does not prove that there was nothing to know." In all likelihood, however, they lacked the Sun Dance and others of "those noisy and gaudy superstitious ceremonies" which Palliser, in 1863, attributed to the later plainsmen, which were a particularly spectacular and impressive feature of the "typical" culture of the historic Plains Indians, and whose presumptive absence in earlier days was probably one of the reasons for regarding the Plains culture as unimportant and nondistinctive in character.

Kroeber's steadfast denial that Plains culture had any historical depth and his insistence that "the Plains traits that have historical depth, on the other hand, seem Woodland, and date from the time when such Plains culture as there was constituted a margin at the fringe of a natural area" must certainly be re-examined in light of

[12] *Loc. cit.*, 105.

the archaeological and ethnohistorical record. The basic ingredients of true Plains culture, including primary dependence on the bison for subsistence, high development of skin-working, portable skin dwellings, dog traction, sign language, etc., are not demonstrably of Eastern Woodlands origin; and the first and most distinctive item, at least, has been shown to have very respectable historical depth in the region, as do the chipped-stone and simple bone tools used in processing the kill and in dressing and adapting the hides to human use. From these circumstances I would rather suggest again, as I was constrained to do twenty years ago, that "acquisition of the horse in the 17th and early 18th centuries thus gave a last colorful fillip to a mode of life old when the first Conquistadores set foot on the Great Plains."

The cultures of the Eastern or Prairie Plains and their origins are another matter. In their pottery, agriculture, stable community life in fixed villages, and other characteristics, these peoples throughout their existence shared much with the inhabitants of the Eastern Woodlands and the Southeast. Wissler pointed this fact out long ago, and archaeology confirms it.[13] But Wissler also recognized these people as culturally "intermediate"; that is, as more or less distinct from the "typical" hunting groups to the west. Here it is undoubtedly true that many of the traits that have historical depth must be regarded as rooted in the older cultures of the Woodlands, or of the Prairie-Woodlands margin, from where came some of the peoples themselves—the Siouans, for example, from the east, the Caddoans out of the marginal Southeast. In part, the way of life of the later bison hunters, including some of their hunting and war practices, appear also to have been an outgrowth of Eastern Woodlands culture, which may reflect essentially the fact that many of these tribes were relatively late intruders from the east. But, as our recital of the archaeological record should have made clear by this time, the Village dwellers were latecomers to the greater Plains; and most of the characteristics that make their sites so much more productive archaeo-

[13] Wissler, "Material Cultures of the North American Indians," *loc. cit.*, 484-85.

logically than are those of the western hunter-folk were demonstrably brought to the Plains long after men had learned how to take bison successfully in the region. I would suggest, then, that much of the confusion over what has or has not historic depth in the culture of the Plains region stems partly from ignorance or disregard of the findings of archaeology, and partly from failure to distinguish, as Linton did, between the two *types* of culture— the semisedentary Village Indians on the east, the nomadic hunters on the west—that together dominated the greater Plains area in historic times.[14]

In considerable measure, as Wissler reminded us long ago, the aboriginal Plains were an area of "great material uniformity with notorious linguistic and political diversity." The uniformity was a result of its geographic distinctiveness and of the strong tendency of its inhabitants to specialize on one subsistence staple, the bison; the diversity reflected the readiness with which outsiders of varied linguistic and cultural origins drifted into the region from all directions throughout its long history. Unfortunately, not very much is yet known about the physical anthropology of these various populations, concerning which we have said almost nothing up to this point.[15] Thus far, perhaps the most comprehensive treatment is Neumann's hypothesis of the trihybrid, or multiple, origin of the Plains Indian, based principally on the form and

[14] R. Linton, *The Study of Man.* 386, 392.

[15] No extended discussions of the physical anthropology of the Plains have yet appeared, but the following papers will be found useful as an index of what has been done: Howells, *loc. cit.*; A. Hrdlicka, "Catalogue of Human Crania in the United States National Museum Collections," U. S. National Museum *Proceedings*, Vol. LXIX, Art. 5 (1927); G. K. Neumann, "The Origin of the Prairie Physical Type of American Indian," *Papers*, Michigan Academy of Science, Arts, and Letters, Vol. XXVII (1942), 539–42; Neumann, "South Dakota Physical Types," *Museum News*, W. H. Over Museum, Vol. XIII, No. 5 (1952); Neumann, "Archeology and Race in the American Indian," in J. B. Griffin's *Archeology of Eastern United States* (1952), 13–34; C. W. M. Poynter, "A Study of Nebraska Crania," *American Anthropologist*, new ser., Vol. XVII, No. 3 (1915), 509–24; T. D. Stewart, "Some Historical Implications of Physical Anthropology in North America," Smithsonian *Miscellaneous Collections*, Vol. C (1940), 15–50; T. D. Stewart, "Skeletal Remains from Platte and Clay Counties, Missouri," U. S. National Museum *Bulletin 183*, Appendix (1943), 245–73; T. D. Stewart, "Description of the Skeletal Remains from Doniphan and Scott Counties, Kansas," Bureau of American Ethnology *Bulletin 174* (1959), 669–83.

height of the cranial vault in skeletal populations. According to this hypothesis, the earlier populations of the Eastern Plains were characterized by high vaults. Those in the northern sector were longheaded and of presumably Eastern Woodlands derivation, while in the south the people were more roundheaded and had affinities with the Southeastern states. Then, at some unspecified time, strong admixture with low-vaulted peoples of northern origin created the hybrid populations of the Plains area.

This trihybrid theory has some basis in fact. The early populations known for the Eastern Plains, including most of the Woodland and Hopewellian groups, the Plattsmouth skulls described by Poynter, and perhaps also those represented by Lansing Man and other putatively preceramic or early ceramic peoples are characterized by long narrow heads with high vaults. Later groups, however, were rounder-headed, the shape doubtless being sometimes accentuated by artificial head-flattening. These groups are represented by the late prehistoric Middle Mississippi peoples, probably by the Wallace Mound crania from near Omaha, and perhaps also by the Upper Republican and Nebraska aspect peoples of the Central Plains. Protohistoric and historic skeletal collections can be identified as yet for only three tribes. The putatively Mandan crania are typically longheaded and high-vaulted, bespeaking their Eastern Woodlands origin. The miscellaneous Siouan skulls described by Hrdlicka, on the other hand, are principally characterized by very low vaults attributed to the northern invaders. Arikara crania, which represent by far the largest available series for the Plains, are almost as low-vaulted, but are less massive than the Siouans. Biological distances between the Arikaras and their more southerly linguistic relatives, the Pawnees and Caddos, are only now being explored.

Some physical anthropologists feel that the weakest part of Neumann's hybridization theory is that there is really no evidence that such a process took place. As we have seen, there have been at least three biologically distinct groups of populations in the Plains—the two high-vaulted groups and the low-headed one. But their distribution in time and space, as well as what may be adduced about their morphology, could be explained on the basis of discontinuity and replacement of populations with perhaps equal ease. According to the hybridization hypothesis, the shift to low-headedness in the Eastern Plains must have been very rapid and very late. Yet low vaults may have a fair antiquity further west, as judged by the McKean skull from northeastern Wyoming, dated at over 3,200 years ago. Without better data and more searching analysis, it is idle to speculate on the antiquity of low vaults in the Plains and the possible movement of this trait to the eastern edges of that area.

All we can be reasonably sure of is that the peoples of the Plains were biologically more diverse than perhaps those in any other North American area. The extent to which this diversity can be attributed to the position of the Plains as a major corridor of movement, and as an ecologically marginal and at times an environmentally hostile area, is a problem for future research. Part of this larger problem is the contrast between the prehorse and posthorse days, where the latter saw a strong drift of peoples into the Plains, undoubtedly involving extensive replacement and intermixture of populations. It is clear that the only feasible approach to the physical anthropology of the Plains must be a multifaceted one. Comprehensive studies on the long-neglected skeletal collections in our museums, on a careful sampling of new ones, and on morphological and serological studies of living Indian remnants need to be carried out against the extensive cultural backdrop that is being developed through archaeological researches. Until these studies are accomplished, more speculation than the broad outlines sketched above is not likely to be very rewarding.

Linton has observed that "any type of culture which has once become established in a particular environment tends to persist there in the face of immigrations and population changes."[16] That immigrations and population changes have taken place in the vast region we know as the Plains, and probably more than once, seems certain. Perhaps, when the physical anthropology of the prehistoric populations has been further studied and reported in

[16] *The Study of Man*, 385.

detail by competent specialists, we shall have additional light on this important point, though it is already clear that there were marked differences in the biological make-up of the peoples through time and space. In any case, if the early bison-hunters of pre-Altithermal times and the later ones of 3,500 years ago in the Western Plains had devised ways and means of procuring food and shelter in the peculiar and often trying environment of the region, it can be assumed that new groups coming in from whatever direction would have adopted quickly the techniques that had proved successful to the earlier residents. In this light, one suspects that as early Woodland and later Village-dwelling Indians pressed or were pushed westward into and across the High Plains, some of them may have altered their way of life and become basically hunters of the bison. Where these erstwhile pottery makers and partly agricultural peoples had not yet entirely given up their sedentary arts, their traces might still include recognizable clues for the archaeologist. On the other hand, small and scattered groups of pedestrian hunter-folk possessing only such largely perishable traits as were recorded for the Querechos would leave on their camp sites little or nothing for the excavator to turn up. We can only speculate as to how often the simple Plains hunters may have been attracted to the earth-lodge villages and, impressed with their stable way of life, reasonably sure subsistence, and apparent affluence, chose to cast their lot with the Village dwellers instead of returning to their earlier life of nomadism.

Our review of the prehistoric Plains, with its glimpses of some of their principal known human inhabitants in aboriginal times, will close here. The specialist, if he has read this far, will be keenly aware that much of what we know and think about these plainsmen of the past has remained unsaid, or has been only briefly and tentatively touched upon. He will recognize, too, as we have repeatedly emphasized throughout this book, that a very great deal remains to be learned about native man and his activities in the greater Plains region. It is encouraging to reflect on the fact that systematic and sustained archaeology, particularly that of the past quarter-century or a little more, has vastly increased our store of information on the peoples who, from a remote and dimly seen past, sought in various ways and without the technological advantages of the white man today, to make a way of life for themselves in the vast expanses of the Plains and Prairies. Important, too, is the fact that new dating methods have helped us to bring progressively better order into our interpretation of the succession of events that transpired here. We may expect, in the years that lie ahead, important additions to our resources of carefully gathered field data, in spite of the ever present menace of the bulldozer and the dragline; more and more, scholars will turn to the impressive stores of still unstudied collections and records already in hand; and finally, new techniques of description and analysis can be expected to give us deeper insights and truer perspectives on the long and complex story of human endeavor that is unfolding.

There are many things, I repeat, about the prehistoric Plains that we do not yet know or understand, but this is as it should be. For, in the last analysis, it is the unknown that leads the archaeologist on.

BIBLIOGRAPHY

Abel, A. H., ed. *Chardon's Journal at Fort Clark, 1834–1839*. Pierre, South Dakota, 1932.

———. *Tabeau's Narrative of Loisel's Expedition to the Upper Missouri*. Norman, 1939.

Agogino, G. A., and W. D. Frankforter. "A Paleo-Indian Bison-Kill in Northwestern Iowa," *American Antiquity*, Vol. XXV, No. 3 (1960), 414–15.

Aikman, J. M. "Native Vegation of the Region," in *Possibilities of Shelterbelt Planting in the Plains Region*, U. S. Forest Service (1935), 155–74.

Alden, W. C. "Physiographic Development of the Northern Great Plains," *Bulletin*, Geological Society of America, Vol. XXXV (1924), 385–423.

Antevs, E. "Geologic-Climatic Dating in the West," *American Antiquity*, Vol. XX, No. 4 (1955), 317–35.

Aronow, S. "On the Postglacial History of the Devils Lake Region, North Dakota," *Journal of Geology*, Vol. LXV, No. 4 (1957), 410–27.

Baerreis, D. A. "The Preceramic Horizons of Oklahoma," *Anthropological Papers*, No. 6 (1951), University of Michigan, Ann Arbor.

Bates, C. G. "Climatic Characteristics of the Plains Region," in *Possibilities of Shelterbelt Planting in the Plains Region*, U. S. Forest Service (1935), 82–110.

Beauregard, Mrs. H. T., ed. and trans. "Journal of Jean Baptiste Trudeau Among the Arikara Indians in 1795," Missouri Historical Society *Collections*, Vol. IV, No. 1 (1912), 9–48.

Bell, Charles N. "Mounds in Manitoba," *American Antiquarian*, Vol. VIII, No. 2 (March, 1886), 108–109.

———. "Mounds and Relics in Manitoba," *American Antiquarian*, Vol. XV, No. 4 (1893), 207–11.

Bell, E. H., and R. E. Cape. "The Rock Shelters of Western Nebraska," in E. H. Bell's *Chapters in Nebraska Archaeology*, No. 5 (1936), 357–99.

Bell, Robert E., and David A. Baerreis. "A Survey of Oklahoma Archeology," *Bulletin*, Texas Archeological and Paleontological Society, Vol. XXII (1951), 7–100.

Birdsell, J. B. "The Problem of the Early Peopling of the Americas as Viewed from Asia," in W. S. Laughlin and S. L. Washburn's *The Physical Anthropology of the American Indian*, (1949), 1–68.

Bliss, Wesley L. "An Archeological and Geological Reconnaissance of Alberta, Mackenzie Valley, and Upper Yukon," American Philosophical Society *Yearbook 1938* (1939), 136–39.

———. "Early Man in the Northwestern Plains," *Proceedings*, Fifth Plains Conference for Archeology (1949), 121–26; University of Nebraska, Laboratory of Anthropology Note Book No. 1.

———. "Archeological Reconnaissance in Wyoming and Montana, 1946–1947," *Proceedings*, Fifth Plains Conference for Archeology (1949); University of Nebraska, Laboratory of Anthropology Note Book No. 1.

———. "Early and Late Lithic Horizons in the Plains," *Proceedings*, Sixth Plains Conference for Archeology (1950), 108–16; University of Utah, Department of Anthropology "Anthropological Papers," No. 11.

———. "Birdshead Cave, a Stratified Site in Wind River Basin, Wyoming," *American Antiquity*, Vol. XV, No. 3 (January, 1950), 187–96.

Bolton, H. E. *Athanase de Mezieres and the Louisiana-Texas Frontier, 1768–1780*. 2 vols. Cleveland, Arthur H. Clark Company, 1914.

———. *Spanish Exploration in the Southwest, 1542–1706*. New York, Charles Scribner's Sons, 1916.

———. *Coronado, Knight of Pueblos and Plains*. New York and Albuquerque, Whittlesey House and University of New Mexico Press, 1949.

Borchert, J. R. "The Climate of the Central North American Grassland," *Annals* of the Association of American Geographers, Vol. XL, No. 1 (1950), 1–39.

Bowers, A. W. "Mandan Social and Ceremonial Organization," University of Chicago *Publications in Anthropology* (1950).

Brackenridge, Henry M. "Journal of a Voyage up River Missouri in 1811," in Vol. VI of Thwaites' *Early Western Travels, 1748–1846*. Cleveland, 1904.

Bradbury, John. *Travels in the Interior of America in the years 1809, 1810, and 1811*. Liverpool and London, 1817.

Brooks, C. E. P. "Geological and Historical Aspects of Climatic Change," in T. F. Malone's *Compendium of Meteorology* (1951), 1004–18.

Brower, J. V. *Mandan: Memoirs of Explorations in the Basin of the Mississippi*. Vol. VIII. St. Paul, 1904.

Burpee, Lawrence J., ed. *Journals and Letters of Pierre Gaultier de Varennes de la Vérendrye and His Sons*. Toronto, The Champlain Society, 1927.

Byers, D. S. "The Bering Bridge—Some Speculations," *Ethnos*, Nos. 1–2 (1957), 20–26.

Caldwell, Warren W. "The Black Partizan Site (39LM218), Big Bend Reservoir, South Dakota: A Preliminary Report," *Plains Anthropologist*, Vol. V, No. 10 (1960), 53–57

Capes, Katherine. MS. "The W. B. Nickerson Survey and Excavations, 1912–1915, of Southern Manitoba Mounds Region," Manuscript in National Museum of Canada.

Carlson, G. G., and V. H. Jones, "Some Notes on Uses of Plants by the Comanche Indians," *Papers* of the Michigan Academy of Science, Arts, and Letters, Vol. XXV (1940), 517–42.

Catlin, George. *North American Indians, Being Letters and Notes on Their Manners, Customs, and Conditions, Written During Eight Years' Travel Amongst the Wildest Tribes of Indians in North America, 1832–1839*. 2 vols. Philadelphia, Leary, Stuart and Company, 1913.

Champe, John L. "The Sweetwater Culture Complex," in E. H. Bell's *Chapters in Nebraska Archeology*, No. 3 (1936), 249–97.

———. "Ash Hollow Cave," University of Nebraska *Studies*, new ser., No. 1 (1946).

———. "White Cat Village," *American Antiquity*, Vol. XIV, No. 4, Pt. 1 (April, 1949), 285–92.

Chapman, Carl H. "Culture Sequence in the Lower Missouri Valley," in J. B. Griffin's *Archeology of Eastern United States* (1952), 139-51.

——. "The Origin of the Osage Indian Tribe, an Ethnographical, Historical, and Archeological Study," unpublished Ph.D. dissertation, University of Michigan (1959).

Chardon, Francis T. *See* A. H. Abel.

Chubbuck, Jerry. "The Discovery and Exploration of the Olsen-Chubbuck Site (CH-3)," *Southwestern Lore*, Vol. XXV, No. 1 (1959), 4-10.

Clements, Frederic E. "Climatic Cycles and Human Populations in the Great Plains," *Scientific Monthly*, Vol. XLVII, No. 3 (1938), 193-210.

Clements, F. E., and R. W. Chaney. "Environment and Life in the Great Plains," Carnegie Institution of Washington *Supplementary Publications*, No. 24 (rev. ed.) (1937).

Collier, Donald. "New radiocarbon method for dating the past," Chicago Natural History Museum *Bulletin*, Vol. XXII, No. 1 (1951), 6-7.

Comfort, A. J. "Indian Mounds Near Fort Wadsworth, Dakota Territory," *Smithsonian Institution Annual Report for 1871* (1873), 389-402.

Coogan, Alan H., and William N. Irving. "Late Pleistocene and Recent Missouri River Terraces in the Big Bend Reservoir, South Dakota," Iowa Academy of Science *Proceedings*, Vol. LXVI (1959), 317-27.

Cooper, Paul L. "Archeology of Certain Sites in Cedar County, Nebraska," in E. H. Bell's *Chapters in Nebraska Archeology*, No. 1 (1936), 11-145.

——. "The Archeological Exploration of 1938," Nebraska History *Magazine*, Vol. XX, No. 2 (1940), 94-151.

——. "Recent Investigations in Fort Randall and Oahe Reservoirs, South Dakota," *American Antiquity*, Vol. XIV, No. 4, Pt. 1 (April, 1949) 300-10.

——. "The Archeological and Paleontological Salvage Program in the Missouri Basin, 1950-51," Smithsonian *Miscellaneous Collections*, Vol. CXXVI, No. 2 (1955), 1-99.

——. "Archeological Investigations in the Heart Butte Reservoir Area, North Dakota," Bureau of American Ethnology *Bulletin 869.* (1958), 1-40.

Cotter, John L. "The Occurrence of Flints and Extinct Animals in Pluvial Deposits Near Clovis, New Mexico," *Proceedings*, Academy of Natural Sciences of Philadelphia, Vol. LXXXIX (1937), 1–16.

Crandell, Dwight R. "Pleistocene Geology of Part of Central South Dakota," *Bulletin*, Geological Society of America, Vol. LXIV (1953), 581–98.

Culbertson, Thaddeus A. "Journal of an Expedition to the Mauvaises Terres and the Upper Missouri in 1850." *Fifth Annual Report* of the Board of Regents of the Smithsonian Institution [for] the Year 1850; Appendix No. IV (1851), 84–145.

Darton, N. H., and W. S. T. Smith. "Description of the Edgemont Quadrangle," The Edgemont Folio, South Dakota–Nebraska, U. S. Geological Survey Geologic Atlas of the United States, *Folio No. 108* (1904).

Davis, E. Mott. "Recent Data from Two Paleo-Indian Sites on Medicine Creek, Nebraska," *American Antiquity*, Vol. XVIII, No. 4 (April, 1953), 380–86.

Davis, E. Mott, and C. Bertrand Schultz. "The Archeological and Paleontological Salvage Program at the Medicine Creek Reservoir, Frontier County, Nebraska," *Science*, Vol. CXV, No. 2985 (March 14, 1952), 288–90.

Deevey, E. S. Jr., and R. F. Flint. "Postglacial Hypsithermal Interval," *Science*, Vol. CXXV, No. 3240 (1957), 182–84.

Dempsey, Hugh A. "Stone 'Medicine Wheels'—Memorials to Blackfoot War Chiefs," *Journal* Washington Academy of Sciences, Vol. XLVI, No. 6 (1956), 177–82.

Dixon, R. B. "Some Aspects of North American Archeology," *American Anthropologist*, Vol. XV, No. 4 (1913), 549–77.

Dondelinger, N. W., and R. M. Tatum. "Preliminary Survey of Sites in Las Animas County, Colorado," *Southwestern Lore*, Vol. VIII, No. 1 (1942).

Dorsey, George A. "An Aboriginal Quartzite Quarry in eastern Wyoming," Field Columbian Museum *Anthropological Series*, Vol. II, No. 4, Pub. No. 51 (1900).

Dunbar, Carl O. *Historical Geology*. New York, John Wiley and Sons, Inc., 1949.

Dunlevy, Marion L. "A Comparison of the Cultural Manifestations of the Burkett (Nance County) and the Gray-Wolfe (Colfax

BIBLIOGRAPHY

County) Sites," in E. H. Bell's *Chapters in Nebraska Archaeology* No. 2 (1936), 147–247.

Eggan, Fred. "The Ethnological Cultures and Their Archeological Backgrounds," in J. B. Griffin's *Archeology of Eastern United States* (1952) 35–45.

Eggleston, Wilfrid. "The Cypress Hills," *Canadian Geographical Journal*, Vol. XLII, No. 2 (February, 1951), 52–67.

——. "The Short Grass Prairies of Western Canada," *Canadian Geographical Journal*, Vol. L, No. 4 (April, 1955) 134–45.

Eiseley, Loren C. "Did the Folsom Bison Survive in Canada?" *Scientific Monthly*, Vol. LXVI, No. 5 (1943), 468–72.

——. "Archeological Observations on the Problem of Post-glacial extinction," *American Antiquity*, Vol. VIII, No. 3 (1943), 209–17.

——. "The Fire-Drive and the Extinction of the Terminal Pleistocene Fauna," *American Anthropologist*, Vol. XLVIII, No. 1 (1946), 54–59.

——. "The Fire and the Fauna," *American Anthropologist*, Vol. XLIX, No. 4, Pt. 1 (1947), 678–80.

Ewers, John C. "The Blackfoot War Lodge: Its Construction and Use," *American Anthropologist*, Vol. XLVI, No. 2, Pt. 1 (1944), 182–92.

——. "The Case for Blackfoot Pottery," *American Anthropologist*, Vol. XLVII, No. 2 (1945), 289–99.

——. "The Indian Trade of the Upper Missouri Before Lewis and Clark: An Interpretation," Missouri Historical Society *Bulletin*, Vol. X, No. 4 (1954), 429–46.

——. "The Horse in Blackfoot Indian Culture," Bureau of American Ethnology *Bulletin 159* (1955).

——. *The Blackfeet: Raiders on the Northwestern Plains*. Norman, University of Oklahoma Press, 1958.

——. "Selected References on the Plains Indians," Smithsonian Anthropological *Bibliographies*, No. 1 (1960).

Fenneman, N. M. *Physiography of Western United States*. New York, McGraw-Hill Book Company, 1931.

——. *Physiography of Eastern United States*. New York, McGraw-Hill Book Company, 1938.

Figgins, J. D. "New World Man," *Proceedings*, Colorado Museum of Natural History, Vol. XIV, No. 1 (1935).

Flint, R. F. *Glacial Geology and the Pleistocene Epoch*. New York, 1947.

———. "The Ice Age in Arctic North America," *Annual Report,* Smithsonian Institution for 1952 (1953), 243–60.

———. "Pleistocene Geology of Eastern South Dakota," U. S. Geological Survey *Professional Paper 262* (1955), 140–43.

Flint, R. F., and E. S. Deevey, Jr. "Radiocarbon Dating of Late-Pleistocene Events," *American Journal of Science,* Vol. CCXLIX, No. 4 (April, 1951), 257–300.

———, eds. *American Journal of Science Radiocarbon Supplement,* Vol. I. New Haven, Yale University Press, 1959.

Forbes, Jack D. "The Appearance of the Mounted Indian in Northern Mexico and the Southwest, to 1680," *Southwestern Journal of Anthropology,* Vol. XV, No. 2 (1959), 189–212.

Forbis, Richard G. "Some Late Sites in the Oldman River Region, Alberta," National Museum of Canada *Bulletin 162* (1960), 158–64.

Forbis, Richard G., and J. D. Sperry. "An Early Man Site in Montana," *American Antiquity,* Vol. XVIII, No. 2 (1952), 127–32.

Forest Service, U. S. *Possibilities of Shelterbelt Planting in the Plains Region.* Washington, U. S. Forest Service, 1935.

Frankforter, W. D. "A Pre-Ceramic Site in Western Iowa," *Journal,* Iowa Archeological Society, Vol. VIII, No. 4 (1959), 47–72.

Fuller H. M., and L. R. Hafen. *The Journal of Captain John R. Bell.* Glendale, Arthur H. Clark Co., 1957.

Gebhard, D. S., and H. A. Cahn. "The Petroglyphs of Dinwoody, Wyoming," *American Antiquity,* Vol. XV, No. 3 (1950), 219–28.

Gilder, Robert F. "Indian Sites Near Frederick, Wyoming," *Records of the Past,* Vol. VII, Pt. 4 (July-August, 1908), 179–82.

Gilmore, M. R. "The Aboriginal Geography of the Nebraska Country." *Proceedings,* Mississippi Valley Historical Association, Vol. VI (1913), 317–31.

———. "Uses of Plants by the Indians of the Missouri River Region," Bureau of American Ethnology *Thirty-third Annual Report* (1919), 43–154.

Gleason, H. A. "The Vegetational History of the Middle West," *Annals* of the Association of American Geographers, Vol. XII (1922), 39–85.

Gould, C. N. "The Oklahoma Salt Plains," *Transactions,* Kansas Academy of Science, Vol. XVII (1901), 181–84.

Great Plains Committee. "The Future of the Great Plains," Report of the Great Plains Committee, Washington, 1936.

Griffenhagen, George B., and James H. Harvey. "Old English Patent Medicines in America," U. S. National Museum *Bulletin 218*, Contributions from the Museum of History and Technology, Paper 10, (1959), 155–83.

Griffin, James B. "Cultural Change and Continuity in Eastern United States Archaeology," in Frederick Johnson's *Man in Northeastern North America. Papers* of the Robert S. Peabody Foundation for Archaeology, Vol. III (1946) 37–95.

Grinnell, George Bird. "The Medicine Wheel," *American Anthropologist*, Vol. XXIV, No. 3 (July- September, 1922), 299–310.

Gross, H. "Mastodons, Mammoths, and Man in America," *Bulletin*, Texas Archeological and Paleontological Society, Vol. XXII (1951), 101–30.

Gunn, Donald. "Indian Remains Near Red River Settlement, Hudson's Bay Territory," *Smithsonian Institution Annual Report for 1867* (1868), 399–400.

Gunnerson, Dolores A. "The Southern Athabascans: Their Arrival in the Southwest," *El Palacio*, Vol. LXIII, Nos. 11–12 (1956), 346–65.

Gunnerson, James H. "Plains-Promontory Relationships," *American Antiquity*, Vol. XXII, No. 1 (1956), 69–72.

———. "Archaeological Survey in Northeastern New Mexico," *El Palacio*, Vol. LXVI, No. 5 (1959), 1–10.

———. "An Introduction to Plains Apache Archeology—the Dismal River Aspect," Bureau of American Ethnology *Bulletin 173*, *Anthropological Papers, No. 58* (1960), 131–260.

Haines, Francis. "Where Did the Plains Indians Get Their Horses?" *American Anthropologist*, Vol. XL, No. 1 (1938).

———. "The Northward Spread of Horses Among the Plains Indians," *American Anthropologist*, Vol. XL, No. 3 (1938).

Hall, E. T., Jr., "Early Stockaded Settlements in the Governador, New Mexico," *Columbia Studies in Archaeology and Ethnology*, Vol. II, Pt. 1 (1944).

Hammond, G. P., and A. Rey. "Narratives of the Coronado Expedition, 1540–1542," University of New Mexico, *Coronado Historical Series*, Vol. II (1940).

Harper, E. A. "The Taovayas Indians in Frontier Trade and Diplomacy, 1719–1768," *Chronicles of Oklahoma*, Vol. XXXI, No. 3 (1953), 268–89.

Haury, E. W., Ernst Antevs, and J. A. Lance. "Artifacts with Mammoth Remains, Naco, Arizona," *American Antiquity*, Vol. XIX, No. 1 (1953), 1–24.

——, E. B. Sayles, W. W. Wasley, Ernst Antevs, and J. F. Lance, "The Lehner Mammoth Site, Southeastern Arizona," *American Antiquity*, Vol. XXV, No. 1 (1959), 2–39.

Hayden, F. V., ed. *Geological Report of the Exploration of the Yellowstone and Missouri Rivers, Under the Direction of Captain W. F. Raynolds, Corps of Engineers, 1859–60.* Washington, 1869.

Hewes, Gordon W. "Early Tribal Migrations in the Northern Great Plains," Plains Archeological Conference *Newsletter*, Vol. I, No. 4 (1948), 49–61.

——. "Burial Mounds in the Baldhill Area, North Dakota," *American Antiquity*, Vol. XIV, No. 4, Pt. 1 (April, 1949), 322–28.

Hibben, Frank C. "The Gallina Phase," *American Antiquity*, Vol. IV, No. 2 (1938), 131–36.

Hill, A. T., and Paul Cooper. "The Archeological Campaign of 1937," *Nebraska History Magazine*, Vol XVIII, No. 4 (1938), 237–359.

——, and M. F. Kivett. "Woodland-Like Manifestations in Nebraska," *Nebraska History Magazine*, Vol. XXI, No. 3 (July–September, 1940), 147–243.

——, and George Metcalf. "A Site of the Dismal River Aspect in Chase County, Nebraska," *Nebraska History Magazine*, Vol. XXII, No. 2 (April–June, 1941), 158–226.

——, and Waldo R. Wedel. "Excavations at the Leary Indian Village and Burial Site, Richardson County, Nebraska," *Nebraska History Magazine*, Vol. XVII, No. 1 (1936), 2–73.

Hill, R. T. "Physical Geography of the Texas Region," U. S. Geological Survey *Topographic Folio 3* (1899).

Hind, Henry Youle. *Northwest Territory. Reports of Progress; Together with a Preliminary and General Report on the Assiniboine and Saskatchewan Exploring Expedition, Made Under Instructions from the Provincial Secretary, Canada.* Toronto, 1859.

Hoard, L. J. "Report of the Investigation of the Meyer Site, Stanley County South Dakota," South Dakota Archeological Commission *Archeological Studies, Circular No. 2* (1949).

Hoffman, J. J. "Comments on the Use and Distribution of Tipi Rings in Montana, North Dakota, South Dakota, and Wyoming," Montana State University Anthropological and Sociological *Paper 14,* (1953).

Holden, W. C. "Excavation of Saddle-Back Ruin." *Bulletin,* Texas Archeological and Paleontological Society, Vol. V (1933), 39–52.

Holder, Preston, and Joyce Wike. "The Frontier Culture Complex, A Preliminary Report on a Prehistoric Hunters' Camp in Southwestern Nebraska," *American Antiquity,* Vol. XIV, No. 4, Pt. 1 (April, 1949), 260–66.

Holmes, W. H. "Notes on an Extensive Deposit of Obsidian in the Yellowstone National Park," *American Naturalist,* Vol. XIII (April, 1879), 247–50.

——. "An Ancient Quarry in Indian Territory," Bureau of American Ethnology *Bulletin 21* (1894).

——. "Flint Implements and Fossil Remains from a Sulphur Spring at Afton, Indian Territory," U. S. National Museum *Report for 1901* (1903), 237–52.

——. "Handbook of Aboriginal American Antiquities," Bureau of American Ethnology *Bulletin 60,* Pt. 1 (1919).

Hopkins, D. M. "Cenozoic History of the Bering Land Bridge," *Science,* Vol. CXXIX (1959), 1519–28.

Howard, Edgar B. "Evidence of Early Man in North America," *Museum Journal,* Vol. XXIV, Nos. 2–3 (1935), 61–175.

——. "Folsom and Yuma Points from Saskatchewan," *American Antiquity,* Vol. IV, No. 3 (January, 1939) 277–79.

——. "Discovery of Yuma Points *In Situ,* Near Eden, Wyoming," *American Antiquity,* Vol. VIII, No. 3 (January, 1943), 224–34.

Howard, James H. "The Southern Cult in the Northern Plains," *American Antiquity,* Vol. XIX, No. 2 (October, 1953), 130–38.

Howells, W. W. "Crania from Wyoming Resembling 'Minnesota Man'," *American Antiquity,* Vol. III, No. 4 (1938), 318–26.

Hrdlicka, Ales. "Catalogue of Human Crania in the United States National Museum Collections. The Algonkin and Related Iroquois; Siouan, Caddoan, Salish and Sahaptin, Shoshonean, and Californian Indians," U. S. National Museum *Proceedings,* Vol. LXIX, Art. 5 (1927), 1–127.

Hughes, Jack T. "Investigations in Western South Dakota and Northeastern Wyoming," *American Antiquity,* Vol. XIV, No. 4, Pt. 1 (April, 1949), 266–77.

——. "Little Sunday: An Archaic Site in the Texas Panhandle," *Bulletin* of the Texas Archeological Society, Vol. XXVI (1955), 55–74.

Hurt, Wesley R., Jr., "Report of the Investigation of the Swanson Site, 39BR16, Brule County, South Dakota, " South Dakota Archeological Commission *Archeological Studies Circular No. 3*, (1951).

———. "Report of the Investigation of the Scalp Creek Site, 39GR1, and the Ellis Creek Site, 39GR2, Gregory County, South Dakota," South Dakota Archeological Commission *Archeological Studies, Circular No. 4* (1952).

———. Report of the Investigation of the Thomas Riggs Site, 39HU1, Hughes County, South Dakota Archeological Commission *Archeological Studies, Circular No. 5* (1953).

———. "Report of the Investigation of the Spotted Bear Site, 39HU26, and the Cottonwood Site, 39HU43, Hughes County, South Dakota," Archeological Studies *Circular No. 6* (1954), South Dakota Archeological Commission.

———. "Report of the Investigation of the Swan Creek Site, 39WW7, Walworth County, South Dakota," Archeological Studies *Circular No. 7* (1957), South Dakota Archeological Commission.

Huscher, Betty H., and Harold A. Huscher. "The Hogan Builders of Colorado," *Southwestern Lore*, Vol. IX, No. 2 (1943), 1–92.

Hyde, George E. *Indians of the High Plains.* Norman, University of Oklahoma Press, 1959.

Irwin, C., and H. Irwin. "The Archeology of the Agate Bluff Area, Colorado," *The Plains Anthropologist*, No. 8 (1957), 15–33.

James, Edwin. *Account of an Expedition from Pittsburgh to the Rocky Mountains, Performed in the Years 1819–20 . . . Under the Command of Major Stephen H. Long.* 2 vols. Philadelphia, 1823.

Jeancon, J. A. "Excavations in the Chama Valley, New Mexico," Bureau of American Ethnology *Bulletin 81* (1923).

Jenks, A. E. "The Problem of the Culture from the Arvilla Gravel Pit," *American Anthropologist*, new ser., Vol. XXXIV, No. 3 (1932), 455–66.

Jennings, Jesse D. "Plainsmen of the Past," National Park Service, Region Two, Omaha (1948).

———. "Danger Cave," Society for American Archaeology *Memoir No. 14* (1957).

Jepsen, G. L. "Ancient Buffalo Hunters," *Princeton Alumni Weekly*, Vol. LIII, No. 25 (1953), 10–12, Princeton, N. J.

Johnson, Frederick. "Radiocarbon Dating," *Memoirs* of the Society for American Archaeology, No. 8 (1951).

————. "A Bibliography of Radiocarbon Dating," *American Journal of Science Radiocarbon Supplement*, Vol. I (1959), 199–214.

Johnson, W. D. "The High Plains and Their Utilization," U. S. Geologic Survey *Twenty-first Annual Report*, Pt. 4 (1900), 607–741.

Johnston, C. Stewart. "A Report on the Antelope Creek Ruin," *Bulletin*, Texas Archeological and Paleontological Society, Vol. XI (1939), 190–202.

Johnston, W. A. "Quaternary Geology of North America in Relation to the Migration of man," in D. Jenness' *The American Aborigines, Their Origin and Antiquity*, Fifth Pacific Science Congress (1933), 9–45.

Kehoe, Alice B. "Ceramic Affiliations in the Northwestern Plains," *American Antiquity*, Vol. XXV, No. 2 (1959), 237–46.

Kehoe, Thomas F. "Stone 'Medicine Wheels' in Southern Alberta and the Adjacent Portion of Montana," *Journal*, Washington Academy of Science, Vol. XLIV, No. 5 (1954), 133–37.

————. "Tipi Rings: The 'Direct Ethnological' Approach Applied to an Archeological Problem," *American Anthropologist*, Vol. LX, No. 5 (1958), 861–73.

————. "Stone Tipi Rings in North-Central Montana and the Adjacent Portion of Alberta, Canada: Their Historical, Ethnological, and Archeological Aspects," Bureau of American Ethnology *Bulletin 173*, Anthropological Paper No. 62 (1960), 417–73.

Kehoe, T. F., and Alice B. Kehoe. "Observations on the Butchering Technique at a Prehistoric Bison-Kill in Montana," *American Antiquity*, Vol. XXV, No. 1 (1960), 420–23.

Kendrew, W. G., and B. W. Currie. *The Climate of Central Canada*. Ottawa, 1955.

Keyes, Charles R. "Prehistoric Indians of Iowa," *The Palimpsest*, Vol. XXXII, No. 8 (1951), 285–344.

Kincer, J. B. "The Climate of the Great Plains as a Factor in Their Utilization," *Annals* of the Association of American Geographers, Vol. XIII, No. 2 (1923).

Kivett, Marvin F. "Archeological Investigations in Medicine Creek Reservoir, Nebraska," *American Antiquity*, Vol. XIV, No. 4, Pt. 1 (1949), 278–84.

————. "Woodland Sites in Nebraska," Nebraska State Historical Society *Publications in Anthropology*, No. 1 (1952).

————. "The Woodruff Ossuary, A Prehistoric Burial Site in Phillips

County, Kansas," Bureau of American Ethnology *Bulletin 154, River Basin Surveys Papers No. 3* (1953), 103–41.

Krieger, Alex D. "Culture Complexes and Chronology in Northern Texas, with Extension of Puebloan Datings to the Mississippi Valley," University of Texas *Publication No. 4640* (October 22, 1946).

———. "The Eastward Extension of Puebloan Datings Toward Cultures of the Mississippi Valley," *American Antiquity*, Vol. XII, No. 3 (1947), 141–48.

———. "Certain Projectile Points of the Early American Hunters," *Bulletin*, Texas Archeological and Paleontological Society, Vol. 18 (1947), 7–27.

———. "Artifacts from the Plainview Bison Bed," *Bulletin*, Geological Society of America, Vol. LVIII (1947), 938–52.

Kroeber, Alfred L. "Native Culture of the Southwest," University of California *Publications in American Archaeology and Ethnology*, Vol. XXIII, No. 9 (1928), 375–98.

———. "Cultural and Natural Areas of Native North America," University of California *Publications in American Archeology and Ethnology*, Vol. XXXVIII (1939).

———. *Anthropology*. (Rev. ed.) New York, Harcourt, Brace and Co., 1948.

Lehmer, Donald J. "The Fort Pierre Branch, Central South Dakota," *American Antiquity*, Vol. XVII, No. 4 (1952), 329–36.

———. "Archeological Investigations in the Oahe Dam Area, South Dakota, 1950–51," Bureau of American Ethnology *Bulletin 158*, River Basin Surveys Papers No. 7 (1954).

———. "The Sedentary Horizon of the Northern Plains," *Southwestern Journal of Anthropology*, Vol. X, No. 2 (1954), 139–59.

Lewis, T. H. "Mounds on the Red River of the North," *American Antiquarian*, Vol. VIII, No. 6 (1886), 369–71.

———. "Stone Monuments in Southern Dakota," *American Anthropologist*, Vol. II, No. 2 (1889), 159–64.

———. "Bowlder Outline Figures in the Dakotas, Surveyed in the Summer of 1890," *American Anthropologist*, Vol. IV, No. 1 (1891), 19–24.

Libby, W. F. *Radiocarbon Dating*. (2nd ed.) Chicago, University of Chicago Press, 1955.

Linton, Ralph. "Origin of the Plains Earth Lodge," *American Anthropologist*, new ser., Vol. XXVI, No. 2 (1924), 247–57.

———. *The Study of Man*. New York and London, 1936.

Lister, Robert H. "Notes on the Archeology of the Watrous Valley, New Mexico," *El Palacio*, Vol. LV, No. 2 (1948), 35–41.

Logan, Wilfred D. "Graham Cave, an Archaic Site in Montgomery County, Missouri," *Memoir*, No. 2 (1952), Missouri Archaeological Society.

Lowie, Robert H. "Indians of the Plains," *Anthropological Handbook No. 1*, American Museum of Natural History, (1954).

———. "Reflections on the Plains Indians," *Anthropological Quarterly* (formerly *Primitive Man*), Vol. XXVIII (new ser. Vol. III), No. 2 (April, 1955), 63–86.

Ludlow, William. "Report of a reconnaissance of the Black Hills of Dakota, Made in the Summer of 1874," Engineer Department, U. S. Army (1875).

Mackintosh, W. A. "Prairie Settlement, The Geographic Setting," *Canadian Frontiers of Settlement*, Vol. I (1934).

MacNeish, Richard S. (Southern Manitoba Archeology), "Notes and News," *American Antiquity*, Vol. XIX, No. 3 (1954), 306–307.

———. "The Stott Mound and Village, Near Brandon, Manitoba," *Annual Report*, National Museum of Canada, 1952–53, *Bulletin 132*, (1954), 20–65.

———. "An Introduction to the Archaeology of Southeast Manitoba," National Museum of Canada *Bulletin 157*, Anthropological Series No. 44 (1958).

Malouf, Carling. "Tipi Rings," *Southwestern Lore*. XXV, No. 4 (1960).

Martin, H. T. "Further Notes on the Pueblo Ruins of Scott County," Kansas University Science *Bulletin*, Vol. V, No. 2 (1909), 11–22.

Maximilian, Prince of Wied. "Travels in the Interior of North America," in Vol. XXIII of Thwaites' *Early Western Travels, 1748–1846*. Cleveland, 1906.

Mayer-Oakes, William J. "Relationship Between Plains Early Hunter and Eastern Archaic," *Journal*, Washington Academy of Sciences, Vol. XLIX, No. 5 (May, 1959), 146–56.

McAdams, William. "Exploration of Apparent Recent Mounds in Dacotah," *American Antiquarian*, Vol. VIII, No. 3 (1886), 156–58.

McDermott, John F., ed. *Tixier's Travels on the Osage Prairies*. Norman, University of Oklahoma Press, 1940.

McKern, W. C. "Preliminary Report on the Upper Mississippi Phase in Wisconsin," *Bulletin,* Milwaukee Public Museum, Vol. XVI, No. 3, (1945).

McNutt, Charles H., and Richard P. Wheeler. "Bibliography of Primary Sources for Radiocarbon Dates," *American Antiquity,* Vol. XXIV, No. 3 (January, 1959), 323-24.

Meleen, E. E. "A Preliminary Report of the Mitchell Indian Village Site and Burial Mounds, on Firesteel Creek, Mitchell, Davison County, South Dakota," South Dakota Archeological Commission *Archeological Studies, Circular No. 2,* (1938).

——. "Report of an Investigation of the La Roche Site, Stanley County, South Dakota," South Dakota Archeological Commission *Archeological Studies, Circular No. 5,* (1948).

——. "A Preliminary Report on the Thomas Riggs Village Site," *American Antiquity,* Vol. XIV, No. 4, Pt. 1 (April, 1949),310-21.

Mera, H. P. "Ceramic Clues to the Prehistory of North Central New Mexico," Archeological Survey *Technical Service Bulletin No. 8,* (1935). Laboratory of Anthropology, Santa Fe.

——. "Some Aspects of the Largo Cultural Phase, Northern New Mexico," *American Antiquity,* Vol. III, No. 3 (1938), 236-43.

Metcalf, George. "Additional Data from the Dodd and Phillips Ranch Sites South Dakota," *American Antiquity,* Vol. XXI, No. 3 (1956), 305-309.

Missouri River Commission. "Map of the Missouri River (From Its Mouth to Three Forks, Montana), 1892-95," in 84 sheets, 1" = 1 mile, and 9 index sheets 1" = 8 miles.

Montgomery, Henry W. "Remains of Prehistoric Man in the Dakotas," *American Anthropologist,* Vol. VIII, No. 4 (1906), 640-51.

——. "Prehistoric Man in Manitoba and Saskatchewan," *American Anthropologist,* Vol. X, No. 1 (1908), 33-40.

——. " 'Calf Mountain' Mound in Manitoba," *American Anthropologist,* Vol. XII, No. 1 (1910), 49-57.

Moorehead, Warren K. *Archeology of the Arkansas River Valley.* New Haven, Yale University Press, 1931.

Morton, Harry C. "Excavation of a Rock Shelter in Elbert County, Colorado," *Southwestern Lore,* Vol. XX, No. 3 (1954), 30-41.

Moss, John H. "Early Man in the Eden Valley," *Museum Monographs,* The University Museum, University of Pennsylvania, 1951.

Mott, Mildred. "The Relation of Historic Indian Tribes to Archeological Manifestations in Iowa," *Iowa Journal of History and Politics*, Vol. XXXVI, No. 3 (1938), 227–314.

Mulloy, William. "The Hagen Site, a Prehistoric Village on the Lower Yellowstone," University of Montana *Publications in Social Sciences, No. 1* (1942).

———. A Prehistoric Campsite Near Red Lodge, Montana," *American Antiquity*, Vol. IX, No. 2 (1943), 170–79.

———. "The Northern Plains," in J. B. Griffin's *Archeology of Eastern United States* (1952), 124–38.

———. "Archeological Investigations in the Shoshone Basin of Wyoming," University of Wyoming *Publications*, Vol. XVIII, No. 1 (1954), 1–70.

———. "The McKean Site in Northeastern Wyoming," *Southwestern Journal of Anthropology*, Vol. X, No. 4 (1954), 432–60.

———. "A Preliminary Historical Outline for the Northwestern Plains," University of Wyoming *Publications*, Vol. XXII, Nos. 1 and 2 (1958).

———, and O. Lewis. "Some Early Types of Points from the Lower Yellowstone Country," *American Antiquity*, Vol. VIII, No. 3 (1943), 298–99.

Nasatir, A. P. *Before Lewis and Clark, Documents Illustrating the History of the Missouri, 1785–1804.* 2 vols. St. Louis, St. Louis Historical Documents Foundation, 1952.

Nelson, N. C. "Camping on Ancient Trails," *Natural History*, Vol. XLIX, No. 5 (1942), 262–67.

———. "Contribution to Montana Archeology," *American Antiquity*, Vol. IX, No. 2 (1943), 162–69.

Neuman, Robert W. "The Truman Mound Site, Big Bend Reservoir Area, South Dakota, *American Antiquity*, Vol. XXVI, No. 1 (1960), 78–92.

Neumann, Georg K. "The Origin of the Prairid Physical Type of American Indian," *Papers*, Michigan Academy of Science, Arts, and Letters, Vol. XXVII (1942), 539–42.

———. "South Dakota Physical Types," *Museum News*, W. H. Over Museum Vol. XIII, No. 5 (1952), 1.

———. "Archeology and Race in the American Indian," in J. B. Griffin's *Archeology of Eastern United States* (1952), 13–34.

Newman, Marshall T. "The Blond Mandans: A Critical Review of an Old Problem," *Southwestern Journal of Anthropology*, Vol. VI, No. 3 (1950), 255–72.

————. "The Application of Ecological Rules to the Racial Anthropology of the Aboriginal New World," *American Anthropologist,* Vol. LV (1953), 311–27.

Newman, Thomas M. "Documentary Sources on the Manufacture of Pottery by the Indians of the Central Plains and Middle Missouri," *The Plains Anthropologist,* No. 4 (1955), 13–20.

Norris, P. W. "Prehistoric Remains in Montana, Between Fort Ellis and the Yellowstone River," Smithsonian Institution *Annual Report for 1879* (1880), 327–28.

————. *Fifth Annual Report of the Superintendent of the Yellowstone National Park.* Washington, 1881.

Opler, Morris E. "A Summary of Jicarilla Apache Culture," *American Anthropologist,* Vol. XXXVIII, No. 2 (1936), 202–23.

Osterwald, Frank W., and Doris B. Osterwald. "Wyoming Mineral Resources," Geological Survey of Wyoming *Bulletin 45* (1952).

Over, W. H. "The Archeology of Ludlow Cave and its Significance," *American Antiquity,* Vol. II, No. 2 (1936), 126–29.

————, and E. E. Meleen. "A Report on an Investigation of the Brandon Village Site and the Split Rock Creek Mounds," South Dakota Archeological Commission *Archeological Studies Circular No. 3* (1941).

Palliser, John. *The Journals, Detailed Reports, and Observations Relative to the exploration by Capt. John Palliser of that portion of British North America Which in Latitude Lies Between the British Boundary Line and the Height of Land of the Northern or Frozen Ocean Respectively and in Longitude Between the Western Shore of Lake Superior and the Pacific Ocean, During the Years 1857, 1858, 1859, and 1860.* British Parliamentary Papers. London, 1863.

Pike, Zebulon M. *An Account of Expeditions to the Sources of the Mississippi, and Through the Western Parts of Louisiana, to the Sources of the Arkansaw, Kans, La Platte, and Pierre Jaun Rivers; Performed by Order of the Government of the United States During the Years 1805, 1806, and 1807. And a Tour Through the Interior Parts of New Spain, when Conducted Through These Provinces.* Philadelphia, C. and A. Conrad and Company, 1810.

Plains Archeological Conference. *Proceedings,* Fifth Plains Conference for Archeology, Note Book No. 1 (1949), Laboratory of Anthropology, University of Nebraska.

———. *Proceedings* of the Sixth Plains Archeological Conference (1948), *Anthropological Papers No. 11* (1950), University of Utah.

Pond, S. W. "The Dakotas or Sioux in Minnesota as They Were in 1834," Minnesota Historical Society *Collections*, Vol. XII (1908), 319–501.

Poynter, C. W. M. "A Study of Nebraska Crania," *American Anthropologist*, new ser., Vol. XVII, No. 3 (1915), 509–24.

Quimby, George I., Jr. "Cultural and Natural Areas Before Kroeber," *American Antiquity*, Vol. XIX, No. 4 (1954), 317–31.

Radiocarbon Dates Association, Inc. "Radiocarbon Date Cards," (1955).

Renaud, E. B. "Prehistoric Cultures of the Cimarron Valley, Northeastern New Mexico and Western Oklahoma," Colorado Scientific Society *Proceedings*, Vol. XII, No. 5 (1930), 113–50.

———. "Archaeological Survey of Eastern Colorado" (1931), Department of Anthropology, University of Denver.

———. "Archeological Survey of Eastern Colorado, Second Report" (1932), Department of Anthropology, University of Denver.

———. "Archeological Survey of Eastern Colorado, Third Report" (1933), Department of Anthropology, University of Denver.

———. "The Archaeological Survey of Colorado, Fourth Report, Seasons 1933 and 1934," (1935), Department of Anthropology, University of Denver.

———. "Pictographs and Petroglyphs of the High Western Plains," *Eighth Report* of the Archeological Survey of the High Western Plains (1936).

———. "The Archaeological Survey of the High Western Plains, *Seventh Report*, Southern Wyoming and Southwestern South Dakota, Summer 1935" (1936), Department of Anthropology, University of Denver.

Riggs, Stephen R. "Dakota Grammar, Texts, and Ethnography," *Contributions to North American Ethnology*, Vol. IX (1893); U. S. Geographical and Geological Survey of the Rocky Mountain Region, 53 Cong., 2 sess., *House Misc. Doc. 173*.

Roberts, F. H. H., Jr. "A Folsom Complex: Preliminary Report on Investigations at the Lindenmeier Site in Northern Colorado," Smithsonian *Miscellaneous Collections*, Vol. XCIV, No. 4 (1935).

———. "Additional Information on the Folsom Complex: Report on the Second Season's Investigations at the Lindenmeier Site in Northern Colorado," Smithsonian *Miscellaneous Collections*, Vol. XCV, No. 10 (1936).

——. "Developments in the Problem of the North American Paleo-Indian," Smithsonian *Miscellaneous Collections*, Vol. C (1940), 51–116.

——. "Archeological and Geological Investigations in the San Jon District, Eastern New Mexico," Smithsonian *Miscellaneous Collections*, Vol. CIII, No. 4 (1942).

——. "A New Site," in "Notes and News," *American Antiquity*, Vol. VIII, No. 3 (1943), 300.

——. "River Basin Surveys: The First Five Years of the Inter-Agency Archeological and Paleontological Salvage Program," Smithsonian Institution *Annual Report for 1951* (1952), 351–83.

——. "River Basin Surveys," *Seventieth Annual Report*, Bureau of American Ethnology (1952–53), 5–29.

Roe, Frank G. *The Indian and the Horse.* Norman, University of Oklahoma Press, 1955.

Ruppé, Reynold J. "Archeological Investigations of the Mill Creek Culture of Northwestern Iowa," American Philosophical Society *Year Book 1955* (1956), 335–39, Philadelphia.

Rusco, Mary K. MS. "The White Rock Aspect," M.A. thesis, Department of Anthropology, University of Nebraska, Lincoln, 1955.

Satterthwaite, Linton. "Stone Artifacts At and Near the Finley Site, Near Eden, Wyoming," *Museum Monographs*, University Museum, University of Pennsylvania, 1957.

Sauer, Carl O. "A Geographic Sketch of Early Man in America," *Geographical Review*, Vol. XXXIV, No. 4 (1944), 529–73.

Sayles, E. B. "An Archeological Survey of Texas," *Medallion Papers, No. 27* (1935).

Schmitt, Karl. "The Lee Site, GV3, of Garvin County, Oklahoma," *Bulletin*, Texas Archeological and Paleontological Society, Vol. XXI (1950), 69–89.

——, and R. Toldan. "The Brown Site, GD1, Grady County, Oklahoma," *Bulletin*, Texas Archeological and Paleontological Society, Vol. XXIV (1953), 141–76.

Schultz, C. Bertrand. "Some Artifact Sites of Early Man in the Great Plains and Adjacent Areas," *American Antiquity*, Vol. VIII, No. 3 (1943), 242–49.

——, and W. D. Frankforter. "Preliminary Report on the Lime

Creek Sites: New Evidence of Early Man in Southwestern Nebraska," *Bulletin*, University of Nebraska State Museum, Vol. III, No. 4, Pt. 2 (1948), 43–62.

Schultz, C. Bertrand, G. C. Lueninghoener, and W. D. Frankforter. "Preliminary Geomorphological Studies of the Lime Creek Area," *Bulletin*, University of Nebraska State Museum, Vol. III, No. 4 (1948), Pt. 1, 31–42.

Schultz, F., and A. C. Spaulding. "A Hopewellian Burial Site in the Lower Republican Valley, Kansas," *American Antiquity*, Vol. XIII, No. 4 (1948), 306–13.

Sears, P. B. "The Archeology of Environment in Eastern North America," *American Anthropologist*, new ser., Vol. XXXIV, No. 4 (1932), 610–22.

Secoy, Frank R. "The Identity of the 'Paduca': an Ethnohistorical Analysis," *American Anthropologist*, Vol. LIII, No. 4, Pt. 1 (1951), 525–42.

———. "Changing Military Patterns on the Great Plains," *Monographs* of the American Ethnological Society, No. 21 (1953).

Secrist, Kenneth G. "Pictographs in Central Montana," Montana State University *Anthropology and Sociology Papers, No. 20* (1960).

Sellards, E. H. "Artifacts Associated with Fossil Elephant," *Bulletin*, Geological Society of America, Vol. XLIX (1938), 999–1010.

———. *Early Man in America.* Austin, University of Texas Press, 1952.

———. Glenn L. Evans, and Grayson E. Meade. "Fossil Bison and Associated Artifacts from Plainview, Texas, with Description of Artifacts by Alex D. Krieger," *Bulletin.* Geological Society of America, Vol. LVIII (1947), 927–54.

Shaeffer, J. B. "The Alibates Flint Quarry, Texas," *American Antiquity*, Vol. XXIV, No. 2 (1958), 189–91.

Shantz, H. L. "The Natural Vegetation of the Great Plains Region," *Annals* of the Association of American Geographers, Vol. XIII, No. 2 (1923), 81–107.

———, and R. Zon. "The Natural Vegetation of the United States," *Atlas of American Agriculture*, Pt. 1, "The Physical Basis; Natural Vegetation," (1924), U. S. Department of Agriculture, Bureau of Agricultural Economics.

Shapley, H. ed. *Climatic Change: Evidence, Causes, and Effects.* Cambridge, Harvard University Press, 1953.

Sheldon, A. E. "Ancient Indian Fireplaces in South Dakota Bad-Lands," *American Anthropologist*, Vol. VII, No. 1 (1905), 44–48.

Shelford, V. E. "Naturalist's Guide to the Americas," Ecological Society of America (1926).

Shimkin, D. B. "Shoshone-Comanche Origins and Migrations," *Proceedings*, Sixth Pacific Science Congress, Vol. IV (1941), 17–25.

Simms, S. C. "A Wheel-Shaped Stone Monument in Wyoming," *American Anthropologist*, Vol. V, No. 1 (1903), 107–10.

Skinner, M. F., and O. C. Kaisen. "The Fossil Bison of Alaska and Preliminary Revision of the Genus," *Bulletin*, American Museum of Natural History, Vol. LXXXIX (1947).

Smith, Carlyle S., and Roger T. Grange, Jr. "The Spain Site (39LM301), a Winter Village in Fort Randall Reservoir, South Dakota," River Basin Surveys *Papers No. 11;* Bureau of American Ethnology, *Bulletin 169* (1958), 79–128.

Smith, G. Hubert. "Archeological Work at 32ML2 (Like-a-Fishhook village and Fort Berthold), Garrison Reservoir Area, North Dakota, 1950–54," *The Plains Anthropologist*, No. 2 (1954), 27–32.

Smith, Harlan I. "An Unknown Field in American Archeology," *Bulletin*, American Geographical Society, Vol. XLII (1910), 511–20.

———. "An Album of Prehistoric Canadian Art," Canada Department of Mines *Bulletin 37*, Anthropological Series, No. 8 (1923).

Snider, L. C. "The Gypsum and Salt of Oklahoma," Oklahoma Geological Survey *Bulletin No. 11* (1913), 203–205.

Snodgrasse, Richard M. "The Skeletal Remains from Pictograph and Ghost Caves, Montana," University of Wyoming *Publications*, Vol. XXII, No. 2 (1958), 236–64.

Snow, E. P. "The Hartville Iron Ore Deposits in Wyoming," *Engineering and Mining Journal*, Vol. LX (October 5, 1895), 320–21.

Spaulding, Albert C. "The Middle Woodland Period in the Central Plains," *Proceedings*, Fifth Plains Conference for Archeology (1949), 105–11. Note Book No. 1, Laboratory of Anthropology, University of Nebraska.

———. "The Arzberger Site, Hughes County, South Dakota," *Occasional Contributions, No. 16*, Museum of Anthropology, University of Michigan (1956).

Stearn, E. W., and A. E. Stearn. *The Effect of Smallpox on the Destiny of the Amerindian*. Boston, Bruce Humphries, Inc., 1945.

Steen, Charlie R. "Two Early Historic Sites on the Southern Plains,"

Bulletin, Texas Archeological and Paleontological Society, Vol. XXIV (1953), 177–88.

Stephenson, Robert L. "Culture Chronology in Texas," *American Antiquity,* Vol. XVI, No. 2 (1950), 151–57.

———. "The Hogge Bridge Site and the Wylie Focus," *American Antiquity,* Vol. XVII, No. 4 (1952), 299–312.

———. "Taxonomy and Chronology in the Central Plains-Middle Missouri River Area," *The Plains Anthropologist,* No. 1 (1954), 12–21.

Stewart, Omer C. "Why the Great Plains Are Treeless," *Colorado Quarterly,* Vol. II, No. 1 (1953), 40–50.

Stewart, T. Dale. "Some Historical Implications of Physical Anthropology in North America," Smithsonian *Miscellaneous Collections,* Vol. C (1940), 15–50.

———. "Skeletal Remains from Platte and Clay Counties, Missouri," U. S. National Museum *Bulletin 183,* Appendix (1943), 245–73.

———. "The Lower Level Human Skull (From the McKean Site in Northeastern Wyoming)," *Southwestern Journal of Anthropology,* Vol. X, No. 4 (1954), 457–59.

———. "Description of the Skeletal Remains from Doniphan and Scott Counties, Kansas," Bureau of American Ethnology *Bulletin 174* (1959), 669–83.

Stirling, Matthew W. "Archeological Investigations in South Dakota," *Explorations and Fieldwork of the Smithsonian Institution in 1923* (1924), 66–71.

———. "Arikara Glassworking," *Journal,* Washington Academy of Sciences, Vol. XXXVII, No. 8 (1947), 257–63.

Strong, William D. "The Plains Culture Area in the Light of Archeology," *American Anthropologist,* new ser., Vol. XXXV, No. 2 (1933), 271–87.

———. "An Introduction to Nebraska Archeology," Smithsonian *Miscellaneous Collections,* Vol. XCIII, No. 10 (1935).

———. "From History to Prehistory in the Northern Great Plains," Smithsonian *Miscellaneous Collections,* Vol. C (1940), 353–94.

Studer, Floyd V. "Texas Panhandle Culture Ruin No. 55," *Bulletin,* Texas Archeological and Paleontological Society, Vol. VI (1934), 80–96.

Suhm, Dee Ann, A. D. Krieger, and E. B. Jelks. "An Introductory Handbook of Texas Archeology," *Bulletin,* Texas Archeological and Paleontological Society, Vol. XXV (1954).

Thomas, A. B. *After Coronado: Spanish Exploration Northeast of New Mexico, 1696–1727.* Norman, University of Oklahoma Press, 1935.

Thomas, Cyrus. "Ancient Mounds of Dakota," *Sixth Annual Report,* U. S. Geological [and Geographical] Survey of the Territories . . . for the Year 1872 (1873), 655–58.

———. "Report on the Mound Explorations of the Bureau of Ethnology," Bureau of American Ethnology *Twelfth Annual Report* (1894), 17–730.

Thornthwaite, C. Warren. "Climate and Settlement in the Great Plains," *Yearbook of Agriculture 1941: Climate and Man,* Washington, 177–87.

Thwaites, Reuben Gold, ed. *Original Journals of the Lewis and Clark Expedition, 1804–1806.* 8 vols. New York, Dodd, Mead & Company, 1904–1905.

Todd, J. E. "Boulder Mosaics in Dakota," *American Naturalist,* Vol. XX, No. 1 (1886), 1–4.

Trewartha, Glenn T. "Climate and Settlement of the Subhumid Lands," in *Climate and Man,* 167–76. Yearbook of Agriculture, 1941. Washington.

Troike, Rudolph C. "Anthropological Theory and Plains Archeology," *Bulletin,* Texas Archeological and Paleontological Society, Vol. XXVI (1955), 113–43.

Tunnell, C. D., and J. T. Hughes. "An Archaic Bison Kill in the Texas Panhandle," *Panhandle-Plains Historical Review,* Vol. XXVIII (1955), 63–70.

Udden, J. A. "An Old Indian Village," Augustana Library *Publication,,* No. 2 (1900).

U. S. Department of Agriculture. *Atlas of American Agriculture.* "Physical Basis Including Land Relief, Climate, Soils, and Natural Vegetation of the United States," Bureau of Agricultural Economics. 1936.

Van Royen, Willem. "Prehistoric Droughts in the Central Great Plains," *Geographical Review,* Vol. XXVII, No. 4 (1937), 637–50.

Vestal, Paul A., and Richard E. Schultes. *The Economic Botany of the Kiowa Indians.* Cambridge, Botanical Museum, 1939.

Vickers, Chris. "Archeology in the Rock and Pelican Lake Area of South-Central Manitoba," *American Antiquity,* Vol. XI, No. 2 (1945), 88–94.

———. "Burial Traits of the Headwaters Lakes Aspect in Manitoba," *American Antiquity*, Vol. XIII, No. 2 (1947), 109–14.

———. "The Historic Approach and the Headwaters Lakes Aspect," Plains Archeological Conference *Newsletter*, Vol. I, No. 3 (April 15, 1948), 31–37.

———, and Ralph Bird, "A Copper Trade Object from the Headwaters Lakes Aspect in Manitoba," *American Antiquity*, Vol. 15, No. 2 (1949), 157–60.

Villiers, Marc de. *La Decouverte du Missouri et l'Histoire du Fort Orleans (1673–1728)*. Paris, Champion, 1925.

Warren, Lieutenant G. K. "Explorations in the Dacota Country in the Year 1855," 34 Cong., 1 sess., *Sen. Exec. Doc. 76.*

Watson, Virginia. "The Optima Focus of the Panhandle Aspect: Description and Analysis," *Bulletin*, Texas Archeological and Paleontological Society, Vol. XXI (1950), 7–68.

Weakly, H. E. "Tree Rings as a Record of Precipitation in Western Nebraska," *Tree-Ring Bulletin*, Vol. VI, No. 3 (1940), 18–19.

———. "A Tree-Ring Record of Precipitation in Western Nebraska," *Journal of Forestry*, Vol. XLI, No. 11, (1943), 816–19.

Webb, W. P. *The Great Plains*. Boston, Ginn and Company, 1931.

Wedel, Mildred M. "Oneota Sites on the Upper Iowa River," *The Missouri Archaeologist*, Vol. XXI, Nos. 2–4 (1959).

Wedel, Waldo R. "Contributions to the Archaeology of the Upper Republican Valley, Nebraska." *Nebraska History Magazine*, Vol. XV, No. 3 (1935), 132–209.

———. "An Introduction to Pawnee Archeology," *Bulletin 112*, Bureau of American Ethnology (1936).

———. "The Direct-Historical Approach in Pawnee Archeology," Smithsonian *Miscellaneous Collections*, Vol. XCVII, No. 7 (1938).

———. "Archeological Reconnaissance in Southeastern Colorado," *Explorations and Field-Work of the Smithsonian Institution in 1938* (1939), 91–94.

———. "Culture Sequence in the Central Great Plains," Smithsonian *Miscellaneous Collections*, Vol. C (1940), 291–352.

———. "Environment and Native Subsistence Economies in the Central Great Plains," Smithsonian *Miscellaneous Collections*, Vol. CI, No. 3 (1941).

———. "Archeological Remains in Central Kansas and Their Possible Bearing on the Location of Quivira," Smithsonian *Miscellaneous Collections*, Vol. CI, No. 7 (1942).

335

———. "Archeological Investigations in Platte and Clay Counties, Missouri," U. S. National Museum *Bulletin 183* (1943).

———. "Culture Chronology in the Central Great Plains, *American Antiquity*, Vol. XII, No. 3 (1947), 148–56.

———. "Prehistory and Environment in the Central Great Plains," *Transactions*, Kansas Academy of Science, Vol. L, No. 1 (1947), 1–18.

———. "Prehistory and the Missouri Valley Development Program ... in 1947," Smithsonian *Miscellaneous Collections*, Vol. CXI, No. 2 (1948).

———. "Notes on Some Plains-Southwestern Contacts in Light of Archeology," in *For the Dean, Essays in Anthropology in Honor of Byron Cummings on his Eighty-Ninth Birthday, September 20, 1950* (1950), 99–116.

———. "Notes on Aboriginal Pottery from Montana," *Journal*, Washington Academy of Sciences, Vol. XLI, No. 4 (1951), 130–38.

———. "Prehistory and the Missouri Valley Development Program ... in 1948," Bureau of American Ethnology *Bulletin 154*, River Basin Surveys Papers No. 1 (1953).

———. "Some Aspects of Human Ecology in the Central Plains," *American Anthropologist*, Vol. LV, No. 4 (1953), 499–514.

———. "Earthenware and Steatite Vessels from Northwestern Wyoming," *American Antiquity*, Vol. XIX, No. 4 (1954), 403–409.

———. "Archeological Materials from the Vicinity of Mobridge, South Dakota," Bureau of American Ethnology *Bulletin 157*, Anthropological Papers, No. 45 (1955), 69–188.

———. "Changing Settlement Patterns in the Great Plains," in G. R. Willey's *Prehistoric Settlement Patterns in the New World*, Viking Fund *Publications in Anthropology*, No. 23 (1956), 81–92.

———. "Observations on Some Nineteenth Century Pottery Vessels from the Upper Missouri," Bureau of American Ethnology *Bulletin 164*, Anthropological Papers, No. 51 (1957), 87–114.

———. "The Central North American Grassland: Man-made or Natural?" *Studies in Human Ecology* (1957), 39–69. *Social Science Monographs, III*.

———. "An Introduction to Kansas Archeology," *Bulletin 174*, Bureau of American Ethnology, 1959.

———, and George B. Griffenhagen. "An English Balsam Among the

Dakota Aborigines," *American Journal of Pharmacy*, Vol. CXXVI, No. 12 (1954), 409–15.

Wendorf, Fred. "Salvage Archeology in the Chama Valley, New Mexico," School of American Research *Monograph No. 17* (1953).

———. "The Archaeology of Northeastern New Mexico," *El Palacio*, Vol. LXVII, No. 2 (1960), 55–65.

———, A. D. Krieger, C. C. Albritton, and T. D. Stewart. *The Midland Discovery*. Austin, University of Texas Press, 1955.

———, and Alex D. Krieger. "New Light on the Midland Discovery," *American Antiquity*, Vol. XXV, No. 1 (1959), 66–78.

Wettlaufer, Boyd. "The Mortlach Site in the Besant Valley of Central Saskatchewan," *Anthropological Series No. 1* (1955), Department of Natural Resources, Regina.

———. "The Long Creek Site," *The Blue Jay*, Vol. XV, No. 4 (1957), 167–69.

———. MS. "An Archeological Survey of Saskatchewan," The National Museum of Canada and Provincial Museum of Saskatchewan, No. 1 (1951).

Wheat, Joe Ben. "Two Archeological Sites Near Lubbock, Texas," *Panhandle-Plains Historical Review*, Vol. XXVIII (1955), 71–77.

Wheeler, Richard P. "Check List of Middle Missouri Pottery Wares, Types, and Subtypes," *The Plains Anthropologist*, No. 2 (1954), 3–21.

———. "Two New Projectile Point Types: Duncan and Hanna Points," *The Plains Anthropologist*, No. 1 (1954), 7–14.

White, L. A., ed. *Lewis Henry Morgan: The Indian Journals 1859–62*. Ann Arbor, 1959.

White, Thain. "Tipi Rings in the Flathead Lake Area, Western Montana," Anthropology and Sociology *Papers, No. 19*, Montana State University (1959).

Wied-Neuwied, Maximilian Alexander Philip, Prinz von. "Travels in the Interior of North America," in R. G. Thwaite's *Early Western Travels, 1748–1846*. Vols. XXII–XXIV, Cleveland, 1906.

Wilford, Lloyd A. "A Tentative Classification of the Prehistoric Cultures of Minnesota," *American Antiquity*, Vol. VI, No. 3 (1941), 231–49.

———. "A Revised Classification of the Prehistoric Cultures of Minnesota," *American Antiquity*, Vol. XXI, No. 2 (1955), 130–42.

Will, George F. "Some Observations Made in Northwestern South Dakota," *American Anthropologist*, Vol. XI, No. 2 (1909), 257–65.

———. "Some New Missouri River Valley Sites in North Dakota," *American Anthropologist, new ser.*, Vol. XII, No. 1 (1910), 58–60.

———. "A New Feature in the Archeology of the Missouri Valley in North Dakota," *American Anthropologist*, Vol. XIII, No. 4 (1911), 585–88.

———. "An Unusual Group of Mounds in North Dakota," *American Anthropologist*, Vol. XXIII, No. 2 (1921), 175–79.

———. "Archeology of the Missouri Valley," *Anthropological Papers*, American Museum of Natural History, Vol. XXII, Pt. 6 (1924).

———. "Indian Agriculture at its Northern Limits in the Great Plains Region of North America," *Annaes do XX Congresso Internacional de Americanistas*, Rio de Janeiro, 20–30 Agosto, 1922, Vol. I (1924), 203–205.

———. "A Résumé of North Dakota Archeology," North Dakota Historical *Quarterly*, Vol. VII, Nos. 2 and 3 (1933), 150–61.

———. "Tree-Ring Studies in North Dakota," *Bulletin 338*, Agricultural Experiment Station, North Dakota Agricultural College.

———, and Thad C. Hecker. "The Upper Missouri River Valley Aboriginal Culture in North Dakota," North Dakota Historical *Quarterly*, Vol. XI, Nos. 1 and 2 (1944), 5–126.

———, and G. E. Hyde. *Corn Among the Indians of the Upper Missouri*. St. Louis, W. H. Miner Company, Inc., 1917.

———, and H. J. Spinden. "The Mandans," *Papers*, Peabody Museum American Archeology and Ethnology, Harvard University, Vol. III, No. 4 (1906).

Williston, S. W. "Some Prehistoric Ruins in Scott County, Kansas," Kansas University *Quarterly*, Series B, Vol. VII, No. 4 (1899), 109–14.

———. "An Arrowhead Found with Bones of Bison Occidentalis Lucas, in Western Kansas," *American Geologist*, Vol. XXX (1902), 313–15.

Wilson, Gilbert L. "Agriculture of the Hidatsa Indians, An Indian Interpretation," *Bulletin* of the University of Minnesota, Studies in the Social Sciences, No. 9 (1917).

———. "The Horse and the Dog in Hidatsa Culture," American Museum of Natural History *Anthropological Papers*, Vol. XV, Pt. 2 (1924), 125–311.

———. "The Hidatsa Earthlodge," American Museum of Natural History *Anthropological Papers*, Vol. XXXIII, Pt. 5 (1934), 343–420.

Wilson, N. L., and Alfred Atkinson. "Corn in Montana: History, Characteristics, Adaptation," Montana Agricultural College Experiment Station (1915).

Winchell, N. H., "The Aborigines of Minnesota," Minnesota Historical Society (1911).

Wissler, Clark. "Diffusion of Culture in the Plains of North America," *Proceedings*, Fifteenth International Congress of Americanists, Tome II (1907), 39–52.

———. "Ethnographical Problems of the Missouri Saskatchewan Area," *American Anthropologist*, new ser., Vol. X, No. 2 (1908), 197–207.

———. "The Influence of the Horse in the Development of Plains Culture," *American Anthropologist*, Vol. XVI, No. 1 (1914), 1–25.

———. "Material Cultures of the North American Indians," *American Anthropologist*, Vol. XVI, No. 3 (1914), 447–505.

———. *The Relation of Nature to Man in Aboriginal America*. New York, 1926.

———. *The American Indian*. (2nd ed.) New York, 1931.

Withers, Arnold M. "University of Denver Archeological Fieldwork, 1952–1953," *Southwestern Lore*, Vol. XIX, No. 4 (1954), 1–3.

Witte, A. H. "Certain Archeological Notes on the High Plains of Texas," *Bulletin*, Texas Archeological and Paleontological Society, Vol. XVIII (1947), 76–82.

Wood, W. Raymond. MS. "The Redbird Focus," M. A. thesis, Department of Anthropology, University of Nebraska, Lincoln, 1956.

———. "A Woodland Site Near Williston, North Dakota," *The Plains Anthropologist*, No. 6 (1956), 21–24.

———. "Two Woodland Vessels from North Dakota," *American Antiquity*, Vol. XXV, No. 1 (1959), 123–25.

———. "The Boundary Mound Group (32SI1): An Eastern Woodland Complex in North Dakota," *Plains Anthropologist*, Vol. V, No. 10 (1960), 71–78.

———. MS. "The Pomme de Terre Reservoir in Western Missouri Prehistory" (1960).

Wormington, H. M. "A Proposed Revision of Yuma Point Terminology," *Proceedings*, Colorado Museum of Natural History, Vol. XVIII, No. 2 (1948), 1–19.

———. "A Reappraisal of the Fremont Culture," *Proceedings,* Denver Museum of Natural History, No. 1 (1955).
———. *Ancient Man in North America* (4th ed.). Denver Museum of Natural History, Popular Series No. 4 (1957).
Wright, Muriel H. *A Guide to the Indian Tribes of Oklahoma.* Norman, University of Oklahoma Press, 1951.

INDEX

Adze-shaped scraper handles, antler: 110, 118, 123, 175, 198
Afton Spring, Okla.: 137n.
Agate Basin, Wyo.: 72, 248
Agate Bluff, Colo.: 102
Age of sites and cultures: 280, 281, 282; early big-game hunters, 68, 69–70; Central Plains, 85, 88, 99, 111, 113, 115, 119, 120, 121, 126, 287, 289; Southern Plains, 135, 137, 138, 140, 144, 145, 147, 150, 152, 287; Middle Missouri, 165, 183, 197, 200, 287; Northeastern Periphery, 213, 224, 235, 236, 237; Northwestern Plains, 247, 251, 258, 277; see also dendrochronology, radiocarbon dating and dates, cross dating
Agriculture, Plains Indian: 80–81, 114; environmental influences on, 29, 31, 32, 34; archeological evidence of, 88, 90, 94, 95, 99, 109, 118, 143, 195, 204–205, 208, 212, 215; crops grown, 173; tools used, 173; see also corn, beans squash, gourd
Alberta, Can.: pictographs in, 276; see also Northwestern Plains
Alibates quarries, Tex.: 140, 143, 153–54
Alignments, rock, in Northwestern Plains: 260
Allen site, Neb.: 72, 74–75
Allis, Samuel: 124
Altamont moraine: 28
Altithermal: 18–19, 254, 255, 282
Anderson focus, Manitoba, Can.: 236

Anderson focus, S. D.: 179
Angostura complex: 71, 74, 235, 248
Angostura reservoir, S. D.: 71, 247, 256, 257
Angus, Neb.: 58
Animals native to the Plains: 40–43, 47, 79; see also bison, deer, elk, antelope
Antelope, pronghorn: 41–42; remains found in sites, 63, 69, 106, 134, 139, 143, 173, 187
Antelope Creek, focus, Tex.: 142–44
Antler artifacts: of the Central Plains, 99, 110, 118, 123; of the Southern Plains, 135, 140, 143; of the Middle Missouri, 175–76, 189, 198; of the Northeastern Periphery, 222, 235, 237; of the Northwestern Plains, 256
Antler Creek, Manitoba, Can.: 217, 219, 238
Apache Indians: 79, 151–52; see also Plains Apache
Apios tuberosa (groundnut): 38, 294
Apishapa River, Colo.: 151
Arahey: see Harahey
Arapaho Indians: 79, 241, 290, 297
Archaic Mandan culture: 180
Archeology: defined, 3; objectives, 3, 6; methods, 4, 5–13
Arikara Indians: 157, 162, 183, 191, 192–93, 194, 201–202, 203, 204, 207–208, 308; Bradbury on corn-growing among, 205
Arizona, early big-game hunter sites in: 57
Arkansas River: 29, 30, 97, 102, 103, 105

archeological evidence on, 279 ff.; Wissler on, 291, 297–98, 307; Kroeber on, 298–99, 305

Plains in prehistory: 297–310

Plains-Southwestern relationships: 103, 114; archeological evidence of, 107, 113, 114, 121, 144, 145, 150, 152–53; *see also* Pecos Pueblo, Taos

Plains Village pattern: 168, 306; *see also* Village Indians, Plains

Plains Woodland culture: 90 ff., 152, 165, 284–85

Plainview site, Tex.: 65, 75, 133; points, 65, 71, 73, 74, 85, 235

Plants, wild, of the Plains, used by Indians: 36–40, 294–97; *see also* vegetation, natural

Platte River, Neb.: 30, 79, 80, 82, 122

Plattsmouth, Neb., Indian crania found near: 308

Pleistocene animals: 279–81; hunted by early man in America, 10, 54–59, 60–77; spread of, between America and Asia, 47; extinction of, 77–78

Pomme blanche (Psoralea esculenta): 38, 294

Pomme de Terre River, Mo.: 137n.

Ponca Indians: 80, 121

Ponil Creek, N. M.: 149

Portales complex: 71

Poteau River, Okla.: 136

Potsuwi'i Incised pottery, N. M.: 152–53

Pottery: 284, 286, 288, 292, 306; of the Central Plains, 89, 90–91, 96, 99, 102, 107, 110, 113, 119, 121, 124, 125, 126; of the Southern Plains, 136, 137, 140, 141, 143, 145, 146, 147, 149, 151, 152–53; of the Middle Missouri, 166, 177–78, 180, 183, 189–190, 197, 205; of the Northeastern Periphery, 212–13, 214, 221–22, 236, 237; of the Northwestern Plains, 244, 256–60

Pottery, mica-tempered (micaceous): in Central Plains Dismal River sites, 113; Southwestern relationships of, 113, 149, 151

Pottery, non-Plains: "Caddoan," on Plains sites, 97, 147; Southwestern, on Plains sites, 107, 113, 121–22, 144, 145, 147; Intermontane (flat-bottomed), on Plains sites, 258, 259

Poynter, C. W. M., on Indian crania from Nebraska: 308

Prairie chicken: 43

Prairie grassland: characteristics of, 36, 40; Indians of, 306–307

Prairie People, mention by La Verendryes: 194

Prairie Provinces, Can.: 163, 254, 261

Precipitation: variations in, 30–32, 48, 59, 63, 68, 131; yearly distribution of, 31–32; nature of, 32–33

Promontory Point caves, Utah: 245

Pryor Canyon cairns, Mont.: 260, 265

Pryor Mountains, Mont., rock constructions on: 265–66

Psoralea esculenta (Indian turnip): 38, 294

Pueblo Indians: 103, 113, 114–15, 150; *see also* Pecos Pueblo, Picuris Pueblo, Taos Pueblo

Puebloan materials on the Plains: Central Plains, 107, 113, 114, 121; Southern Plains, 143, 144, 145, 149

Pueblo Revolt (1680): 114, 151

Pumice: 89, 175, 188

Punished Woman's Hill, S. D., boulder outlines on: 230–31

Purgatoire River, Colo.: 151; Apache agriculture on, 152

Qu'Apelle (Fishing) Lakes, Saskatchewan, Can., Indian corn grown at: 238

Qu'Apelle River, Saskatchewan, Can.: 241

Quarries, aboriginal: 128–29, 275; Peoria (Okla.), 81; Nehawka (Neb.), 82, 128; Republican Valley (Neb.-Kan.), 129; Alibates (Tex.), 140, 143, 153–54; Timbered Mounds (Okla.), 106, 140; Pipestone (Minn.), 159; Knife River (N. D.), 160; Crowley (N. D.), 160; Spanish Diggings (Wyo.), 271–72; Flint Hill (S. D.), 272–73; Parker Peak (S. D.), 273; Battle Mountain (S. D.), 273; Obsidian Cliff, (Wyo.), 274

Querechos Indians: 103–104, 114, 289, 301–305

Quivira: 82, 102 ff., 132; identified with Great Bend aspect, 107; identified with Wichita Indians, 107

Sign language: 302; early Spanish reports of, 104

Signal Butte, Neb.: 85–86, 102, 247, 253, 283

Simonsen set, Iowa: 87

Sims mound, Manitoba, Can.: 221

Sioux Falls, S. D., Indian mounds near: 217

Sioux Indians: see Dakota Sioux Indians

Sisseton Dakota Indians: 211

Skeletal remains: 78, 83, 307–309; from the Central Plains, 91–92; from the Middle Missouri, 166, 167; from the Northeastern Periphery, 218, 219, 220, 221, 226; see also physical anthropology

Skin-working: 22, 298, 302; archeological indications of, 89, 91, 95, 104, 112, 123, 126, 140, 143, 153, 174–75, 188, 235, 242, 250

Slant Village, N. D.: 195

Sloth, ground: 47

Smallpox: 201, 207

Smoking River, possible identification with White River: 192

Smoking Earth River, identified by Capt. Raynolds with White River: 192n.

Smoky Hill aspect: 94

Smoky Hill River: 105

Snake Butte, S. D., boulder outlines on: 232

Soapstone: artifacts, 207, 237, 244, 250, 257, 273; quarries, 273–74

Soils, buried: 73, 74, 84; as indicators of past climate, 17–18; as indicators of grassland, 45

Son of Star, and the Great Northern bean: 208

Souris River: 215, 217, 218, 219, 221, 222, 225, 238

South Dakota: 121, 153, 228, 233–34, 286, 289, 308; early big-game hunter sites, 71, 85, 90; quarries, 160, 272–73, 275; bone paths, 233–34; boulder outlines, 229–33; tipi rings, 262–63; cairns, 265; pictographs, 275; see Middle Missouri, Northeastern Periphery

South Pass, Wyo.: 241

South Platte River: 102

Southern Plains: subarea defined, 130; historic tribes of, 131–32, 146–48; archeology of, 132 ff.

Southwestern-Plains relationships: see Plains-Southwestern relationships

Spanish Diggings, Wyo.: 271–72

Spanish Fort site, Tex.: 147

Spiro Mound, Okla.: 137

Spring Coulee site, Alberta, Can.: 270

Springs: 26, 30, 145, 300

Squash remains: 90, 95, 97, 109, 122, 134, 187, 195

Staked Plains: Tex., 26; N. M., 56

Stanton site, Neb.: 117, 120

Star Village, N. D.: 203, 207–208

Steatite: see soapstone

Steed-Kisker site, Mo.: 81

Steppe: see short-grass plains

Sterns, F. H.: 83

Sterns Creek focus, Neb.: 83

St. Helena focus, Neb.: 81

Stone artifacts, chipped: of the early big-game hunters, 54–58, 61–74, 85, 86, 87; of the Central Plains, 89, 91–92, 95–96, 99, 106, 110, 112, 123; of the Southern Plains, 133, 135, 136, 140, 143; of the Middle Missouri, 166, 173–76, 188–89, 198; of the Northeastern Periphery, 213, 222, 235, 236–37; of the Northwestern Plains, 244, 248, 249, 250, 255, 256, 259, 272

Stone artifacts, ground: of the early big-game hunters, 54, 63, 69, 70, 71, 73, 74, 87; of the Central Plains, 89, 91–92, 96, 99, 106, 110, 123; of the Southern Plains, 133, 140; of the Middle Missouri, 166, 174–76, 187–89, 198; of the Northeastern Periphery, 213, 222; of the Northwestern Plains, 244, 250, 256, 273

Stony Beach site, Saskatchewan, Can.: 258

Storage pits: see cache pits

Stott site, Manitoba, Can.: 236

Stratigraphy: 4, 8, 62, 64, 65, 69, 73, 86, 102, 179, 182, 184, 246, 247

Strong, W. D., on the Mandan: 162

Stump Lake, N. D., drought evidence at: 16–17

Subsistence economies: hunting and gathering, 51, 59, 75–77, 79, 86, 100,

Prehistoric Man on the Great Plains is set in Linotype Janson. Janson is one of the most widely used faces for fine book work in this country.

UNIVERSITY OF OKLAHOMA PRESS
NORMAN